Man

The Mane Event

*By "Firestone",
as dictated to several of the editors at
Reiman Publications—the publishers of
Country and Reminisce magazines—which
sponsored our cross-country trek.*

"I want to thank the nearly 50,000 people who climbed aboard our red wagon to become part of this historic trip (the first-ever, coast-to-coast, by a six-horse hitch), and the thousands more who came to our Maine-to-California route to say 'Hi' to me and my five Belgian buddies. I also want to thank each of the hundreds of amateur photographers who took pictures of us along the route and let us use them in this book.

"Some of you may also have come to wish our driver, David Helmuth, his wife, Vikki, and the rest of the crew good luck on our journey, but I'd like to think most of you wanted to meet me and my mammoth teammates. To these people, thanks for the encouragement during our 3,800-mile walk...thanks for the fistfuls of fresh grass you little kids pulled out and fed us daily...and special thanks to little Kathy back there in Concord, Massachusetts—that apple core was the best of the entire trip!"

Firestone

(See actual size of Firestone's foot on pages 52-53.)

Publisher: Roy J. Reiman
Contributing Editors: Rick Van Etten, Bob Ottum, Hal Prey, Deb Mulvey
Assistant Editors: Kristine Krueger, Sherri Congleton
Art Director: Jim Sibilski
Art Associates: Julie Wagner, Maribeth Greinke
Editorial Assistant: Mary Ann Koebernik
Production Assistants: Melody Trick, Kathy Bloskey, Karen Ellenbecker, Patty Hudy, Tina Severson

© 1994 Reiman Publications, L.P.
5400 S. 60th St., Greendale WI 53129

Country/Reminisce Books
International Standard Book Number: 0-89821-132-8
Library of Congress Number: 94-69027
All rights reserved. Printed in U.S.A.

For additional copies of this book or information on other books, write:
Country Store, P.O. Box 990, Greendale WI 53129.
Code number of this book is 19528. Credit card orders call toll-free 1-800/558-1013.

Contents

Ocean to ocean...
Maine to California...

Millions of hoofprints between...
"Pulling for Seniors"

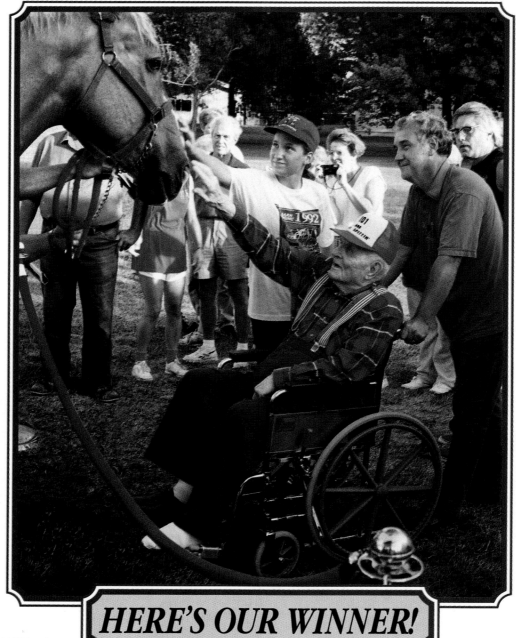

HERE'S OUR WINNER!

IT WASN'T EASY selecting a single winner from the *thousands* of excellent photos submitted by hitch enthusiasts from all along the cross-country route. We'd offered a single prize—*$1,000.00*—for the *best* photo submitted by amateur photographers, and photos *poured* in from Maine to California!

We looked at great pictures of the hitch moving along rural roads and interstate highways…we chuckled over "comic relief" shots of the Belgians rolling on their backs or of astonished children getting "up close and personal" with these gentle giants…we smiled fondly at the many touching photos shot on the day of Vikki and David's wedding.

One photo in particular genuinely touched our hearts.

That's the photo you see above, our $1,000.00 Grand Prize winner, taken by Emerson Eckstein of Galeon, Ohio. The picture truly exemplifies what the entire trip was all about—recognizing, honoring and bringing a bit of happiness to our country's seniors.

The photo shows Mr. Lloyd Hinkel, 101 years old, reaching up to pet Firestone. Also in the photo are Mr. Hinkel's step-granddaughter, Crystal McCown (in red cap and 1992 T-shirt), and his stepson, Gordon McCown (behind Mr. Hinkel's wheelchair).

Mr. Hinkel himself personifies much of what has made our nation great. He was born in a log cabin in Little Wyandot, Ohio in 1892. He spent all of his life on Ohio farms and began driving his father's draft horse teams when he was 12. At the age of 66, he married (for the first and only time) a widow with several children. He retired from farming in 1972 and now resides in a nursing home in Mt. Gilead, Ohio.

Emerson says he was simply "in the right place at the right time" in capturing this poignant picture. Our judges obviously agreed. They felt that, while many excellent photos were entered in the contest—this one *best* exemplifies the purpose and spirit of this trip while "Pulling for Seniors".

'Giddap!'

In people terms, this is the "Foreword" of the book, where Firestone, the Editor, provides an overview of what lies ahead.

By Firestone

I THINK you're going to love this book. It's going to make you feel a real part of this historic cross-country trip. It's going to make you feel you were *there*, sitting right on the driver's seat between David and Vikki Helmuth, looking down over the broad backs of me and my five Belgian buddies day after day as we walked—about 10 miles a day—*more than 3,800 miles* across the diagonal width of the United States, from Maine to California.

Talk about *really* seeing rural America! Most people see it at blurring speeds along superhighways. David and Vikki and the rest of the crew saw it at a horse's gait, taking in beautiful rural scenery and meeting friendly country people all along the way.

This casual pace allowed them to notice gradual changes in the land, the trees, the crops and livestock. (I even noticed gradual changes in the taste of the hay and grass along the way.) But they noticed other subtle changes as well—such as in the accents of folks (they called us "haa-ses" in Maine and "horr-ses" in Kansas), who sometimes even invited the crew into their homes for family gatherings and home-cooked meals around the kitchen table.

As you read this book, it will be as though you're up there behind us on the wagon every day of this 17-month trip, waving at all the smiling faces lined up along the road ("It was like a small-town Fourth of July parade every day," says David), answering the same questions hundreds of times, having an outdoor breakfast with the crew every morning, and making camp at a new site almost every night.

From Laughs to Lumps

While you'll feel you're a part of all the laughs, greetings and handshakes, you're also sure to get a lump in your throat now and then when you find

Chris Manzella

what *Country's Reminisce Hitch* meant to senior citizens along the way, some of whom didn't say a word but got teary-eyed as they watched us huge Belgians prance by, and even more so when they had a chance to pet me and the other members of *their* team.

As one nursing home patient said when David brought me right inside the building's front lobby, "I dearly miss horses. I read books about horses, I study pictures of horses, but what I've

---

> ## *"This trip was a lot of fun, and that's what we've tried to bring you…"*

---

really missed is the *smell* of a horse. Thanks for bringing that to me today." And then tears flowed down his cheeks.

There were many touching moments like this as my teammates and I fulfilled our mission of "Pulling for Seniors". One man in New England related how his 84-year-old mother wouldn't leave her home; she hadn't stepped outside for more than 2 years. But the day *we* came through her town, she asked him to take her to the route to see *her* team.

Likewise, several senior center officials told of residents who hadn't spoken for long periods, but suddenly began talking excitedly during our vis-

it to their center's grounds. Since the mission of this cross-country trek was to salute seniors during the 50th anniversary of the country's 15,000 senior centers, these testimonials regarding the effect of *Country's Reminisce Hitch* on seniors have been highly rewarding.

Older people often got emotional when they came up to pet us, and it made all of us feel good that we were able to bring back some fond memories of their earlier days with horses.

Hurrahs and a Hayride!

Even the big red wagon we pulled wouldn't hold all the highlights of the trip…such as the day we arrived in a Kansas town on the day of the Christmas parade. Vikki put some of her lipstick on Cody's nose and attached some "antler-like" twigs above his ears. Then she and David joined the parade, riding the biggest "Rudolph" the delighted locals ever saw!

(The rest of the team and I sure kidded Cody about that lipstick, though. He got so mad he kicked Magic in the rump when we were turned out in someone's pasture one night. So we don't bring it up anymore.)

The crew was treated like royalty along the route. They were presented keys to small towns…made honorary mayors of others…and became the featured attraction of two towns' Fourth of July parade on the same weekend.

And one day the six of us Belgians were the sole source of power for "The World's Largest Hayride"—17 hay wagons hooked up one behind the other loaded with more than 460 laughing-and-loving-it riders. Me and my five Belgian buddies didn't have trouble pulling it once we got it going, but David said he did see sparks come out from our metal shoes on the asphalt street when we first leaned into our harnesses and got under way.

You'll learn about many more highlights as you page through this book. They're well illustrated with hundreds of candid pictures, many of them taken by amateurs along the way and entered in our "Hitch Photo Contest", which awarded $1,000.00 for the *best* picture of the thousands submitted. (The winning photo is at left.)

You'll also enjoy dozens of little vignettes detailing fascinating "happenings" and incidents along the coast-to-

↻

coast route. And I *hope* you enjoy the daily "diary" I kept for this book. I let the other editors handle much of the rest of the book, but the diary portion was my assignment all the way.

As fans of the hitch already know, I'm sort of the cornerstone of *Country's Reminisce Hitch*, since I was the first team member bought and (ahem) was named the top Belgian gelding in the country the year prior to this trip.

I've also been described as kind of a "character", I absolutely love people, and—okay, I'll admit it—I've rather enjoyed the "celebrity" status I've attained in the draft horse industry.

So, to make the day-by-day "travel-ogue" of the trip a little more interesting, the editors let me put the entire daily diary in my words, so readers of this book could "hear it right from the horse's mouth". I'll be the first to admit that Vikki aided me immensely in filing the "diary report" every single evening of the entire trip—her handwriting's easier to read than mine.

East to West, Then West to East

While we're on the subject of the daily diary, I'd better explain that, about halfway through our trip, we had to revise our game plan. (I've noted this in the corresponding diary entries, but I wanted to provide a bit more explanation to prevent any confusion.)

Our original intention was to make the cross-country trip from Maine to California in *one continuous nonstop journey*. But the rainy weather that plagued much of the Midwest last summer put us well behind schedule, and when it became cold and uncomfortable for the crew and riders (didn't bother us horses at all) in southern Iowa during late October, David finally yelled "Whoa!" at us and we switched to our "contingency plan".

Ann Fosnaugh

WHO SAYS this trip was all work and no play?

At Centerville, Iowa, David and the crew implanted a "Golden Horseshoe", a la the "Golden Spike", to mark the point we'd reached east to west. Then they loaded us horses on our special semi and hauled us all the way to the end of our planned route at San Diego.

Almost immediately after arrival, we splashed our hooves in the Pacific and began walking back along the same route in the opposite direction. This put us and the crew in the southern part of California, Arizona and New Mexico during the best time of the year to be there—December through February—and had us headed north through Texas, Oklahoma, Colorado and Kansas as spring moved north with us.

While David would have preferred to traverse the entire route east to west in one continuous trip as we'd planned, he was determined from the beginning to always do what was best for us Belgians and the crew. (He really treats us well and cares about us. I know he likes Vikki best, but it's obvious all of us in the team are a very close second.)

I'd also like to add one more observation about the trip, and I think it's something you'll see reflected throughout the entire book: This trip was a whole lot of *fun*!

I heard plenty of people along the way ask David and Vikki and the rest of the crew if they were getting tired of being on the road. Invariably, their answer was a resounding "No way!"

The fun and excitement of this journey are what we've tried to capture for you in this book, because—let's face it —we all can use a little more fun in our lives. Everybody should take time to "horse around" now and then. (For example, see the "tough duty" pictures of me and my buddies at right.)

Before I hoof off (sign off) here, I want to share one little incident that happened near Kennebunkport, just before this trip began, which captures the challenge and immensity of this trip.

Early one morning, while we were staying at the Parsons Farm right on the Atlantic Coast, making final preparations for the trip (you'll read about those preparations in my diary, which starts on page 25), one of our crew members strolled into a little restaurant along the beach for a cup of coffee. The place was called "The Old Salt", and the elderly fellow behind the counter was the "Old Salt" himself.

There was only one or two peo-

ple in the restaurant, and the owner began chatting with our crewman. "What are you up to today?" he asked.

"Well, we're up to something pretty big," Mike Bartel, our crewman, responded. "We're going to take our six-horse hitch and run it through the water along the edge of the beach, to officially make this an ocean-to-ocean trip, and then we're going to take off clear across the country for San Diego."

The old gentleman looked at Mike, blinked, was quiet a few seconds and then said, "Too bad you weren't in here yesterday."

"Why's that?" asked Mike.

"Because every Thursday, I give a free lunch to the person who tells the biggest whopper. And *that* story would have won for sure!"

Later that morning, Mike and the rest of the crew wondered—when they splashed in the Atlantic and took off for California—whether the "Old Salt" was watching. He and a lot of other people—including many experienced draft horse people who didn't believe this trip could be made—would have seen a "whopper" become a reality.

Wagonload of Memories

Now, I'm going to let some of the other editors "take over the reins" for some of the upcoming pages. They've also assembled a whole wagonload of short stories about unusual incidents along the way...about touching comments from people who came to the route (plus humorous comments from children overheard by the crew)... they'll introduce you to my teammates ...and share dozens of photos taken by amateurs who were capturing some memories on film for themselves and others.

So, I'll be back with my day-by-day diary beginning on page 25, which provides the only official permanent record of this trip. Farther back, beginning on page 152, is a list of the names and hometowns of many of the nearly 50,000 riders who—by climbing on board—became a part of this historic achievement.

You're sure to enjoy other aspects of this book as well. But I'm sure you'll agree (and keep in mind that I'm a lot bigger than you are) that the daily *diary* is the best part by far. With that, welcome to *The Mane Event*, a "travel-ogue" of the first-ever walk from Maine to California by six proud horses, including yours truly.

Allan Kaulbach

Schelly Odom

"UNBRIDLED" AFFECTION is an obvious title for the above photo. Firestone tried not to let such overtures go to his head!

"I'VE ALWAYS BEEN a sucker for a blond ponytail!" declared Firestone when he met the cute tyke above.

Sharon Arnold

Dave Herrewig

Phyllis Eckert

ONE GOOD NUZZLE deserves another (above)! Belgians' easy-going temperament delighted hitch fans all along the route.

BELGIANS were big hit with kids and adults alike and enjoyed the attention of thousands.

Dottie Clarke

Sheila Seme

A Bit of Background About Our Belgian Editor

LEST you think I'm partial to Firestone, let me first point out what the best judges in the draft horse industry think of him:

He's been named the Grand Champion Belgian eight times at major shows throughout the country, and has won First Place in cart competitions 19 times. To top it off, in 1992 he was named "All-American Belgian Gelding", the highest award bestowed in this field.

The facts are, Firestone is already a legend in the draft horse industry. He's won more awards than many horses win in their whole lifetime, and he still has 6 to 7 years left to compete!

His superb physical characteristics represent all the finest qualities of a Belgian, and he's become the standard used to measure against in competitions.

Honestly, when I get him ready for competition, I hardly know what to do to try to improve his appearance! He has perfect feet, perfect breed features and the most beautiful head I have ever seen on a draft horse.

Plus, he has personality and charisma —everybody who sees him or comes up to him just immediately likes this horse. And he likes them, too—he just loves people!

He Ranks with Secretariat

To me, Firestone is to the draft horse industry what Secretariat was to the horse racing industry. He's what John Wayne was to men and cowboys. He's simply the best Belgian draft horse gelding that has ever been seen in the show world. That's not just my opinion. Ask the judges who gave him all the awards.

Let me tell you how I found Firestone. I was working at the Grupe

Editing this book was a BIG job—that's why we harnessed Firestone with that task. We knew he had the credentials to pull it off, as evidenced by these comments from his driver and best friend.

By David Helmuth

Farms in Stockton, California, and we decided to put together the *best* six-horse hitch in the nation. All in all, we checked out and screened over 60 horses to find the six that would make up this champion hitch.

But it started with Firestone. We knew we needed the horse of all horses to build around. So, early in our search, I got a call from Julie Hunt in Vermont, who with her husband, Donald, have bred some outstanding Belgians.

She'd heard about our quest, and she said she thought she had the perfect horse for me. "His name is Firestone," she said, and at the moment she said

that, he whinnied in the background. "That was him," she chuckled. (Maybe he was saying "Hi" and sending me a message!)

Liked Proud Manner

Julie explained that he was a tremendous horse, and a very proud animal, "but he's so spirited he's a little too much for me to handle! So, while this is difficult for me, I think it's best that I sell him to someone who can control that spirit and put all that energy to good use."

Firestone was then between 3 and 4 years old. Since we were at opposite corners of the country, she agreed to send me a videotape of him—a local TV station had done an interview of the Hunts recently and had shot a lot of footage of Firestone.

When I watched that film, what sold me on him was an unusual move when they were filming him. An umbrella being used in the background to reflect light caught Firestone's eye. He straightened up and cocked his head in such a proud manner that I played that short segment back and forth over and over again.

Then I said, "That's him! That's the horse!" I dialed Julie's number and bought him over the phone, without having seen him in person. When he arrived in California a week later, he was everything I'd hoped for, and more.

And every day I work with him, my regard for him grows. He has such a great disposition—he's always glad to see me and he's always eager to get in harness and go to work. We've become so "in tune" with each other, it seems he often anticipates what I want him and the team to do before I tell them to do it.

I just love this horse. I regard Firestone as one of my best friends.

"THANK YOU!"

By Rick Van Etten
one of Firestone's co-editors

COMPLETING THE TRIP were (above, back row, from left) Steve Zbornik, David Wright, Marlene Thompson, Mark Feckers and Junior Kauffman. Also assisting David and Vikki were Dalmatians Coachman (left) and Ashley.

ON BEHALF of all the employees of Reiman Publications, we want to sincerely thank the entire crew of *Country's Reminisce Hitch* who—while obviously enjoying the "trip of all trips"—also put in *many* long, hard hours, endured some weather and low-comfort conditions that proved mighty challenging (living in a fifth-wheel trailer unit or the "dormer" behind a semi tractor for a year and a half is not like staying at the Ramada!), yet always kept a smile on their faces and a friendly greeting on their lips.

There was some turnover and changes among David and Vikki's "support crew" along the way, but three members of the crew stuck it out for the *entire trip*. They are Marlene Thompson of Winchester, Ohio (Vikki's mother and crew cook who turned out *thousands* of delicious meals in the "cook's trailer"), Eli "Junior" Kauffman of Waverly, Iowa and Steve Zbornik of Ft. Atkinson, Iowa.

Other crew members who performed well for a large segment of the trip included: Dan Bisbee of Portsmouth, New Hampshire; Mike Bartel of Milwaukee, Wisconsin; Don and Lois Garrett of Douds, Iowa; Dave Wright of Venedocia, Ohio; Ron Page of Leicester, New York; and Mark Feckers of Parkersburg, Iowa.

We thank each of these crew members for their help and their patience while answering the same questions hundreds of times, day after day, yet usually with a smile.

Most of all, we want to thank David and Vikki Helmuth, who began the trip as an engaged couple, got married along the way and then took what is probably the most unusual year-long honeymoon trip known to mankind—crossing the country behind a six-horse hitch!

Roy Reiman, who heads up our company, had always dabbled in the draft horse industry, and he knew a lot of good drivers before we began this trip. "David was my pick from the beginning, and he never gave me or any of our staffers a reason to regret that choice," Roy says.

"Instead, he enhanced that decision again and again with his treatment and knowledge of the horses, with the on-the-road and spur-of-the-moment decisions he had to make almost daily, and his constant upbeat attitude and polite treatment of people as he represented our company along the way.

"Nor can I say enough about Vikki, who (and David would confirm this) was the best 'crewman' David had (she *knows* horses and can do about anything that needs to be done around them). Her delightful demeanor, ready laugh and zest for life makes her fun to be around, and that added greatly to the enjoyment of the thousands who visited the hitch."

After the regular updates of the trip in our company's magazines and the numerous pictures we featured of this handsome couple (especially after their wedding in Ohio), these two became such "celebrities" among our magazines' subscribers that our home office staff began lightheartedly referring to the trip as the "Elvis and Loretta Lynn Show"!

After a while, it seemed *everyone* along the way wanted David and Vikki's autographs, and while that was sometimes an inconvenience in the midst of their activities, they never hesitated to sign as many as time allowed. (Several of us remember standing next to Vikki shortly after their wedding ceremony when she said, "Hey, this is the first time I signed 'Vikki Helmuth' on anything!")

Again, all of us at Reiman Publications sincerely thank the entire crew—and particularly David and Vikki—for their help, for their caring and their dedication in making this dream trip a reality, for us as well as our readers. We truly regard them as *friends*.

> "*We appreciate their upbeat attitude and the way they treated our subscribers...*"

Wherever Hitch Went, The Cameras Clicked

WE KNEW THIS HITCH was photogenic, but we didn't fully appreciate that fact until the pictures started pouring in...*by the thousands!* Some folks sent us entire photo albums, complete with captions. No doubt about it—the hitch drew "shutterbugs" like a clover field attracts bees!

Rose Burling

Mrs. Norman Denlinger

THE HITCH was captured on everything from videotape to 35-millimeter film (above) during its historic cross-country trip.

"GETTING A LEG UP" on the situation, the young lady at left finds just the right angle for her shot of the semi.

WILLING SUBJECT. Members of the hitch—in this case, Cody (below)—were always happy to pose for admirers.

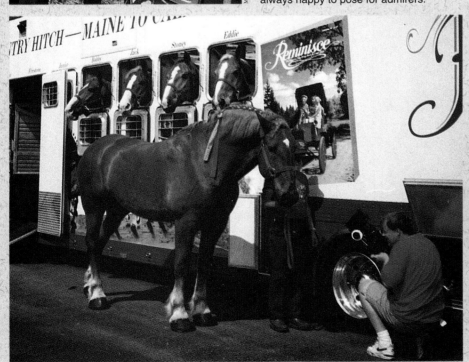

Phyllis Slaughenhaupt

BIRD'S-EYE VIEW of the hitch was obtained by this clever farmer (above), who used the lift on his tractor to gain altitude.

Julie Rybal

DEDICATION

By Roy Reiman
CEO, Reiman Publications

I'm dedicating this book to my dad…and to all the other farm dads just like him, who instilled in their children a love and respect for the land and all it gives us…for instilling in some of us the zest for "never wasting daylight" by getting up early every morning, enjoying that special part of the day and looking forward to the challenges that face us…and for finding great satisfaction in *working* and feeling you've accomplished something worthwhile before the sun sets at the end of each day.

My dad did that for me. He got me and my four brothers up by 5:30 every morning so that we "wouldn't waste daylight". If there wasn't obvious planting or harvest work waiting for us, it seemed we looked for things to do. And there was always plenty of work to be found on our rented northwest-Iowa grain-livestock farm.

As a result, I still get up early every morning, and have learned that the other "ex-farm kids" in our company do, too. If I wake up and see it's light outside, there's just no way I can go back to sleep. I know the day has begun, and I fear I'll "miss something" if I don't get up. Worse, I seem to experience a sense of guilt—it's as though my father would chide me if I laid there wasting away part of a day that was beginning without me. My father didn't just dislike laziness; he loathed it.

So I credit my father for a good deal of my "get up and go" attitude. I also credit him for a good deal of my success. I've taken a good many business risks in my life, even quitting a good-paying full-time job to go on my own at a time when we had four young children and my wife, Bobbi, was pregnant with the fifth.

I—nor she—ever considered these to be big risks, because we both always knew that there wasn't any kind of job "below" me. If whatever project or direction I was working on didn't pan out, we knew that I could and would work at whatever job that was available to put food on the table.

After growing up on a farm, I'd already done most of the worst jobs, so if it meant working at a tannery, a gas station or at a garbage disposal firm, I knew, sure, I could do that.

Dad *Enjoyed* Hard Work

I also credit my dad for the sense of satisfaction I have from putting in a good day of work. Dad actually *enjoyed* hard work. I saw it in his face as he stood back and admired a huge, well-

> ## "*My* parents taught me there's a period in life when it's time to 'give back', and that's why we made this trip…"

molded stack of hay that he and "his boys" had hauled in and completed in a single day, and in many of the other things we did on those nonstop sunup to sunset harvest days back in Iowa.

These days, I love golf, tennis and most other sports…I love gardening (especially growing tomatoes) and trying new kinds of flowers…I love traveling and our frequent family gatherings…but I still also really enjoy just plain *working* and seeing the results of personal efforts.

Finally, I credit my dad for my love of horses. Especially draft horses. *Especially* Belgians. It stems from growing up on that same Iowa farm.

I was a kid during the "in-between" years of agriculture—that is, in between horses and tractors. When I was a little squirt, my dad often let me ride up there in front of the wagon with him when he drove our team, "Dan" and "Mabel". And now and then he handed me the lines.

I guess I've been holding onto those lines ever since…and to the memories that go with them. In fact, one of the main reasons I organized and carried out this first-ever six-horse trek across 18 states is in memory of my father.

He'd Be Part of the Crew

If he were still alive, he'd have thought this was a wild and wonderful adventure, and it would have been hard to keep him from coming along.

And he wouldn't have been just one of the "riders"; he would have insisted on being one of the *crew*—he would have been brushing, braiding, harnessing and helping with the hitch every day.

I, too, wish I could have been with the hitch every step of the way. But I'm married and have kids and have regular issues of our magazines to turn out, so I couldn't take a year and a half out of my life and spend it on the road.

Yet, if I hadn't been faced with these realities, *you couldn't have kept me away from these horses and this trip for a single day!*

I absolutely *ached* to be a regular part of this magnificent journey every time David Helmuth called me from the road to describe his most recent experiences ("It keeps getting better every day!" he often said). I desperately wanted to be there for the experience of meeting, shaking hands and thanking thousands of our subscribers for their support over the years.

Better yet, I wanted the opportunity of personally *seeing* subscribers' reactions as *their* hitch approached…I wanted to watch their faces as these champion horses pranced by their real "owners".

Yes, I Drove the "40"

Unfortunately, I was only able to be with the hitch now and then during this journey. Still, when I was there, helping to get these beautiful Belgians ready for their day on the road...smelling the sweat and the harnesses...busting up bales of hay and feeling the lines as I threw them up to David or Vikki in the driver's seat...all this took me back to those days with Dad that I so fondly remember.

And it was obvious when I was out there that it brought back the same kind of memories for thousands of people along the route. There's something about draft horses that brings back those "kinder, gentler days" George Bush used to talk about. I base that on personal experience.

You see, I'm fortunate to count Dick Sparrow among my friends. And after Dick put together his famed 40-horse hitch at Zearing, Iowa and took it on the road, I had the opportunity to ride up next to him in the driver's seat. (He even let me *drive* them once—believe me, that was quite an experience!)

Looking out over the backs of those 40 Belgians—stretched out about half the length of a football field—was an experience in itself. But the memory that has always stuck with me was the faces of the elderly farmers along the parade route—they absolutely *glowed* and looked 10 to 20 years younger as their eyes ran over that hitch.

Hitch Pulls Back Memories

You could tell those fellows were seeing way beyond those horses. They were seeing way back to the days when "horsepower" wasn't something measure under a hood. They were remembering the days when it was them and *their* "Dan" and "Mabel", working together in the field to pull a crop out of stubborn land that still hadn't been introduced to hybrid seed, granular fertilizer and liquid herbicides.

If *Country's Reminisce Hitch* had the same effect on the thousands of retired farmers—and I contend it did—who came to our cross-country route to see

GETTING ACQUAINTED. In top photo, Roy Reiman holds Firestone as children pet him. Children of all ages love this horse—and he loves them—as evidenced in the lower photo.

their team, and brought about a better understanding and appreciation of early agriculture for thousands of others, then I feel this trip was worth doing.

Likewise, if these horses gave a lift to thousands of senior citizens (we took the hitch—or at least one of the horses—to senior centers all along the route) for just a day here and there,

then this trip was worth doing, and the "We're Pulling for Seniors" slogan on the hitch wagon had merit.

And, in the face of all the crime and graft and negative news that seems to dominate the nation's newspapers and TV screens these days, if the "personal appearance" of these beautiful Belgians in hundreds of small communities along our 3,800-mile rural route added a bright note to a dull day, then this trip was worth doing.

Trip a Way to Say "Thanks"

Lastly, my dad taught me more than just things about getting up early, enjoying hard work and how to drive draft horses. He and my mother instilled certain values that still linger. They taught me there were just certain things that were "the right thing to do".

One of those values was that, if you're blessed with success, you have an obligation to share part of your good fortune with those who are less fortunate. In other words, you "give back" to the community that helped you get where you are.

So that's what I decided to do—to "give back" something to the community of more than 10 million people who now subscribe to our company's eight magazines.

As I see it, since we used part of their subscription payments to buy this champion hitch, that makes them "part owners" of these beautiful Belgians. And I couldn't think of a better way to show our appreciation for their support and loyalty than to bring *their* hitch to them to see, meet and pet.

If this gave thousands of them a good deal of satisfaction...if this "sharing" experience made them feel closer to us and to other members of our subscriber "family"...and if this cross-country trek allowed our hitch crew, other staff members and me to look many of them in the eye, shake hands and say, "*Thank you!*", then this trip was worth doing.

James Panetta

CHAPTER ONE

HOOFING IT
ACROSS AMERICA

Getting Ready Was a Trip in Itself!

WHEN anyone saw them coming, their pulse picked up. For anyone along the cross-country route, the first sighting of *Country's Reminisce Hitch* was an inspiring, heart-pounding experience—massive steeds over 7 feet tall, ears erect, proud heads tossing, 24 legs rising and falling in unison, huge hooves pounding the ground.

Soon you'd hear shouts from others around you, "The hitch is coming! *Our hitch is coming!*" It happened wherever they appeared.

Then, when these six huge horses got up close and passed by, onlookers could *feel* the power of these champion Belgians, as their combined weight of over 6 tons actually shuddered the ground so that it vibrated people's feet!

Preparations Began in 1992

For subscribers to our company's eight magazines, the best part of this experience was that it was *their* hitch. That's because these horses were purchased with a portion of their subscription money, making it the only hitch in the world with over *10 million owners!*

Up until this cross-country trip began, these 10 million co-owners had gotten to know these horses only through pictures and features about them in the Reiman Publications magazines. Even so, it was amazing how quickly our readers became attached to this team and developed a special feeling for them.

Gradually, this team became "Amer-

Here are the complete details of the planning, the routing and the mission of this cross-country trip…plus behind-the-scenes tidbits of how we selected these six beautiful Belgians, the driver and the crew.

ica's Hitch", as our subscribers spread the word about these exceptional horses and our trek across the country.

This trip allowed *thousands* of these readers to see *their* team up close, to meet them, pet them, smell them and call them by name during this no-hurry, no-schedule journey…and provided our staff an opportunity to personally thank all these people for their years of supporting our ad-free magazines.

While the idea for this first-ever

"It's the world's only hitch with 10 million co-owners…"

---

cross-country trip by a six-horse team was born nearly 5 years ago, serious planning didn't begin until early in 1992. And the more we discussed it and checked out the details, the more we realized how great an undertaking this

really was. But once we announced tentative plans for this cross-country trip in the fall of 1992, there was no backing down.

Excitement immediately began building among our readers. Letters, phone calls and even fax messages *poured* into our offices from people eager to learn more about the trip.

Many of these readers simply had questions about the route and wanted to know when and if the hitch would reach their area. But others wanted to help out and get involved in any way they could, even offering to "Have the crew eat and stay at our place—you can put the horses in our new barn!"

Needed a 24-Hour "Hotline"

The phone calls were so incessant we found the need to establish a "900 HITCH HOTLINE", which allowed subscribers to call in any time, 24 hours a day, to listen to a recorded message about the hitch's training and details even before the trip began.

Later, it allowed them to regularly check on the location and progress of the hitch along its route. We received an average of *more than 3,000 calls a month* on this 900 line to listen to the recorded updates.

Our readers loved the idea of this cross-country trip from the outset…and their enthusiasm never let up as the team inched across America. This team not only left its prints on miles of rural roads, but on the minds of *thousands* of appreciative people as well.

For Special Trip, We Needed Special Wagon

WELL IN ADVANCE of the trip, we made arrangements for building a special wagon.

When a wagon is going to be used to cover over 3,800 miles of rural roads from Maine to California, it has to be well constructed. And when it is going to carry thousands of people as passengers and be seen and photographed by thousands more, it has to *look* good, too.

That's why we went all the way to Ontario, Canada to talk to Tom Penhale, who's regarded in the draft horse industry as one of the best wagon builders available today. Tom, who owns Penhale Wagon and Carriage Works in Bayfield, Ontario, is in such demand he's sometimes fully committed to

wagon orders for as much as a year in advance.

But when we explained our plans for this first-ever cross-country trip and why we were doing it, he became enthralled with the challenge as well, and agreed to fit us in and build a "special wagon" worthy of the trip.

"What makes this wagon particularly unique is the fold-down set of steps and the handrails we added to the back of the wagon to help people board with ease," Tom explains.

Has "First-Ever" Features

"We never made a wagon with a ladder like this before. After the passengers are loaded, the ladder and handrails slide conveniently into a slot below the floor of the wagon between the bench seats along the side so people won't trip on them."

(Our crew can attest to how well this idea of Tom's worked, after taking out and putting back the ladder and handrails *thousands* of times over the past year and a half, to load and unload more than *38,000 passengers!*)

Tom painted the wagon currant-red metallic to match the hitch semi and other vehicles, then used a metallic gold on the wheels, undercarriage, striping and lettering.

"This wagon has lots of brass on it, and features special solid brass coach lights," Tom points out proudly. "I think it's one of the prettiest wagons I've ever built."

It was obvious people along the route agreed with him.

EYE-CATCHING CONVEYANCE was custom-designed and constructed by Tom Penhale of Bayfield, Ontario. Steps used to board wagon (shown in top left photo) fold up and slide into slot between seats shown in photo at top right.

Our Historic Cross-Country Route, On

April 13, 1993 to August 12, 1994

Planning a route across the country for a trip in your car is one thing. Planning such a trip for a six-horse hitch is quite another!

We learned that after we started organizing this trip early in 1992. We began with a basic plan of starting in the northeast corner of the U.S., right off the coast of New England where the early settlers landed, and then heading west just as they had.

Next we decided to make it a "diagonal" trip across the width of the country, to touch the states of as many of our magazines' subscribers as possible. So, Maine to California would be about

---

"The advice of draft horse people in each area proved highly reliable..."

"as far as we could go". With that in mind, we began charting our course, closely studying the highways, the topography, the rivers and other aspects of each state map.

We contacted state highway officials and local county sheriffs...we got in touch with draft horse owners in each state we were crossing and used their local knowledge of the roads to ask which route *they* would take if they were driving a six-horse hitch across their state...and we read dozens and dozens of letters from subscribers pleading with us to please, please, *please* come through *their* state.

We were getting so many letters and phone calls asking about our planned course that we put down a "temporary" route and published it in a winter issue of our magazines. In retrospect, we probably shouldn't have done that.

Pennsylvanians Disappointed

Why? Because later, when we had to make a number of minor changes to the route, we got another logjam of letters from readers disappointed with changes.

To begin with, any and every change

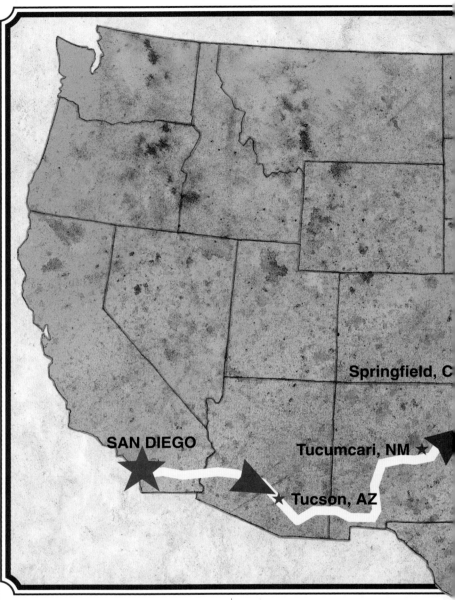

we made in the route was for the *horses*, not for anyone or anything else. It seemed each week we were confronted with a new regulation...a highway department official with different restrictions...newly announced road construction plans...unforeseen safety hazards...or a mountain in our planned path that some "locals" warned us was too steep and too hard on the horses.

As a result, many of the changes we had to make were out of our control. And often a minor change in the route at one point meant a major change down the line.

For example, our early "temporary" route had us going through the middle

of Pennsylvania, where we have thousands of enthusiastic subscribers. But some un-crossable mountains in lower New York pushed us on a line farther north, and—to the dismay of many Pennsylvanians—we crossed only the northwest corner of their state. We had no other choice.

We'd liked to have stayed on a straighter line diagonally southwest from Ohio to southern Kansas, but we have so many subscribers in Iowa we felt we just *had* to stay north long enough to at least cross the southern edge of The Hawkeye State.

We'd also have liked to continue along the same line, gradually heading

Step at a Time, 10 Miles a Day

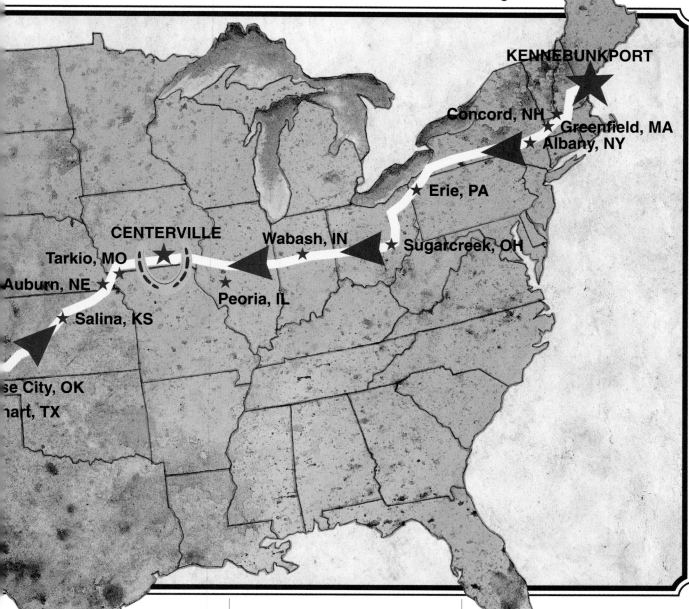

KENNEBUNKPORT

Concord, NH
Greenfield, MA
Albany, NY

Erie, PA

CENTERVILLE
Wabash, IN
Sugarcreek, OH

Tarkio, MO
Peoria, IL

Auburn, NE
Salina, KS

se City, OK

hart, TX

southwest through Colorado, Utah and Nevada, but with the length of this trip time-wise (we were still thinking of one continuous walk, East Coast to West Coast, at that time), we had to think about the weather at that point.

Five States in Short Order

We knew if we left Maine at the start of spring, it would be late summer by the time we hit the central states, and we had to start heading south to avoid cold temperatures in fall and early winter.

So, our route started cutting south through Nebraska and dropping down fast through Kansas. Still, we wanted to allow as many subscribers as possible to say, "They went through our state!", so we cut across the corners of Colorado, Oklahoma and Texas before heading into New Mexico—you'll see by the map that we crossed the borders of five states in less than 100 miles!

Again, through New Mexico and Arizona, we'd liked to have taken a straighter, shorter line to the California coast, as our earlier published route had indicated. But the "locals" shooed us away from that planned route due to steep mountains (we found they knew what they were talking about—while some of the mountains in New York were a challenge, the ones in the extreme Southwest proved to be the steepest by far of the entire route).

All in all, we couldn't be more pleased with the route we eventually settled on. The advance advice—especially from other draft horse people—proved highly reliable. And we couldn't be more appreciative of all the help we received along the way, from highway officials, county sheriffs and small-town policemen, who all seemed glad we came and provided a "lift" for the people of their community, especially the senior citizens.

LOTS OF HORSEPOWER was on hand at the Denver Draft Horse Show, where the hitch took top honors in the six-horse hitch division. At top right, David (on left) and a handler show four members of the hitch "in halter"; Firestone (right) looks over just a few of the hitch's recent awards.

We Chose *Best* Team to Make a '3,800-Mile Victory Lap'

THEY'RE the "Champs". In 1992, the year before this cross-country trip began, the team that was chosen for *Country's Reminisce Hitch* won more awards at major shows than any other six-horse hitch on the circuit. It's an indication of the regard that judges and experts in the draft horse field have for these particular horses.

This hitch was not only rated the top Belgian six-horse hitch in the country at those shows, *this hitch also ranked over any other six-horse team* of Clydesdales, Percherons, Shires or whatever. This team was named the *Nation's No. 1* six-horse hitch!

How did they come by that title? Well, draft horse shows are run a lot like the Indy 500 race car circuit. If an Indy driver places first at one race, it's worth so many points. If he places second at another, that's so many points, etc. And then these accumulated points are added up at the end of the year to determine which Indy 500 circuit driver is best.

We decided at the outset that if we were going to have a hitch represent our company and make history as the first six-horse hitch to cross the U.S., only the finest hitch in America would do.

The same approach is used on the draft horse circuit—points are awarded based on the placing at each of the shows recognized by the draft horse industry.

Country's Reminisce Hitch appeared at most of the major draft horse events across the country in 1992, and by the time they competed at the Live Oak Invitational Horse Show at Ocala, Florida, the number of points these champion horses had accumulated put them far ahead of any other six-horse hitch in the

nation. It's one of the reasons we decided to put these horses "on the road" for this trip, showing and sharing them with our subscribers, rather than go on the show circuit again.

It's our opinion that if you have already won the "Super Bowl" of the draft horse industry, it isn't much of a thrill to simply go out on the circuit and see if you can win it again.

Instead, it seemed more appropriate that we take these horses on the road, on a no-hurry, no-schedule, rest-on-Sundays "victory lap" through 18 states, so their 10 million co-owners and their families and friends could see and touch these champions.

Why Use Champions for Trip?

Those who had a chance to see these Belgians up close during the trip found it easy to understand why they so readily caught the eye of experienced draft horse judges. These horses stand over *7 feet tall*, weigh up to *2,400 pounds* each and can pull *five times* their

lishing company, we wanted it to be one that would reflect the kind of quality our magazines have become known for.

Besides, if these horses were going to make history as the first six-horse hitch to cross the width of the U.S., we felt it only fitting that America's finest hitch represent the task.

See Them, You've Seen Best

What's more, this hitch was perfect for the role, because one of the things that makes this particular hitch unique is that it's both a "show hitch" and a "parade hitch". Not all hitches are good at both roles.

"Show horses" are simply more refined animals. They represent years of training and often an enormous investment in time and money. "Parade horses", such as the great Budweiser Clydesdales, may have minor deficiencies not obvious to the untrained eye, but exhibit a lot of size, spirit and friskiness that people standing along a parade route like to see.

Country's Reminisce Hitch fares well in both roles. As confirmed by the nation's top judges, they possess the refined characteristics that draft horse people look for in both breeding and the way they perform together, and yet their enormous size and head-tossing "hamminess" make them a hit with any parade crowd.

Prior to this trip, in July of 1992, this hitch appeared at the Great Circus Parade in Milwaukee, Wisconsin. Dozens of draft horse teams had already passed, but when this particular hitch came prancing by, the crowd not only burst into applause, many of the people on hand began rising to their feet to give the team a "standing ovation".

This outstanding team has that kind of effect on people. If you haven't as yet had the opportunity to see this hitch pass by up close, try to get out and see them at one of the many appearances they'll be making around the country in the future.

You'll likely react the same way—there's simply some sort of charisma, something "magic" about this particular team that makes them instantly endearing and memorable. On the following page you'll learn how this team was put together, and then further into the book, you'll learn how they were trained, etc.

But you have to *see* them to fully appreciate them. You'll come away convinced like everyone else. *They're the "Champs".*

weight. Yet, these enormous steeds move with a kind of grace that defies logic.

They're *perfectly matched*. (One woman observed along the route, "They look like six brothers!") They're the same size, which makes them look good together...and they move with the same style, which is why they work together as a *unit*.

Despite their size and power, these massive horses have the patience and temperament of the family dog. And when you observe them for a while, it becomes obvious that they enjoy all of the attention and affection they get. You watch 'em—you'll agree there's a little "ham" in these horses! That's what makes them such great performers in the show ring.

Actually, there are people in the draft horse business who asked us why we wanted to take a hitch of this caliber on this cross-country trip. They point out that it would have been easier and cheaper to throw together a "publicity hitch", simply made up of decent-looking horses, and call it *Country's Reminisce Hitch*.

They say—and perhaps rightfully so—that the majority of people across the country who aren't really "into horses" wouldn't know the difference. We didn't consider that for a minute. We knew from the outset that if we were going to have a hitch represent our pub-

How This Hitch of All Hitches Was Assembled

PUTTING TOGETHER a champion hitch is a gigantic undertaking. As evidence, David Helmuth spent 3 years searching for the right six horses for *Country's Reminisce Hitch* and then training them to work as a *unit*.

Draft horses by nature are very willing workers. Most of them would much rather pull something than stand idle in the pasture.

Yet, they still require a lot of patient training before they fully cooperate with the driver…and the rest of the team. They have to do their job individually, and yet function as part of a smooth-working unit that moves almost as one.

These things are true even if you have a two-horse hitch, but the larger the hitch is, the greater the degree of difficulty. Making six horses perform as a unit is a formidable challenge even for experienced drivers and trainers.

Keeps "Picture" in Mind

In addition, in order to win on the show circuit, each individual horse in the hitch must be an outstanding animal to pass the judges' exacting criteria on the basis of their physical appearance, their breed characteristics and their markings. Each horse has to exhibit muscle quality, alertness, proper carriage and an eagerness to perform.

David had all this in mind as he set out in 1989 to put together "the hitch of all hitches". The team that made this cross-country trip is the result of a 3-year search for just the right horses, which even included trips to Canada.

In that time, David changed his "starting lineup" almost continually. Dozens of horses were bought and sold, shuffled in and out of the hitch in those 3 years, as he struggled to create the *ideal* team.

"I always carry a vision of what the perfect team should look like," David explains. "And no matter how good my team is at the time, I know it can get better. So that means keeping your eyes open as you travel the show circuit and attend horse sales, and always staying flexible."

As David slowly developed this team, he constantly looked beyond an individual horse's characteristics—he always kept in mind how the horse would *fit in with the others*.

To give you an idea of how much attention he paid to that detail—even though these horses are nearly 7 feet tall—there is only a *1-inch difference* in height between the lead team and the swing team! (The lead team is, obviously, the two horses up front, and the swing team is the two horses in the middle of the hitch.)

Likewise, there is a 1-inch difference in height between the swing team and the wheel team. What's more, there is only a *1/2-inch difference* between the height of each *pair* of horses in each of the three hitch positions!

"No Foot, No Horse"

There's a host of other physical factors an experienced driver/trainer like David looks for when assembling a great team. The feet of draft horses is given a high priority because it best measures a workhorse's usefulness. ("No foot, no horse", draft horse experts are proud of saying.)

A wide heel is considered essential to withstand the strain of the constant pounding of a heavy horse. Good long hocks…a strong, well-shaped back and withers…a nicely shaped head with alert eyes—all these are desirable characteristics of a top draft horse.

After covering these physical aspects, David begins talking about the disposition of the horse, and his voice gets even more enthusiastic. He likes to refer to the disposition as "heart".

"If a horse has a big heart, I can train him," he says. "He has to have a fire in his belly. The best feet and head and markings in the world don't mean a thing if he doesn't have the desire to perform."

The horses also have to be able to get along with the rest of the team. Teamwork is the name of the game; one cantankerous horse can lead to one cantankerous team, David points out.

If One's Wrong, All's Wrong

"If the team doesn't perform well, I never single out one of my horses and blame it on that horse," he explains. "When one horse makes a mistake, it's the whole team's mistake. That's the way I train them, and that's the way I want them and myself to think. And it's *my* mistake more than that individual horse's or the team's mistake, because somewhere along the line I must not have done my job."

Still, David doesn't forget the individuality of the members of his team. "Each one of my horses has a distinct personality, and that's fine. Just like people, each of these Belgians is unique. Only sometimes I think they're a little smarter than people!"

While it's obvious he's extremely fond of each of these horses, he says he's careful not to get too attached to any of them. "These guys are not pets," he explains. "They have to know who's in charge.

"They know when they get that harness on, they have a job to do and they're going to work. That doesn't mean they can't have a little fun when the day is done, and they do. But they have to realize that when they're in harness, they're all business."

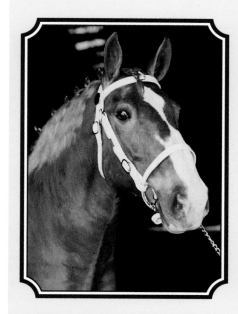

THE TRIP BEGINS!

You'll learn more about the team and their training on the following pages, but here's the beginning of Firestone's day-by-day "diary", which will wend its way throughout this book…just as this team wended its way across the country, one huge hoofprint at a time.

By Firestone

Apr. 9—Well, after months of training and preparing back in Iowa, we're finally here at our starting point—Kennebunkport, Maine, just down the road from former President Bush's home.

We rode 5 days in the semi from Waverly, Iowa, but we traveled comfortably—with our modern semi (see photos and details of it on pages 54-55), we even ate and drank while the semi was purring down the road.

Here we're being stabled in barns at Parsons Farm (the Parsons were nice enough to take us in) until we officially start our trip. Right now my teammates and I and the crew are getting accustomed to the Northeast. Most of us have never been here before.

Crewmen Junior and Steve rode each of us Belgians into the Atlantic today to get us used to water, since David plans to drive us all in the surf as we begin our trip to make it officially "ocean to ocean". Then he hitched all six of us to the wagon, and we took a "practice run" in the surf.

The photographer who's doing a ♂

Let Us Introduce You to Each Member of This Champion Team

On the following pages is a bit of background on each of the horses…when each one was bought and why…and what each one's role is within the hitch.

FIRST OF ALL, you should know that a six-horse hitch is made up of three pairs of horses. Up front is the "lead team", in the middle is the "swing team", and in front of the unit being pulled is the "wheel team".

On the next few pages, we'll introduce the members of *Country's Reminisce Hitch* to you in that order, with driver/trainer David Helmuth's comments on each pair of horses and their role in the hitch, followed by his comments on the quality and desirability of each individual horse.

Front pair is the LEAD TEAM

Middle pair is the SWING TEAM

Nearest wagon is the WHEEL TEAM

THE LEAD TEAM

"A LEAD TEAM is born, not made," David emphasizes. "They have to be born with certain instincts, desires and reflexes.

"The lead team should be willing to go wherever the driver wants them to go. If you've trained them right and you want those two horses to walk right over a car, they should be willing to do it!"

In a "show hitch", the lead team is the most important team in the hitch. They are the first horses the judges and the audience see when the team enters an arena or appears along a parade route.

These horses not only set the pace for the whole team, they often set the tone of the whole performance. By holding their head high, thrusting their ears forward alertly and picking up their feet with a high knee bend, they present an air of dignity and pride that sets the standard for the horses following them.

They have to show good action, which refers to the height they lift their feet in a trot. High action is especially desirable in the lead team because it's the most noticeable indicator of a well-trained, high-spirited hitch. It gives the team a majestic appearance and a graceful gait.

"Chip" and "Magic", the lead team in *Country's Reminisce Hitch*, are regarded by many people in the draft horse industry as the top lead team in the country. They're true "performers" who love their job. They seem to relish having a crowd around them when they're in harness—you can actually see them react to an audience.

And as for David's comment that the lead team should be willing to go wherever the driver wants them to go, "even right over a car", we're reminded of when David had this team on the edge of the Atlantic at the beginning of the trip.

These horses had never seen an ocean before they got to Maine, but when he turned them straight toward the water and got them up to their knees before turning back, those two lead horses didn't hesitate for an instant—they charged right in and kept going straight out until he turned them!

"Chip"

Position: Right lead
Height: 18 hands
Weight: 2,000 pounds
Acquired: 1990
Age: 9 years

Prestigious Awards:
8 times first place award in Men's Cart competition. 10 times first place award in six-horse hitch.

"CHIP was the second horse acquired in the hitch—after Firestone —and in many ways he's the real leader of the team," says David.

"No other horse can 'out-proud' him. He simply will not allow it. He is definitely one of the great personalities of the hitch, and a real crowd-pleaser.

"Chip has the highest knee action of any horse I have ever seen in my life! I also feel he's the most intelligent horse in the hitch. He just never stops amazing me.

"Chip was extremely energetic when we bought him, but not a good horse to be around. He was so excited, you had to keep an eye on him. But after a lot of work, I've managed to harness all of that energy and put it to good use.

"Now Chip is one of the best lead horses that the draft horse industry has ever seen. That's not just my opinion, either.

"On this cross-country trip, he never wanted to be out of the lineup!"

Interesting Fact: *In addition to being part of this champion six-horse hitch, Chip regularly competes in the Men's Cart competition, where he was undefeated for 2 years straight.*

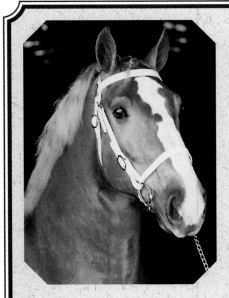

"Magic"

Position: Left lead
Height: 18 hands
Weight: 2,000 pounds
Acquired: 1991
Age: 6 years

Prestigious Awards:
Grand Champion Stallion.
4 times first place in Men's Cart competition. 8 times first place in six-horse hitch competition.

"IT TOOK us 3 years to find a horse that could keep up with Chip," David relates. "In January of 1991, we saw Magic named Grand Champion Stallion at the Fort Worth Stock Show. We looked him over closely, and knew we'd finally found our horse.

"Yet, it took me 3 months to convince his owner to part with him. That was a lot of talking and bartering, but Magic has proven it was well worth the effort. He was the easiest horse I've ever had to break. He's a true born show horse!

"Magic has filled a huge hole for us. His action and spirit are just incredible. He seems determined to give Chip a run for his money every chance he gets.

"As a result, a real healthy competition and respect seems to have developed between them, and that's an ideal situation. They just keep getting better and better. At 6 and 9 years old, they're both young, so these two horses have a great future ahead of them."

Interesting Fact: The team took first place in a major competition the very first time that Magic performed as part of the lead team. That normally doesn't happen until a horse gets a good deal of experience, but when these two got together, everything "clicked" from the get-go.

video of the trip filmed us making the splash. Wouldn't you know it? I was the only horse in the hitch to lose my footing on the first try—a wave hit me just as I stepped on a submerged tree branch, and down I went!

Waves splashed right over my back. Didn't hurt any more than my pride, though, and once they got my harness untangled and fixed part of the wagon's hitch structure (yep, busted that, too), we took a second run and it was picture-perfect!

Apr. 10—Saturday. Rainy and chilly today; high of 45°. The crew members all got their "official uniforms" for the trip today, and they were pretty excited. Guess that's only fair— me and my buddies all got fancy new custom-made harnesses for the trip with lots of brass and class.

The other horses and I spent the day resting in our stalls after "taking the plunge" yesterday.

Apr. 11—Easter Sunday. Everyone up at 5:50 a.m. David, Vikki, Marlene, Junior and Dan attended Advent Christian Church's sunrise service at Narragansett Point. Chip went, too!

See, the minister wanted one of the horses on hand for the service, and he said a prayer and offered a special blessing for the team and crew. That was very graceful of him.

Church members treated the crew to a bacon-and-egg breakfast afterward. At 10 a.m., David and Vikki took Ashley, the team's Dalmatian mascot, and Stoney to Barron Center, a rest home in Portland, Maine. It was raining and the residents couldn't come outside, and the Activities Director said the residents were so looking forward to the visit that she didn't want to disappoint them. So she asked David to bring Stoney right inside!

From what Stoney whinnied to me later, the director hadn't told the receptionist, and when she saw David lead that 7-foot horse right up to her desk, her eyes got as big as Stoney's!

Apr. 12—Crew got up at 4 a.m. in the rain to groom us and braid our manes. They'd hoped to start our cross-country trip this afternoon, but it rained all day, and they finally decided to wait another day.

Everybody's getting *awfully anxious* to get under way. Wonder if astronauts get this antsy before a launch?

Apr. 13—WE'RE OFF! Still a gray day, but David says a little drizzle isn't going to hurt any of us, and it's ♂

THE SWING TEAM

"PEOPLE think they can hide horses behind their lead team," says David. "They are wrong. To win in really good competition, you can't hide anything.

"Every horse in our hitch is a top-quality animal. In fact, both horses in our swing team could be used as a lead team in most other hitches. I've actually put them there a few times when a need has arisen, and they performed well there.

"The pair of swing horses has to fill a unique position in a six-horse hitch. First of all, it takes an even-tempered horse to perform in the middle slot with a pair of horses in front and behind them.

"The swing team has to have what is known as 'medium action'. (Again, action refers to how high a horse lifts its feet in a trot.) While you want each team to be progressively taller as you go from the front to the back of the hitch, you want just the opposite when it comes to action.

"That is, you want the most action in the pair up front, and then have it decline gradually with each pair from front to back, with the wheel team having only a slight amount of action. The action of our swing team meshes perfectly with the two other teams."

Firestone has become so well-known that one of the first and most frequent questions that's asked is, "Where's Firestone?" Then, when David points him out, they're shocked to find that the top Belgian gelding in the nation isn't among the lead team—he's in the swing team!

"Moving him to there was a hard decision for me," David admits, "because you'd like to have a beautiful horse like him up front. But it raised the quality of our team a whole notch. And when judges know you have a horse like Firestone in swing rather than lead, they figure you must have some awfully good horses in front of him!

"Again, Firestone is one of the best draft horses I've ever been around and I'm proud to have the privilege of driving him."

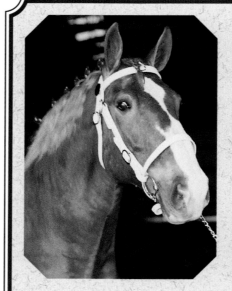

"Firestone"

Position: Right swing
Height: 18:2 hands
Weight: 2,200 pounds
Acquired: 1988
Age: 9 years

Prestigious Awards:
8 times Grand Champion Belgian at major shows. 19 times First Place in cart competitions.

"FIRESTONE is the first horse we acquired for this hitch, and he's the cornerstone around which this team is built. After we bought him in 1988, we used him as a standard and tried to find five horses to complement him.

"Actually, Firestone is already a legend in the draft horse industry. He's won more awards than many horses win in their entire lifetimes, and he still has several years left to compete!

"He's not only an excellent harness horse, but he's become the horse to beat in halter competitions for Grand Champion Belgian Gelding at major shows. Firestone's physical characteristics represent all the finest qualities of a Belgian.

"As I've said lots of times before, I don't really have anything much to do to get him ready for competition. He comes just about as close to being the 'ideal' Belgian as any horse I've ever seen!

"He also has one of the best dispositions you'll ever find in a Belgian. He's made the whole nation open its eyes to the offspring of his sire, 'Master's Eddie', a stallion that sold for a record public price."

Interesting Fact: *In 1992, Firestone was honored as the "All-American Belgian Gelding". That's the highest award bestowed in this field.*

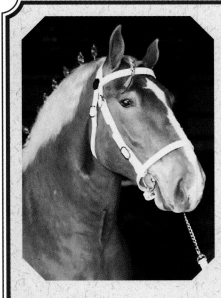

"J.R."

Position: Left swing
Height: 18:1 hands
Weight: 2,100 pounds
Acquired: 1992
Age: 5 years

"WE didn't buy J.R. until late in 1992, but he's already showing excellent promise and is responding nicely to his new teammates. He's just what we needed to make this the 'hitch of all hitches'.

"Want to know why I'm so high on this horse? J.R. is Firestone's younger brother! And now these two brothers are working right next to each other as our swing team.

"Because Firestone is such an outstanding horse, finding a mate for him was really a chore. Even though we did extremely well with this hitch and won most of the top awards in '92, I felt the swing horse we had then was the weak link in the chain.

"That horse was sometimes un-cooperative—he was a high-quality horse, and he'd do well for the first 5 to 10 minutes in the show arena. But if the judging stretched out and the judge wanted the teams to make several more laps around the arena, that swing horse—I won't name him here—sometimes just got tired of the whole affair and began acting up. He cost me first place at a major show.

"So, I looked for a long time, trying to find a teammate for Firestone, but every horse ended up looking pale by comparison. Actually, that's one of the problems when you're dealing with a horse as good as Firestone—even a pretty high-quality horse can look bad next to him.

"But now, with this full brother of Firestone in this slot, it's just a matter of time before he makes what was the weakest link in the hitch into one of its strongest assets."

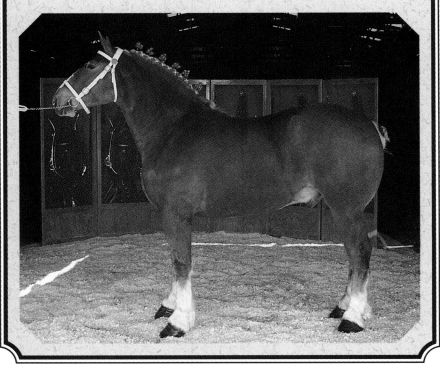

time to get this historic journey under way.

Crew hitched us up at 7:30 a.m., David and Vikki climbed up onto the seat and he yelled, *"Team! Walk!"* for the first time. With that, this trip of all trips began, and we left the coast and headed for the small town of Kennebunkport.

When we got there, David had some trouble getting my pal Magic up there in the lead team to cross the bridge into town, but once he saw his teammate Chip was going, Magic decided he could do it, too!

Stopped at Laver Village senior center at 9 a.m. Vikki and Steve of the crew stayed on at the center to teach the residents some line-dance steps after the rest of us left.

Had 115 riders on this first day on the road, including a lady who donated a blanket she'd made for Ashley. As wet as it's been, she should have made her a rain jacket!

Apr. 14—Finally better weather, so the videographer did a lot of filming today. After we were done with today's miles, David put Magic and Chip in the trailer and hauled them back to the beach and did some "Roman riding" for the photographer, so some pictures could be taken in the sun instead of the gray weather we've had so far. Lots of other people were there to watch, and cameras *really* started snapping!

Later, the crew washed, fed, watered us and called it a day. They found the salt water from the ocean was not only hard on our harnesses, but affected the rubber pads that cushion our horseshoes, so they did a lot of cleaning tonight. Guess they're no more used to the ocean than we are.

Apr. 15—Up at 7 a.m. and, as my country music friend Willie Nelson says, we were "on the road again". Lots of people stopped by to see us. Ones who don't read any of the Reiman magazines don't know what this trip is all about, but others who subscribe quickly fill them in.

Tonight the crew groomed us while David and Vikki drove to Wells, Maine to check out our next stop.

Apr. 16—Another cool, quiet day, with 45-50 riders. We're starting to get a little more used to the routine.

The crew put brand-new rubber pads (the salt water ruined the old ones) in our "Scotch Bottom" shoes, and they really feel great—our shoes are as com- ☞

THE WHEEL TEAM

"THE WHEEL position is where you will always find the largest and the strongest horses of the team, because they tow the largest portion of the load.

"It is the duty of the pair of wheel horses to negotiate the turns of the wagon. This requires an intelligent, responsive horse, much like what you look for in your lead horses. Turning can be a tricky undertaking, and the wheel horses have to be especially sensitive to the most subtle commands of the driver.

"While most drivers look for sheer power in the wheel position, we're fortunate to have a lot of 'style' as well in our wheel team of Bobby and Jack.

"Yet, these two are amazingly powerful as well. In the 1992 Rose Bowl Parade, my six-horse hitch pulled the float that weighed 24 tons, and the team never flinched while pulling it over the long 5-mile route. And these two big horses in my wheel team did most of the work!"

The "Spare Team". We had extra horses along on the tour at all times —sometimes two extras and sometimes four, depending on the terrain we were passing through and whether our "first team" would need more days off.

For these rides, we'll use our "spare team"—that is, the extra horses in the semi trailer that weren't on the hitch that day. These two horses will also be rotated in the hitch from time to time to give the other six horses a day's rest.

These extra horses (or the "regular" that was "off" that day) were hauled in the semi to the next camp site on their day off, and allowed to rest. Two of these "spares" were extremely gentle around people, and were used most often for visits to senior centers. The others, while gentle, too, were a little high spirited for this duty, and often got anxious and fidgety when their teammates were not in sight.

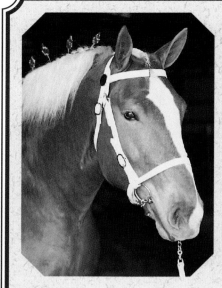

"Bobby"

Position: Right wheel
Height: 18:2 hands
Weight: 2,400 pounds
Acquired: 1991
Age: 7 years

Prestigious Awards:
Grand Champion Gelding.
3 times first place in Men's Cart competition. 8 times first place in six-horse hitch.

"BOBBY is probably most famous for making history in 1991 by selling for $21,000. This still stands as a record price for a gelding at a public auction.

"I remember that while everyone who knew horses recognized Bobby's high quality, they wondered whether he would pay off in the show ring later.

"Well, he has. So far he's placed first in every cart competition he's entered! He also was named the 'Grand Champion Gelding' at the National Belgian Show in Davenport, Iowa in '92, and when you consider the country's best Belgians were there, that's quite an achievement.

"Bobby is the best wheel horse in the country. Most people in the industry would agree with me. He has the quickness and agility of a lead horse (sure, I could actually put him up there in front if I wanted), but he has the size and strength of a wheel horse.

"He is the second smartest horse in *Country's Reminisce Hitch*, and is one of the proudest horses I have ever seen.

"Bobby has proved to me—and many other people—that in horses, like in most other things, you get what you pay for. He was worth every dollar paid for him."

Interesting Fact: In Bobby and Jack, experienced observers say that our wheel team has as much action as many people's lead teams.

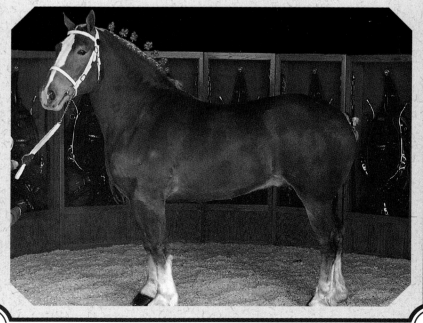

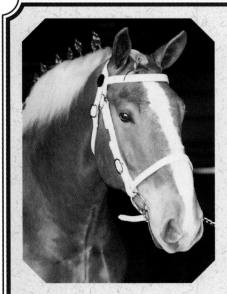

"Jack"

Position: Left wheel
Height: 18:2 hands
Weight: 2,350 pounds
Acquired: 1991
Age: 10 years

Prestigious Awards:
Grand Champion Gelding.
7 times first place in Men's Cart competition. 8 times first place in six-horse hitch competition.

"FINDING a partner for Bobby was another huge task for us. Just matching Bobby's size at 2,400 pounds was hard enough. But, because Bobby is so spirited and eager, we had to be doubly careful in this match-up.

"I finally remembered seeing Jack a year earlier at a show in Canada. It took 3 weeks of long telephone conversations with his owner up there until I finally convinced him to sell—I bought Jack without seeing him a second time until he was delivered to our farm.

"Jack was (see item below) a major key to the hitch's success. He was just one tremendous horse."

Unfortunate Fact: Jack was the only tragedy of our trip. While standing and waiting for a group of people to climb on the wagon in Audubon, Iowa on November 9, he suddenly collapsed and died instantly of a heart attack. The veterinarian who performed the autopsy found he'd had a heart murmur, and said, "The best thing you could have done for him is what he was doing—regular light pulling strengthens the heart when a horse has this condition. So you actually prolonged his life in this hitch."

Said David: "The only good part of this tragedy is that Jack died doing what he loved best. He loved the feel of the harness and getting to work. He'd always much rather be pulling something than spending a day in the pasture. I miss him—he was a wonderful horse."

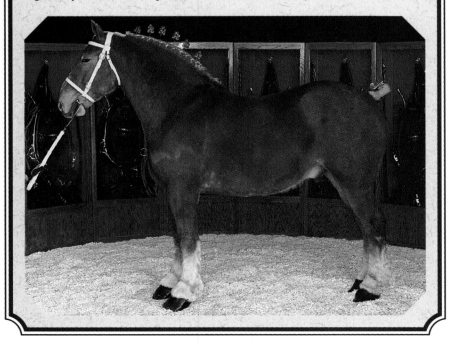

fortable as old sneakers for us now.

David and Vikki drove to the airport in Boston to pick up an awning for the semi. Marlene went to town to do grocery shopping for the crew's meals. When she fills up three or four grocery carts, I bet people gawk and wonder how big a family *she* has!

Apr. 17—Up at 6 and on the road under sunny skies by 8:30. Drove through Sleepytown, Maine (love the name of that town!). Had 45 riders today.

E. Clair Russell of Hartland, Maine brought gifts—he'd made a small horseshoe for each crew member and put them on key chains. Hope that brings us good luck! Put in 10 miles today. No sweat. Literally.

Apr. 18—Sunday. Hurrah, our first day off! The "policy" for this trip is that we're on the road 6 days a week and have a full day's rest on Sundays. Looks like the crew appreciates it as much as we do.

Bruce Littlefield of North Berwick, Maine made the day for me and my Belgian buddies by donating 14 bales of timothy hay for us. Good, fresh hay, too! He also brought some homemade muffins for the crew. They really enjoyed them, but they just don't know what they're missing. Timothy hay, *uummm!*

Apr. 19—Another beautiful day and we're back on the road. We left with David at 8; the crew got the campsite cleaned up and followed at 9.

Passed through North Berwick, then crossed into New Hampshire. We're already in our second state of the 18 we'll be crossing. The crew was flattered when they stopped to fuel up the vehicles—people wanted their autographs!

Cynthia Plaisted of Berwick gave Marlene a kitchen wall hanging. Reached Holy Trinity Church in Somersworth at 11 a.m.; traveled 10 miles. Had 17 riders plus nearly 300 visitors.

Eddie, one of the "spare horses", rode in the trailer today, and later, while the rest of us got our baths, he was still stomping his feet in protest—all of us draft horses would rather *work* and be part of the team each day rather than being hauled around in a trailer. But David thinks we should each have an extra day off now and then, so we have two extra horses along to switch in and out as he determines.

Apr. 20—Wow! People get up early here! There were 70 visitors at the campsite this morning, watching us get ♂

hitched up before we left at 7:50 a.m.

Passed through Dover, where someone left the crew a cake that read, "Welcome to Maine and New Hampshire!" Traveled 10.4 miles today and arrived at Calef's General Store in Barrington at 10:10 a.m. Owner Harlan Calef invited the crew to eat at his seafood restaurant.

Afternoon visitors keep bringing food. Marlene was given maple syrup, cheese, spices, homemade bread, coffee cake and a cookbook today. People are sure making us feel welcome!

Apr. 21—Left camp at 8:55 a.m. under cloudy skies. Had 29 riders through Nottingham and Northwood. One group was chanting, "Our hitch is here!" as we arrived.

Chip lost a shoe about 7 miles out, so we took a break while David put it back on. This area's beautiful, but hilly; steep grades were quite a pull for us.

We'd gone 12 miles when it started raining at 11:45. We all got pretty wet but it didn't stop us. The crew has umbrellas for the people riding in the wagon, and me and my buddies rather enjoy the cool rain on our backs.

Arrived at Deerfield Fairgrounds at 12:25 p.m. Tonight Jim and Lynda Barnes' family of Northwood invited crew to their home for corned beef hash, potatoes, carrots, biscuits, steamed cabbage, beets and *three* desserts! They had a wonderful evening.

Apr. 22—A rainy 40° this morning, almost sleeting, so we're not traveling today. The crew used the time to clean our harnesses, then Dan vacuumed us and brushed our coats.

David and Vikki took the pickup and drove ahead to check out the next 20 miles of route. Marlene fixed pizza for supper. Me and my teammates are still munching on Bruce Littlefield's timothy hay. Thanks again, Bruce!

One of the crewmen drove to the Manchester airport to pick up Jim Rupple, one of the top farriers in the country, who'll put new shoes on us tomorrow. The plan is to get us new shoes every 6 weeks. We're checked over periodically by the team vet, Dr. Clarence Meeusen of Cedar Grove, Wisconsin, so we're being well taken care of.

Apr. 23—*Brrr*—a chilly 20° when David got us up. Too cold and wet to travel again; the passengers would get too uncomfortable on the wagon. We're already getting behind schedule.

Had over 500 visitors today, though,

EACH HARNESS (above and below) was custom-fitted to a specific horse in the hitch—thereby ensuring maximum comfort—prior to beginning cross-country journey. Keeping brass trim polished was an ongoing task for crewmen.

HARNESS-UP time came early so that the hitch could be on the road by 8 a.m. each travel day.

Photos: Ginne Farnsworth

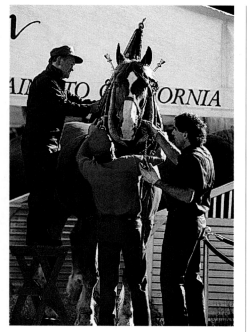

IT TOOK 45 minutes to harness all six horses, after which they were led to their respective positions (below).

RARIN' TO GO! Firestone's alert ears signal his eagerness to "get the show on the road" in the photo above.

some from as far as 150 miles away. Irene Tasker of Concord said seeing us was "a dream come true"!

After lunch, Vikki gave the visitors a "seminar" about draft horses, etc., using me to "model". I like Vikki a lot, and obviously she thinks a lot of me, too.

Later, Chip, Magic, Stoney and I got our new shoes. The "Smoke Shed" in Deerfield gave the crew some beef jerky, and they sampled a little of it before Marlene fixed them pork chops for dinner tonight.

They say she's a great cook. I just know she's a great lady—she kisses me and each of the other horses on the nose several times every day!

Apr. 24—Saturday. Up early again and had big crowds on hand—850 today! Colleen Towle of Chester, New Hampshire brought the crew some homemade cookies. If they keep eating this well, they're going to be a load to haul before this trip's over!

The remaining horses were re-shod today and the farrier left. David and Vikki took Stoney, one of the spare horses, to a senior center, the Sharon Home in Deerfield this afternoon.

David takes Stoney instead of me on some of the senior center visits because Stoney's about as laid-back as an old dog. David says I'm sometimes too spirited (hey, that's just *me*) for those confined areas. Plus, I've heard David explain to people that when I don't have my other teammates in sight, I get a little antsy—I'm always afraid they're going to get hitched up and leave without me, and that's *my* team.

The Deerfield Draft Horse Club treated the crew to dinner tonight— lasagna, ham, scalloped potatoes, beans, salad, corn bread and biscuits. I heard the dessert was cake with our picture on it! Wonder if they got the white marking on my face right.

I'm known for that "diamond" on my forehead; I've heard David tell people that I have "the most beautiful head" he's ever seen on a horse. Hmmm …wish somebody made a mirror big enough for Belgians.

Apr. 25—Sunday. Warm and beautiful for a change—sunny and 70°. More than 1,100 visitors showed up today. I was petted and talked to a *lot*. Loved every minute of it.

We've had a few days off this week, so even though this is supposed to be our "rest day", David decided to give us some exercise and put on a driving ex- ↪

Meet Our Driver...*David Helmuth*

He's come a long way since growing up in an Amish family. He's driven hitches since he was 10, and eventually was named "Top Driver" at one of the draft horse industry's major shows.

DAVID HELMUTH admits this cross-country trip allowed him to "live a dream". "From the time I was a very young boy, growing up on an Amish farm, I wanted to drive a team of big horses—a 'show team'—and compete with others in the field.

"And I wanted to travel, to see as much of the country as I could. This trip let me do both. I couldn't ask for more out of life. My dream has come true."

When you get to know David, you become less surprised that he's living his dream. His focus on everything he does is as targeted as a laser beam. When he sets his mind to something, he's so determined to succeed at it and make it a reality that he makes it come true.

"I'll admit to being very dedicated to what I do," he says. "But I believe people need to set goals. The only way you can achieve those goals is to believe in them first.

"I actually envisioned this hitch and the individual horses before I saw any of them. I even envisioned the wagon and the equipment before they were made. I envision things like this, then I follow through, and just do whatever it takes to make it happen."

Different Type of Childhood

David feels that growing up as part of an Amish family has had a great deal to do with his success. "I left my Amish family when I was 17, and at the time I was glad to get away from that conservative way of life," he explains. "But as I look back today, I can honestly say, 'Thank you, God, and thank you, Mom and Dad, that I was born Amish.'

"That way of life taught me the value of hard work and dedication. It brought me my love for horses. All of our 'English' neighbors had already switched to tractors and mechanization, so I wouldn't have learned so much

about draft horses at an early age if I hadn't had that Amish upbringing.

"I think I knew from the time I was 6 years old what I wanted to do with my life. How many people are lucky enough to know exactly what they want to do at such a young age? And then succeed at it?

"Actually, this trip across America with a champion team of Belgians is the perfect ending to my dream. I don't know what I'm going to do for an encore!"

David was born in 1958, and his childhood on that Amish farm near Hazelton, Iowa was definitely different from that of many children at that time. While other little boys were playing with Tonka trucks, David was already riding ponies.

While other kids were reading comic books, David was reading *The Draft Horse Journal*. While other teenagers were playing baseball and experiencing their first date, David was already deeply involved in training and breeding champion Belgians that weighed over a ton apiece.

David has walked off with numerous awards during his career. But likely none was more coveted than when he was named "High Point Driver" (the driver who accumulated the most points) at one of the industry's major shows, the National Western Stock Show in Denver, in 1992.

It took a lot of calloused hands, long conversations sitting on hay bales, and learning while watching and listening to others to get him there. He's only 36 years old now, but due to his unique background he's probably had more experience with horses than some people twice his age. "I was actually training ponies when I was 6 years old," he relates.

"When I was 10, I graduated to draft horses. Between the ages of 10 to 16, I drove draft horses. I wasn't just exercising them—I was working in the field with them, planting crops, hauling hay and plowing. I was just a little guy, too —I only weighed 100 pounds when I was 18 and only weigh 140 today—but I could handle them. I would feed and water these horses, clean out the barn and spread new bedding every day before I went to school. Even then I was already breeding mares and training colts.

"When I was 16, I competed in my first draft horse show. A man who believed in me, Everett Steege, gave me the opportunity to show a yearling filly in a group class. I won, and I was 'hooked' on showing horses! I still have the picture of myself (at left), in my Amish clothes, with my horse.

"Once I got into showing horses, there was nothing that could keep me away from it. We didn't get many magazines, but Dad got *The Draft Horse Journal*, and I studied it like the Bible. I'd dream and wake up wanting to own and show Belgian horses. I was just obsessed with it."

Began New Way of Life

That first taste of success in the show ring is likely what changed David's life. His admiration grew for

Dick Sparrow of Zearing, Iowa, who had already become famous for putting together and driving the 40-horse hitch.

"I was 16 when I sneaked away with Dick Sparrow to the Draft Horse Sale in Columbus, Ohio," David says. "I'd never been out of Iowa before, and this show and sale—with hundreds of draft horses and hundreds of draft horse people—was an unforgettable event. In fact, that's 20 years ago and I have never missed attending that annual sale since.

"Even though I was only 16 when I was at that first show, people there already knew of my ability with draft horses, and I received a number of job offers. One of them was from my 'hero', Dick Sparrow. He didn't encourage me to leave the Amish order. He simply made it clear that if I ever decided to do so, I could come to work for him.

"That was early in 1976, the bicentennial year. I gave it a lot of thought, and finally joined Dick. I promised my parents before I left that I would be back in the fall to help them harvest the corn. I was the oldest in the family—I had two brothers and a sister—and since we picked all our corn by hand, I knew they needed me. And I did come back for that harvest, but then left again when we were done.

"With the 40-horse hitch, I was responsible for four of the horses, and we traveled all over the United States. I learned an awful lot from Dick during those couple of years, and I'm ⤵

> *"I left the Amish order when I was 17, but I thank God today that I was born Amish..."*

THE BEGINNING. David, at left in his Amish clothes, is shown competing in his first draft horse show. He won, and he has been "hooked" on showing horses ever since.

hibition for all the folks over at the fairgrounds. So after Marlene, Steve and Lois returned from church, the crew got us hitched up.

We really strutted our stuff—figure eights, fanning to right and left, backing up, 360-degree turns, everything. The crowd loved it, and got a better understanding of why we hold the title of the No. 1 six-horse hitch in America. We don't wear that title lightly, and now and then we enjoy a chance to show we're worthy of it!

There were so many people on hand that Lois even sold out of hitch souvenirs today! After enjoying Marlene's chicken dinner, the crew began getting the equipment ready to get back on the road.

Apr. 26—Headed out at 8:30 a.m. Passed Deerfield and many stone fences on the way to Bear Brook State Park at Allenstown. Arrived at 11 a.m. after putting in 10 miles.

Over 400 people greeted us along the way. Had 58 riders, including a woman who told us she'd walked a mile to get there. She said she'd been reading about us in *Reminisce* magazine and had been waiting for this for a full year!

Started raining at noon and never stopped after that—glad we'd already made camp.

Apr. 27—Wow! Woke up to an inch of *snow* this morning! Got up to 50° by noon, though, so it melted quickly. Left at 7:10 a.m.; stopped at Pembroke Academy at 8 a.m. Drove through towns of Allen and Pembroke and covered our usual 10 miles but only had seven riders. Guess the snow scared them off.

Arrived at Agway Feed in Concord at 9:40 a.m. Had 300 visitors there. Today was Marlene's birthday! David and Vikki took her out to celebrate. I gave her a nice nuzzle.

Apr. 28—Left at 9:15 a.m. and drove to the Capitol building. (Concord's the capital of New Hampshire; most of you humans likely knew that, but it's news to a horse, of course.)

David gave a seminar for about 500 there, then gave Gov. Stephen Merrill a wagon ride through Statehouse archway and right up to the Capitol steps. I heard several people comment on how well-mannered we were. Hay (that's not misspelled), we're *always* on our best behavior!

David and Vikki signed lots of autographs, then took us to Concord Odd- ⤵

fellows Home. The seniors there sure seemed to like us, as the seniors at each center do. Remember, we're making this trip in honor of the 50th anniversary of senior centers in the U.S. That's why our wagon says, "We're Pulling for Seniors!"

Had 35 riders on our 13-mile route today, the most miles we've put in on a day so far. No problem, though; hay, other Belgians around the country are walking farther than that easy, pulling a plow or whatever. Our red wagon pulls so easily any two of our crewmen often move it by hand.

Rested at noon at the Sandy Heino real estate office. Learned the building was once a blacksmith's; it's in the *Guinness Book of Records* for having the world's largest pile of horseshoes! Naturally, I've seen a lot of horseshoes in my day, but that *was* a big pile!

Apr. 29—Left camp at Foster's Quarry at 9:45 a.m. after our usual morning grooming. After traveling only a mile, David stopped to adjust lines for Jack and me—I was working with him in the wheel position today.

Had 26 riders along our 10-mile route, including Bette McBride of Henniker, New Hampshire, who'd baked her specialty, "bundt cakes", to "help feed hungry crew". How can they be hungry?

Arrived 11:50 a.m. at Maine Auto in Hillsboro. This town, established in 1772, is President Franklin Pierce's birthplace. I love these New England towns. I especially like all those pretty white church steeples.

Apr. 30—I was back on the swing team today when we pulled out at 8:30 a.m. Passed through the town of Antrim and had 31 riders.

The crew was given sweatshirts advertising the Deerfield Fair; established in 1876, it's New England's oldest fair. Vikki was interviewed by reporters from Peterborough, which is tomorrow's destination. We walked our usual 10 miles and stopped at a park near Bennington at 11 a.m.

The crew set up a temporary hot-wire pen and turned all eight of us horses loose so we could exercise. Felt good to run and kick and snort a bit. They got some exercise, too, playing softball with some of the locals.

May 1—Saturday, and we were on the road at 8:35 a.m. Had 21 riders... and saw 700 folks along the route! We visited the Pheasant Wood Nursing Home in Peterborough, and David

HORSE PLAY. David takes "Bobby" for a brisk run on his Iowa farm, where the hitch wintered and was trained for the upcoming cross-country trip.

still using what he taught me today."

That traveling experience also ignited David's wanderlust. While he was still a teenager and the "40" fizzled out, he was so determined to see more of the country that he tried to get a job as a semi driver. When no one would hire him, he bought his own semi and hauled independently.

One adventure on the road found him in Miami with a sunburn so fierce he coated the inside of his coveralls with Vaseline in order to get back on the road and head home!

Gave Amish Life Second Try

In the late '70's, at his parents pleading, David agreed to come back home and give the Amish life-style another chance. He lasted only a year.

"I gave it an honest try," he says. "I think the world of Amish people and their way of life. But I had so much drive in me, a zest for travel and showmanship, that I just couldn't hold still. Sometimes I think I was born like one

of my 'lead horses'. I had to be in the lead; I loved the limelight of showing horses and winning. (The Amish aren't allowed to go to horse shows; only horse sales.)

"I couldn't have that and be Amish, too. The Amish are very happy people—they probably enjoy their life as much as I enjoy mine. But I love competition. It makes the world go around. It fills me with energy and excitement.

"When it comes to Belgian draft horses, no one scares me. I will compete with anyone in the country. That's how confident I feel about what I do. And that's the way you have to feel in order to compete and win.

"The only way I've gotten better was by getting beat. Losing teaches you a lot; it just gives you that much more incentive to get better and win."

With all this zest for showmanship in his blood, David moved to a small ranch near Littleton, Colorado and started "Helmuth Belgians, Inc."

"I started my operation there by buying four horses from Dad that I'd bred back when I was 12 years old," he recalls. "I bought them at a fair price, too—I probably could have gotten them for less, but I wanted to 'give something back' to my parents.

"I remember when I started that breeding program without my dad's knowing it. I was just 14 then, but I could already see we weren't going to get anywhere breeding and selling the kind of horses Dad had then.

"So I got in touch with Andrew Nielson of Merritt, Michigan. I knew Dad couldn't afford to buy the kind of stallion that Andrew had, but I eventually worked out a deal where we could lease a stallion named 'Lakeledge Sonny' from him for 1 full year.

Hoped Stallion Would Do It

"I still hadn't told Dad after Andrew agreed to bring the stallion to our place on the way to a sale, because I knew he wouldn't approve of it. I felt if he saw the stallion and it was already there on our place, he might listen and eventually agree to the deal.

"So I started building a big box stall in the barn, and Dad kept asking me about it. I kind of let him conclude that I felt we needed a better stall for the stallion we already had. Then, finally, Andrew drove the truck in and started unloading 'Lakeledge Sonny'. He was beautiful. As expected, Dad was pretty upset and wasn't having any part of it. But after an hour of talking and leading that stallion around and around him, he finally consented to the leasing deal.

"The investment paid off right away. The first filly Lakeledge Sonny sired for us was the top-selling filly at the Tri-State Sale in Hawkeye Downs at Cedar Rapids, Iowa. And after that he just kept turning out one winner after another.

"So it was with four of those horses that I started my breeding program. Those Belgians helped put me on the map in the draft horse world.

"At the National Western Show in Denver, every one of my entries won first place awards, and I had the Grand Champion Mare. I showed there for 7 years, and always had either a Grand Champion stallion, mare or gelding at that national show."

Started New Program

Despite this success, David's budget limited him in how much he could ex-

JUST FOR FUN, David assumes a "tough guy" pose for one of our photographers.

> ## *"I'm not a big person, so I use my voice to show them that I mean business..."*

pand his operation and how many shows he could compete in. So finally, in 1986, after several unsuccessful earlier attempts, Phyllis and Fritz Grupe convinced him to head up the growing Belgian operation on their Stockton, California farm.

David was back "on the road again", driving the Grupe six-horse hitch and competing across the country, and giving "draft horse clinics" to grade school children in various parts of California. (He estimates that he has given these clinics to more than 30,000 children over a 6-year period.)

The Grupes gave David the funds and the latitude to put together the top hitch in the country. Beginning with Firestone, he did exactly that. "I can't say enough for the Grupes," he emphasizes. "Phyllis is extremely knowledgeable about draft horses.

"She drove and competed regularly with members of this hitch in cart and unicorn events, so she not only knew their quality but how they performed."

Roy Reiman, head of Reiman Publications in Greendale, Wisconsin, also has a healthy interest in draft horses —especially Belgians. (He once asked his wife for a Belgian mare for Christmas, and got it!) Roy noticed how this Grupe Hitch kept walking off with more and more awards each year.

In the summer of 1992, when it became the No. 1 six-horse hitch in the country, he and the Grupes worked out an arrangement with Reiman Publications to sponsor the hitch on the show circuit.

Readers Fell in Love with Hitch

Subscribers to the company's publications—especially those who subscribed to *Country* and *Reminisce* magazines—responded so well to the hitch that, at the end of the year, when the Grupes decided to sell the hitch, Reiman Publications bought it.

Soon after, the small Wisconsin publishing company announced plans for a cross-country trek, from Maine to California, to allow thousands of subscribers across the U.S. to come see, meet and pet their hitch. Just as importantly, they hired David to help choose the route, hire and organize the crew, and drive the team on this memorable journey.

The rest, now, is history.

drove us right up to the front door so residents could pet us.

Then we headed for the Peterborough Plaza shopping center, where we'll rest until Monday. Saw lots of forests and ravines on our trip this morning and noticed the grass is really "greening up"—there's nothing we horses like the looks of more than a nice green pasture!

After a meat loaf dinner, David and Vikki went to the opening of the New Hampshire International Speedway in Concord. I can't figure out the attraction; if it was a *horse* race they'd gone to watch, that I could understand!

May 2—Sunday, so the crew "slept in" this morning, and we got some extra rest, too. After church, David and Vikki went back to the speedway; Junior and Steve had the day off.

The crew sat outside this evening, discussing the coming week's schedule. We're enjoying New Hampshire; folks have been friendly and generous, offering water for us and even volunteering the use of their barns!

May 3—We were "rarin' to go" this morning and the crew was, too. Left Peterborough at 8:40 a.m. David stopped in Jaffrey to chat with schoolchildren lined up on sidewalk. Had 36 riders on the way to Fogg's Mini Mart in Rindge.

Vikki told us we worked better today as a group than we have yet on this tour. She's a sharp gal, and sure knows how to win over a horse's heart!

We saw Richard and Margaret Baker of Rindge again—they visited us at Peterborough, watched us along today's route and were among the 75 folks who stopped by tonight. They're starting to feel like old friends!

Tim Ojala of New Ipswich, New Hampshire also brought horseshoes and a ring-toss game for Roy Reiman (our owner and boss!). People around here sure are generous!

May 4—We broke camp early and headed out under overcast skies. Ran into (I mean, happened upon!) a construction crew on Route 202; they motioned us to follow behind their ground roller. So we got to walk on freshly leveled dirt—a nice change of pace from the hard paved road!

We crossed into Massachusetts at 9 a.m. and in Winchendon, just over the state line, crowd was chanting, "Welcome to Massachusetts!" Nothing like a little fanfare to get us stepping lively!

We had 34 riders today and stopped ♂

for the night at the Royal Paddock Restaurant in Winchendon. (Any place with the word "paddock" in its name sounds fine to me and my buddies!) Owners Robert and Robin Hicks treated the crew to dinner.

May 5—Woke to drizzle and threat of rain, so we stayed put in Winchendon. Crew turned us out in hot-wire pens, so we had a lazy day, eating grass and rolling on the ground. (For some reason, everyone gets a kick out of watching us roll—maybe they're afraid we're like turtles and can't get up if we're on our backs!)

Crew chatted with visitors—nearly 500 today! They also organized our tack boxes while David and Vikki scouted the next 40 miles of the route.

May 6—Rained all night but was clearing when we left at 8:50 a.m. Went all the way through Baldwinville, then on to Templeton, where children were on the sidewalk shouting, "This is our best field trip ever!" We enjoy seeing the kids get so excited; kinda brings out the streak of colt in all of us.

Pretty panoramic views today, but Vikki said prettiest sight *she* saw was a woman holding a sign reading, "Welcome, Dave and Vikki—I have doughnuts!" (She had a whole bag full!)

Arrived at 11 a.m. at the Woodside Variety Store in Phillipston, Massachusetts. Owners treated crew to ice cream; Junior and Steve ate theirs while giving us our baths—talk about dedication!

May 7—On the road by 8:15 a.m. Huge crowds along sunny 10.2-mile route—over 1,000 people turned out! Had 54 riders. In Athol, police escorted us through town—good thing our harness has blinders; they helped block out all those flashing lights!

David took us to drive-through at McDonald's; you should have seen the girl's face at the pickup window! Her mouth fell open wide enough to eat a Big Mac in one bite.

In Orange, a lady dodged traffic to bring crew a big box of doughnut holes. Muriel Charlonne of Rindge gave crew a porcelain statue of Dalmatians; Ruth MacEwen of Athol gave Vikki a bouquet.

Arrived at the King Sing Chinese restaurant in Orange at 11 a.m. David, Vikki and Marlene ate dinner there—Marlene's first Chinese food. (Personally, I'll stick with hay and oats.)

May 8—We left Orange at 8:20 a.m. under sunny skies. We walked to the

Meet Vikki Helmuth

She's not only David's top assistant, she became his wife during this cross-country trip. She's also an experienced horse-woman and was a valuable member of the hitch crew.

SHE'S such a pretty, petite and fine-featured young woman, you're surprised when she uses an authoritative voice and gives one of the big Belgians a firm pat on the rump to move him around during grooming.

Then she crouches down and grabs one of the huge hooves to clean and polish it, with seemingly no concern for the danger of what a kick from one of these massive steeds could do.

You quickly conclude that this beautiful blond has obviously been around horses like this before. And you're right.

Vikki Lyn Thompson was raised on a crop and livestock farm in Ohio, and her parents loved horses—they always had a few Belgians and Arabians around. So, beginning at the age of 7, Vikki showed Belgians and Arabians at the Adams County Fair, then graduated to other shows.

As a 4-H member, she competed in riding events with Arabians, and competed in driving events with Belgians. Eventually she became a 4-H riding instructor for other kids in her rural community.

But just because she enjoyed working with horses, she didn't become a "tomboy". She started studying dance at age 6, and studied at six schools, learning advanced ballet, jazz, tap and gymnastics. She even instructed dance for 2 years, and has danced to entertain at various civic functions and senior centers.

Vikki's mother, Marlene Thompson, who was along on the cross-country trip as the crew's cook, proudly says, "Vikki's a natural—she's always been a terri-

> *"She put her background to good use by teaching line dancing during stop at senior center…"*

fic dancer. I've always just loved watching her perform!"

Vikki put her teaching talent to good use on the cross-country trip. For example, when David and Vikki brought one of the Belgians over to a senior center in Maine shortly after the beginning of the trip, they were getting ready to leave when the activities director said, "Too bad you couldn't stay. Tonight's our night for country line dancing."

Vikki perked up and said, "Really? Hey, maybe I could stay a little while longer and teach you folks a couple of new line dancing steps I just learned."

Steve Zbornik, one of the other crew members, quickly chimed in, "I know how to line dance, too—I'll stay and help you."

With that, David headed back to the campsite with the horse, and several dozen seniors fell in line behind Vikki and Steve, trying to emulate her steps.

The shuffling feet of all these dancers soon caught the eye of the cameraman who taped the videos of this trip. He dropped down low, first focusing in tight on Vikki's tasseled, shiny-tipped boots, then drew back to show Steve's big cowboy boots, then drew back even further to show dozens of house slippers and old shoes trying to stay in step.

Finally, as the music thumped on, he

pulled back to show the smiling faces of the pretty blond, the big cowboy and all those happy seniors behind them.

Has a Great Way with People

It resulted in some fantastic footage that captured part of the fun people had wherever the hitch showed up, and carried out the slogan painted on the big semi, "We're Pulling for Seniors!"

Obviously, Vikki loves people and is gracious with her time. Her talents aren't limited to horse training and dancing, either — she graduated from Southern State Community College in Ohio with an Associate of Arts Degree, and she loves to get involved in anything dealing with marketing and public relations.

But her interest in horses has never diminished. She's served as the coordinator for several horse shows, and was chosen the 1988-1989 Southern Ohio Draft Horse Queen. In 1990, she was given the crown of Ohio Belgian Queen.

Won Many Industry Prizes

She continued competing in various riding and driving competitions. In 1989, Vikki was named Reserve Champion Showmanship Winner of the Arabian Division at the Ohio State Fair.

In 1992, she won Second Place in the Ladies Cart Class at the Michigan State Fair, driving a Belgian, and then won Third Place in the same event at the 1992 Indiana State Fair.

Prior to starting this cross-country trip in April of 1993, Vikki and David had been engaged for more than a year. "We were going to be married on June 12, 1993, but then we had the chance to take this trip," she explains, "and that changed a lot of things.

"We decided it would be exciting to get married somewhere along the way when we're on the road with the hitch. For a while, we were leaning toward getting married on the Fourth of July, regardless of where the hitch happened to be on that date, because this is such an 'All-American trip'.

> ## "We thought it would be exciting to get married somewhere along the way…"

Got Married Near Home

"But finally we decided to get married when we reached Sugarcreek, Ohio, whenever that might be. That made it awfully convenient for many of my relatives and friends to be on hand, since I'm from near there.

"And, while my dad—who kept running our home farm while Mom and I were on the road—visited us often along the way, it made it more convenient for him, too."

And so they were wed in the charming Amish town of Sugarcreek, on August 14, 1993. For details and photos, turn the page.

French King Bridge—wow, what a structure! I'd have to say, that's the highest elevation me and my buddies have ever been!

As we were crossing the bridge, which spans the Connecticut River, a helicopter flew above us, shooting footage of us for the videotape they're producing of the first part of our trip. I'll bet it's going to be spectacular!

May 9—Sunday. Spent the day taking it easy—not a bad idea, since the high today was near 90°, our warmest weather yet.

One lady told Marlene she'd asked her family to bring her to see us for Mother's Day—a 4-hour trip, but she said it was her best Mother's Day ever!

The crew also got some much-needed rest. Steve rode his bike to unwind, and Don, Dan and Junior went to a plowing match. I'll bet those tractors couldn't do anything a top team of Belgians couldn't do…

May 10—Got another early start this morning, and we stopped in Turners Falls to visit the senior center there. The seniors really enjoyed seeing us, and the feeling was mutual. It's nice to be a part of this trip and know that we're bringing some happiness to so many people.

Then it was on to Greenfield, another very nice town. While relaxing in my stall this afternoon, overheard a couple of the crew members saying rain's predicted for tomorrow.

May 11—It's 70°; no rain in sight! We visited the Mohawk Trail Regional High School in Shelburne Falls, Massachusetts today, and gave rides to quite a few students and townspeople.

People everywhere are amazed by our size and how well-behaved we are, but hay, what did they expect, a bunch of undisciplined colts? We're all professionals in this outfit!

May 12—Rainy, so the crew slept in until 8. Owners of Gould's Maple Farm in Shelburne Falls provided breakfast for everyone—the humans, that is.

Busy evening—David gave presentation at 5:45; gave rides from 6-7:15. Once we were tucked in, crew attended a benefit concert for children whose mother had died. David and Vikki danced with a group from Greenfield Senior Center. Patty Roberts of Colrain brought a wedding gift for David and Vikki—Tupperware and towels.

May 13—Up at 8 a.m. After morning chores and breakfast, David and ♂➙

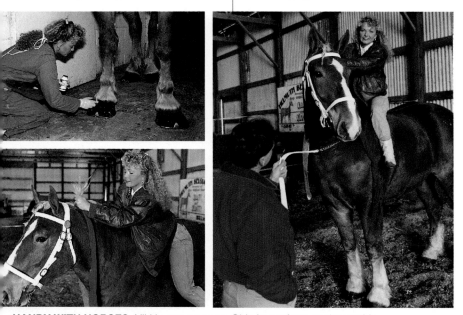

HANDY WITH HORSES. Vikki grew up on an Ohio horse farm, and uses this experience to handle all sorts of duties on the trip. "She's the best and fastest mane braider we have on the crew," says David. "She can do about anything with horses."

The Day They Got Hitched in Ohio

It was the wedding of weddings! With subscribers from 22 states on hand, it was truly a special day for two special people.

IT WAS the kind of day that memories are made of. The sun was shining, the bride and groom were beaming, and so were more than 5,000 subscribers who showed up to share the day with them.

It was August 14 in Sugarcreek, Ohio, the heart of Amish Country. The hitch had crossed six states so far, and on a beautiful sunny Saturday, David and Vikki got married.

The wedding took place at a small church out in the country, about 2 miles north of town. It was the perfect spot—up on a hill, surrounded by cornfields, trees and pasture—plenty of pasture to provide plenty of parking.

It was needed! As David drove the hitch about 3/4 mile from the "camping" area where the horses and semi were set up, cars and pickups lined both sides of the gravel road. Video cameras were everywhere—people were sitting on hoods of cars, standing on embankments near the cornfields, taking pictures, waving and cheering.

The church, Valley View Community Church, held about 500 people. After the invited guests were seated, subscribers were invited to fill the remaining seats. Others on hand quickly filled the more than 500 chairs set up under a huge tent outside. Still more just milled around the six patient horses and listened to the program over the public-address system.

The minister who married the couple, Rev. Charles Jarvis, estimated "5,000 to 7,000 people" for the weekend. We had no way of getting an exact count, but our staffers checked notes and found we'd talked to subscribers from 22 different states (from as far as Connecticut, Colorado, Tennessee and Florida) plus Canada!

We ordered a huge wedding cake that served over 600 people, and made sure everyone on hand got a cup of lemonade (for a real "country toast") as well as a copy of the wedding program to take home as a souvenir.

> ***"It was the largest 'family' to ever attend a wedding!"***

FESTIVE AFFAIR. These pictures provide an idea of the atmosphere, the crowd and the excitement at the wedding. Photos at right show Vikki's wedding gown and David and Vikki dancing. Below shows crowd gathered around the country church near Sugarcreek and special cake made by one of our subscribers; the wedding party driving off is above.

The special cake was made by one of our subscribers, Mary Ann Williams of Valencia, Pennsylvania, who with her husband, Mark, transported the cake in their car more than 140 miles from their home north of Pittsburgh.

The four main tiers were surrounded by six smaller cakes, each with the name of one of the six horses in *Country's Reminisce Hitch*, plus a smaller cake in the shape of a horseshoe.

At the end of the ceremony, Rev. Jarvis said, "I've been holding back this line all day, and now that the formalities are over, I'm going to use it: I just want to say that I knew this ceremony would go smoothly, because the rehearsal last night went off without a hitch!"

The church erupted with laughter and applause, and continued as the handsome couple smiled their way down the aisle and out the back of the church. When they emerged, the waiting crowd outside cheered, threw rice and shouted good wishes as the couple joined the rest of the wedding party on the wagon.

It was quite a sight to see a pretty bride in her white satin gown standing on the wagon, holding

the lines while David briefly addressed the crowd on a portable microphone, thanking them for coming and being "part of the largest 'family' who ever attended a wedding!"

Then he pulled on leather gloves, whistled at the team and took off down that same crowded gravel road to the camping site, where hundreds more cheered when they arrived.

"I must have signed 5,000 autographs this weekend," David said later. "Me, too," echoed Vikki. (She signed some of them "Mrs. Helmuth".)

It was truly a special day and a special wedding for two special people. And then they headed across the country on one of the most unusual honeymoon trips ever—on a slow-moving wagon behind six beautiful Belgians.

Vikki left to buy tack supplies. Then the crew harnessed us for our walk to historic Deerfield, and we left after lunch.

Arrived at 5 and gave rides in town from 6-7 p.m. Camped for the night at Yeswinski dairy farm. Steve's a former dairyman, so he was thrilled—but we arrived too late for him to help with the milking!

May 14—I had the day off to rest my neck; collar's been rubbing a bit. Hitch left at 8:30 a.m.; had 11 riders and 700 spectators on route to Williamsburg.

Arrived at The Lunch Box restaurant just in time for lunch. George Smith of Chesterfield (he'll be 84 next month) drove to visit us. He can't walk far, so Vikki took Stoney right up to his car for a visit.

David was interviewed by a reporter from North Hampton. Brent Young of South Deerfield took Steve sight-seeing after crew got us settled.

May 15—I had a day off again; the other guys left at 8:20 a.m. for 8-mile trip. Had 44 riders, nearly 800 spectators.

Stopped at Goshen Center School at 10 a.m.; David talked with 400 folks there. Arrived Country Corner restaurant in Goshen just after 11.

While Don was parking the semi, he got hung up on a berm. Good Samaritans Bob Kabat and Peter Luchiner cut logs with a chain saw and put them under the tires to get him "unstuck".

May 16—Sunday. Sunny skies for our "day of rest". Crew gave us baths. Marlene was busy cooking, as usual, and cleaning the motorcoach.

I'm getting anxious to get moving again—I'm a draft horse, and all of this "taking it easy" stuff just isn't my style!

May 17—On the road at 8:25 a.m. Saw over 700 people on 10-mile route and gave rides to 42 people.

Vikki drove the hitch part of the way. As we passed Hillside Terrace Nursing Home, residents stood outside waving. Also saw 400 people at Berkshire Trail Elementary School.

Dorothy Beebe of Williamsburg came by with a wedding gift for David and Vikki—an oil painting she'd done herself! Arrived at 11 a.m. at a rest stop on Hwy. 9 near Cummington.

May 18—Hitch left at 8:35 a.m.; David's still letting my neck rest, so I rode in the semi again. Saw fewer people today (about 200 on 11-mile route); maybe cool weather kept them home.

It was a beautiful drive past Windsor ♂

State Forest. Arrived at Dalton General Store at 11:30. This afternoon David gave a seminar at Craneville Elementary School.

Native American Robert "Big Bear" Stevens of Williamsburg, one of 170 visitors today, gave us Indian blessings for a safe journey.

May 19—Another gorgeous day! I'm *finally* back in swing with J.R.—good to be back on the job! Left at 8:15 a.m.; had 34 riders on 10-mile trip to Pittsfield.

Arrived 10:30 a.m. after stopping at a day-care center.

May 20—Traveled down to the Shaker Village stable in historic Richmond, Massachusetts today. The crew turned us out in a field; we ran together and kicked up our heels as the videotape cameras rolled.

The crew also took all of the rigs to Western Star Trucks near Pittsfield for a wash—we're a classy outfit and determined to keep everything looking sharp!

May 21—Left at 9:10 a.m. for 10.5-mile trip into New York State. Over 900 people came out today, despite overcast skies and slight rain.

Gave 30 people rides; arrived in New Lebanon, New York at 12:15 p.m. Crew broke for lunch (Coney dogs, slaw, baked beans), then visited with more than 200 people.

The crew's hard work was rewarded tonight with a 3-hour cruise on the Hudson River, aboard the *Spirit of St. Joseph*. Junior Kauffman was especially thrilled; he'd never been on a riverboat before. Marlene was excited, too—she got to be "captain" for a few minutes!

May 22—Saturday. Nicer weather today. Left 8:30 a.m. for 11.7-mile trip. Stopped at 9:50 so David could replace Chipper (one of our new "spare" horses) with Magic in left lead; Chipper was getting tired as he's not quite as accustomed to the road as the rest of us!

Passed through Nassau; had 48 riders. Arrived 11:45 a.m. at the Agway Feed Store—definitely *my* kind of place—in Schodack. Bazan family of East Nassau brought David and Vikki homemade goodies—jelly, honey, banana bread.

May 23—Sunday. We ordinarily

Trip Began with Horses'

TO MAKE this an official "Atlantic to Pacific" coast-to-coast trip, David wanted to dip the horses' hooves into the surf at Kennebunkport on the coast of Maine. We'd all been waiting for this dramatic moment, but none of us anticipated just *how* dramatic it would be!

Junior and Steve rode each horse separately into the water first, to get them used to the feel of waves crashing around their feet. They, like most of the crew members, had never seen the ocean before. Then all six horses were hitched up and David and Vikki drove them in.

The team charged confidently into the crashing surf, responding without hesitation to David's commands, prancing proudly as the videographer and dozens of sightseers filmed the impressive sight.

Then Firestone, in the swing position with Stoney, tripped on a submerged tree branch and fell. He wasn't hurt, but his harness was tangled around the branch.

"It's all right, boys," David calmed the other horses. "He's okay. Just stand quiet." And they did, nearly knee-deep in the water with more waves coming in.

The other crew members hurried into the cold water to Firestone's side to keep him calm and keep him down (if a horse gets up and finds himself tangled in the harness, he'll often panic and try to run, worsening the situation for him and the rest of the hitch).

Firestone stayed down and stayed calm. As David said later, "It was as though he was lying there saying, 'Hey, I'm Firestone, I'm the star of this show. I fell down, and everybody's going to come to my aid and take care of me, so I'll just lie here and wait.'"

The crew, getting splashed with cold waves above their waist, worked quickly to untangle Firestone's harness. Everybody got completely soaked, and Don even

Dramatic Splash in Surf

lost his new crew hat. He contended later that a whale was probably wearing it now!

After a few minutes, they got Firestone free and he stood up. Since part of the wagon hitch needed repair, they unhooked the rest of the team and led them out of the water.

A while later, the crew hitched up all of the horses again and got set for another try. This time things were picture-perfect, as some of the other surf-side photos in this book attest. In fact, the "splashing through the surf" picture has proved to be our best-selling poster.

Sunrise Service on Beach

Another memorable event as the trip got started was the special Easter service on the beach at Narragansett Point. Several congregations participate in this inter-denominational service each year—but this was probably the first time a big Belgian horse was part of the service!

Chip came with the crew and stood in the back row throughout the service. He was very well-behaved, although he did add a few whinnies as Pastor Paul Johnson said a special blessing for the crew and horses. "We pray for the protection and safety of everyone involved in the trip," the pastor said, then quipped, "and Chip's 'comments' seem to be very positive!"

Pastor Johnson said his parishioners were thrilled to be part of this event. "My wife and I have been fans of *Country* magazine for years and have shared it with a lot of people. Having *Country's Reminisce Hitch* here was wonderful!"

After the service, David and Vikki took Chip for a ride in the ocean—a majestic sight Marlene will never forget. "Seeing these great forces of nature come together made chills run up my spine," she said. "This was truly one of my most memorable Easter Sundays!"

don't travel today, but made an exception since the videographer is with us.

We walked to Albany, the capital of New York. I was in swing with another new horse, Spike. He's doing just fine!

Had 49 riders on 11-mile route through Rensselaer and Albany and across the Hudson River to the Capitol building in Albany.

Once we got to the Capitol, we took 12 Russian dignitaries from the Capitol to the governor's mansion!

Lois helped them on the wagon but couldn't talk with them much; she doesn't speak Russian and they don't speak English! But they got into the spirit of things anyhow, and all donned official hitch caps for their ride!

May 24—Since we traveled yesterday, we took the day off and spent it at our campsite near Albany. Jim and Kathy McNamee of Claverack brought the crew a bunch of homemade muffins; bet they tasted good with Marlene's meat loaf!

May 25—Rain! We decided to sit tight another day.

May 26—A beautiful day—quite an improvement! Left at 9 a.m. and stopped at 10:30 at the Guilderland Elementary School, where David gave a seminar for 500.

Passed through Westermere and McKownville; had 50 riders. Arrived 12:30 p.m. at O'Connor's Auction Service. Crew received gifts from Candy Kraft of Altamont, Bob and Donna Pikalingis of Schenectady, and Suzanne Aldi of Palatine Bridge.

Had 150 more visitors tonight—people sure seem to get excited when they hear we're in town!

May 27—It rained all morning, so David decided we wouldn't travel today. Then—wouldn't you know it—it turned bright and sunny in the afternoon. Some days you just can't call 'em!

May 28—Rained again this morning, so we didn't leave until noon. We went through Princeton and Duanesburg, then arrived at the Elks Lodge in Esperance, New York at 3:30 p.m. Da- ↻

vid wanted to make up for some of our rain delays, so we traveled 13.2 miles today.

The crew got us settled in, then broke for dinner—steak, asparagus and baked potatoes. About 175 people stopped to visit this evening.

May 29—Saturday. After our "long haul" yesterday, David decided to give us the day off. The crew fed and groomed us, then we relaxed in outdoor pens. Had over 1,000 visitors! Lions Club treated the crew to a barbecue dinner this evening, then invited them to stay for a dance afterward.

May 30—Sunday. After the crew bathed, vacuumed and brushed us, they spent the day relaxing. Some went bowling, others to a movie. About 2,000 visitors today—the crowds are growing faster than a Belgian colt!

May 31—Memorial Day. Hitch was to participate in town's Memorial Day parade, but it rained so hard that Vikki rode Magic instead. He looked great in white show bridle. Rain didn't bother him a bit. Had over 2,000 visitors again!

June 1—Left at 8:30; route went up two steep hills. We were really "digging in"—David had to tighten shoes on Stoney and me later! Had 22 riders on 9.2-mile route through Sloansville.

Arrived Carlisle Fire Department, 11:20 a.m. Windstorm this afternoon—crew had to tighten tent ropes several times, and two tent bars broke in half!

Goodies for crew—June Collins of Sloansville brought cookies, and Kenneth Mays of Sharon Springs gave David and Vikki a plaque for their upcoming wedding. Reporter from Cobleskill interviewed David, too.

June 2—Cool, windy. On the road at 8:25 a.m. Gave 26 folks rides on 11.2-mile trip through Sharon, Sharon Springs and Leesville. Arrived Burton's Dairy at 11:45 a.m.

Ethel Benninger, director of Office for Aging in Cobleskill, provided lunch for crew. Rod's Welding, Cherry Valley, welded tent bars back together. David gave a seminar at Central School, Sharon Springs.

John and Donna Schuttig of Central Bridge brought Marlene some pot holders with horses on them. We thought those were mighty stylish!

June 3—On road at 8:25. Had 32 riders through pretty dairy country. Seeing fresh-cut alfalfa in fields made us hungry!

Walked 11.6 miles through historic

ENTHUSIASTIC SENIORS (above and below) made the most of every opportunity to admire and pet the champion Belgians whenever hitch paid a visit to senior centers and nursing homes. Riders (bottom photo) frequently lined the hitch route for miles.

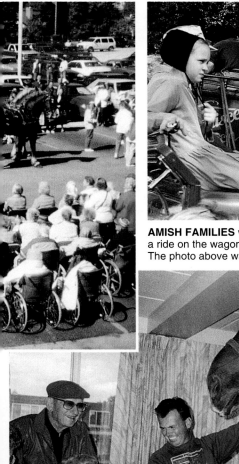

AMISH FAMILIES were among the many who enjoyed taking a ride on the wagon when the hitch passed through their area. The photo above was taken between Perrysville and Lucas, Ohio.

PACKED HOUSE! Gentle giant Cody always filled the room (above) whenever he paid a "personal" visit to delighted nursing home residents. Photo below shows Cody making the acquaintance of a miniature "cousin" during the hitch's stop at Ft. Madison, Iowa.

Cherry Valley and stopped at Senior Outreach Center in Springfield Center, New York.

Arrived Burger World restaurant, Springfield Center, at noon. Crew ate well—topped off sub sandwiches at lunch with brownies from Win and Connie Osterhout of Oneonta. Bruce Hargrove of East Springfield brought muffins, too.

June 4—Great day, with nearly 1,500 visitors. Walked 6.5 miles through Warren and Richfield. Had 32 riders.

Stopped to visit folks in Disabled American Veterans van; David took us right up to the van door so people in wheelchairs could pet Magic and Chip.

Arrived at Dari-Creme in Richfield Springs at 10:25 a.m. Owners Karen Meehan and Sheryl Maine treated the crew to both lunch and dinner. Went to the town's Central School later. A television crew interviewed David and took pictures of Vikki and me. (The photographers obviously knew a great subject when they saw one.)

June 5—Saturday. Left at 8:25 under cloudy skies. Had 69 riders on 11.4-mile trip through Brighton. David stopped at 10:15 to readjust lines on Stoney and me.

In Winfield, the auction house stopped its sale when we walked by; everyone applauded us! It was raining when we arrived at Winfield Memorial Town Park at 12:15 p.m. Had 480 visitors in the afternoon and evening.

June 6—Sunday. Crew was up at 7 a.m. Rained on and off, but nearly 700 people came to see us. Spent the day resting under tent while crew took it easy.

Marlene took a break from cooking and bought fried chicken for dinner. Crew celebrated Junior's and Steve's birthdays with cake and ice cream. Chip and I were trying to guess their ages in "horse years".

June 7—Back on the road at 8:25. Beautiful weather! Saw 400 people on route. Had 82 riders. Walked 13 miles through Bridgewater and Waterville.

Stopped at Harding Nursing Home in Waterville. Arrived Rich's Feeds (I wish they'd let me go in and *browse*) in Sangerfield at 12:20 p.m. Had 750 visitors. David was interviewed by a TV reporter from Syracuse.

June 8—Set a new record today— 94 riders! Walked 11.7 miles; passed through Madison and Bouckville and arrived at 12:30 p.m. at a rest area out- ↷

side Eaton, New York. Madison Central School bands serenaded us along Hwy. 20! They were awarded a $200 check for participating in the *Reminisce* Club's Communicating Through Music & Actions Program.

Stopped at Methodist church for Time Out for Care Givers program; excited seniors were waiting for us. Had 925 visitors at evening stop, including six Mennonite men from Swanton, Maryland who were in area on business and made a special trip to see us.

June 9—Left 8:30 a.m. for 11.4-mile trip to Nelson Inn. Had 53 riders. Stopped at two schools in Morrisville, plus Madison County Office for Aging and Crouse Community Center. Arrived in Nelson at noon. Had 750 visitors.

June 10—Warm and humid when we left at 8:20 a.m. Had 55 riders on 11.3-mile route—steepest grades yet, so we stopped to rest a lot!

Passed through Cazenovia, which will use horse-drawn vehicles in its centennial on Sept. 18. Arrived 12:20 p.m. at Mabe Stables, Pompey.

Gave seminar for 800 at Burton Street Elementary School; students had lots of good questions! Welder fixed two new stalls Featherlight made for us. We needed extra room—there are 10 of us now!

Marlene bought the week's groceries—cost $176—that's a hungry crew she's got to feed! Had 450 visitors tonight. Steve went home for his brother's wedding.

June 11—Cool, cloudy weather kept crowds small. Had 30 riders on 12-mile trip to La Fayette. Wind was a challenge—it's harder to pull when it's in our faces.

Stoney and I needed new nails in our hind shoes; Dan did Stoney's and Junior did mine. (Good thing we're not ticklish!)

Mary Anne Lelakowski of La Fayette brought food for the crew—rhubarb-apple pie, pancake mix, honey and syrups—what a spread!

June 12—Saturday. Left 8:20 a.m.; at 11:45, Dan brought Cody from camp to replace J.R. who was prettty well tuckered out. He's still a young horse, and the humidity and hills were pretty tiring, even for us old veterans!

We had 95 riders on our 12.6-mile walk through Navarino; we arrived at Vic Johnson's drive-in outside Skaneateles at 1:05 p.m.

Heat got to the crew also, but they

How David Trains Belgians— Probably Like No One Else

Every trainer likely has his own unique methods, but David's include actually riding each horse.

"WHEN I train a horse, he becomes almost a part of me. I get inside his head. I get to know every habit or personality quirk of his, and he gets to know me just as well."

That's how David Helmuth describes his personal approach to training a draft horse, an approach that he's developed and groomed since he started training ponies at 6 years old, and training draft horses at 10.

"To get to know each other better, I also do something that very few trainers still do. I ride every draft horse I train. When I'm on their back, they are listening to my voice commands within 3 feet of their ears. It's strictly one-on-one. I haven't found a better way to communicate with a horse.

"It takes me about 18 months of concentrated attention to make a draft horse perfect. And I mean perfect. That means he'll do everything I want him to, immediately and willingly.

"It takes a certain horse as well as a certain person to make it work. The horse has to have a big heart and be willing to work, and so does the trainer. You can throw a bushel of patience in there, too, for the trainer.

Must Have Mutual Admiration

"There are dumb horses, just like there are dumb people. But for the most part, all horses are pretty trainable. I can pretty much look at a horse—see how he holds his head and whether he has pride and a good look in his eye—and tell whether he can be trained.

"But by the same token, I think a horse knows pretty quickly whether a trainer knows his stuff. He knows a 'true horseman'. He can spot an imposter in an instant. Point is, the two of them have to trust each other."

Ideally, David likes to start working with a colt within a week after it's born. "I put a little halter on him and lead him around. I want him to get to know what a human being is and that I'll be kind to him and take care of him.

"I like to get him out in the pasture and let him get a lot of exercise. I give him just enough feed to fully nourish him, but don't overfeed him; if you overfeed they can grow too fast. I like horses to grow and develop naturally.

"I also want him outside to get used to the weather. If you pamper him and baby him, he'll be a baby all of his life. I want him to get used to the elements, so by the time he's 2 years old, he's tough and has a lot of spirit and confidence in himself."

Small Size No Problem

While David has gained stature in the draft horse industry, he's not of large stature himself, and he's keenly aware of it. It comes up often in his conversation. You soon get the idea his 5-foot-8-inch stature is what has always given him his determination to compete with "the big boys". More importantly, his size never mattered to the horses—they have always known he was "in charge", even when he was a 10-year-old boy driving 2,400-pound horses.

"I'm not a big person," he says matter-of-factly. "When I was 18, I only weighed a hundred pounds. And I only weigh 140 today. A Belgian can walk all over you if he doesn't respect you and the way you command him. So I learned real quick to use my voice in a way that shows him I mean business!"

David has never trained or shown any other breed of draft horse but Belgians. "I owe a lot to this breed," he explains. "First, as a kid on an Amish farm, that's the only breed we had. But even in the years since then, no horse has ever excited me the way a Belgian does.

"I don't think there's an animal alive that has more 'willingness' to work than a Belgian. They're just unreal. They love to be in harness and do something. You can tell they prefer it to standing in the barn or lolling around in the pasture. They're achievers.

"And Belgians have a great temperament. They're easier to work with than most horses. They have distinct personalities, they have a great deal ♂→

worked extra hard to get *us* bathed and comfortable! Good crowds—450 this morning, 700 at evening stop.

June 13—Warm, pleasant weather for our Sunday off. David probably liked having day off, too—it's his birthday! He and Vikki visited the beautiful Finger Lakes area.

Had over 1,700 visitors today; souvenir stand was swamped! Crew ate their meals at drive-in.

June 14—Left 8:15 a.m.; had 122 riders on our 11-mile walk through Skaneateles, Sennett and Auburn. Magic and Chipper spooked a bit when 20 Holsteins saw us and ran up to a fence along the road—guess you could say they were really "mooooved" by the incident!

Passed Skaneateles Lake, part of Finger Lakes—that cool water looked mighty inviting. Later, we visited 50 children at Skaneateles Early Childhood Center, and 500 more at Herman Avenue Elementary School in Auburn.

Chipper seems to be the kids' favorite—they like the fact he's the youngest horse and in the lead team! (Obviously, they're still a little too young to appreciate maturity when they see it—did I mention that I was named Grand Champion Belgian *eight* times?)

We arrived at the rest area in Aurelius at 12:10 p.m.; 900 visitors there.

June 15—Crew got rained on while breaking camp. On road at 8:50 a.m. for 11-mile trip through Tyre to Seneca Falls.

Had 61 riders and arrived at our stop at 12:05 p.m. Helene Newell of Skaneateles brought doughnuts for crew; John and Lucille Cardinell, Union Springs, brought rolls. Marilyn Strickland, Williamson, gave Vikki a cookbook, a bouquet and fresh asparagus.

June 16—Cool weather for 10.7-mile walk through Waterloo (celebrating its bicentennial), to Geneva.

Had 49 riders and visited 120 seniors at New Horizons Adult Day Health Care Center, Waterloo. Arrived 11:40 a.m. at Lakeshore Park in Geneva. Had over 600 visitors, including a tour bus from World Wide Country Tours, a division of Reiman Publications—the same company that's sponsoring our journey!

David talked about the trip; Vikki brought me out for petting! (They loved it when I tossed my head and whinnied!) Crew had generators serviced. Dan picked up shavings and supplies for ♂→

"I know each of these horses as well as I know members of my family. I know what to expect of them even before they do it. They're like a part of me, and I'm a part of them..."

us, and tightened Stoney's hind shoes.

June 17—Left 8:30 a.m. for 12.1-mile walk through Seneca, Flint and Aloquin. Busy route—lots of traffic!

Had 97 riders. Arrived 1 p.m. at the Finger Lakes Livestock Exchange. Had 650 visitors, including Judy and George McAllaster of Watertown, who drove over 100 miles to see us!

Crew went to Price Champion barn to pick up hay donated to us—now that's what I call a meaningful contribution!

June 18—Dan fed us at 5:15 a.m., and we left at 8:30 for 9.7-mile walk through Canandaigua and Centerfield, New York. We passed several strawberry farms and arrived at the convenience store in East Bloomfield at 11:20.

Today was much quieter than usual. Had 48 riders and then 90 visitors at our evening stop.

June 19—Saturday. J.R. left for Vikki's dad's farm in Winchester, Ohio today to rest awhile—David says he's a little too young to keep up with the rest of us. He'll be grazing in green pasture and drinking fresh creek water, so he shouldn't find the adjustment too difficult!

Dan took the ladder off the wagon; a welder needs to fix one of the steps.

June 20—Sunday. Spent the day relaxing. Junior had set up hot-wire pens in a grassy area near the convenience store. We really enjoyed being able to roll around, soak up some sun (I think my mane is beginning to show some blond highlights) and eat fresh grass!

June 21—Very cold and rainy today, so we stayed put for some additional rest.

June 22—On the road by 8:20. Weather's warmed up to 70s. Had 104 riders on 10.7-mile route through Bloomfield, West Bloomfield and Lima.

We arrived 12:20 p.m. at Shanks Agricultural Service. Sandy Lunch of Honeoye Falls gave Vikki some handmade doilies. Had 550 visitors.

June 23—Left 8:30 a.m.; walked 9.1 miles through East Avon and arrived in Avon at 12:20. Had 125 riders, including a lady from Pinehurst Nursing Home, Honeoye Falls, who was 99!

David gave a seminar for 200 at St. Agnes School.

Among 750 visitors tonight were Jack's former owners, Keith and Margaret Dennis of Ontario, Canada. Jack

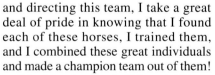

of intelligence and, most importantly, they have a big heart."

While David stresses the importance of training each horse in his hitch, he says all that training is wasted if any horse in the hitch thinks of himself as an individual rather than a member of the team.

Emphasis on Teamwork

"As their driver, trainer and 'coach', my job is to make these six horses work together as a single unit," he explains. "Six great individual horses doing their own thing won't win anything or anyone's respect. They have to like each other, respect each other and work together, as a team.

"When you make that happen, it's a beautiful, satisfying thing. Driving this champion six-horse hitch is the most satisfying thing I've ever done. When I'm up there on that wagon, holding the lines and directing this team, I take a great deal of pride in knowing that I found each of these horses, I trained them, and I combined these great individuals and made a champion team out of them!

"And you know what? I can tell these horses enjoy that same feeling as much as I do! They cherish the spotlight. They have a lot of pride and enjoy performing. It's so obvious when you watch them closely—they'll be plodding along, just sort of keeping to themselves as I approach the parade grounds, looking sort of old, tired and disinterested.

"But as soon as they get in front of

RIDING each Belgian he trains helps David get "better acquainted" with the horse. "When I'm 3 feet from his ear, he knows that I'm talking to *him*." At right, he rides "wide open" during winter training. At left, he drives a "practice lap", and above he "Roman rides" at Kennebunkport, Maine.

that crowd, they'll perk up their ears, hold their heads high and swing them from side to side, bring their knees up and prance like they're all colts! The bigger the crowd, the more the applause, the more they prance. I'm busy up there in the seat, but it still brings a smile to my face every time, just to see them 'showboating'.

"These six horses are real characters. They're a bunch of hams, and because they just crave attention, they loved every day of this trip, with thousands of people coming out to watch them all along the way."

As he talks about these beautiful Belgians, the excitement of that 10-year-old kid fascinated with draft horses can sometimes still be seen in his eyes.

told me later that it was good to see them again, and that they told him they were mighty proud of his part in "Pulling for Seniors"!

June 24—Had 137 riders on 12.4-mile walk through Geneseo. Shirley Smith of Linden, Pennsylvania came 175 miles to ride!

Arrived 12:30 at A.R. Christiano Farms, Cuylerville. Had 900 visitors tonight. One said our shoes, "Scotch Bottoms" with a rubber pad between the shoe and our hoof, reminded him of Air Jordans. David laughed and said maybe Michael Jordan should try a pair. (I wonder who this Michael Jordan is—some guy who does a lot of running, maybe?)

June 25—Busy 10.5-mile trip; 156 riders. Went through Leicester. David gave seminar at Silver Lake Day Treatment Center for the handicapped.

He was turning the hitch when Magic's lead line broke. Vikki jumped down to catch him, then taped the line together. (Of course, *I* knew that Magic had things under control the entire time.)

Arrived at Charcoal Corral (funny name—I've never seen a corral made of charcoal!) in Perry, New York at 12:30 p.m. Stopped by a Belgian farm, too, so we got to visit some "relatives"!

Luther Reynolds of Perry, age 103, visited us. Vikki brought me out so Luther could pet me. Bush Hill Florist, Perry, gave the crew flowers.

June 26—Saturday. Gave rides to 148 people on 12.5-mile walk through Castile. When we got to railroad tracks, Magic spooked and jumped to the left. Chip led him back by tugging on his inside line, pulling Magic toward him. (We have to watch out for each other, you know.)

Arrived at the Wyoming County Fairgrounds in Pike at 12:30 p.m. We put on an exhibition and David talked about the trip. Had over 4,000 visitors. Theodore Roy drove 3 hours from Towanda, Pennsylvania to see us! Sheila Seme of Lima brought fruit for the crew, and Becky Broughton of Castile brought strawberry pies. Talk about a warm reception!

June 27—Sunday. Quieter today—occasional rain kept crowds down to about 1,700. I stayed in the tent with Bobby to meet the public; other horses stayed in a barn, each with his own exercise pen.

Western New York Draft Horse and Pony Club treated the crew to a picnic ♂⃗ lunch. Some crew members went sight-seeing later.

June 28—Still at fairgrounds—rained on and off all day. We stayed in hot-wire pens until 4 p.m.; then Junior and Steve washed us and brought us to our stalls for dinner.

George Bancroft of Danville brought some equipment for us, including a lightweight swing pole that'll take some weight off our shoulders. David and Vikki were interviewed by a reporter from Arcade.

June 29—Walked 11 miles through Bliss and Eagle, New York; had 168 riders. Magic did much better crossing tracks. Spike and Jack wore work collars with sheepskin pads to keep necks comfortable.

Chip and I stayed behind to rest.

Had 150 folks waiting when we arrived at evening stop in Arcade. Pammy Macauley of York brought crew home-made goodies; Fred and Agnes Boberg of Delevan brought maple syrup.

June 30—I was back on the road today; walked 10.9 miles through Arcade. Had 132 riders; another 300 people were waiting when we stopped at Suburban Adult Services, a sheltered workshop.

We snacked on grass there, then headed on to the Sardinia Town Park in Chaffee. Had over 1,500 visitors!

July 1—Dan was up at 5:15 to feed us; rest of crew was up between 7 and 10:30. David said this was to be a rest day, so everyone took it easy.

All vehicles were washed, and an RV dealer added two propane tanks to the motorcoach. Vikki gave a seminar while Marlene showed me off to the people—this time *I* got to wear a fancy white show bridle!

July 2—After breakfast, the crew bathed, vacuumed and brushed us, and also cleaned the harnesses and wagon. Then following dinner, they braided our manes and tails and put red, white and blue ribbons in our forelocks.

All this "dolling up" was to get us ready for Chaffee's Independence Day parade, where we pulled our wagon filled with local seniors. Ann Bean of Sardinia said that sight was the highlight of the whole parade!

Lots of folks brought out magazines for David and Vikki to autograph. About 4,500 people were waiting for us when we returned to the park after the parade.

July 3—Saturday. Film crew ar-

What the Crew Went Through Each Day to Get Horses Ready for The Road

If you think these horses looked sharp when you saw them, they probably didn't wake up in the morning looking that way!

HORSES, just like people, need a little grooming and "makeup" to get them looking their best. And getting a draft horse ready for the show ring appear-

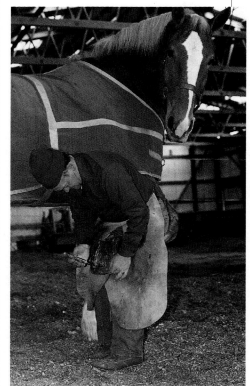

ances or parades takes a lot more time than for any of us people-types to get ready for a night out with our friends. At least we don't need to get our tails braided!

Driver David Helmuth was determined to have these champion horses looking just as good each day on the road as they did when they entered the show ring. ("After all, these horses were going to be 'judged' by hundreds of different people each day," he says, "and more importantly, the subscribers among these people are the real owners of these horses. Most of them would be seeing this hitch for the first and perhaps the only time, so they needed to see these horses at their best.")

With that in mind, we thought you'd be interested in what David and his crew went through each morning of the trip to get these horses ready for another day on the road.

After the team was fed and watered each morning, each horse was brushed down. Any soiled spots were washed off, dried and brushed. Next, the mane and tail on each horse was brushed and combed thoroughly, preparing them for rolling and braiding.

If a mare is part of a show hitch, the mane is normally not rolled—mares are believed to look more feminine without the roll. But since our horses are all geldings (males not used for breeding), their manes were rolled to look their best.

Some horsemen refer to this process as "braiding" the mane; David and many others use the term "rolling" the mane, since the process involves "rolling" various strands of hair over and over each other. David's 15-step method of rolling (called the "Aberdeen Plait", the same method used in preparing most American draft horses for show), is too complicated to describe step-by-step, but basically it involves using four strands and braiding them together with a bunting (a thin piece of colored fabric).

Complicated as it is to describe, it is still "Easier said than done…until you can do it; then it is easier done than said," according to Maury Telleen, editor of *The Draft Horse Journal*.

Usually five rosettes (rose-like ornaments or ribbons) were inserted into the mane roll. A light wire attached to the mane makes this possible. These rosettes can be purchased, but many draft horse owners prefer to make their own from silk, foam or chenille.

While most owners roll the mane by standing next to the horse, David and Vikki prefer to sit on the horse to do this task. They say it's easier and faster that way (David wouldn't hire any crew member who can't roll a mane or braid a tail in 7 minutes with "perfect" results).

Next, the tail was prepared for braiding. First it may be docked (cut) to make it even at the bottom and the same length as that of the other horses'. Then, as with the mane, it has to be brushed free of any tangles before the braiding begins. This braiding, too, is a 15-step process difficult to describe until you're shown how it's done.

Lastly, the head of each horse was closely inspected, and a small scissors was used to clip and trim long hairs around the ears, muzzle and jaw. A good clip job can greatly enhance the appearance of a horse's head.

All This Really Necessary?

David—and other knowledgeable horse people—feel this type of grooming and care is highly essential to a horse's health and to improving its appearance. "It's not something you can do at the last minute," says David, "or it will show. Experienced horsemen can tell in an instant if a horse has been groomed regularly—its hair will be short, well-managed and glossy, which indicates a healthy skin below it.

"What's more," he points out, "regular grooming is one of the best ways for a horseman to establish a good relationship with his horse. Grooming gets the horse accustomed to being handled, and consequently, it makes him more docile and easier to handle. When we climb right up on these Belgians' backs twice a day—to roll the mane in the morning and unroll it at night—our horses and crew get to know each other pretty well."

There are other practical reasons for thorough grooming. The tail is braided for hygienic reasons, and because it allows the judge a clearer view of the horse's buttocks and legs. Likewise, rolling the mane makes the horse's neck more visible to the judges. In each case, it keeps the showman from "hiding" something from the judge.

"More than anything, getting these horses fully groomed each day not only made them look better to people, it made these horses feel better about themselves," David says.

"Horses, like people, know full well when they're getting 'all dolled up', and they then act a little different and conduct themselves better when people come to see them."

rived at 9 a.m. to shoot interviews with David, Vikki and our visitors. Crew spent much of the afternoon grooming us. Pizza Hut provided pizzas for dinner. Spent rest of the evening relaxing.

July 4—Sunday. Broke camp this morning; drove up to F.E. Brown & Sons Funeral Home in Orchard Park to set up camp and prepare for another parade.

Bob Brown's daughter, Heidi Gardner, treated the crew to a dinner of hot dogs, potato salad and coleslaw—even *I* know that's about as all-American as you can get!

The parade began at 7, and once again, people were lining the route to see us. (I have to admit, we get a "kick" out of showing off like this!) Afterwards, we returned to our camp for quick baths.

David and Vikki were presented with a plaque of appreciation from the village. Crew sat outside to watch the fireworks—what a display!

July 5—Crew was up at 7 to feed us, clean the equipment and get everything loaded back in the semi. After lunch, they washed us, conditioned our manes and tails, and put us aboard the semi for the trip back to our previous overnight stop at Chaffee.

July 6—Donald Vacinek of Sardinia came by with 10 bales of hay— my kind of guy! We waited until things ♂

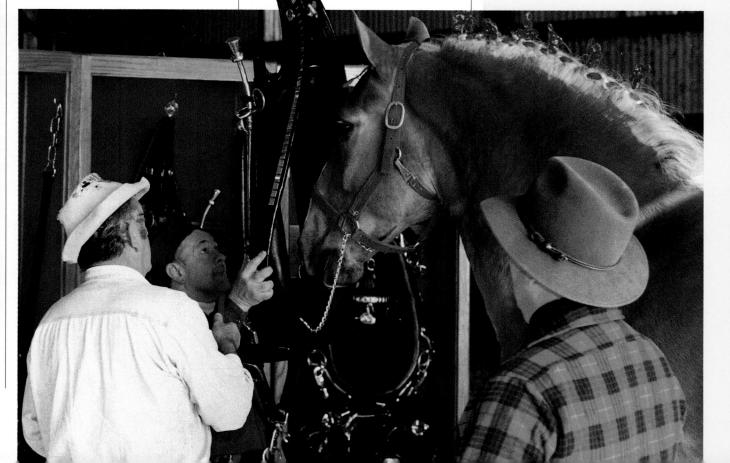

began to cool off in the afternoon before leaving Chaffee for our walk to Agway Feeds in Springville.

Started raining at 6:45, but we kept going; riders (we had 101!) just got out their umbrellas, and those of us in harness found the rain pretty refreshing!

The high school band welcomed us into Springville. Later, David gave a seminar at Le Lans Restaurant, then the crew enjoyed a roast beef dinner. Ron Page from Leicester, New York joined the crew today.

July 7—Scent of fresh-cut hay filled the air on route today—needless to say, that had all of our nostrils flaring!

We left at 8:45 a.m. and stopped a few minutes later for David to give a seminar for 82 residents at Fiddler's Green Manor nursing home in Springville.

Had 63 riders today, including Dr. Wesley Potter of Great Valley, who was so excited about the trip that David let him drive us one block!

We walked 10.2 miles and arrived at the old milk house in Collins, New York at 12:20 p.m. Hot and muggy, so crew hosed us down as soon as we arrived!

July 8—Another humid 90° day. Left 8:05 a.m.; walked 11 miles through Gowanda and past the old Quaker cemetery to Perrysburg, where the Pine Valley Central School marching band serenaded us when we arrived.

Dan and Junior washed us under a shade tree after lunch and put two more fans on us. The crew got another fan for the souvenir stand, too.

July 9—Whew! Up to 92° today! If I wore a bandanna, I'd be using it to mop my brow!

We left at 8 a.m. while it was only 75°. Walked 9.5 miles to Forestville; along the way we had 101 riders. (I mentioned this number to Ashley and asked if it meant anything special to her; she just chuckled!)

As we got to town, the middle school and high school bands fell into step ahead of us creating quite a fanfare. Arrived American Legion Post at 11 a.m. Had over 1,000 visitors.

July 10—Saturday. Nice 11-mile walk through Sheridan to Dunkirk; 80 riders. People seemed especially excited to see us—many came running out of their offices for a closer look!

Arrived Dunkirk Fairgrounds, 11:30 a.m. While crew was having lunch, Vikki and Marlene gave autographs! We

Firestone's BIG FOOT!

"NO FOOT, NO HORSE" is a common adage among draft horse enthusiasts, inferring that if a draft horse doesn't have four sound feet, there's no use looking at or evaluating the rest of the horse.

This being the case, we thought many of you might be amazed to see just how large the feet of high-quality draft horses really are. That's the reason for this *actual-size* photo of Firestone's right front foot. If you put a ruler against it, you'll see it's exactly 9 inches wide.

Now you know why David, Vikki and the other crew members always have to be careful that Firestone or one of the other horses in the hitch doesn't accidentally step on their feet. After all, the feet on each of these horses is supporting over a ton of weight!

Note the shoe under Firestone's foot, which was custom-designed just for this foot, just as each shoe is for each horse in our hitch for maximum comfort. There's even a special rubber pad between the shoe and the hoof to cushion each step.

Just as humans have to trim their toenails regularly, Firestone's hooves have to be trimmed regularly, too. This doesn't "hurt" the horse any more than it hurts to cut your toenails. Nor does attaching the horseshoe to the foot—the nails are driven into the outside edge of the foot, where there are no nerves or feeling.

If some of you who read this book weren't fortunate to get to the trip route to see these magnificent Belgians in person, this picture should put you a little closer to *your* hitch—with this actual-size photo of Firestone's foot, we hope you'll feel this beautiful horse stepped right into your home!

Horses Got New Shoes Every 6 Weeks

Special rubber pads made their shoes comfortable as "old sneakers".

TAKING CARE of the feet is the No. 1 priority of any draft horse hitch. As mention above, the saying in the draft horse industry goes, "No foot, no horse."

With this in mind, a lot of attention was paid to the

ACTUAL-SIZE PHOTO

feet and the shoes of the horses in *Country's Reminisce Hitch* while they were on the road. The horses were re-shod every 5 to 6 weeks.

Special "Scotch Bottom" shoes from Scotland were used on the horses, with each shoe custom-fit for each foot of each horse. For extra comfort, a rubber pad was placed between the shoe and the hoof for cushioning, and each shoe had a heel support.

Don't Worry About the Nails

"These shoes are about as comfortable to these horses as a pair of sneakers are for you," says David. "The Scotch Bottom shoe has a particularly large base, and that provides more surface area to spread out the weight."

If you're inexperienced around horses and see someone pounding a nail into a hoof, don't be concerned—the nails attaching the shoes are driven near the edge of the hoof, where there's no more feeling than you have in the edge of your toenail.

"You have to trim the hoof every time you change shoes," explains David. "You always take a little more off the back and the sides than you do in front.

"This keeps the heel down and makes it more comfortable for the horse. It also results in a lot more flex and action in the toe movement. You want the legs of these horses to go down the road like a sewing machine!"

got baths while Lois, Don and Marlene visited Niagara Falls.

July 11—Sunday. Junior and Steve fed us at 7:45 a.m. Had about 1,500 visitors today. We got baths after lunch, but spent most of the day in our stalls.

Magic and Chipper exercised in arena tonight. Vikki and David took Ashley to Lake Erie for a swim. Vikki ordered her bridesmaids' dresses. (We've all heard we're going to be in the wedding. I don't care what they say; I'm not wearing any dress!)

Marlene bought $316 in groceries, $148 in supplies for the campers.

July 12—Had 144 riders on 10-mile trip from Dunkirk through Pomfret, Fredonia and down to Brocton.

We visited the seniors at Park Shore ♂

Health Care Center before leaving Dunkirk this morning. Arrived West's General Store in Brocton at 11:40 a.m. Had over 1,100 visitors today.

David and Vikki went golfing tonight at Sugar Hill Golf Course. The course's well-groomed fairways looked mighty inviting, but I'm sure the greenskeeper wouldn't appreciate a bunch of 1-ton-plus Belgians thundering over his turf!

July 13—Sunny skies for our 9.5-mile trek through Westfield along Lake Erie; had 95 riders.

Lost a rubber tube off the front left wagon wheel about 10:30 a.m. (Guess that's sort of like throwing a shoe!) Wagon's builder promised to replace any tires that came off, so we're sure he'll fix it.

Sherry Robson, Portland, had a sign in her yard reading, "Good luck to David and Vikki and the team", so we stopped to chat with her. Arrived Ottawa Park 12:30 p.m.

July 14—Cool, cloudy when we left at 8:05 a.m. Walked 11 miles through Barcelona and Ripley. Rain started at 10:30, but we still had 100 riders!

Crossed into Pennsylvania; arrived

Our Special Semi Is One of a Kind!

*The tractor is a limited-edition model…
and the trailer is loaded with features never before seen
in any other horse carrier.*

AT SOME stops along the hitch route, there were almost as many people checking out the truck as the horses! Little wonder—it's a beauty. And it's huge.

With its currant-red finish and its *Country's Reminisce Hitch* artwork, this powerful brute is definitely an eye-catcher.

The huge trailer behind the tractor turns heads, too, but let us tell you about the tractor first, the trailer later. It's a Ford "Hardrunner" Aeromax with a 3406 Caterpillar engine and a 15-speed transmission. It features Alcoa rims and wheels and has a 60-inch

sleeper with 7-1/2-foot standup space.

On top of an already-loaded Hardrunner is the most complete accessory package available, including stereo, CB, air ride seats, motor mirrors, TV and VCR in the sleeper and a host of other amenities.

This particular semi tractor is unique for a lot of reasons. For one, when Ford decided to get into the truck business in a big way in 1990, this very truck was the prototype that was used to turn out a limited edition of just 200 models just like it.

Being a prototype, this tractor was

not made by machines—every bolt was put in by hand and everything else was hand-assembled. Until Ford got this one finished, they couldn't set up anything on an assembly-line basis.

The Hardrunner package included a lot of things that Ford had never put into a truck before. And the testing was extensive—this prototype was tested for wind resistance and dynamics in the same tunnel that was used for the space shuttle at Cape Kennedy.

Up until the start of our cross-country trip, this tractor had never been "put to work". It was Ford's "show truck", and it had never pulled a trailer during the time it was exhibited at truck shows and in dealerships all over the U.S.

"It was built to show, and that's what we did with it," says David. "We wanted a classy, eye-catching tractor that would match the caliber of the rest of what we were taking on the road.

"We really appreciated how the executives of Ford Motor Company and their dealer—Don's Truck Sales of Fairbank, Iowa—worked out an agreement on this particular tractor that

proved mutually beneficial—it brought a lot of positive exposure for them while being appreciated by the thousands who come to see it.

First-Ever Trailer Like This

"During the 5 years prior to this cross-country trip, while transporting horses, I'd been thinking of ways I could put together the best horse trailer that has ever been built," says David.

"I did a lot of homework. I talked to a lot of people, and I studied other horse units—the Budweiser, Coors and Walt Disney rigs—which are the leaders in horse transport.

"The one problem I kept seeing with all horse trailers is that the horses are walked in and backed out. That's when most of your injuries occur, when you're backing out a horse and it steps off the ramp or whatever.

"Secondly, I wanted to haul all eight of my horses, plus the hay, the feed, the water, the harnesses, the equipment and even the wagon *all in one trailer*. (Budweiser uses a separate truck to haul its wagon.)

"I also wanted an office as part ♂➜

Lake Side Farm near the town of North East at 11:45 a.m. I heard owner George Felton tell David and Vikki that his grandfather started the farm in 1875.

George has grape vineyards, like many farmers in the area. Stephanie Ziegler of North East donated crew's dinner—pizza!

July 15—Sun's out today. Took 137 riders on 13-mile trip along the shore of beautiful Lake Erie; lots of vineyards here!

Visited Parkside North East Senior Center on our way out of town this morning. Arrived Shades Beach, Harborcreek Township Park, 12:20 p.m. TV crew filmed us—that's the third crew in 3 days!

Esther Pearsall brought a wedding gift for David and Vikki—glasses from North East Chamber of Commerce. Crew had baked fish and broccoli casserole for dinner. We had 850 visitors!

July 16—Had 117 riders on 11-mile walk to Erie. Pennsylvania National Guard helped direct traffic on busy route—pretty impressive!

David gave a seminar for 300 at Bre- ♂➜

villier Village Nursing Center. We also took several seniors there for a ride; the oldest, Mary Glasgow, was 106!

Another seminar at Erie Day School; we really "knocked the kids' socks off" when we did a figure eight on the playground as we were leaving.

Arrived Erie Fire Department at 11:55 a.m. Over 700 visitors there.

July 17—Saturday. Warm, sunny weather for 11-mile walk through Avonia and Girard to Lake City, Pennsylvania. Had 112 riders *en route* (pretty fancy for a workhorse, eh?) to YMCA's Camp Sherwin in Lake City.

Crew put up our stalls under shade trees. Ethel and Paul Dzmura of Fairfield brought crew homemade breads and jams. David and Vikki left at 6:30 p.m. for the 4-hour drive to Sugarcreek, Ohio to finalize wedding plans.

July 18—Sunday. Crew relaxed today; they even got a chance to take naps! (Of course, they can't sleep standing up like me and my buddies can.)

Don and Lois took the semi to Tantivity Trailers in Vernon, New York to have new doors installed. David and Vikki got back from Ohio this afternoon; sounds like they're getting the plans for this wedding thing pretty well nailed down!

July 19—Laid over an extra day; it was raining this morning, and semi's still being worked on. Crew did regular chores—up at 7 a.m. to clean stalls, water and feed us, then turned us out in pairs in pens.

Dan and Ron cleaned harnesses, too. Several crew members went swimming later in the camp's pool. Ann Young of Corry brought Vikki crocheted pot holders; Jeanette Otteni of Erie brought two ceramic Dalmatians.

July 20—Crew got us up at 6 a.m. to be fed, vacuumed and brushed. Over 300 visitors today. Cody attended two seminars with David—one at camp for 100 people, another at Pleasant Ridge Manor senior center in Girard.

The rest of us relaxed in hot-wire pens. David bought 23 bales of hay for us today, plus shavings and 2 tons of feed. That'll keep us going for a while!

July 21—Back on the road! 300 folks cheered us along our 11-mile route to the home of Ellie Whitsett in East Springfield. Had over 900 visitors there.

Doris Reel of Palm Springs, Florida grew up in this area and flew back just to ride the wagon! (I gave her a little nuzzle when she came over to pet me;

of the trailer, so we'd have a place to do business or relax when we park it.

"So, I put all of these things down on paper and went to see Conrad Clement, president of Featherlight Trailers in Cresco, Iowa. We decided to build the 'trailer of the century', and I think we did it!"

Has Many Unique Features

This trailer-of-all-trailers is 53 feet long, 8-1/2 feet wide and 13 feet high. The horses are led in one side of the trailer when loading, and led out the other side when unloading. "I've been in the horse business for a long time, and this is the only trailer I know of with that feature," David emphasizes.

To achieve that, horses are led one at a time up the ramp near the right rear side of the trailer through 6-foot-wide double doors (most doorways are 4 feet wide). The first horse is led into its stall near the front, turned with its head toward the left side of the

> *"We decided to build the horse trailer of the century, and I think we did it!"*

trailer, and then a cushioned gate is swung in place to close off the side of its stall.

Each of the other horses is led in and locked in in the same fashion. The stalls are set at an angle rather than perpendicular to the front of the truck—that takes some of the sway out of the ride that horses experience when they face directly forward or directly sideways during transit.

To unload, 6-foot-wide double doors on the opposite side of the trailer—near the left front—are opened, and the horses are led out one by one. The stall gates are hinged on both ends and can move both ways—they can be opened one way to put the horses in and the other way to let them out.

The trailer rides extremely low—just 12 inches off the ground on the road. Then, rubber air bags under the frame are released when the unit is parked, lowering the trailer to just 8 inches off the ground for easier load-

ing and unloading. (While in this position, the trailer box rests right on the tires, which concerned many visitors—"How can you drive with the trailer scraping on the tires like that!" many asked, as the crew explained once more that the trailer body is raised before it's moved.)

Rode in Trailer Himself

The 12-inch clearance on the road benefits the horses, too—the lower the ride, the smoother it is for the horses. The air bags also cushion the ride for them. (David confirmed this personally by riding back there himself while a crew member drove the truck.)

To eliminate the never-ending job of replacing bedding and cleaning the stalls in the trailer, David had a 4-inch-thick rubber matting installed in the stalls. "We just take a power washer and wash everything right off the rubber and out the drains in the floor," David points out. "This rubber floor also cushions the ride for the horses."

The transport area for the horses is 8 feet 6 inches high. The 5 feet above that is used for hay storage, tack storage and everything else that needs hauling.

Above the lounge area in front is a 200-gallon water tank concealed in the frame of the truck. Ingeniously, David used baffles in the tank to keep the water from splashing back and forth and swaying the truck.

The water flows by gravity to the stalls, where watering is as easy as turn-

EASY DOES IT. After the harnesses are stored in cabinets along right side, wagon is put on ramp. Hydraulic lift hoists wagon up, then cable-winch pulls it in on pair of tracks.

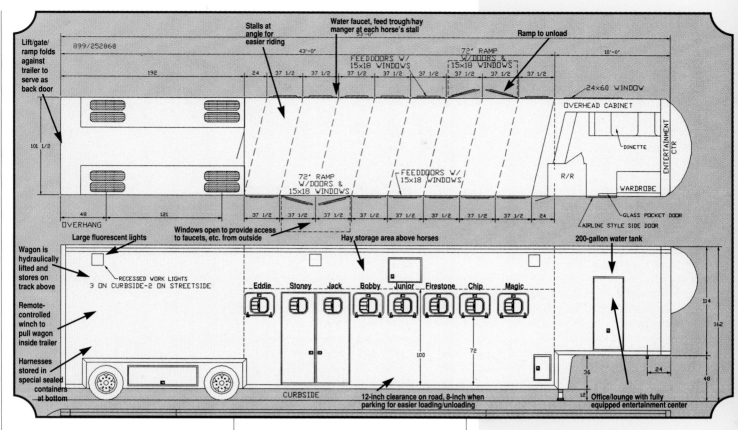

Labels on diagram:
- Lift/gate/ramp folds against trailer to serve as back door
- 899/252868
- Stalls at angle for easier riding
- Water faucet, feed trough/hay manger at each horse's stall
- 53'-0"
- Ramp to unload
- 43'-0"
- FEEDDOORS W/ 15x18 WINDOWS
- 72' RAMP W/DOORS & 15x18 WINDOWS
- 10'-0"
- 192
- 24x60 WINDOW
- OVERHEAD CABINET
- ENTERTAINMENT CTR
- DINETTE
- 101 1/2
- 72' RAMP W/DOORS & 15x18 WINDOWS
- FEEDDOORS W/ 15x18 WINDOWS
- R/R
- 48   121
- WARDROBE
- OVERHANG
- Windows open to provide access to faucets, etc. from outside
- GLASS POCKET DOOR
- AIRLINE STYLE SIDE DOOR
- Large fluorescent lights
- Hay storage area above horses
- 200-gallon water tank
- Wagon is hydraulically lifted and stores on track above
- RECESSED WORK LIGHTS 3 ON CURBSIDE-2 ON STREETSIDE
- Eddie   Stoney   Jack   Bobby   Junior   Firestone   Chip   Magic
- Remote-controlled winch to pull wagon inside trailer
- 114
- 162
- Harnesses stored in special sealed containers at bottom
- 100   72
- 36   24   48
- CURBSIDE
- 12   12-inch clearance on road, 8-inch when parking for easier loading/unloading
- Office/lounge with fully equipped entertainment center
- 37 1/2 (repeated dimension marks)

ing each stall's faucet knob. Water can also be drawn into buckets for watering horses while they're hitched up. Each stall has a window (with the horse's name above it) that opens out.

This allows crew members to feed and water the horses without opening the large doors to get inside as is the case with most horse trailers—they can simply reach in through the window to water each horse, give it feed and put a large measure of hay in its manger.

"From the outside of this trailer, we can put in enough feed and water to carry them comfortably for over 100 miles," David says proudly.

When he's transporting horses, he likes to feed them around 5 a.m., load them up and be on the road by 6 a.m. He stops after 20 minutes to make sure everything is okay, then stops every hundred miles for about 20 minutes to do the same thing.

"Most people don't let their horses eat while they're moving," David says. "But I like to keep hay and water in front of them while we're on the road. I try to fool them into thinking they're at home in the barn, and make them as comfortable as they would be there."

This all-in-one trailer has 15 feet of specially designed space for the 14-1/2-foot wagon, too. First the harnesses are

stored in boxes at the bottom of this space ("I got tired of dealing with the soiled harnesses stored below the horses as they are in many trailers").

Then a remote-controlled winch with a cable attached to the wagon pulls it onto a ramp at the back of the truck. Next a powerful hydraulic lift raises the wagon straight up before it's winched forward on a pair of tracks over the harnesses. The lift/gate/ramp then folds up to serve as the trailer's back door.

Still Many More Features

Lighting had always been a problem at night with trailers David used in the past, but not with this one. There are four large fluorescent lights on each side of the trailer and two in the rear, plus eight lights inside.

These are powered by a generator on the back of the semi tractor, as are all the amenities in the 10-foot x 12-foot plush lounge in the front of the rig. It opens with an airplane-style door to an office area that includes a desk, a fax machine, a telephone, a dinette with a microwave, a bathroom and shower, plus a sleeper sofa.

The lounge also includes a complete entertainment center with a color TV, VCR and stereo system. "You can see why we feel this is the best horse trailer ever built," David says.

hope I wasn't being too forward!)

Marlene made a hearty dinner for crew—steak, deviled eggs, corn, scalloped potatoes. Don and Lois got back with semi—new doors look great!

July 22—Nice sunny day for 11.2-mile walk into our sixth state—Ohio, the Buckeye State. (Here's a piece of trivia—did you know buckeyes are also called *horse* chestnuts?)

Had 134 riders on our way to Conneaut—saw lots of covered bridges along the way!

Arrived at the Church of God, 11:45 a.m. More than 1,200 visitors—one man brought his children more than 300 miles to see us!

July 23—We traveled 9 miles through Bushnell and Monroe Center; arrived at the Pierpont Fire Department at 11 a.m. Had 149 riders on route.

Cindy Rothermel of Kutztown, Pennsylvania drove 8 hours for a ride! Earlier, the team gave rides to nine seniors during our visit to the Care Ace Home before we left Conneaut.

Had over 1,100 visitors, including Everett Smith of Jefferson—a champion yodeler!

July 24—Saturday. Beautiful weather for 11-mile walk through North Richmond on the way to Andover, Ohio. Chip was enjoying himself—his ♂

ears perked up whenever the Holsteins came close to fences along the road!

Had 196 riders. Ralph and Margaret Thomas and Ruth and Carol Keeney drove 375 miles from York County, Pennsylvania to get on board; they said it was worth it, though!

Arrived at Thurman and Ernestine Bullis' Andover farm, 11:45 a.m. We had lunch in barn's box stalls. Junior, Steve cleaned semi so our 1,800 visitors could walk through it. Terry and Elaine Wrahood of Andover brought cheese and meat tray for crew.

July 25—Sunday. Muggy weather; glad we had the day off! We spent most of the day in our stalls. Crew gave us baths and chatted with over 1,000 visitors.

Marlene had the night off from cooking, but had to drive 25 miles to do laundry! Me and my buddies aren't the only ones working on this trip!

July 26—I was resting today, but it was another humid, busy day for the rest of the team. Flies were a real problem; Vikki had to buy vinegar to pour on their backs to repel those nasty critters. Take it from me; a bite from a horsefly is not a pleasant experience!

Had 211 riders on 11-mile route through Williamsfield to Kinsman. Riders Roger and Sheila Larwood of Marion, New York came 280 miles—their third visit with us, but their first ride!

David gave seminar for 200 seniors at Miller Memorial Health Care Center in Andover this morning. Folks there gave Vikki a photo album of clippings about the trip.

Arrived Badger High School, Kinsman, 12:15 p.m. Crew stayed busy answering questions from nearly 1,800 visitors. Dale and Estelle King of East Berlin, Pennsylvania drove 340 miles to see us.

July 27—I was back in swing with Spike for 11.5-mile trek to Cortland Quality Care Nursing Center in Cortland; center treated crew to lunch.

Tammy and Greta Trecker of Kinsman brought coconut pie for crew, too. Kathleen Weik drove 356 miles from Harrisburg, Pennsylvania to visit.

July 28—I rested again while the team walked 13 miles through Warren to Lordstown; had 132 riders.

Stopped at two senior centers—Gillette Nursing Center and Scope Nursing Home, which had a seniors band playing. Arrived at an open field at Hewitt Gifford Road and Todd Av-

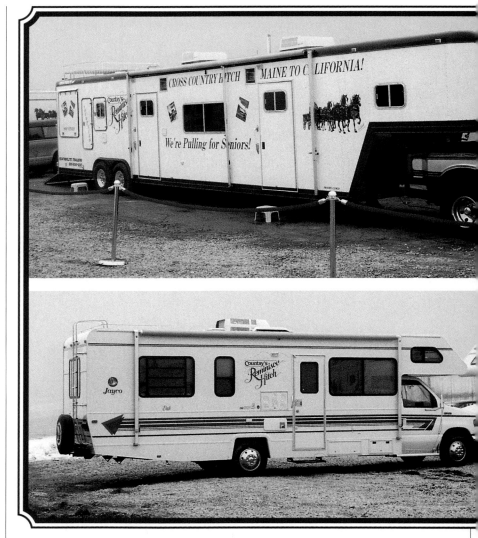

Comfortable Units Provided Crew's 'Home on the Road'

Several large mobile units offered crew modern sleeping quarters, cooking facilities and a "souvenir stand".

"AFTER we got the semi horse trailer under way, I went back to Featherlight with the idea of designing and building a mobile home trailer that's just as good," David explains.

"In my opinion, the problem with most mobile homes is that once you reach your destination, you have nothing smaller to drive around in—you have to keep wheeling this big mobile unit around. I wanted a fifth-wheel unit—I wanted a big trailer I could pull behind my pickup, so I could unhook it and use the truck to run around for whatever needs to be done."

That's what he got. The motorless mobile home (shown at top) is huge—a full 43 feet long—and has about every convenience known to be available in such units. "When you're going to live in something for a full year or more solid, you

CONVOY accompanying hitch across the country includes 43-foot trailer (top left) with souvenir stand at back (above), plus two big mobile homes for sleeping quarters.

want it to have as many conveniences as you can get," David contends. "This had to be a real 'home away from home'."

Crew Sheltered While Eating

The attractive-looking unit includes a master bedroom with bathroom and shower, a complete entertainment center, a kitchen and dining room with couch, a washer and dryer, a second bedroom for the cook with a separate shower, bathroom and TV, plus two heating and air-conditioning units.

In the center of the unit is a complete kitchen filled with modern appliances—including a stove, oven, microwave, sink, refrigerator, freezer, dishwasher, etc.—used to cook for the crew (see details on next page).

At the back of the trailer is a 10-foot-wide souvenir stand (shown above). A large half-door folds out and up to provide a shelter over the vending area like those used in "popcorn wagons", revealing souvenir items displayed on the interior walls of the area. The unit also boasts a large fabric awning that pulls out from the top of the trailer to cover the outdoor barbecue unit, chairs and folding table that add to the crew's comfort while eating outdoors.

Two other large mobile homes (shown above left) complete the convoy, and each of those is loaded with amenities, too. All of these units are painted and decorated exactly alike, to give an attractive classy, "together look" to the vehicles.

"We tried our best to keep them clean, too," David says. "When we moved down the road, we wanted this whole operation to look as sharp as a Disney World production!"

enue in Lordstown at 12:40 p.m. Had 550 visitors this afternoon, but only 170 in evening—thunderstorms started about 7 p.m.

July 29—Weather cleared for today's 13-mile walk. Chipper, Chip, Spike and I were hitched with our new, light harness for the first time. These rest under the neck and along the sides instead of atop our necks.

Had 176 riders, 900 people along route. Stopped for the night at the Ellsworth Fire Department; saw another 2,200 people there. David and Vikki were so busy giving autographs that we were already in our stalls eating before they got off the wagon—guess that's what they mean by "the price of fame"!

July 30—Cool, wet weather kept us off the road. Had over 500 visitors, despite the rain. Crew clipped all of us while David went to pick up a new breast harness for the wheel team.

Crew watched rain while eating their lunch (fish sandwiches and chili) under a picnic shelter. Fire Department treated crew to dinner.

July 31—Saturday. Back on the road—one of our busiest days yet! Had 378 riders, the most yet, on 13-mile walk through Berlin Center and Stratton. Arrived at the junior high school in Damascus, Ohio at 1:15 p.m.; had over *6,000* visitors there!

Aug. 1—Sunday, and pretty quiet. Stayed in our stalls but had about 1,500 visitors looking us over—taking a close look at the semi-trailer, too.

David gave a seminar at 10 a.m. By mid-afternoon, it was getting mighty hot; David bought a large floor fan for the semi to help keep us cool.

Local folks treated crew to a delicious lunch and dinner. David's uncle, John Helmuth, also stopped by. Nancy Sutton of Homeworth brought David and Vikki a homemade basket.

Aug. 2—Unbelievable crowds today! Had record-breaking 522 riders on 13.5-mile walk through North Georgetown, despite brief showers along the way.

Trip took longer than usual—left at 8, arrived post office in East Rochester at 2. Met about 2,700 visitors there.

Were lots of Amish and Mennonite families along route. Judy and David Miller of Minerva invited David and Vikki to dinner with about 125 Mennonites. They brought us a load of fresh hay, so we did all right, too!

Aug. 3—It was cool and cloudy this morning. Kishman's IGA in Minerva ♂

brought crew snacks, doughnuts and T-shirts—a nice way to start the day.

Walked 10 miles with 174 riders through Bayard and Minerva (where Mayor Jim Waller gave a plaque to David and Vikki), Pekin and Oneida. Arrived at the Woods Grocery in Malvern at noon.

On our best behavior for some 46 seniors at Minerva Convalescent Center, where we stopped on our way through town. Also stopped at Great Trail Care Center in Minerva. Two bands played for us along the route—"Marching Dukes" from Alliance, and Minerva High School Band.

Aug. 4—Rainy and miserable today. Got soaked on 10-mile walk to Sandyville—so did the 21 brave folks who rode wagon anyway! Others just pulled their cars off the two-lane road and watched from under umbrellas.

Arrived Grace Lutheran Church, 11:15 a.m.; had about 200 visitors. May Shepherd of Barnesville brought Amish cinnamon bread; wish I could have tasted it! Barbara Romano of Malvern brought drinking glasses; Shirley and Frank Mapes of Carrollton brought a bouquet in a heart-shaped basket.

Aug. 5—Nice weather returned for our 13.6-mile walk through Mineral City and Zoarville. Had 113 riders. Rubber started to peel from one wagon wheel; David patched it with duct tape!

Had about 800 visitors at our evening stop, the fairgrounds in Dover, Ohio. Crew put us in barns there; mighty cozy!

Aug. 6—Relaxed today in fairgrounds stalls. Crew gave us baths and Steve cleaned harnesses. We got new shoes today—our second set since the trip began.

Vikki's dad brought us a new spare lead horse, "Dale". Crew chatted with about 650 visitors.

Aug. 7—Cody got to show off today to a big crowd; David used him for a demonstration during a seminar. Ron cleaned the wagon and Steve finished cleaning the harnesses—we're getting ready for David and Vikki's wedding, only a week away!

Aug. 8—Sunday. Taking it easy in our stalls again today. Vikki and Junior "pulled" our manes today in preparation for braiding.

Pulling all that hair raised four blisters on Vikki's fingers. Maybe I should fix my own mane next time!

Aug. 9—Poor Marlene went to the ♂➙

'That's 1,248 Eggs, 19,710 Slices of Bread...Oh, My!'

WHEN you rise with the roosters and stay on the move till the last dog howls at dusk, you build up a powerfully big appetite. And, just as the army moves on its stomach, our crew moved on the meals turned out by the cook, Marlene Thompson.

This great country cook prepared many a delicious menu on the family farm she and her husband, Virgil, still operate in Ohio. (He visited the hitch regularly during the trip but couldn't come along—he couldn't get anyone to run the farm for a year, yet didn't want to deny Marlene the once-in-a-lifetime opportunity to accompany daughter Vikki on this memorable trip across the country.)

All the crew's meals were cooked in the modern kitchen (see its features in preceding article)

"COME AND GET IT!" Lunch—one of *hundreds* Marlene Thompson served on trip—is almost ready.

inside the 43-foot-long trailer pulled behind the 3/4-ton pickup.

Rural grocery stores along the hitch route loved Marlene! And she likely attracted a few stares from people wondering how big her "family" was when they saw her fill up one grocery cart, then go back for another...and another!

To get an idea of how much food it took to feed this hungry crew for over a year and a half on the road, we asked Marlene to go over what they'd consumed the first 2 weeks, and then estimate what the amounts would come to for a year.

"The biggest meals were breakfast and supper," she pointed out. "Since the crew got up early and the rules for this trip were that the horses always got taken care of first, everyone worked for at least an hour or more each morning before they sat down to eat.

"By then they were pretty hungry, and it took about 2 dozen eggs a week for breakfast alone. That came to about 1,248 eggs in a year! Wow! And it took a lot of bread for toast and a lot of coffee—we sometimes went through about 24 cups a day. Let's see...that came to about 8,760 cups for the year. Gee, I shouldn't be doing this—no wonder I was tired nights!"

Marlene spread butter or margarine on many a slice of bread over the year, too—around 19,710 slices, we figured! That's due to all the toast in the morning, plus all the sandwiches for the crew's noon lunch, which was usually eaten on the move.

Potato growers, meat producers and dairymen also played a big part in feeding this crew—these horse handlers put away about 20 pounds of potatoes a week (that's 1,040 pounds over a year), 70 pounds of meat a week (3,640 pounds/year) and 7 gallons of milk a week (364 gallons/year).

Other estimates Marlene provided on groceries needed to feed the crew for 365 days on the road include these interesting items: Eight boxes of cereal a week (416 boxes/year); 15 heads of lettuce a week (780 heads/year); 10 pounds of fruit and vegetables a week (520 pounds/year); three cakes or pies per week (156 cakes/pies/year); and 4 gallons of ice cream a week (208 gallons/year).

See what we mean when we say rural grocery stores along the route surely loved Marlene? And, since this writer was fortunate enough to be on the road with the crew on a number of occasions and sampled Marlene's menus, I'm sure the crew learned to love her even more!

Harness Features Brass and Class

When you learn about its background, you'll find this team is gussied up in some pretty fancy custom-made harness!

IF YOU GOT within petting distance of *Country's Reminisce Hitch* and took a close look at the harness, you no doubt quickly discovered it's not just some everyday work harness that's thrown on a team to haul in a load of hay.

Each of the harnesses on the horses in this hitch was built by one of the most famous harnessmakers in the business—Garnett Shanahan of Ontario, Canada. He insists on doing all of the work himself, with no hired help. Each harness is handcrafted and hand-stitched from imported leather, then decorated with real brass.

"He's the best in the business," says driver David Helmuth. "He's in such demand that if you ordered a new harness from him today, it would probably take him 2 years to finish it for you."

With this kind of craftsmanship, Garnett's harnesses don't come cheaply. "Yet, buying a harness for a horse is like buying clothes for yourself," says David. "You normally get what you pay for."

Not only is a Shanahan-made harness highly attractive, it has features that make it more comfortable for the horse. For example, each harness—which weighs about 130 pounds—has adjustments that allow a perfect fit for each horse. Each horse in *Country's Reminisce Hitch* had its own individually fitted harness that was his for the entire trip.

The collar is by far the most important part of the harness—fit smoothly around the horse's neck and against its shoulders, it's what allows the horse to pull. Says Maury Telleen, editor of *The Draft*

Horse Journal, "The collar on a horse is akin to boots on a marching soldier." The fit and comfort level have a great deal to do with endurance.

Collars—which weigh around 80 pounds each—come in different sizes. After the size is selected, the back of it is molded to fit each horse. This is done by soaking the collar in warm water for about an hour. Then the collar is placed on the horse and allowed to adjust itself to the exact shape of the horse's neck and shoulders. The result is a custom-fit collar.

Polishing a Nightly Job

Keeping this kind of "show" harness looking its best was a time-consuming job on the cross-country trip. First, the leather needed to be cleaned every night, and treated with a lubrication regularly.

But it's the ample supply of brass on

"ELBOW GREASE" was put to good use daily during the trip as crew members such as Dan Bisbee cleaned the harnesses' hand-stitched leather and polished its decorative real brass.

these harnesses that took even more time. Any ex-military people can remember how much work it took to keep the brass on your uniform shining each day. With that background, you can appreciate how much "elbow grease" it took to keep all the brass on these harnesses glistening every day!

"We could have bought harnesses highlighted with chrome," says David. "But this is the No. 1 six-horse hitch in the country, and we felt these horses deserved the best. Brass is class!"

The harness on all the horses in the hitch is identical except for two things: The lead team up front wore ornamental brass-decorated "martingales" (the eye-catching straps across the chest of the horses), and the harness on the wheel team had "breeching" across their rumps (sturdy straps that helped these two horses stop the load or back the wagon).

You can see there's a lot more to harnessing a horse and making regular adjustments to assure the animal's comfort. Yet, an experienced crew member can harness a draft horse in about 10 minutes or less.

One last note: If you're around any draft horses when they are being harnessed, watch the excitement and anticipation build in each horse. Most draft horses love to be harnessed up and "put to work".

It's obvious they prefer it to a day in the pasture or relaxing in the stall. Just as great athletes love to play the game, draft horses like to pull something.

emergency room to have a swollen foot treated. And speaking of doctors, the vet was out today to check all of us and floss our teeth.

Getting ready for a wedding is a lot more complicated—and time-consuming—than I would have imagined! That's why we haven't traveled for several days.

Aug. 10—Slightly rainy in the afternoon, but some 350 people still turned out to see us. David and Vikki took time out from their wedding preparations to attend the Ohio State Fair, where they saw Belgians (none as handsome as me, I'm sure!) and also some of those "other" breeds—Percherons and Clydesdales.

Actually, I wouldn't have minded visiting with some of those big fellows myself—thought I might run into one or two of my old friends from our competition days!

Aug. 11—Got back on the road! Covered 14 miles and drove through Sugarcreek, the "Little Switzerland" of Ohio. What a quaint place for David and Vikki's wedding!

Also stopped at home of Ray and Cora Bark, who subscribe to all of the Reiman magazines. He's 95 and she turned 91 yesterday!

This was also the first day we used the new guy, Dale, next to Chip in the hitch. He handled himself like a real pro!

Nearly 1,000 people greeted us at end of day. We're camping at Belden Brickyard No. 8 in Sugarcreek, where we'll be staying until after the wedding.

Aug. 12—Met another 1,000 people today. Got a change of "sheets"—well, not exactly; crew filled our stalls with fresh sawdust! And Vikki decorated our stalls with flowers and bows in honor of her upcoming wedding.

Vikki took her wedding gown to the cleaners to have it pressed, and David drove to the Columbus airport to pick up his best man, Pete. (Wonder what a "best man" is; anything like "Grand Champion", maybe?)

Aug. 13—The day before the wedding, and wow, another 1,100 people showed up today!

Vikki and Marlene finished making rice bags for the wedding. (Is that what the guests get to eat?) David and Pete went to New Town Mall to pick up their tuxedos for the wedding. The rest of the gang was getting ready for the rehearsal dinner. And lots of wedding gifts are arriving—maybe we'll be

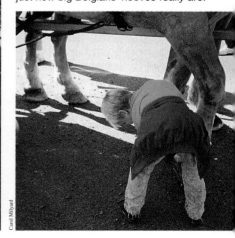

SEEING DOUBLE? Girls shown above won T-shirts for being the only twins present when the hitch traveled through Abilene, Kansas.

KIDS OF ALL AGES enjoyed visiting the hitch. Youngster below and little ones at top right decided to see for themselves just how big Belgians' hooves *really* are.

AN ARMFUL OF PUPPY has the little girl and her companions (above) smiling, while another set of twins (below) shares the driver's seat with David.

asked to haul them all in our wagon!

Aug. 14—Vikki and David's wedding day! And we were a *big* part of it! (Bet you didn't know that horses could make puns.) There were more than *5,000 people* in attendance!

We were all gussied up with bows and flowers in our manes. At 1:30, David drove us to the Valley View Community Church, then went inside to change into his tuxedo. (Vikki arrived later by limousine and went in a different door—I overheard someone saying it's bad luck for a bride and groom to see each other on the wedding day before the ceremony.)

The wedding was at 3, and we waited patiently in the parking lot, listening to the service over the loudspeakers that had been set up outside. Then at 4, the new Mr. and Mrs. David Helmuth came out of the church for the public reception under a tent that was even bigger than the one above our stalls!

After that, we gave the bridal party the ride of their lives back down the road to our campsite...but only after David wheeled us through a couple of figure eights in the church parking lot!

I think I'm safe in speaking for the rest of the hitch when I say there's never been a prouder moment in our entire lives than when we pranced down the road carrying the bridal party.

Later, after we'd all been unharnessed and returned to our stalls, we talked briefly among ourselves and vowed that we would do everything possible to make their cross-country honeymoon trip a happy one, and to carry them safely every step of the way.

Aug. 15—Sunday, and pretty quiet after yesterday's big event. Just rested our hooves today while crew cleaned our harnesses.

Nearly 1,100 people stopped by to see us and talk with the crew. David and Vikki spent the day opening wedding gifts. Great stuff, but nothing much a horse would be interested in!

Aug. 16—Hit the road again today; did 10 miles, driving through Walnut Creek to Berlin, Ohio.

We're in Amish Country, and lots of Amish families rode on our hitch. Two Amish buggies passed us on route—they were moving at a faster clip than we were!

The Amish Door Restaurant in Wilmont presented Amish hats to crew. Ap- ↷

parently, they didn't have my size.

Aug. 17—Crew got us up at ungodly hour—5:30 a.m.—to pretty us up for pictures with the wagon. I shouldn't nag (little pun there!); I looked mighty handsome—again!

Grass was still wet this morning, causing wagon to slide a bit during picture-taking. Went through Berlin and Millersburg (platted in 1824) in the heart of Amish Country. Staying the night at Holmes County Fairgrounds.

Aug. 18—Just a half day's work today. Got us up at 6:30 for usual beauty treatment to look our best for David's noon demonstration in grandstand arena at Fairgrounds.

We showed our stuff, doing figure eights, pinwheels and docking the wagon for some 1,500 spectators. Crew let us relax in the afternoon because of the heat.

Gave another demo this evening. Talk about doubleheaders!

Aug. 19—Warm, sunny, in 70s. Good crowds—670 in morning, 700 in afternoon, 1,300 when we stopped at Nashville Elementary School for the night.

West Holmes High School Band serenaded us as we went by their school. Lee Smetzer of Big Prairie, Ohio donated 20 bales of alfalfa and timothy mix for us. I'd shake his hand if I could!

Aug. 20—Slight sprinkles of rain, but big crowds: 700 in morning, 900 in afternoon. West Holmes Fire Department truck escorted us through Loudonville. From there, Hillsdale High School Band led the way into Perrysville with their music.

Nearly 1,000 people greeted us as we stopped at the Perrysville Fire Department for the night. Vikki took me—just me!—to Colonial Manor Health Care Center so people there could pet me. I was in horse heaven!

Aug. 21—Covered 10 miles. Land needs rain soon; hot and sunny, 79°. Walked to 150-year-old town of Lucas, meeting 1,300 people during the day, another 750 at night.

People in town put up signs welcoming us and asking for David's and Vikki's autographs. (No one ever asks for mine; maybe because it's 9 inches wide and would require a mighty big piece of paper!)

News crew from local television Channel 51 interviewed David and Vikki this afternoon. Dr. Alan Jones of Mansfield made pumpkin and raspber-

"These Horses Wouldn't Want to Hurt You, But..."

FREQUENTLY, a youngster along the cross-country route would ask a crew member, "Mister, do these horses ever kick?"

Here's the answer David Helmuth gave to a young boy one day—it has a lot of merit in helping both children and adults understand horses:

"Don't ever let anyone tell you that any horse never kicks," David answered emphatically. "Now, Firestone here and the other horses in our hitch are very gentle animals. They all love people, and they would never willingly try to hurt anyone.

"But you have to understand that all horses are defensive—they keep their guard up against one another, because it's the nature of these animals to teasingly sneak up behind and nip or bite each other. When a horse is surprised that way, it sometimes impulsively kicks at the other animal to defend itself.

"That being the case, the worst thing you can ever do is surprise a horse. If you walk up to one from behind and slap him on the rump or pet him, you may surprise him and he may kick out at what he thought was another horse!"

Just a "Flick of Leg"

David then walked up to the young boy and asked, "What are you going to do if I flick my hand at your face like this as though to slap you?" The boy quickly brought up his hand to defend himself.

"There, see, you weren't really striking out at me—you were just jerking your hand up to protect yourself. And that's likely all a horse intends to do when it's surprised—just flick its leg out to protect itself. To you, it's a kick; to him, it's simply a defensive move. But with the size of these horses' legs and their sheer power, a mere 'flick' by them can be a serious 'kick' to you.

"So, it's best never to believe anyone when they say a horse doesn't kick. And never surprise a horse—as you approach him, always talk softly and let him know exactly where you are before you touch him.

"In fact, if you watch experienced horse owners, you'll notice that as they walk around a horse, they often never lose touch of him—they'll just keep one hand running alongside the horse to let him know exactly where they are at all times.

"Again, these horses in our hitch love people, and they're gentle as puppies. But all horses are animals. That makes them unpredictable, and anyone who approaches a horse should respect that."

FUTURE COWBOYS. David poses with the two young sons of crew member Mike Bartel.

When Tragedy Struck, Crew Pitched in to Help

AS THE HITCH neared Shelburne Falls, Massachusetts, the crew had no idea the community had just suffered a tragedy.

Judy Almeida, a young wife and mother, lived in nearby Colrain with her husband and eight children. Her oldest, Mary, sang in Mohawk Regional Trail High School's show chorus, and Judy rarely missed a performance.

At a spring concert, the chorus sang *Danny Boy*. Judy was so moved by it that she told the school's music director, Nick Waynelovich, "I would want the chorus to sing that at my funeral."

One week later, Judy Almeida was killed in an automobile accident. The students were shocked and shaken, but insisted on honoring her request.

"I was a little nervous about it," Nick confessed. "No one could have blamed them if they'd fallen apart singing that song. But they did a great job."

But Nick wanted to do more. He began planning a concert to benefit the Almeida family.

In the meantime, the hitch was on its way. Nick had contacted David about videotaping the school dance band. That band would be the first to receive a $200 check for its participation in the *Reminisce* Club program. Why not film the band at the benefit?

"We had seniors participating at the benefit, too," Nick said, "so this provided a showcase for them as well as the kids."

The concert featured the band and choir, and a moving vocal solo of *The Rose* by Mary Almeida. Then Vikki tap-danced with the Greenfield Senior Center's Golden Steppers and Belles, and danced with David to *Boogie-Woogie Bugle Boy*.

"We had a wonderful time," Vikki said. "It was such a treat to watch these talented kids perform to benefit a fellow student."

The crew had made camp at the school's parking lot, so everyone was able to enjoy the program. The hitch also donated $600 to the Almeida Fund.

"Having the hitch involved probably doubled the publicity for the event," Nick said. "The community support was tremendous. We ended up raising nearly $2,500 for the family. It was quite an event, and we were glad the hitch and crew were part of it."

BAND AID? High school marching bands turned out all along the route to welcome and escort the hitch into their communities. For this gesture and agreeing to play a concert featuring "golden oldies" at a local senior center, plus devising a creative way to improve communications with seniors, each participating band was awarded $200 by the *Reminisce* Club.

ry muffins for the crew. Wish they could make 'em with alfalfa!

Aug. 22—Sunday. Still in Lucas. Day of rest, cooler, down to 60s. Dale acted up during the night; broke the rear bar on his stall and pushed over a side panel. My guess is that he had a bad dream; too many oats right before bedtime can do that to you.

Laura Flockenzier presented a fruit pizza plate to David and Vikki.

Aug. 23—Did 10 miles today, which took us to Lexington, Ohio. Lots of company along the way: 500 in the morning, 800 in the afternoon and another 600 at our evening stop.

During our walk, a kind lady rode up on her horse and told us about a short cut we could use to avoid the steeper hills on our planned route—that was mighty nice of her!

NBC Channel 4, out of Columbus, interviewed David and Vikki and took pictures of our hitch during today's run. Wish somebody'd think to rig our stalls with a portable TV so we could see ourselves on the evening news!

Aug. 24—Carried 138 riders on our 13-mile walk to Iberia, where 800 more people were waiting. It started raining about 10 and kept it up for 3 miles; crew used umbrellas.

Charles and Sylvia Martin gave crew gift certificates for McDonald's. Iberia Methodist Church treated crew to dinner. I'm feeling a little miffed this evening; that's because I didn't work in the hitch today.

Aug. 25—Back at swing for another big day; 115 riders, even though it was 92°, sunny, hot and sticky. That's in addition to crowds of 400 in the morning, 500 in the afternoon and 850 at our evening stop in Caledonia.

Merrill Sheets of Delaware, Ohio and his hitch of six pony-sized mules met us on the road and followed for about 3 miles Another new horse, "Tim", joined us today; he and Dale look almost like twins!

Aug. 26—Short day, did 7 miles to Marion in the 92° heat. Had 85 riders. Treated residents of Marion Multi-Purpose Senior Center to rides in the center's parking lot.

David and Vikki were interviewed there by Ed Johnson, who has a local farm program. The interview will air on TV Sept. 25.

Also stopped at the Mental Retardation Adult Center in East Marion, where we showed off with a demon- ↪

stration of figure eights and pinwheels.

Aug. 27—Sunny, humid and 74° as we "hitched" our way through Big Island and on to Meeker, Ohio. Had 62 riders. Corn and bean fields along the way need rain badly.

Vikki was in the spotlight again, interviewed by Jim Petsche of the *Daily Chief-Union* newspaper from Upper Sandusky. Tim got into the act, posing beside the wagon with Vikki—I gotta speak up more!

Some 1,400 people were on hand to greet us at our evening stop, the United Methodist Church in Meeker.

Aug. 28—The church treated the crew to breakfast. Then we traveled 10 miles through Hardin County, seeing upwards of 800 people, with 170 riders.

Also saw three buffalo in a field alongside Rt. 309, a comfortable blacktop road. It was a big night for David and Vikki; they saw Billy Ray Cyrus in concert at the Allen County Fair and got to talk with him and his manager.

Big night for us, too. We're staying at Rodney Evans' horse farm—my kind of place, with nice big paddocks!

Aug. 29—Sunday. Got a good night's sleep. What a great life!

Stayed in separate outside pens, eating grass and relaxing, but had to come inside tent in morning to get away from the flies that were pestering us.

Marlene grilled steaks and bratwurst, and the crew really chowed down. Everybody had a nice relaxing day.

Aug. 30—It worked! I got in on Channel 35's interview with David and Vikki, standing proudly beside wagon!

Saw about 1,200 people today plus 1,000 at our evening stop, Don Steinman's place in Kenton.

Busful of seniors from Corinthian Center met us at Hardin County Council on Aging. Maud Williams, who's *109* and the oldest resident at Hardin County Home, got to pet us.

David also gave a demo at the Senior Center and gave many of the seniors a ride around the parking lot.

Aug. 31—Traveled 11 miles today and gave 145 people rides. A few raindrops in early morning, but nothing more. That's a shame because they really need rain; crops are starting to burn up! (Coming from a farm myself, I hate to see that sort of thing!)

Busy with some 1,250 visitors this evening. Channel 35 gave us coverage on the 5:30 news. I like this celebrity stuff! Seniors from Green Acres Center

We Salute Seniors!
And Senior Centers on Their 50th Anniversary!

That was our mission and message during trip as senior centers hit the half-century mark.

IT'S NO COINCIDENCE that we picked 1993 for *Country's Reminisce Hitch* to strike out on this memorable cross-country trip.

You see, 1993 marked the 50th anniversary of senior centers in America, and since more than one-third of the U.S. population is now over 50, the mission of these mammoth steeds was to "elevate the concern, respect and service for seniors".

And likely to "bring them a little fun", too, as this champion six-horse hitch stopped at numerous senior centers along its cross-country route and gave rides in the custom-designed red wagon.

The very first senior center was opened in 1943 in Hudson, New York, and that pioneering effort led to improved care and concern for senior citizens at what now numbers more than 15,000 senior facilities across America. In view of this, our small publishing company is doing a variety of things to involve and salute these 15,000 senior centers, thereby carrying out the "We're Pulling for Seniors" theme painted on the wagon and semi.

For example, we're using funds from the sales of this book plus the Official Hitch Program and other souvenir items to give a *free subscription* of *Reminisce*

magazine to each of those 15,000 senior centers across the country. Each issue mailed to these centers is accompanied by a "lesson plan" filled with questions and suggestions to aid the activities director in conducting a regular "*Reminisce* Hour".

The response from this program has been tremendous. Several therapists at these centers have even reported that stroke victims who haven't spoken for a long time suddenly started talking and relating personal memories after studying pictures in *Reminisce*.

The sales proceeds were also used to launch the "*Reminisce* Club" in February of 1994. The Club already has more than 2 million members and offers folks over 50 a wide variety of activities and benefits.

"Firestone's Coming!"

As pointed out in other articles in this book, David Helmuth took our most famous horse, Firestone, to many senior centers along the route to let people there see and meet him.

There has been a great deal of evidence in recent years regarding the therapeutic effect of pets on senior citizens. This being the case, a visit by this huge, beautiful, gentle horse proved to be a welcome, memorable experience for thousands of seniors along our trip route.

It's too bad everyone reading this book couldn't be there to see the broad smiles and twinkling eyes of these seniors, as this giant steed brought back proud memories of "horse and buggy days" for many of these people! Can you imagine their excited conversations at dinner that evening?

"Honestly, the experience of taking Firestone or Cody or Stoney to these senior centers was sometimes so moving that I can't put my feelings into words," says David. "In most cases, the entire building seemed to empty when we brought the horse over," he relates. "Elderly people surrounded the horse, and then these people talked softly to him and began sharing memories of their own about horses in 'the good old days'."

"Bring Him in!"

It began to rain when David brought Stoney and "Ashley", the team dog, to one center in Maine. "I guess it's too wet for the folks to come outside," David said to the activities director. "Should I just bring the dog in and talk about the trip a bit?"

"No, bring him right in," said the Activities Director. "We have big double doors to our lobby, and the people have been so eager to experience this, I don't want them to miss it."

"Well, this is certainly a first!" David said as he unloaded Stoney and led him inside. Stoney's metal shoes clopped loudly on the lobby's tile floor—he weighs over a ton—and his ears were only inches from the 8-foot ceiling. David talked to the residents about the trip and the horses for more than a half hour, and the seniors loved it. Wheel-

chairs and even a few rolling beds were pushed close so people could pet the horse.

Some of the elderly residents just wanted to smell a live horse again. Stoney stood quietly, minded his bathroom manners perfectly and seemed to relish the attention.

"Ashley" Made Personal Visit

When Vikki learned that a dozen or so of the seniors at the center weren't able to come down to the lobby to see Stoney, she took Ashley up to their rooms. The seniors appreciated this personal visit by Vikki and this beautiful Dalmatian dog as much as their friends had enjoyed Stoney's visit.

These kinds of things gave us a good feeling about this trip. You should feel good, too, about all this, because your purchase of this book and/or our other souvenirs items—photos, posters, garments and other items, all offered by the hitch crew along the road—helped to make all this possible and will help similar things to continue at senior centers through efforts of the *Reminisce* Club.

Proceeds from these sales helped fund the trip, the senior center visits and the 15,000 free *Reminisce* subscriptions, and support the Club's program for high school band donations (part of which urges them to

> "*You can feel good about helping provide 15,000 free subscriptions for America's senior centers.*"

play concerts for seniors featuring songs from the '30s–'50s), and many other things involving senior centers across America. By purchasing this book, you—like this hitch—are "Pulling for Seniors".

LIKE THE SLOGAN. Seniors crowded around the hitch and our wagon at each of our stopovers. As shown below, they appreciated our slogan and what trip did for folks over 50.

in Kenton also came to hobnob with us.

Sept. 1—Wow! Saw 1,000 people along route in morning, 1,250 in afternoon, and—get this—3,000 during our evening stop at the Allen County Fairgrounds in Lima, Ohio! Also, 153 people rode wagon, including Cecil Sawyer, who's blind. He said he could feel our power—we were really touched!

Something cute, too: Katherine Stephens—she's only 3—donated a roll of pennies to the crew. Hope it goes into our horsy bank!

Channel 35 out of Lima did a live interview with David at noon. Stopped at Lost Creek Care Center; they gave Vikki bouquet of red and white carnations. And someone left a huge plate of nachos and salsa at souvenir stand for the crew. All that in 11 miles!

Sept. 2—Good thing we didn't travel today. Hard rain started in morning, then continued on and off all day. Crew relaxed in their campers; we stayed in our stalls.

Somehow, Spike got out of his box stall last night. Crew found him in hallway of the fairground barn in morning. Never knew horses walked in their sleep!

Indiana Democrat newspaper reporter came and interviewed Vikki and also took pictures of her and Bobby.

Sept. 3—My day off, but the other horses were busy. In just 10.8 miles, they visited the Oak Care Center, Lima Convalescent Home, Day Center and Lima Memorial Hospital!

Crossed the Ottawa River to spend ♂

the night in the parking lot of Bethel Chapel Church in Allentown.

Sept. 4—Another 10.8 miles today. Crossed Auglaize River—we've sure been getting plenty of practice at going over bridges! We had 255 people ride the wagon on our way to Dan Klausing's farm near Spencerville.

Spike was sure feeling his oats today; seemed like he wanted to pull the wagon all by himself! Junior and Dan gave us baths this afternoon and Ron and Steve cleaned our harnesses—talk about room service!

Sept. 5—Sunday. Still taking it easy at Klausing's Farm—what a beautiful place! They're taking pictures of it to appear in *Country* magazine.

Crew resting in campers. The family is treating us like kings; made dinner for crew. Got pretty chilly this evening, so Dan put our blankets on us.

Sept. 6—Labor Day. Had 225 riders even though we went through a really small town today—Converse, Ohio: population, 7!

Also went through Elgin. Reporter from Van Wert newspaper talked with Vikki for a story. Also took pictures of Tim in front of wagon. Gotta find out when it's my turn again!

Sept. 7—Weather's cooling off; 50° at 7, up to 65° during the day. Good traveling weather for horses, take my word for it!

Parkway Band performed and led us through town of Willshire, where we're staying at the J&J Grocery Store. Ashley climbed aboard wagon and rode for 4 miles. Channel 15 interviewed Vikki. We were featured on both the 5 and 11 o'clock news!

Sept. 8—Gained an hour (I'm not real sure what that means) as we crossed into Indiana today, driving to Monroe.

We also showed off our figure eights and pinwheel turns at the elementary school in Monroe. Crowd got up to 1,750 in afternoon, growing to 2,500 at our evening stop, the Adams County Fairgrounds.

In the afternoon, a group of fiddle players performed for us. Virgil Sprunger, Monroe Township Marshall, played a *saw* in the barn where we're staying—humans can come up with some of the darnedest things!

Sept. 9—Virgil Sprunger escorted us to the county line this morning. There, Wells County Sheriff Tim Meade led us into Bluffton. Along the route, the Christian Care Center had a beauti-

Seeing Spots? That's 'Ashley'!

How this team dog won the hearts of seniors...and some fascinating facts about Dalmatians, right here in black and white.

The Dalmatian dog that accompanied the crew on this trip sometimes got as much attention as the horses! Especially when this team dog wagged its way right into senior center rooms for "personal visits".

"Ashley" was the one getting all the attention during most of the trip. Earlier in the trip it was "Baron". You see, David and Vikki own two Dalmatians, and Baron was along for the first week or so. But "he proved a little too hyper and didn't want to stay on the wagon for long terms," Vikki says. "So we sent him back to our farm in Ohio where he has all the running room that he wants.

"But Ashley loved the the trip and loved all the people she met. It seems that everyone felt that way about her, too."

During some of the stops at senior centers, Vikki took Ashley right up to the rooms of people who weren't able to come outside to see Firestone, Stoney or Cody. The elderly people were delighted by these personal visits from this friendly spotted dog.

Little History Lesson

People always asked a lot of questions about this unusual breed. So we decided readers of this book might like to learn a few facts about this black and white spotted dog as well.

For example, ever wonder why one of these dogs is seen at nearly every firehouse? Why do Dalmatians and firehouses go together like smoke and fire?

It all started in the days of stagecoaches. Horse theft was so common back then that many stagecoach drivers strung a hammock between two stalls at night, then slept behind their horses to guard against thieves.

Unless they had a Dalmatian, that is. If they had one of these dogs, the drivers could sleep in the house or the stagecoach hotel. Why? Because Dalmatians, they knew, formed an amazingly tight bond with horses. When they became close to a team, no stranger would dare lay a hand on them.

Therapeutic Effect on Horses

When the knowledge of that trait spread, more stagecoach drivers went to great lengths to get Dalmatians to watch over their teams. In fact, this practice became so common, Dalmatians were first called "coach dogs".

"Dalmatians have always gotten along well with horses," says Esmeralda Treen of Milwaukee, a recognized authority on the breed. "Horses are gregarious and feel the need for company. You can't leave them alone too long. Dalmatians take to horses and become their 'companions'.

"Back in the stagecoach days, the 'Dals' would run alongside the coaches, or under the rear axle of the moving

ON THE SPOT when seniors were around, Ashley loved her role as official "crew dog".

coach. They'd keep up with the team as far as it went—that was sometimes more than 20 or 30 miles a day.

"When the coach reached the inn, the coachman left the dog to guard the team as well as the luggage in the coach," she explains. "If the coachman stayed on guard, a robber would sometimes distract him in conversation while others pilfered the goods. But they could never pull that ruse on a Dal—they're very alert dogs."

Since every firehouse back then had a set of fast horses to pull the pumper wagon, it became common for each group of firemen to keep a Dalmatian.

The horses are gone now, but the Dalmatians aren't. The tradition has continued, due to the appeal of these dogs and nostalgic ties to yesteryear.

NEW FAMILY MEMBER. Georgia Ward of Tucson, Arizona named her new puppy "Vikki" in honor of the litter's "stepmom".

Hitch Receives a 'Special Delivery'

ONE of the many highlights of the hitch's cross-country journey occurred in early January near Sidewinder, California, just before the hitch crossed the state line into Arizona. There, official mascot Ashley delivered eight purebred Dalmatian puppies. The litter, sired by Baron, included five females and three males.

"Surprisingly, Dalmatian puppies are born pure white," Vikki relates. "Their spots don't begin to show until the puppies are about 3 weeks old—that's when they begin to look like Dalmatians are supposed to!"

The "hitch puppies" proved to be a popular attraction for the many folks who visited the hitch during its trek across Arizona. One of the puppies was purchased by crewman David Wright; another was kept by Vikki and David, who gave their new mascot the very appropriate name "Coachman".

The remaining six puppies were purchased by hitch enthusiasts; the first of these was Georgia Ward of Tucson, who promptly named her pup "Vikki"!

ful blanket hanging on a clothesline; it read "Welcome *Reminisce Hitch*".

When we got to Bluffton, Everett Faulkner presented us with a key to the city—the first we've received. Quite an honor for a horse, don't you think?

Southern Wells High School Raider Force Band escorted us with music into Riverside Park, where we're staying tonight.

Sept. 10—You won't believe what Cody did today. He visited patients in the United Methodist Memorial Home in Plum Tree, Indiana. Yep, I mean *in* the home!

He walked right in the door and through the halls—even right into several rooms! Patients loved him. I hear he was on his best behavior; no horsing around.

While he was there, an announcement was made over the PA system: "Attention: there is a big Belgian horse walking around inside the building." Bet that made everybody sit up and take notice!

Sept. 11—Lots of riders today—about 210, all in just 9.6 miles! Arrived in Mt. Etna, Indiana's smallest town and the "Purple Martin Capital" of the Hoosier State.

One rider, Abby Bollenbacher, who's 11, wrote a note saying, "I like the way you treat the horses." Nice of her to notice—the crew really does go all out for us!

Sept. 12—A windy Sunday, with a few sprinkles. We're camping in the parking lot of Joe and Peg's Grocery in Mt. Etna.

A few people stopped by this afternoon, but all in all, a pretty quiet day.

Sept. 13—Back on the road. Gave about 100 people rides on wagon today. Stopped at Southwood Elementary School along Highway 124, where David gave a seminar to students.

School's playground was ideal for stopping tonight; lots of grass and trees all around. Junior gave us baths, and Steve and Ron cleaned our harnesses.

Sept. 14—Got mobbed today. More than 1,000 people turned out along route in morning, and some 1,500 in afternoon.

Staying tonight at the headquarters of the Belgian Draft Horse Corporation of America in Wabash—what could be more appropriate?

Seniors from Miller's Merry Manor in Peru came by bus to visit us there. Tim had the honors, showing off and ↻

getting petted. We learned that Wabash was the first city in the world to get electric lights, back on March 31, 1880. We really found this piece of trivia illuminating!

Sept. 15—Busy, busy day! Walked 15 miles; sheriff's department escorted us into Peru. Blaire Point Elementary School students stood out in school yard as we passed.

Peru High School Marching Band accompanied us through town, around courthouse and to seniors' nursing center at Miller's Merry Manor. Cody again went into all the rooms, and actually laid his head down on one patient's bed. Such a show-off!

Mayor of Peru presented us with a Certificate of Appreciation.

Sept. 16—Today is our 100th day on this hitch! Seems like just yesterday when I dipped my hoofs in the Atlantic Ocean—time's passing at a good clip!

Traveled 13 miles today to Logansport, Indiana. Mayor William Verne presented David and Vikki with a key to the city. David and Cheryl Wilson of Roanoke, Indiana donated 24 bales of hay to us—my kind of people, and my kind of donation!

Sept. 17—I had the day off. Bobby stepped into a hole in the road and bent his shoe; Junior re-tacked it when we stopped for the evening.

Approximately 2,000 people greeted us along our 10.5-mile route. Nearly 200 people rode on wagon, including Logansport Mayor Verne. Also escorting us was a deputy sheriff all the way to Worman's Lake Campground, where we're staying tonight.

Sept. 18—Theo Kintigh of Jonesville, Michigan brought us a really unusual gift today, a Petrosky stone, named after Petrosky, Michigan. The stone is actually a coral fossil formed millions of years ago when Michigan was under water.

In the note accompanying his gift, Theo mentioned that David and Vikki were married on his birthday…and he was born in 1913! Now if I've figured correctly—took me quite a while to hoof this out—that means he's 90.

Kenny and Mary Watts of Logansport also presented us with an arrowhead for good luck. We're spending the night at the fire department in Idaville. Junior, Dan and Steve put up hotwire fences for us on the adjoining field.

Sept. 19—Sunday, so we stayed put, but David and Vikki drove 25 miles

"He's 18 'Hands' High? What Does That Mean?"

THE more you hang around draft horse people, the more you become aware they have a language all their own. Terms such as "croup", "spring of rib", "underpinning", "clean boned" and "low in the heels" fall off the tongues of draft horse enthusiasts like oats out of a bucket.

But the one you will likely hear most often is "hands". If you go back to page 28 of this book, for example, you'll see that Firestone's height is "18:2 hands". What's that mean?

Well, let's go back a bit. In the days before there was a standard system of measurement, horse owners needed some way to determine the height of a horse. So, since most people's hands—across the palm from finger to thumb—were about the same width (4 inches), the height of a horse was measured by placing one hand over another and totaling it up.

On that basis, Firestone's height is 74 inches (18 hands times 4 inches plus 2). But, don't conclude that he's only 6-foot-2 to the top of his ears! (Actually, he's well over 7 feet at that point.)

You see, a horse's height is measured from the ground to the top of his "withers", which is the high point of the back of a horse, located at the base of the neck and between the shoulder blades.

Despite all the modern methods of measurements, "hands" is still the standard used in referring to the height of a horse. Why? Maybe it just adds a bit of nostalgia or "character" to the industry.

Or maybe, as one draft horse owner responded, "It's worked just fine for years. Why change it now? All of us in the industry know what we're talking about, and if we're all comfortable with it, so be it."

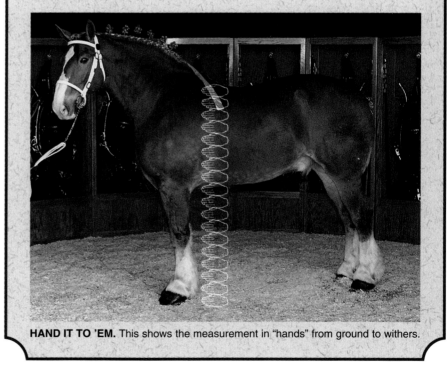

HAND IT TO 'EM. This shows the measurement in "hands" from ground to withers.

Glad You Asked… When Frances B. Murphey, a reporter from the *Akron Beacon News*, visited the hitch in Sugarcreek, Ohio, she asked crew member Steve Zbornik, "Why is the one horse named Firestone?"

Without missing a beat, Steve replied, "Because that's what his mother always called him!"

It Was Great To Meet You!

Several of the editors of Reiman Publications' magazines rode with the hitch from time to time...and had a chance to meet and thank thousands of our subscribers.

AS has been mentioned several times in this book, the main reason Reiman Publications sponsored this cross-country trip was to honor the nation's senior centers during their 50th-anniversary year...offer some enjoyment to these seniors by bringing one of the horses or the whole hitch to centers located along the route...and use proceeds raised through the trip's souvenir sales and the sale of this book to fund activities and programs at the nation's 15,000 senior centers.

But this trip also provided our editors a chance to personally meet thousands of our subscribers along the way, to shake their hand and thank them for their loyal support over the years.

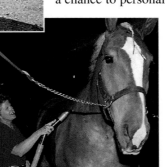

ON THE ROAD. Reiman Publications' editors often rode with the hitch, including Ann Kaiser, Editor of *Country Woman*, right and top, and Roy Reiman, Publisher of *Country* and *Reminisce*, above.

Of course, it wasn't possible for an editor to be along every day of the trip—we had our usual issue deadlines to meet. But as often as possible, our staffers went out in the field and rode along for a few days, to enjoy the experience and the chance to meet "our public" on a personal basis.

While out there, each of these editors helped gather material for this book. They also took pictures during their stint in the field to help illustrate this book.

To further help with this effort, we urged each member of the hitch crew to keep a "diary" and make notes every evening regarding their day—we gave each crew member a "log sheet" to use each day in jotting down the answers to these four questions: What was the most touching comment you heard today? What was the funniest quip you heard today? What was the prettiest scene or scenery you saw today? What was the highlight of your entire day?

Many of the items in this book are the result of those crew "diaries". Our editors were able to go over these diaries and "coach" the crew members in what kind of material to look for. But mostly, our editors used the visits to the hitch to personally meet and thank our subscribers for supporting our eight "ad-free" magazines. As a result of these trips to the field, they now feel they *know* many of our subscribers, and are better equipped to regularly produce what they feel their "friends" along rural routes will enjoy in future issues.

ahead to Remington. When they got back, they said it was full of very friendly people.

Fellows in the fire department fixed breakfast, lunch and dinner for crew—mighty nice of them! I dined on fresh grass and hay.

Sept. 20—As we left Idaville this morning, townspeople put up a sign reading "God Bless All of You". Even brought a lump to *my* throat!

Covered 12 miles and saw 1,650 people along route. Crossed Lake Shafer. About 125 people rode wagon, including Monticello Mayor Richard Cronch and his wife as we got to that city.

Nearly 900 Roosevelt School students greeted us. And Thelma Griffin of Belleville, Michigan says she drove almost 300 miles just to see us! We're staying at the White County Fairgrounds.

Sept. 21—Humid today, 94° and windy. Cornfields blowing in the wind reminded me of our manes and tails when we gallop across a pasture.

Traveled 10 miles, passed through Reynolds on our way to Wolcott Park, where we're spending the night.

Vikki braided our manes this morning. (I like it when she runs her fingers through my hair!)

Sept. 22—Traveled 13 miles, passing through Remington and Goodland in Jasper County. South Newton High School Band, directed by Joyce Stowers, performed and accompanied us into Goodland.

Stopped at Newton Council on Aging. Also stopped at Goodland Elementary School. A reporter from the *Daily Journal* in Kankakee, Illinois interviewed crew.

Mike and Glenna Minniear of Towne & Country Floral Shop presented Vikki with six red roses, and also served the crew dinner. Good people! We're staying at their place tonight.

Sept. 23—Traveled to Kentland, where we visited with residents at Kentland Nursing Center. Also treated students at Kentland Elementary School and Kentland Catholic School to figure eights and pinwheels.

Then on to our eighth state—Illinois, the Land of Lincoln! Stopped for the night in Effner, just over the state line. Staying next to A&J's Flea Market (hope the fleas don't come visiting during the night!).

Sept. 24—Brrr! Coldest morning so far—46°. Still, lots of people came ♂

Sandy Lebeck

CHAPTER TWO

MEANDERING WEST

out to see us—500 in the morning, 300 after lunch and 750 at our evening stop in Watseka, a town of 5,500 wonderful people.

Visited residents of Sheldon Nursing Home. One, Harold Clarke, was a premier horseman in his day. And another, James Light, says he judged Clarke in a horse show many years ago.

Mayor of Watseka presented David with a key to the city. Bunking at Bernes Implement Store tonight.

Sept. 25—Warmer—in the 60s—but very rainy. Dedicated group of students from Gilman High School, dressed in raincoats, led us through town.

Crew got soaked putting up our tent. Butch and Elsie Wauthier of Martinton, Illinois presented David and Vikki with a jewelry chest. (The kind of stuff I wear wouldn't fit in that one!)

David and Vikki scouted route ahead. Staying at K&W Truck Stop in Gilman.

Sept. 26—Sunday. Finally, some sun! Still pretty chilly, though, so we snuggled up with blankets and stayed in our stalls today.

Don and Lois had relatives from Iowa visit them. Also, David Wright, our newest crew member, enjoyed a visit from his parents.

Sept. 27—Did 10 miles today into Piper City, Illinois. About 30 students of the Piper City School Band marched us to Palmwood Health Care Center, where David gave a seminar.

In the evening, he returned with Cody. Some 300 pairs of eyes popped as Cody pranced through the doors of the center and neighed his way around. What a ham!

David, Vikki and Ashley went with him. They also visited Tri-Point Community School, where David held another seminar. And to top it off, we all made the 5:30 news on Channel 3!

Sept. 28—Passed through Chatsworth, where students at the elementary school were dismissed for the day to come visit us at the United Methodist Church.

Then on to Forest—population 1,200—where Ray McBride, bus driver for Meadowbrook Elementary and Junior High Schools, brought four busloads of kids to see us.

Dorothy Nelson of Racine, Wisconsin brought us—just us horses and Ashley—oats, horse pellets and dog bones. My kind of gal!

Sept. 29—Prairie Central High School Band marched with us to the

John Forrest

Crew 'Buckled Down' to Give Visitors Souvenirs

THE FRIENDLY NATURE of the hitch crew impressed many visitors along the route—especially three Amish farmers who unexpectedly received cherished souvenirs of the trip!

The farmers caught up with the hitch in New England, several weeks into the trip. They flagged down driver David Helmuth and, after chatting for a while, asked where they could buy three of the hitch's souvenir belt buckles. David directed them to the hitch's souvenir booth.

But when the men got to the booth, they learned that the last of the buckles had been sold earlier that morning. A new supply wouldn't arrive for several days.

AMISH FARMERS—who possess a fine eye for a good draft horse—were frequent visitors to the hitch (top). Three of them came away with special souvenir belt buckles (above).

Three crew members, seeing how disappointed the men were, removed the buckles from their own belts and said, "Here, take ours. We'll replace them when the new supply comes in."

A visitor who witnessed the exchange said the three Amish men were delighted. "Not only did they have their souvenir buckles," he said, "but these meant even more because they'd been worn by crew members all the way from Maine!"

"I DON'T KNOW how you're going to get all of this into one book—we've only been on the road about 2 weeks, and we already have enough stories and experiences to fill 200 pages!"

Now There's an Idea...

I WONDERED when I read the souvenir progam what happened to David and Vikki when it rained. But after studying the pictures of the wagon, I concluded that there was an enclosed area under the open seat where they could probably take refuge if necessary!

—*Eleanor Spraker*
Malden, Massachusetts

One for the Heart...

THE EXHILARATION I experienced when I rode the hitch on April 27, 1993 will remain with me forever!

The hitch had spent the previous night at Bear Brook Park in Allenstown, New Hampshire, a short distance from my home. I met the horses and crew there and got so excited thinking about being a part of their trip that I hardly slept a wink all night.

The next morning I headed for Concord, ride coupon in hand. I spotted the hitch as it was passing the city limits and cautiously passed so I wouldn't spook the horses. Then I parked on a side street and dashed back to the route, holding up my ticket.

As they drew near, David whoa'ed the horses and said, "Lady, climb aboard!" I sure didn't hesitate. A young boy and two little girls joined me.

I rode all the way to the AgWay store, where the hitch was stopping for the night. I had a chance to pet Firestone, and I can still remember the feel of his velvety muzzle.

Please excuse me for going into so much detail, but you see, I was scheduled for open heart surgery 2 weeks later, and this happy experience helped me through my many days of convalescence. I will hold these dear memories in my heart forever!

—Jessie Emerson, Suncook, New Hampshire

FEELING THEIR OATS! The Belgians made the most of any opportunity to kick up their heels, treating amused onlookers to quite a display of genuine horseplay.

Can't Dampen Spirits!
WE DIDN'T HAVE our usual mild spring weather in Kennebunkport, but you'd never have known it from watching the wagon's enthusiastic riders. They were waving to their friends along the route and singing *Home on the Range*!

—Peter Valeska, Kennebunkport, Maine

Nursing Center in Forest. Then we covered 12 miles and were led into Fairbury, Illinois by the town's ambulance and fire truck.

Lots of people—I'd guess 1,200—sitting on lawn chairs in their yards and cheering as we drove to Fairview Haven Nursing Home. Also visited Fairbury Hospital.

Sept. 30—My day off. The others did 13 miles, driving through Chenoa and on to Gridley for the night.

Some 135 people got aboard wagon, including Phoebe Collins of Pontiac, Illinois. "You really made my 83rd birthday!" she told David and Vikki.

Visited Meadows Mennonite Retirement Community in Chenoa, where David gave a seminar and we showed off our tricks. We're staying at the Heinold Hog Market tonight.

Oct. 1—Did lots of visiting today! Walked 10 miles into El Paso, Illinois (I always thought El Paso was in Texas!) and the Gridley High School Band serenaded us into the Town Park. The rest of the students—about 400—were waiting there to greet us.

Stopped at Heritage Manor Nursing Home and at El Paso Health Care Center for David to give seminars and answer questions. El Paso Community Band accompanied us to El Paso Center and played *Amazing Grace*—I love that song!

Also stopped at Virgil Reeves' home just to take a picture of the railroad car in his yard. Didn't see any tracks; wonder how it got there!

Oct. 2—Another 10.8 miles into Eureka, where the Eureka Marching Band led us to the Apostolic Christian Center and performed several numbers for residents there.

Walter Christ made the arrangements for us at the center. His wife, Kathleen, had worked there until she died of cancer in July. Walter said she'd been looking forward to seeing our hitch, and he somehow felt that she knew we were there now.

David gave residents a ride around the center's parking lot. Crew members were guests for lunch at the center. No room at the tables for us, I guess!

Oct. 3—Sunday. Spent the day in our stalls in the parking lot of the Eureka Dairy Queen. On our best behavior for visitors, some 1,700 of them!

The crew enjoyed lots of ice cream at the Dairy Queen. They also ate dinner there. This afternoon David and Vikki ♂

drove the route for the coming week.

Oct. 4—Back in the harness. Gave 135 people—and Ashley—rides along the 10-mile route into Washington, Illinois in Tazewell County.

Met 122 residents at Washington Christian Village Center, including 98-year-old Bertha Burnett, who proudly said she once owned draft horses. Rosemary Martin, the center's Activity Director, treated us great.

Steve Johnson of Metamora, Illinois wrote a nice note to crew: "This young couple driving the hitch is such a class act. Makes you keep faith in America!" I just know he thinks the same of us horses.

Oct. 5—Lot of traffic today, going through Pekin and on to East Peoria, where we're staying at the Community Plaza. Lots of people working at mall came to see us, some 700 in afternoon and 850 in evening. Also visited Faith Christian Center.

Oct. 6—A long story but worth telling: Walter Christ from the Apostolic Christian Center in Eureka came to Hanna City where we are now and presented crew with a special quilt titled "Trip Around the World".

The quilt had made quite a trip itself. It was designed by Margaret Fortenbacher of Apostolic Christian Church in Kitchener, Ontario, and quilted by a group of Mennonite ladies in Kitchener.

Then it was purchased by Martha Jane Siebenthal of Princeville, Illinois and donated to the '93 bazaar auction at the Apostolic Christian Home in Eureka. Now our hitch has it. Unique memento of our trip!

Oct. 7—Passed through Trivoli on our way to Farmington, a town of 3,100 wonderful people. Traffic was heavy as hundreds lined the route to see and pet us, and get rides. A farmer in his field saw us driving by, hopped off his John Deere combine, ran to the road and took some pictures.

Stopped at Riverview Retirement Community. Pamela Berendy, editor of *Times Record* in Aledo, drove quite a distance to get a story about our trek. Bill and Betty Steinbelle of Minonk, Illinois gave crew cookies. Bill once was a clown with Ringling Bros.!

Oct. 8—Passed through Middle Grove; the Spoon River Valley High School Band escorted us into London Mills. Big day there!

The annual Spoon River Drive—a

Hitch Evokes Fond Memories of Father-in-Law

MY FATHER-IN-LAW loved horses more than anything in this world, and when the hitch spent a night on land he used to own, I'm sure he knew those Belgians were there.

Forrest Lowe was a mild, soft-spoken man who used horses to pull logs at his sawmill. Although he worked around rough-and-tumble loggers all his life, he never smoked, swore or drank anything stronger than coffee. The only oath he ever uttered was "Thunder"—and then only when one of the loggers was hollering at the horses. "Thunder!" he'd say. "What seems to be the matter with him, anyway?"

I worked for Forrest for many years and saw for myself how much he loved his teams. When the mill moved to another lot, the first thing he built was the horse barn. When he bought a brand-new 1926 Essex, he removed the backseat, filled it with hay and drove it over the rugged logging roads to feed the horses.

Once he had a beautiful roan that went lame. The veterinarian said the horse shouldn't work in the woods anymore, so Forrest gave it to a local farmer. Later, when the mill moved out of the area, my in-laws drove about 30 miles every Sunday for more than 2 years just to visit that horse.

So I'm sure my father-in-law was looking down from Heaven when your Belgians stopped to rest at his old place. And I'll bet there was a big smile on his face!

—*Philip Traxler, Bennington, New Hampshire*

HAVIN' A LOOK-SEE. Belgians enjoyed checking out their surroundings (at top) as they were trucked from Centerville, Iowa to the West Coast. Above, they head out for another day's trek.

READY TO ROLL. David addresses early-morning visitors before departure.

"THIS IS A DREAM come true for me. I love the traveling, meeting the great people and seeing all of the different places. And I feel very privileged to be on a trip like this, considering that I'm the youngest one in the group!"

3,000 Miles of Pure Delight

How we envy David and Vikki,
3,000 miles of pure delight!
Peaceful valleys and rushing rivers
Flowing through hills of grandest height.

Beautiful Firestone is their leader,
That huge giant gentle horse.
Ashley thinks of herself as their guide
And that she keeps them on their course.

There's the goodness of the people
Holding out a welcoming hand,
The wonder in the countryside
And the majestic beauty of our land...

Yes, we truly are quite envious
In the challenge of this trip,
But we wish them a safe journey
With a prayer from every lip.

—Amy McIntyre, Tionesta, Pennsylvania

Photos: Rick Van Etten

LOAD 'EM UP...and move 'em out! Throughout the Midwest, the hitch stopped nearly every half mile during its day's walk to take on a new group of riders.

huge craft show and flea market that encompasses a number of towns in the area—begins tomorrow. They tell us it's always held on the first two weekends of October. (I finally figured out that they don't sell fleas at a flea market—what a relief!)

We overheard someone say they expect 35,000 people this year! Folks from every state attend—Vikki said one of our riders today, Janet Cressy, was from Tampa, Florida, and another, Julie Williams, was from Chino, California!

Oct. 9—Cool, windy and 58°, but lots of people at the flea market and visiting us—1,500 during the day and 800 at night.

We're staying in London Mills again tonight.

Oct. 10—Sunday. Stayed put in London Mills today. Big crowds again in the nice sunny weather, with temperatures in the 60s.

We're attracting quite a crowd, too: 500 visitors in morning, another 1,500 in afternoon, about 750 tonight!

Oct. 11—Walked 8 miles to St. Augustine, where we're staying tonight. Had nearly 185 riders, with hundreds of people cheering us along the route.

David, Vikki and Cody visited the nursing home in Avon, Illinois. Nancy Stenger, administrator, hosted them. Cody's sure getting to show off a lot lately—need to have a word with David about that!

Amy Garrett of nearby Abingdon gave David and Vikki a cute homemade teddy bear. *We* got 15 bales of hay from George Coursey of St. Augustine. Way to go, George!

Oct. 12—Really clip-clopped along today—14 miles to Roseville, home of Boy Scout Troop 336 and 1,250 other nice people, including 94-year-old Naomi Kurtane who rode on our wagon.

The Roseville Band gave us a musical welcome. And Ron and Sandy Huston greeted us with a "WELCOME" sign on which they'd pasted all Reiman magazines. Guess who got to go again with David to the nursing center—Yep! Cody!

David bought us another 15 bales of hay from Kirkpatrick Hay Service in Roseville.

Oct. 13—Walked 11.6 miles into Raritan. Nedra Stewart, local postmaster, wrote us a nice note saying, "Thanks for stopping at our 'Village at the edge of the West'."

Mary Brokaw, of nearby Strong-

Dear Hitch
Is it difficult to drive the semi with the horses in back?
Your friend,
Larry Capron

Dear Hitch ☺☺ I love your horses. Where did they come from? Your FRiend, Kayla

Dear Hitch,
How did Vikki learn to braid the manes so fast and pretty? Your friend, Heidi Studer

hurst—she's 95—rode our wagon. So did Harvey Dohrmann, of Rochester, Minnesota, who's in a wheelchair. Tom and Ellen Rank of Abingdon gave Vikki a dozen red roses plus two Western shirts for her and David.

And the good folks at Lotsawork Ranch (honest, that's the name!) in New Windsor donated 20 bags of sawdust. Practical gift for horses, you know; it makes great bedding!

Oct. 14—Last day in Illinois. Stopping tonight in Lomax, home of 600 nice people. Can't believe the flood damage we're seeing—water lines from the Mississippi clear up to the second story of some houses, and whole cornfields under water!

Staying at Farquher Farms. Crew had a great time at a bonfire tonight; sat on straw bales and roasted hot dogs and marshmallows. (Must have lost my invitation.) Then they began getting us ready for filming tomorrow—brushing, clipping, making our hooves shiny and black…the works!

Oct. 15—Historic day! Film crew shot footage of us crossing the mighty Mississippi River into Fort Madison, Iowa, our ninth state.

We were all decked out in our fancy show harnesses—really looked sharp. But before that, on our last leg in Illinois, the La Harpe Band led us to the Lomax and Carmen senior centers, and the Dallas City High School Band per-

Hitch Is a Hit with New York Students

WHILE the hitch's cross-country trek was primarily designed to honor seniors and senior centers, its appeal was ageless. One special-education teacher even used the trip as part of her lesson plan!

Ann Marie Knight of Camden, New York displayed the route on a map in her classroom (above). She called the "Hitch Hotline" regularly to update her second and third graders on the hitch's progress and posted magazine photos of the horses and crew on her bulletin board. The students also wrote letters to various crew members.

Although Camden wasn't on the hitch's official route, a fellow teacher took pictures to share with Ann Marie's class when the team stopped at *her* school in nearby Morrisville.

"The children just fell in love with the horses, and following the route also provided them with an ongoing social studies lesson for the year!" Ann Marie said.

A FIELD DAY. Hitch's daily progress (and rest stops) were tracked by schoolchildren (top).

THE MANE EVENT

Happy to Oblige...

MY DAUGHTER doesn't get home from kindergarten until 11 a.m., which meant the hitch would pass through our town before she got home. I was so disappointed!

But the hitch was going right past her school, so I asked David if he could stop there—and he said yes! All 500 elementary pupils were let out of class to ask questions and share in the excitement. They were so thrilled!

Thank you so much for bringing joy to many, many people across the country.

—Bernice Parks, Guilderland, New York

CLOSE-UP LOOK. Gentle giants like getting up close and personal with their visitors.

STUCK ON YOU? Curious youngster checks to see if Ashley's spots will rub off.

SNACK TIME. Grazing is extra easy when someone offers you a handful of sweet grass!

"LIFE on the road was full of surprises, and we were frequently amazed by the effect the hitch had on people.

"While we were in New England, a man passed us in a classy car, then turned around, stopped right in front of us and jumped out. He was very well-dressed in a nice suit and wearing lots of gold jewelry, and was handsome enough to be a movie star.

"He walked right up to the wagon and said, 'This is a beautiful thing you're doing, giving senior citizens a ride on this wagon.' Then he peeled a $100 bill off a thick roll, pressed into one of our riding senior's hands, hurried back to his car and drove away without another word!"

formed a concert. Many of the 160 riders we had today were victims of the recent floods. Glad we could bring them a moment of happiness!

Oct. 16—Big, big crowds: 1,500 in morning, some 2,000 in afternoon and another 1,500 at evening stop! David gave a seminar to residents at the Fort Madison Health Center; also visited Fort Madison Health Hospital.

Crew had dinner right out of *Taste of Home* magazine: barbecued chicken made by a local subscriber! Staying in Donnellson, Iowa tonight, where Russell, John and Janet Pletscher arranged for us to camp at the Lee County Fairgrounds, site of the oldest county fair in the state.

Oct. 17—Sunday. Wow! People really turning out to see hitch: 1,300 in the morning, 2,800—yep, 2,800!—in the afternoon and 900 in evening. David and Vikki took Cody to Donnellson Manor Care Center.

Cody also got into a picture with a miniature horse named "Cherokee", owned by Judy Young of Donnellson. Only 21 inches tall, Cherokee posed *under* Cody!

Oct. 18—Saw a llama today on road to Farmington, Iowa (smallest village in Van Buren County)—what a strange-looking critter! Kind of like a cross between a sheep and a giraffe!

Girl Scouts from local Troop 120 gave David and Vikki a Native American dream catcher. Girls' advisor is Pat Millmier.

We stopped for the night at the United Methodist Church in Farmington.

Oct. 19—David and Vikki took Cody to visit the Van Buren Good Samaritan Center in Keosauqua, about 13 miles up the road from Donnellson. (*Finally* found out why they keep choosing Cody—it's because he's so "laid back". And here I'd been afraid it was because they thought he was better-looking than me!)

Crossed Des Moines River during our 12.6-mile walk. Damp and chilly weather held down the number of riders. Stocked up on hay today—25 bales of timothy mixed with alfalfa, one of my favorite combinations. Staying at Phillips Pallets tonight.

Oct. 20—Magic had a "family reunion" today—Don Schnelclothe came to see us. Don raised Magic from a colt; he must be proud his "kid" made the big time!

Fox Valley High School Band gave ♂

Mom's in Her Element

MY HUSBAND and I took my elderly parents to see the hitch near Malvern, Ohio. My father, Walter McAllister of Adena, Ohio, rode in the wagon with me.

Mother is 89 and confined to a wheelchair, so she was not able to ride on the wagon, but we did place her over near the trailer so she could watch the crew set up the stalls and feed the horses after their morning's trip.

When I returned from parking our car, Mother was all alone with Bobby tied up next to her, eagerly awaiting his lunch. It was plain from the look on Mother's face that she was having a ball! She grew up on a farm working with horses and wasn't the least bit afraid.

As the crew led the horses into their stalls, Mother called out to each of them by name, laughing and asking them to please not step on her! Of course, they behaved in a very gentlemanly fashion, and she was delighted to be that close to horses again.

We've enjoyed sharing this story with many others since last August. Thanks for bringing so much joy and so many happy memories to so many people! —*Mary McElroy*
Gibsonia, Pennsylvania

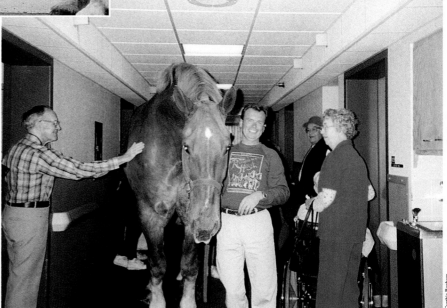

HORSE IN THE HALL! That call was frequently heard in senior centers along the route as David led one of the team right inside the building so residents could get a good look. When the weather was nice, the entire hitch pulled up outside (top left) instead.

us a musical salute, leading us into Milton, where we're staying tonight next to the Phillips 66 station. Some band members marched alongside Dale, petting him as he walked.

Oct. 21—Brrr! Cold, windy and only 30°! Kept going, though, 16 miles into Bloomfield, arriving at Davis County Fairgrounds for the night.

Musical escort was Davis County High School Band, directed by Linda McConnell. Visited Davis County Hospital and Senior Center. Met Julia Kinsinger, who's 100 years old, and June McClure, only a youngster at age 90.

Hazel Croft, mayor of Bloomfield, gave Vikki a bouquet of pink carnations. Crew from Iowa Public Television station shot footage of us.

Oct. 22—Better weather; up in mid-60s and sunny. Crossed into Appanoose County, traveling 13 miles to fairgrounds in West Grove.

Vikki blacked our hooves today. (That's horse talk for shining our shoes.) She also filed the chestnuts off our legs. More horse lingo; chestnuts are what humans call calluses.

Heading for Centerville, Iowa tomorrow. Me and my buddies have heard there are big doin's in the works...

Oct. 23—Our 131st and last day on the road for a while! Traveled 14 miles, crossed the Raritan River and made a

Burning up the Wires...

WE COULD hardly wait for the hitch to reach Marion, Ohio. We kept the Hotline hot and nearly wore out our program sharing it with friends and family.

As we watched for the horses to round the bend on Route 309, we were like kids waiting for a circus parade. What a thrill to see it all up close! —*John and Mary Dean, Marion, Ohio*

MOTORISTS WHO were slowed along Route 5 in Erie County Thursday could hardly believe the reason when they saw it—a team of six Belgian horses pulling a wagon filled with people who were smiling so hard their faces hurt.
—*Robin Cuneo, Erie (Pennsylvania)*
Daily Times, July 16, 1993

"THE HORSES are handling this trip extremely well. On the days that it's more humid, they need a few more breaks than usual. But in general, they're gaining a lot of muscle. They're holding their weight just beautifully.

"They seem to have a lot of energy when they get in parades and different kinds of social activities where we have a lot of people and a lot of excitement going on. They seem to perk up and get in the spirit of things and realize it's time to put on a show for everybody!"

ARE THEY HERE YET? A visit from the hitch was a special occasion for seniors, who often waited in front of their residence for the team to arrive.

NICE CAP, MISTER! Team's diet included plenty of hay and oats, plus carrots and other treats…but apparently not enough caps, figured Firestone (right).

OKAY FOR SHORT HAUL…As delighted riders looked on, David and Vikki tried out an alternate means of transportation. Such horseplay didn't seem to impress the team much.

grand entrance into Centerville.

Radio station KMGO aired a live broadcast of the hitch approaching town. Selected local bands and cheerleaders escorted us. A Senior King and Queen rode the hitch to the town square.

Then about noon, community and school representatives joined the crew in laying one of *my* horseshoes—which they'd had *gold-plated*—in the pavement of the town square. Mighty impressive ceremony, let me tell you!

From listening to David, Vikki and the crew, me and my buddies have learned that we're going to be laying over in Centerville awhile—the cold weather has really gotten to everybody, including the folks coming out to see us.

Chip said he heard David telling Steve and Junior that after we rest a bit, we're going to head for California aboard our semi, and that when we get there, we're going to walk in the Pacific Ocean (just like we did in Maine, only that was the Atlantic) and then walk *back* to Centerville.

So, my golden horseshoe marks the "halfway point" of our journey, and when we get back to it, we'll have completed our walk across the whole country!

Oct. 24—Sunday. You know, I'm happy the way this is gonna work out. If they'd have asked me in the beginning how to plan this cross-county trek, I could have told 'em then to do it this way.

Never really cared for the colt-er-cold, and this new plan will have us in the Southwest during the winter months. I have to hand it (or hoof it, rather) to them for coming up with this contingency plan!

Oct. 25—Warm and sunny in Centerville today. We hitched up and gave rides around the town square (the world's largest, by the way) to celebrate Seniors' Day.

Some of our riders included these "youngsters": Barbara Duncomb, who's 89, from Kirksville, Mississippi, and Roy Lansbury of Albia, Iowa, who won a contest as the oldest person to ride the wagon today—he's 91.

Also Lloyd and Ann Landre rode the wagon as a gift to one another on their 64th wedding anniversary. (Wonder if I could stay "hitched" that long!)

Pat Slater came all the way from San Jose, California to see her 103-year-old mother in Zearing and to see our hitch. Bob and Sally Adler of La Grange, Illinois left home at 3 a.m. just to see us.

Oct. 26—David, Vikki and Cody ♂↱

visited Centerville Care Center. One resident, Doris Jean Woodward, had a wish; wanted to sit on Cody. She got it; David helped her up.

Today was Kids' Day at the square; our youngest rider was Ethan Miller, only 11 days old. Oldest to visit the hitch today was 90-year-old Ruby Seylo of Centerville.

In all, 630 riders today. Laurie and Stacey Hoch at the end of the line almost didn't get to ride. So David invited them to ride with him and Vikki back to the fairgrounds!

Oct. 27—David and Vikki really "put on the feed bag" today—had lunch with Dave McNichols, director of the Centerville Chamber of Commerce, at 18-80 Seniors Club, along with Shirley Payer, club director. Then they were dinner guests of Mr. McNichols at the Rotary Club.

Mamie Bolender came farthest to see hitch today—all the way from Seattle, Washington! Oldest to see hitch: Clyde McGee, 97, of Centerville.

Oct. 28—Shared limelight with 13 other classy hitches today—we all paraded around the square. Barbara Cole of the Chamber of Commerce did great lining up hitches.

Oldest hitch driver was 65-year-old Donald Dudley of Centerville. Bill Little came farthest to see our hitch—from San Francisco.

Also met Ruth Toothman of West Des Moines, who said she was Roy Reiman's teacher in school.

Three couples celebrated their wedding anniversaries by riding the wagon today. They were Merwyn and Leona Thompson of Russell, Iowa, their 60th; Tom and Alta Reynolds of Centerville, their 61st; and Howard and Margaret Yeigh, their 51st.

Oct. 29—Almost 500 people rode the wagon around the town square. Paul and Josie Toole drove down from Alaska to Michigan to pick up their daughter and then came here to see us!

Highlight of the day: the world's largest hayride. Even *The Guinness Book of Records* may not believe it, but over *450 people* rode on *17 wagons* hitched together, which me and my five colleagues pulled without a bit of trouble!

TV Channel 3 was on hand to video-

WEATHER OR NOT. Like the U.S. Mail, the hitch's progress was unimpeded by rain, cold and even snow (opposite). Bundled up or huddled under umbrellas, David and Vikki still had a warm welcome for riders and visitors.

"WE NEVER KNOW if it's going to rain during our trip or not. A lot of people have asked us, 'What do you guys do when it rains?' Well, we all found out early in the trip what we do—we let it rain!

"Our slogan along the side of our wagon says, 'We're Pulling for Seniors.' We *are* pulling for seniors. That's the main reason that we're here. This trip is all about people, and we're not going to let a little rain get in the way!"

THE MANE EVENT

AWESOME AWNING. The loading ramp at the rear of the semi (above) also served as a shelter for crew members during stopovers in the rain. Below: A few flakes are no problem!

Angela Myers

Kathy Purdum

Rain Didn't Dampen Spirits!

WE SAT in the rain on deck chairs under golf umbrellas along State Route 288 for a couple of hours waiting for the hitch. There were truckers and cars going by continually, tooting and waving and wondering about this bunch of crazy people sitting along the road in the rain!

When the hitch finally arrived, we had a delightful time riding down 288 toward the little town of Iberia, where the hitch spent the night. David, Vikki and the crew were super. We enjoyed meeting all of them and, of course, seeing and petting the beautiful horses!   —*Raymond and Eleanor Predmore, Galion, Ohio*

tape us. I think everyone was amazed by what they saw!

Oct. 30—Today's our last day on display at the fairgrounds. Weather's not fit for horses—in the 30s with snow flurries.

Still, some 500 people were thrilled to climb aboard our wagon for rides. The Centerville Band escorted us to the town square for afternoon rides. Vikki says we did so well we deserve a week's rest!

Oct. 31—Sunday. We're relaxing in our stalls today, and the crew is taking it easy in their campers. It's vacation time. I'm going to make the most of it before we head off on a circuit around the state for special showings.

Nov. 1-7—We're taking it easy in the fairgrounds barn this week, which isn't a bad idea, considering the cold, wet weather we're having.

Because we're just "kicking back" (I love that expression!), Vikki said I could take a break from making my daily diary entries. I'll second that proposal with a big whinny!

Should note, however, that next week we're going to be making a quick tour around the state by semi. I'll keep you posted!

Nov. 8—Monday, and away we go! Sure enough, we headed out in our semi today, traveling northwest 110 miles to Madrid, Iowa.

When we arrived about 3 p.m., the crew unloaded us, harnessed us up and drove through town, escorted by the Madrid High School Band. Mayor Lou Galetich extended a hearty welcome.

We stopped at Madrid Nursing Home on North Street, where David held a seminar and gave 11 residents a ride. Thomas Ball of Cortland, New York was honored for coming the farthest to see us today.

Nov. 9—This entry is mighty tough for me to write. All of us in the hitch lost a close friend today. Our buddy Jack, ♂

who proudly pulled in the left wheel position, died suddenly of a heart attack this afternoon in Audubon, Iowa.

We had traveled 75 miles on the semi and arrived in Audubon at about 2. We were hitched up for a parade into town, and as we neared the town's senior center, Friendship Home, Jack fell.

David immediately "whoa'ed" us, and Vikki jumped down and ran to Jack. He raised his head, then fell back and died in her arms.

Jack was a champion in every way. He loved to be in harness and was proud of his role in our hitch. I can only guess how deeply David, Vikki and the rest of the crew feel his loss. We're all going to miss him, but take comfort from the fact that he died doing what he loved best—pulling with us!

Nov. 10—Extremely foggy and cold today; kind of matched our mood after losing Jack yesterday.

Traveled 150 miles in semi to Orange City, where 800 people met us at noon. Stopped at Heritage Home, Orange City Municipal Hospital and Merry Manor. David and Vikki drove the hitch to Todd Mouw's house for a special visit with the well-known horse lover who has been in a wheelchair since a car accident in 1984.

It was sad not seeing Jack get into harness today. Tim was in his place, and he was the first to admit that he's got some mighty big shoes to fill!

Nov. 11—Trucked east 133 miles to Britt, known for its Draft Horse Show each September. Met nearly 2,000 people; 380 took rides on the wagon, including Mayor Pat Byers.

Britt High School Band, 30 of 'em plus six flag girls, marched us into town. David visited residents of West View Care Center.

Nov. 12—Arrived in Decorah; met nearly 3,000 people along the way and had about 300 riders. Drove to John Cline School, thrilling some 300 kids. Also chatted with residents at Case Home, Eastern Star Home and Oneata View Center; later stopped at West Side School.

Nov. 13—Back in our semi for a 140-mile hop to Maquoketa; arrived at fairgrounds at noon. Brownie Girl Scout Troop held up "Welcome!" sign on Main Street as we drove hitch to River Village Senior Housing Department and to Crestridge Senior Center.

Met "shirt-tail" (maybe that should be "horse-tail"!) relatives today: Dale

"OUR TRIP through central New York was a memorable one. Here are just a few of the highlights:

"At a rest stop near Eaton, a woman asked us if she could pull her car close to the horses. Her mother, 92-year-old Ethel Neff of Madison, had watched the horses from her wheelchair earlier in the day, but just had to have a closer look.

" 'We had horses on our farms,' Ethel said. 'When we took the team to auction, I cried when they were bought. This brings back many wonderful memories for me.'

"At Edward R. Andrews Elementary School in Morrisville, band members serenaded us as we drove up, while hundreds of pupils and teachers looked on. Ten-year-old Mark Reed of Bouckville was wide-eyed when he saw the team. 'They're *big*!' he said in awe. Later, at Morrisville-Eaton Central School, students greeted us with signs reading 'Clip Clop' and 'Happy Trails'!

"At the Madison County Office for the Aging in Morrisville, aging specialist Christine Sears gave us a certificate recognizing the hitch for 'its dedication to older Americans'.

" 'It's wonderful what you're doing,' she said. 'I'm impressed with the awareness of you young kids of older Americans. One nice thing about letting seniors ride the hitch is that you're portraying this segment of the population as active and healthy!'

"Later, we visited with 110 residents of the Crouse Community Center, bringing the hitch right to the front door and giving everyone a chance to pet them. It was a thrill to see so many smiling faces. The administrator gave me a T-shirt, and an employee loaded us up with pastries!

"Another special moment was giving a ride to a gracious lady in a wheelchair. Leona Root, 79, of Waterville, New York was gently lifted onto the wagon so she could enjoy the ride. 'It's very considerate to let someone else enjoy the pleasure the crew is experiencing on this trip,' she said afterward. 'I wanted to keep riding all the way to California!'

"As we munched on cinnamon molasses cookies from Polly Hedblom of nearby Earlville, we knew the Belgians were in for a big surprise at our next stop in Nelson—meeting *another* six-horse hitch!

"At a pre-determined site, our horses met a majestic team of Percherons owned by the Price Champion grocery chain in Syracuse. Driver Joe McCullough said they decided to meet the hitch after reading about the trip in *Country*.

"Paul Rebuck, the company's transportation manager, said most of his employees were horse enthusiasts, and were eager to get the two champion teams together.

"To show their support for the trip, Price Champion donated a ton of hay for the Belgians, plus three bulging bags of groceries for the crew.

"They realize how hard this trip across the country really is, and the meeting of these two teams proves that people still use hitches!"

They Enjoyed Keeping Tabs...

JUST WANTED you to know how much the residents at the nursing home where I work appreciated the souvenir hitch program. A nurse's assistant brought it to us at one of our morning programs, and the residents were so interested that I began reading them a page a day.

Now, whenever I walk into the day room, the first thing I hear is, "What's happening now with the hitch?" The residents know all the horses' names, and ask every day if David and Vikki have gotten married yet. Thanks for your dedication and support for senior citizens!

—*Helen Dykeman*
The Baptist Home, Rhinebeck, New York

Picture This: Her Dad, Son, Niece Appeared on Trailer!

WHEN THE HITCH traveled through the Finger Lakes region of New York, Joanne VanAken was determined to see it. After all, her father, son and niece were pictured on the Belgians' semi!

Their picture had first appeared on a cover of *Reminisce* magazine. It shows William VanAken driving his Model N Ford down a country road with Joanne's son, William Bay, and her niece, Becki VanAken, after an antique car meet in the 1960s.

When the horses' custom-built trailer was painted, a large reproduction of that cover was added near the stall windows. When Joanne heard that, she knew she had to see it!

Joanne lives in Canandaigua, so she visited the hitch at the nearby Finger Lakes Livestock Exchange as the crew prepared for that day's trip. She was so fascinated that she was late getting to work, but she said it was worth it.

She only wished her late father could have seen it, too. "He was such an active man," she said. "This trip is definitely something he'd approve of!"

Joseph Wysocki

Right: Jane Burke

M. Lacivita

OLD-TIME HORSEPOWER. *Reminisce* magazine cover reproduced on the side of the semi trailer (inset) was of special interest to Joanne VanAken of Canandaigua, New York —it shows three members of her family rolling along in her father's prized Model N Ford.

and Shel McMain, owners of my daddy, Master's Eddie. Guess that makes 'em my grandpa and grandma in a way, huh? We're staying at their barns where they have classy, comfortable box stalls for us.

Nov. 14—Sunday. Had breakfast, then drove out to Paradise Acres, David and Vikki's farm in Nashua. Crew gave us deluxe room service; they filled our stalls with fresh shavings and made sure we had plenty of hay.

All of us are ready for a little R&R after our big swing around Iowa. We're going to "lay over" here for a week, then head back down to Centerville. I'll pick up this diary again then.

Nov. 21—Sunday. After breakfast, we loaded up and covered the 260 miles to Centerville; arrived at the fairgrounds about 4 p.m.

Learned something interesting today—John Wayne was born in Winterset, just a little ways southwest of Des Moines. In my opinion, he was a real "horse's man"!

Nov. 22—Left Centerville this morning bound for San Diego, California! Traveled 120 miles to Clarinda, Iowa, birthplace of bandleader Glenn Miller.

In a ceremony attended by Mayor Jim Smiley, David and Vikki placed official *Country's Reminisce Hitch* route sign in the ground at Nodaway Valley Historical Museum, signifying that we'll be passing through Clarinda on our way back to Centerville.

Nov. 23—Wow! It was only 20° when we left this morning. We're driving the same route we'll be covering on foot on our way back to Centerville.

Traveled 40 miles, crossing into Missouri and stopping in Tarkio.

Nov. 24—Traveled to Auburn, Nebraska today. Miserable weather, 19°, sleeting with slight snow. Roads were slippery, but some 1,500 people turned out along route to welcome us. Barbara Corvette came all the way from West Virginia to see us and her family.

Nov. 25—Thanksgiving Day in Auburn; still cold. Overheard the crew talking about the great turkey dinner they had at the Church of Christ. Sounded like a good time—I'd like to try a holiday sit-down dinner some day!

About 900 people came out to the ♂

fairgrounds to see us. Local radio broadcaster Judy Coe presented David and Vikki with a poem she wrote about the hitch. Haven't read it yet; wonder if she mentions me in it. What rhymes with "Firestone"?

Nov. 26—Drove 100 miles to Marysville, Kansas, one of the famous stops on the Pony Express route. Now *that* was a way to carry the mail!

This afternoon David and Vikki took Cody to visit the residents of Cambridge Place. In the evening, the three of them joined in the parade to welcome Santa to town. Get this: Cody wore red garland around his neck, his white show bridle with sleigh bells attached and had his nose was painted red (with Vikki's lipstick) like Rudolph the Red-Nosed Reindeer.

Nov. 27— Trucked another 100 miles to Abilene. Starting to feel warmer; 48° at noon. Crew laid in a supply of hay and the fire department brought us water— mighty nice of them!

Nov. 28—Sunday. Arrived in Great Bend, Kansas after a 99-mile trek on Route 56, which follows the old Santa Fe trail.

Pretty town with Main Street decorated with Christmas tree lights—the holiday season is definitely upon us!

Nov. 29—Still getting warmer; sunny and 55° as we trucked 83 miles to Dodge City, Kansas. David and Vikki thrilled some 300 people at Manor of the Plains Nursing Home, showing off Cody.

Staying tonight at stable on the grounds of Dodge City Community College; they offer courses in horsemanship—talk about progressive education! We all got a great night's sleep in heated box stalls.

Nov. 30—Onward to Ulysses, Kansas, another 81 miles. On the way there, we stopped in Montezuma; 500 people waiting for us at Bethel Home.

Montezuma kids were also bused to see hitch there. Interesting landscape— oil wells all over the place for about 20 miles leading into Ulysses.

Dec. 1—Another state—we're now in Oklahoma! Actually, we've been in *three* states today; we left Ulysses, Kansas this morning, followed the hitch route west to Springfield, Colorado, then turned south to Boise City in the Oklahoma panhandle.

As we rolled into Boise City, me and

Once a Horseman...

I RODE with the hitch on both July 5 and 6 at Springville, New York.

I'm seen on the first video as the rider waving with a glove on my right hand. I wore gloves since David had promised that I could drive for a few minutes at Springville.

I have an 8 x 10 picture of the hitch. On the back, David and Vikki certified that I drove the hitch. It is my prize possession!

I'm a retired Baptist pastor. I grew up on a farm in western New York and drove our team before I was big enough to hitch and unhitch them by myself. I enjoyed all of the farm work that could be done with horses. My big disappointment as a teenager was the fact that I couldn't milk cows with "lines" in my hands!
—*Dr. Wesley Potter*
Great Valley, New York

PERFECT FIT. Frequent fittings of new shoes ensured team's comfort every step of the way.

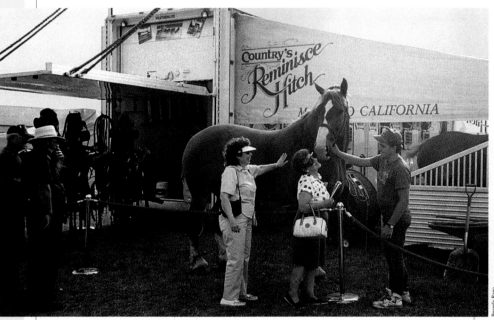

Hitch Salutes the Red, White and Blue

THE HITCH wasn't originally scheduled to visit Orchard Park, New York, but residents invited David and Vikki to appear in the Fourth of July parade there.

The small community, founded by Quakers, is surrounded by the foothills of the Allegheny Mountains. "It required some extra planning on our part to include the hitch in our parade, but it was worth it," said Nancy Conley, acting executive director of the village's Chamber of Commerce.

"The hitch was the highlight of the day, and we had a record crowd of approximately *20,000* people! The hitch generated a tremendous amount of excitement."

Resident Victoria Twarog agreed. "Their participation made our parade the best ever," she said. "What better way to celebrate the pioneer spirit of the horses and crew than on the Fourth of July?"

Victoria also was grateful for the personal attention given to her husband, who is in a wheelchair and couldn't get as close to the horses as he would have liked. "When the crew saw that he was in a wheelchair, they gave us a chance to have a private visit with the team," she said. "That made things much easier for us. The visit will always be a very special memory."

Visitor Gives Hitch High Marks

I WAS in Amish country to do some shopping when I heard the news—the hitch had arrived! Even without phones and fax machines, the word spread quickly. You can't believe the excitement!

My husband and I had to see it for ourselves, so we visited the stables…and we got excited, too. Every detail of this tour was first-class. We loved the way the horses were displayed, their roped-off stables surrounded by nice flowers and mulch.

We liked being able to mingle with the staff, buy a booklet and have bride-to-be Vikki autograph her wedding program without having to stand in a line. We thought Marlene Thompson was a delight, making rice-filled souvenirs for the wedding and letting the dog snitch one or two while she worked. It was all so homespun. We loved it!

—*Mrs. Glenn Blair Jr., Medina, Ohio*

A CLASS ACT. Visitors were impressed by tidy portable stalls, neatly landscaped (above). Parades (below) were a highlight of hitch's visit to many small towns along the route.

"ORCHARD PARK, New York is obviously one of this country's great 'small towns'. The difference between a big capital city and a small town is that here, people still appreciate a great parade!

"We felt just as good being in your parade tonight as we did in the Pasadena Rose Bowl parade. These parades are a bunch of fun for us, and it takes people like you to make them happen!"

my buddies all had our heads out of our windows and—*holy cow*—there was a life-size dinosaur at the edge of town! Turns out it's a statue that was erected there to signify some important fossil finds in the area.

We stayed at the fairgrounds just across the road, and in the evening, David rode Cody, decked out as Rudolph again, into the town square for the official turning on of the Christmas lights. Crowd of 1,000 cheered, "Here comes Rudolph!"

Dec. 2—We're really covering the countryside! Trucked into big ol' Texas today, covering 48 miles through major cattle country. Over 1,500 people came to see us this afternoon in Dalhart, including a busload of seniors from Amarillo.

David, Vikki and Cody visited Dalhart Senior Center, then went to Coon Memorial Home, visiting seniors there, too. Cody also gave tots at Dalhart Kindergarten School a thrill, walking halls and chumming with kids sitting on hallway floors.

Dec. 3—Drove 95 miles to Tucumcari, New Mexico (I like the way "Tucumcari" rolls off my tongue). Got clipped today by Vikki, who did our ears, faces, muzzle, eyes and chin. Then we were brushed and vacuumed—that's the best way to keep us looking sleek!

Dec. 4—Lovely 70° as we rolled 216 miles to Vequita, New Mexico. Chuck Heckman came farthest today to see hitch—all the way from West Palm Beach, Florida! We're staying ♂→

tonight at Jordan and Bev Pareo's place. They raise Belgians that have competed against me and my hitch buddies at previous shows. We enjoyed a good visit with some of our former rivals while we were there!

Dec. 5—Sunday. Covered 192 miles; saw nearly 1,200 people en route to Deming, home of the Southwestern New Mexico State Fair.

Easy day; we stayed in our stalls while Cody performed in arena pen, rolling on ground and generally showing off.

George and Ruth Hollingworth got prize for coming farthest today—from Lake City, Florida. Esther Koppers of Deming was the oldest person to visit our hitch. Being a lady, she wouldn't tell me her age.

Dec. 6—Crossed another state line today. We're spending the night in Benson, Arizona, about 40 miles southeast of Tucson. California, here we come!

Dec. 7—Headed on up to Casa Grande, Arizona today. Roy Reiman surprised all of us by showing up at the seminar David was conducting this afternoon!

Dec. 8—Covered 171 miles today; staying at the fairgrounds in Yuma, Arizona. Some 300 people visited this morning, and 1,000 or so were on the route we drove this afternoon.

Beautiful fields along the way, filled with alfalfa and cotton. They're kept lush by irrigation.

Dec. 9—We've made it to California! We're spending the night in Calexico, which is only a couple of miles north of the border between the United States and Mexico. Tomorrow it's on to San Diego.

Dec. 10—We're on the West Coast! While we'd originally planned to arrive here on foot, I really do think this alternative plan has worked out for the best.

We're going to rest up for a couple of days here in San Diego, then splash in the Pacific and head back east on the second half of our journey.

Dec. 11—Believe it or not, we're staying at a hotel! That's right, the Town and Country Hotel in San Diego! (Well, actually, we're quartered in the hotel's parking lot, not in the hotel itself.)

It's beautiful here, palm trees, golf course and swimming pool. Crew groomed us and polished our harnesses. Some 800 stopped by this afternoon to see us.

Vikki and Marlene went to Sea

Good Samaritan Proves Faith Was Well-Founded

GETTING a ride on the hitch was the highlight of our summer in 1993, and my experience was rather interesting!

I parked our car at the Sugarcreek encampment while the hitch was still on the road headed there. Since my husband, Milton, doesn't drive, I was perplexed as to how I was going to get from the encampment out to Highway 39 to get my ride.

A kind lady volunteered her services to take me out to the highway, as she and her husband had already ridden with the hitch.

Just a mile east of town we saw the hitch approaching. She pulled over, and I left my camera with her so she could take pictures of me on the wagon. I also left my purse and car keys.

She waved good-bye as the wagon started moving, and I thought, "There goes my camera, purse and car keys with a complete stranger. I don't even know her name!"

All was well when we pulled into the encampment, however—her husband and mine were chatting, and we all had a good laugh over how trusting I'd been!

Their names are Robert and Shirley Lee of Carrollton, Ohio, and we've since corresponded with them and exchanged photos we shot of the hitch. We think it's wonderful that the hitch is helping to remind everyone that there are still plenty of decent folks out there…and helping some of us to make new friends!

—*Mildred Boehler, Ashland, Ohio*

TESTING THE WIND. Belgians often enjoyed the fresh air during their truck ride from Iowa to the West Coast.

Linda Jenkins

Adventurous Seniors Thrilled by Hitch

SEEING "our" hitch was such a joyful experience that there aren't words to express it. We'd been trying to make the trip for some time, and one day we just decided to "take off" and find it! The good Lord was surely with us, because it was a perfect adventure.

I'll never forget that moment when we rounded a curve in the road and there they were. Just writing about it gives me goose pimples. I even got to ride on the wagon!

Thanks from the bottom of my toes (the bottom of my heart isn't deep enough!) for one of the most wonderful days of my life.   —*Glada Russell, Logan, Ohio*

"AS WE pass by on the road, some people have yelled out, 'You light up my life!' The effect these horses are having on people is just wonderful!"

Hitch 'Drops in' on Amish Family

BEFORE the hitch arrived in our area, we shared our souvenir program with some Amish neighbors and had them all excited about seeing the horses.

The hitch was to pass their farm after performing at the Millersburg, Ohio fairgrounds, so they rounded up all their married daughters—some from as far away as 10 miles—to see it.

The whole family waited and waited in their buggy-filled yard, but the hitch never showed up. Later, we learned it had been too hot to move the horses, so the team had extended its stay at the fairgrounds.

My husband and I went to the fairgrounds to see the hitch, and I told David about our Amish neighbors. Well, next day the hitch pulled up and *stopped* at their farm! That was the most thoughtful thing David could have done.

—*Mim Blair, Medinah, Ohio*

I was so moved by the beautiful pictures and touching interviews in the hitch video that I picked up my phone and called three local senior centers to ask if they would like to show it.

All said yes, and I've already had several seniors thank me. It gave me such a good—no, *great*—feeling to help brighten these seniors' lives, just as riding on the hitch brightened mine. —*Valerie McFadden, Millersburg, Ohio*

World and saw the Budweiser Clydesdales. I was all set to be jealous until Marlene came around afterward and kissed each of us and told us she still loved *us*.

Dec. 12—Sunday. Crew brushed and vacuumed us, getting us ready for our walk in the Pacific. The film crew shot some footage of San Diego and checked out the beach where we're going to take our "dip". We're excited about getting back on the road!

Dec. 13—Started east today! Crew got us up bright and early this morning and we headed out into the Pacific surf at Mission Beach. The hotel owner, Terry Brown, and his wife came down to watch, and the film crew captured the whole event. Let me tell you, we really turned the heads of those early-morning beachcombers!

Then we headed out onto Mission Village Drive, passing Jack Murphy Stadium where the San Diego Chargers play football. We're spending the night in Lemon Grove—what a great name for a town!

We're all delighted to be back in harness and on the road. After all, pulling is what we do best!

Dec. 14—Heading east in sunny, 65° weather. One man was standing at the on-ramp to the highway when a policeman came by and told him he was in dangerous spot and asked him to move.

The man said he was waiting to ride our hitch. The policeman looked in his rearview mirror, saw us, laughed and told the fellow to go right ahead and wait for his ride!

Dec. 15—Crowds are picking up: 200 this morning, 400 this afternoon, another 100 in evening. Did 6 miles today and staying at Don and Toni Daly's beautiful 5,000-acre ranch.

Lots of Christmas tree lights decorating their house and surrounding fences; looked very pretty this evening. Even a horse gets into the Christmas spirit!

Dec. 16—Only walked 5 miles today; David let us make quite a few stops to relax and catch our breath because the roads are very curvy and hilly in this area.

Arrived in Dulzura, California at about 12:30.

Dec. 17—Well, it *must* be the Christmas season even though it's 67 and sunny; a lady wearing a Santa Claus hat and chanting "Merry Christmas" greeted us along route this morning!

Eye-catching scenery on our 7-mile ♂

walk today—mountains, canyons and rocks. Saw lots of caution signs for rock slides. Crew presented with raisin banana pumpkin bread by Judy Hatfield, local mail-lady; also got goodies from the kitchen of Margaret Corders.

What did *we* get? A nice refreshing bath before we bedded down at Mike and Marty Taylor's ranch south of Dulzura.

Dec. 18—It was mostly an uphill pull today; we covered 7 miles and David gave us plenty of rest stops. Sheriff's department blocked traffic for us along this stretch of busy Highway 6.

Crew ate dinner with the firemen at the Potrero Fire Station. We're spending the night at Potrero Valley Ranch just 2 miles from the Mexican border.

Dec. 19—Relaxed today at Potrero Valley Ranch on this beautiful sunny Sunday in California. Can you imagine, it was in the 70s even though it's December!

David and Vikki went sight-seeing this afternoon and visited the movie stars' walk in Hollywood. I wonder if Trigger has a star—he sure deserves one after helping Roy Rogers capture all of those bad guys over the years!

Dec. 20—Got rolling at 9 a.m. Covered about 11 miles in high winds and heavy traffic on very curvy roads. Overheard the crew saying these are called the Santa Ana winds.

Also had to watch out for rock slides, which are pretty common in this area. Passed some beef cattle grazing in nearby fields. They "mooed" a welcome and we whinnied in reply.

Spending the night at Cameron Corners in Campo, California.

Dec. 21—Left Campo at 9 o'clock, escorted by sheriff's patrol. Traveled about 10 miles and got out into desert country.

Not many people here; three little kids were standing on the rocks of a nearby canyon wall waving to us. And a burro hee-hawed at us—he's jealous, I guess!

Staying in a highway pull-off in the desert tonight.

Dec. 22—Traveled another 10 miles, passing through Boulevard, California on our way to Jacumba for the night. Passed the Wisteria Candy Shop, famous for sending candy to all parts of world.

Santa Ana winds still blowing. Lots of cactus and tumbleweeds in this remote desert area, ringed by scenic

Belgians Spark Fond Memories

DELBERT AND ARDITH BATES traveled to Sugarcreek, Ohio from Palmyra, Michigan after following the progress of the hitch through *Country* and numerous calls to the Hitch Hotline.

"When I was 18, I bought a Belgian colt for $100," Delbert recalled. "I named him 'Champ', and I'd give him a sugar cube every morning when I went out to the barn. It wasn't too many mornings before he started nickering when he saw me leave the house—he knew his sugar was on the way!"

Delbert sold Champ after 2 years, and the young horse went into a farm hitch near Adrian, Michigan. Nowadays, Delbert and Ardith live just north of a farm where Belgians are raised. "Last year, one of their mares dropped a foal less than 300 yards from our house," Ardith said. "We really enjoyed watching the little fellow take his first few steps!"

SMILES ALL AROUND. The hitch generated ear-to-ear grins among visitors from coast to coast. Young and old alike enjoyed coming out to meet the Helmuths, check out the special vehicles and, of course, get personally acquainted with the Belgians.

On their way from Maine to California,
they stopped in to visit us.
The young, the old and the in-between
will all remember how it was.

They put a twinkle in many an eye
and a smile on many a face.
They did a lot for a horseman's pride,
these steeds of strength and grace!

The wedding held in our midst
Not only joined a man and wife,
But brought to our hearts and minds
Memories that will last for life.

Good-bye, David, good-bye, Vikki,
and a sincere farewell to the crew.
May each turn of the wagon's wheels
bring your dreams closer to you.

Every time the sun sets in the west,
We'll all wish upon a star;
We'll pray Godspeed for everyone
and fondly wonder where you are.

Yes, these ambassadors for seniors
invaded Ohio's heart, and won.
Now it's westward, ho the wagon—
California, here they come!

—Delbert Harmon
Holmes County, Ohio

Baker's Dozens...

BAKING A CAKE to feed 540 people would be a big job even for a professional bakery—but imagine doing it in your own kitchen!

Mary Ann Williams of Valencia, Pennsylvania did just that for David and Vikki's wedding. Guests were dazzled by her four-tier main cake, six heart-shaped cakes and another in the shape of a horseshoe. Mary Ann designed and stitched the cake top, too.

What went into those cakes, besides a lot of hard work? Mary Ann's list of ingredients included 56 cups of flour, 48 cups of granulated sugar, 16 pounds of powdered sugar, the grated peels of 7 lemons, 20 pounds of shortening and 104 eggs!

canyons and mountainous terrain. I'm beginning to sound like a tour guide!

Dec. 23—Reached 3,000-foot elevation as we along Highway 8 East. As we left Jacumba, a helicopter flew over and took pictures of us.

Lots of truck traffic today, but we were well over on the nice blacktop shoulder. The wind got the best of David's favorite hat today; it blew off into the path of an oncoming semi, which slowed and moved into another lane so as not to crush it.

Dec. 24—No travel today. It's a warm and sunny Christmas Eve, 73°, and we're staying at Chuck and Shirley Wilbonic's place in Ocotillo.

Heard on Steve's portable radio this morning that the high wind blew two semis over yesterday on Highway 8, right along the same stretch where we walked! Guess we were mighty lucky that David's hat was our only casualty!

Crew celebrated by roasting wieners over a bonfire and exchanging presents. David hung Christmas lights and set up a decorated tree at our stalls. *We celebrated by kicking up our heels and rolling in the desert sand!*

Dec. 25—Merry Christmas! This is a first for all of us, spending Christmas in the desert—needless to say, we sure don't have to worry about getting snowed in!

The crew enjoyed a holiday meal of stuffed turkey and all the fixin's, then watched a couple of movies on videotape. We horses, not being much for movies, played again in the open desert sand. As Jimmy Stewart would say, it's a wonderful life!

Dec. 26—Sunday. Still taking it easy at the Wilbonics' place, but we're beginning to feel a little restless and anxious to get on the road again. Crew tightened the shoes on Chip and Magic; mine are still okay.

Later, Bob and Kathleen Mathews treated the crew to a big barbecue at their home, which they enjoyed. When they got back, we all celebrated Vikki's birthday, which is today, with a chocolate cake Marlene made for the occasion.

Dec. 27—This desert country is certainly different—miles and miles of cactus and tumbleweed. Noticed coyote loping along the highway; wonder if we'll hear him and his buddies serenading the moon this evening!

David let us trot in the desert alongside the highway for about 2 miles; ♂

PERFECT FIT? With the assistance of crewman Steve Zbornik, a hitch enthusiast "gets the feel" of a horse collar (top). In photo above, farrier and crewmen re-shoe the Belgians during a layover; horses were re-shod at least once every 6 weeks.

feels good to dig our hooves into sand! (You humans who enjoy walking barefoot on the beach know what I'm talking about.)

Dec. 28—Our last day in the Yuma Desert. Same sunny 60° weather as we traveled 9 miles to Seeley, California, where we're staying at Walter Brundy & Sons' 4,000-acre farm.

Our route is close to a major earthquake fault line—certainly hope we don't encounter any of those! We also heard that this area is the carrot capital of the world! I *love* crunching on fresh carrots!

Dec. 29—Walked through Calexico today escorted by city's police officers. The desert we've been traveling across is beginning to look more like farmland. Because of the weather, the farmers here are able to farm 12 months a year, getting as many as 11 crops of alfalfa annually—wow! Maybe I should think about this place for my retirement...

We passed a number of buses with Mexican auto plates. *Calexico Chronicle* interviewed David, and city's Mayor Antonio Tirado visited hitch.

Dec. 30—Lots of interesting sights along today's route—a palm tree farm, lettuce farms, a huge sheep farm—and we crossed five canals on our 12.6-mile walk.

Just a dozen riders in this deserted area. Lots of cars, though. Saw one with Oregon plates and another with Montana plates.

Max Leingruber of Holtville, California gave us 10 fresh bales of alfalfa hay. We're staying at Jim and Sue Edna Holdredge's campground in Holtville tonight.

Dec. 31—It was 78° and sunny this New Year's Eve as we traveled 12 miles in the Imperial Desert, a bare sand dune area. We're stopping in this spot because it has access to water.

We're not the only attraction here this weekend; locals expect 30,000 people to attend a four-by-four and three-wheel dune buggy celebration. Certainly a different way to spend a New Year's Eve—we're a long way from Times Square!

Jan. 1, 1994—Happy New Year! No travel today; we're just sharing the area with campers. Many have come 3 to 5 days early for this yearly event.

Dune buggies were bombing around all day. Chip and Magic got carried away by all the excitement, broke out

Rider Happy to Help

AFTER my ride on the wagon, I started trying to find a ride back to my car. A man approached me and said, "We're escorting the hitch. Would you like to ride along? We'll bring you back when we're finished."

So I got to "escort" the hitch along with a police sergeant and the mayor! I rode in the back of their van, facing the hitch. What a thrill to watch the horses trot along no more than 12 feet away!

I even got a chance to help David when Bobby, the right swing horse, stepped into a pothole and threw a shoe. David tried to nail the shoe back in place, but that didn't work, so he opted for a temporary repair with heavy-duty tape.

When I saw David was having trouble unrolling the tape and holding the horse's foot at the same time, I hopped down and helped. It made my day to give him a hand. It was an experience I'll never forget! —*Bob LeMon Mishawaka, Indiana*

COVER GIRL. "It looks like I'm on the cover of *Country* magazine!" joked Jane Burke of New Castle, Indiana, when she submitted this photo shot by husband Harry. "We visited the hitch near Peru—what a beautiful outfit! You can be mighty proud of this endeavor!"

"THE PEOPLE have been just super all along the route. Everyone has been very cooperative, generous and pleased to see us. The farther west we get, the more people show up every day."

GETTING ACQUAINTED. Whether relaxing (above) or in harness (far right), Belgians were always willing to make new friends with folks along the hitch route.

Bluffton First to Give Hitch Key to City; Thousands Turn Out; 'Greatest Reception'

THE HITCH took Wells County and Bluffton (Indiana) by storm.

And the people here literally captured the hearts of the hitch folks too.

"Our greatest reception" were the words given community representatives here.

Reflected was that the hitch is gaining tempo and excitement with rolling momentum as the entourage rambles farther across America on the Maine-to-California journey.

The numbers that saw the hitch in Wells County from the Thursday morning arrival to this morning's departure had to be in the thousands.

And there was a definite first here.

"This was the first time we were presented a key to the city," declared elated driver David Helmuth for the six-horse hitch.

Mayor Everett Faulkner and Bluffton Horizons Chief Executive Officer Robert Hayden were on hand by the Dutch Mill when the hitch made the triumphant arrival just before noon with throngs of people lining the roads and at every possible vantage point.

Mayor Faulkner had the large key ready for the presentation and official welcome to Helmuth and his wife, Vikki.

Minutes earlier, this *News-Banner* reporter was above Highway 124 in a bucket rig to get overhead photos of the hitch advancing into the city—and to exchange waved greetings with the Helmuths and wagon passengers.

At the east edge, the Southern Wells High School Raider Force Band had filled in ahead of the hitch, marching and playing to lead the hitch to Dutch Mill.

—Jim Barbieri, Bluffton-News Banner
September 10, 1993

Hitch Followed Colorful Hoofprints

AS the hitch passed through Wabash, Indiana, we thought the following excerpt from the Wabash County Indiana History book of 1976 might be of interest:

"Wabash resident J.D. Conner Jr. started the Belgian Draft Horse Association of America and was its secretary for 51 years. He was knighted by King Alfred of Belgium and was later given a medal of recognition by King Leopold.

"J.D. was a very dapper gentleman with an extremely good sense of humor. However, he was notorious for driving on the wrong side of the road because it was smoother over there...and he wasn't averse to removing a few fence posts along the way!"

—Tom and Virginia Martin, Branson, Missouri

of their pen and galloped to the top of a nearby sand dune to check out the surroundings. Crew promptly rounded them up. Notice, please, that *I* behaved myself!

Jan. 2—A sunny Sunday, 75° and breezy, blowing sand all around. The crew treated us by letting us out of our pens to roll around in the sand—man, that felt good!

Ashley was pretty restless; she's expecting puppies any day now. Her favorite spot is the couch in David and Vikki's trailer.

David and the crew watched football most of the day on TV; my favorite team (for obvious reasons) is the Denver Broncos.

Jan. 3—We had 37 riders today through the sand dunes and mountains, including one very happy 4-year-old, Alex Whelan of Trabuco Canyon, California, who got to ride on the wagon seat between David and Vikki.

Covered 9 miles on busy Highway 16, arriving at the gas station on Sidewinder Road alongside a motor home park in Winterhaven.

Ashley had her puppies—five females and three males. That's a lot of pups! Mom and puppies are doin' fine!

Jan. 4—Good-bye, California; hello, Arizona! Crossed into our second state on the trek back east at 11:40 a.m.

A California Highway Patrol officer stopped us 2 miles from the state line and asked us to leave the interstate. David talked with him and showed him our souvenir program. After he read it and listened to the riders on the wagon, ♂

COMPANIONS IN HARNESS. The hitch was occasionally visited by other teams like the Belgians (foreground) and Clydesdales (at rear) in the above photo. At left, upon seeing team of miniature burros, hitch leader Chip seems to be saying, "You won't believe what's back there!"

Thanks for the Memories!

I'M 70 YEARS young, and when I was a kid I drove Belgians to load and unload hay. Why? My parents had four girls before any sons showed up!

Dad had "Hap" and "Mary Jane" and their fillies, "Lula Belle" and "Lady Jane". We showed them at colt shows in Berne, Indiana way back when. Later, a McCormick Deering steel-wheeled tractor replaced them—but not in my heart!

My late husband would have loved that hitch semi. He was a trucker, and his first love (well, after me, anyway!) was the road and the big rigs.

Thanks so much for the memories, and the wonderful ride on the hitch! —Barbara Reimer, Craigville, Indiana

he offered us an escort to the state line!

We had 74 riders and made 12 miles today, passing the Quechan Indian Reservation on the way to our stopover location in Yuma.

Jan. 5—About 100 people watched us hitch up this morning at 7:30 for our 6-mile trot to the Yuma County Fairgrounds. Even more people greeted us when we arrived! This is a big area for seniors, many of 'em "snowbirds", staying in RV parks all along the highway.

While the rest of us relaxed in our stalls, David, Vikki and Cody stayed at the fairgrounds' racetrack so the public could get a close-up look at a Belgian. He probably signed autographs, too, the ham.

Jan. 6—Traveled 11-1/2 miles today and gave 83 people rides, including 20 students bused out from Yuma County Elementary School.

Gene Baer of Lexington, Nebraska also rode with the hitch after driving 1,300 miles to see us. Says he's ridden now in two states and he's shooting for four or five, so I guess we'll be seeing more of him along the way!

Chip, Bobby and Tim were sure feeling their oats tonight—they got out of their stalls and were spotted by two policemen at 5 a.m. in the Wal-Mart parking lot about a half mile from our barns! Vikki and David went with Junior and Steve to bring the wanderers home. What can I say…there must be a little mustang in all of us!

Jan. 7—A short day; only walked 8 miles to the Ligurta Station RV park, a sandy desert area. About 600 people came over and chatted with the crew about our historic trip.

Overheard some interesting facts: Ligurta, Arizona, founded about 1860, was a stage-stop for the Butterfield

SISTER ACT. The four sisters shown above, three from Ohio and one from California, enjoyed souvenir shopping while crewman Steve Zbornik was minding the store.

Well-Traveled Program…

WE'VE BEEN following the hitch all along the route. We visited it at five locations along U.S. 24 in Indiana and Illinois, and I got to ride at Idaville, Indiana. Our Official Souvenir Program has been with us in 16 states as we've traveled on vacation! —Don Forgey Logansport, Indiana

Emotional Moment…WE

DROVE about 70 miles to see the horses and met them between Monticello and Reynolds, Indiana. What a delightful sight to see those beautiful horses coming down the road!

The feeling is hard to explain, but as I glanced around the crowd, there were tears in the eyes of many—including me! —Mrs. J.M. Perschke Michigan City, Indiana

Hoosier History

Dear Vikki and David,

I'm writing to tell you a little about our state. Abraham Lincoln spent 14 of his 56 years here, a fact that is often overlooked by historians. I have done extensive research on Lincoln's time in Indiana and often travel to Lincoln's home in the southwest corner of the state to perform a program based on my research.

My family also came to Indiana by flatboat soon after the Lincolns, but they settled in a different area. As you can tell, I'm very proud of my state, and I'm pleased to welcome you and the hitch! —Leelia Cornell Greentown, Indiana

"I'M VERY EXCITED about this trip. We're usually in cars going 65 and moving right along, and we just kind of fly by things. But I really like this slow pace, because you can actually see everything in great detail.

"You don't miss any signs, and I always look at the fields around us and see the different crops growing. I love to go past houses and see the little kids out playing in their swings or flopping around in a swimming pool.

"I also love it when the drivers that pass us slam on their brakes, pull over in the ditch in front of us and start waving—it's wonderful to know that so many people across the country enjoy seeing us!"

She's a Big Firestone Fan

I AM 82 and have loved horses all my life. We used to live in the country, and I was literally raised on ponies. I also helped my father in the fields when he needed extra help; I rode our lead horse when Dad and I cared for our huge garden and truck patch. What happy memories!

I was waiting at Road 303 when the hitch passed by and was lucky enough to get to ride in the pretty wagon! This was certainly a thrill, but an even bigger thrill occurred when I asked David if I could pet Firestone when we stopped. David said yes, and I could hardly wait to get out of the wagon!

Another lady and I went up to Firestone and began talking and calling his name, but we didn't touch him until he perked up his ears and turned his head to see us. Then we rubbed his nose—I had prayed for this—and petted his glossy neck. Those horses are the most beautiful animals on earth!

I also shook hands with Vikki—she's even prettier than her picture—and wished everyone a safe trip. My son bought me a program, and I've read it cover to cover. Even now I can barely stand to close it. Thanks again for this most wonderful experience!

—*Frances Hanen, Hagerstown, Indiana*

Stagecoach line from Tucson to Yuma. The population, once over 1,000, is now only 5—yes, 5—in the summertime.

Jan. 8—Covered 11 miles, arriving at Olsen's Market and Texaco station in Wellton. Lots of car traffic on the way here; also watched a couple of farmhands on John Deere tractors spreading fertilizer in the fields alongside highway. Cabbage and lettuce are big crops here.

Some 400 visitors in the afternoon, another 200 in the evening. Shirley Northness of Kalama, Washington presented the crew with homemade strawberry jam. We all got baths today—mighty refreshing after our walk through the desert!

Jan. 9—Sunday. Nearly 750 people visited us today at Olsen's Market. There are lots of RV parks in this area for seniors who come down here to escape winter up north.

Vikki left her notebook on the tailgate this afternoon, so I got a chance to read some more comments written by people who've ridden with us during the last several days.

Dell Jean Van Fossen and her mother, Evelyn Wonderly, came from San Bernardino, California to Ligurta just to see us. They brought along Dell Jean's 90-year-old grandfather, Joe Moravetz, and her daughter, Wendy, age 11, so four generations got to ride the hitch all at once! Also can't forget Robert, Evelyn's husband; he probably drove the car while they were on the wagon!

Jan. 10—Back on the road, a quiet 10.5-mile trek in this flat desert area filled with tumbleweed and blowing sand. Only noise was car traffic on highway—desert can be a mighty lonely place!

Tonight we're staying at Shay Oil and Chaparral Motel in Tacna, Arizona.

Jan. 11—Traveled another 12 miles today; still not many people in the area. Stopped at a gravel parking area in a desert canyon tonight.

Crew built a bonfire and enjoyed a wiener roast. Sitting around afterward, they heard a pack of coyotes nearby. Vikki told David the sound was pretty ♂

HITCH AFICIONADAS. Various groups of women, including Navajos from Crystal, New Mexico (above left) enjoyed visiting the hitch.

eerie. Of course, *I* could tell her that coyotes are harmless.

Jan. 12—Route today took us alongside the Mohawk Mountains. Not much excitement during our 13.5-mile trip except lots of cars on the highway.

David picked up the mail for crew today; they were all happy to hear from relatives and friends. Melanie Owens and her family visited from Virginia on their way to Guam, where Melanie's husband is stationed at a military base. (And we thought *we* were far from home!)

Tonight's stop is the Dateland Farm Plaza in Dateland, Arizona.

Jan. 13—Still traveling in desert country; 75° and sunny. Only had five riders today. David drove hitch on the desert sand of a service road between the highway and some railroad tracks.

Three trains passed alongside us, but we never flinched. I still can't figure out why those things are called "iron horses"—they don't look like any horse I've ever seen!

We're staying on Spot Road just off Interstate 8. There's no water or power hookup here; good thing we carry our own!

Jan. 14—Walked 9 miles today to Ruben and Carmen Conde's gas station and food mart in Sentinel, Arizona. They keep busy running the station and a 24-hour towing/tire service.

An Amish family was among our 11 riders today. And a fellow parked along the highway, took our picture as we passed, then left his camera on the roof of his car when he came over to talk.

Later, when he drove off, the camera fell onto the highway. Two cars managed to straddle it so it wasn't smashed before he could retrieve it. Wonder if his photos will turn out black and blue!

Two couples from Washington, Leslie and Gerry Brokaw of Renton and Bill and Lisa Webb of Kent, stopped along the route to wish us good luck.

Jan. 15—Walked 10 miles today. A jackrabbit bolted across the road in front of us. They're kind of silly-looking with their big long ears!

Kids from the Sentinel Elementary School paid us a visit and watched us exercise in our pens this afternoon. Only riders today were family of five from Los Angeles.

We're staying tonight in an open parking area in the desert.

Jan. 16—Sunday, 70° and very pleasant. About 40 people stopped by to visit and tell us they are very impressed

Happy Hoosiers Hobnob with Hitch

MY SISTER-IN-LAW was so enthusiastic after seeing the hitch in Idaville, Indiana that she convinced my wife, Avalynne, and me to catch up with it at its next stop.

We did just that the next morning in Wolcott. Avalynne hopped on the wagon and I drove to the next intersection to wait for my ride. Two young women and their five children were waiting there, too. They'd heard of the hitch's arrival early that morning, and left in such a hurry that the youngsters were still in their pajamas!

When the hitch arrived, Avalynne changed places with me, and I got to ride the wagon as it crossed the Interstate 65 overpass. What a thrill to watch cars and semis driving in both directions, and to see the surprised drivers waving at the hitch and passengers overhead!

I tried to relate to what the early settlers must have experienced as they crossed the country in their wagons, but I'm sure their ride was much rougher and more difficult. And I'm sure they never crossed, or even imagined, a bridge like that interstate overpass!

After my ride, I left to tell former neighbor Clarence Schuette, 83, and retired blacksmith William Small, 94, that the hitch was here. "Smalley" perked right up when I offered to drive him out to see it. He seemed a bit reluctant as he waited in line for his ride, but when he climbed onto the wagon, his smile said it all.

Clarence and son Rick showed up east of Goodland, and the older man gingerly climbed aboard. By the time the hitch reached its next stop, Clarence had worked his way up to the front of the wagon and was standing behind the driver's seat, reminiscing with David and Vikki about his horse-driving days!

Clarence proudly stayed on the wagon as the high school band led the hitch all the way through Goodland and on to an implement dealer's west of town. "For someone so reluctant to get on," his son said, "I sure had a hard time getting him off!"

—Roy Cooper, Newton County, Indiana

"RIGHT AFTER we crossed the Ohio border, we encountered some of the biggest horseflies I've ever seen—some of them looked as big as bumblebees! We've pretty much got them under control, though—we're using Dairy-Plus 44, which is high-powered stuff.

"Vinegar works pretty well, too, when you rub it into the horses' coats, but I don't like dealing with the smell of that any more than the flies do!"

Happy Campers

WORMAN'S LAKE Inc. would like to thank Reiman Publications and the hitch for selecting our campground as an overnight stop on the "Maine to California" trip for seniors.

The enjoyment brought into Cass County and Worman's Lake was a "once in a lifetime" experience to be remembered for many years to come.

Also, we would like to extend our personal thank you to the crew for their very important role. They are to be commended for the cleanliness of the campsites after their departure.

—Kenneth Worman
Logansport, Indiana

Smart Kid! I WANT to thank you for the many people in the Logansport area who were thrilled by the hitch's visit here. I took my 4-year-old grandson to see the hitch while they were staying at our local mall. He thought I'd look good in a hitch cap…and asked for the money to buy me one!

He's right—I *do* look mighty good in my new cap. Thanks again from Brandon and his papaw!

—Rich Wild, Logansport, Indiana

BEST SEAT IN THE HOUSE! Fellow above brought his lawn chair to be sure he wouldn't miss any of the action!

THREE GENERATIONS turned out (above) to see the hitch in Sugarcreek, Ohio. At left, attendants help senior get acquainted.

SIGN OF THE TIMES. There certainly wasn't any question about Hoosier sentiments regarding the hitch when it passed through Monroe, Indiana in September 1993.

with what the hitch is doing for seniors across America.

David and Vikki took a drive this afternoon to check out some Arabian horse farms. Heard them telling Marlene later that they saw some mighty impressive spreads!

Jan. 17—The crew had a rude awakening this morning at about 5 a.m., when everything started to tremble and shake!

We horses were already awake and feeling pretty uneasy about something, but we couldn't quite figure out what. Then Magic let out a whinny, and we all lurched against our stalls—it felt like the earth was moving under us!

As we found out later, it *was*—we were feeling the shock of the earthquake that hit southern California! David and Vikki and the crew came running from their mobile homes a minute or so later to check on us, and we were all thankful (horses and humans alike!) that no one was hurt. After that rather unusual start to our day, I'm happy to report that things settled down.

We covered 11 miles; at a breezy 68°, it was a perfect day for walking. About 40 people rode with us, which is pretty good, considering it's still deserted out here.

Someone told us it was about 15° warmer here than usual, and that last year it rained for almost the entire month. Guess that bucket of used horseshoes is continuing to bring us good luck!

Jan. 18—Still in desert country. Very dusty today; now the locals are saying they *need* rain.

We walked another 11 miles in about 3 hours. Stopped at the Paloma Elementary School, where David talked to the students about our trip.

Poor Ashley brushed up against a cactus. The crew had to pull a few spines out of her legs with pliers. Ouch!

Jan. 19—Rolled into Gila Bend, Arizona at noon after walking 10 miles. Passed a huge cattle ranch on the way; heard later that it sold recently for $60 million!

Also got a kick out of Gila Bend's welcome sign: "Population 1,700 people and five old crabs".

We're staying at Southwestern Wood Creations, where we were visited by ex- ↻

governor Rose Mofford. Also had a visit from a vet from Scottsdale; he gave all of us (just the horses, not the crew) our annual checkup and vaccinations.

Jan. 20—Saw some huge cactuses (or should that be cacti? I'm never sure!) during our 12-mile trip this morning.

About 30 people rode with us today; among them were Carl and Ivalou McDorman of Harrod, Ohio. They said they saw us in Lima last September, then made a special trip to see us in Arizona. Great to have fans like that!

A semi loaded with beautiful, fragrant alfalfa hay passed us; boy, did our ears perk up!

Dale and Tim bumped into a cactus as we arrived here. David had to give them the pliers treatment—that'll teach those youngsters to keep their eyes open!

Jan. 21—More cactus along our 13-mile walk today. John and Jo Navicki, originally from Michigan but now living in East Mesa, Arizona, gave Vikki a beautiful rock and cactus memento.

The crew groomed us, and Glenn Kriz, the blacksmith, visited us today, so we're all wearing shiny new shoes. They're getting us ready to show off at a barbecue tomorrow.

Mert Kohn of Lake City, Minnesota said his hitch ride today took him back 55 years to when he was 6 and had his own horse and wagon. Mert said every boy should have a horse. Do I ever agree with that!

Jan. 22—Big doin's today! Ed Short and the "Over the Hill Gang", an organization of retired Arizona state troopers and other Public Safety employees, hosted a barbecue which started at 2 p.m. Rose Mofford paid us another visit, and guess who else joined us—Roy and Bobbi Reiman!

Everyone had a wonderful afternoon watching us show off with our manes rolled and tails tied. (That's the closest I'm ever gonna get to wearing a tux.)

Evelyn Heringer, who left winters in Alberta, Canada, 2,000 miles to the north, to live in Arizona City, left us a

'America's Team' Ambling West

THOSE who thought of the "old-time" Dallas Cowboys as "America's Team" had best reconsider.

They've been replaced.

Eased from communal memory by the arrival of the heaviest front line in the league.

A ponderous phalanx of California cuties, plodding coast-to-coast on behalf of senior citizens and others young of heart.

The *"Reminisce Hitch"* pulled into Goodland, Ind. Wednesday, led by the South Newton High School Band—an event, which in the life of this sleepy farm town might only be rivaled by the clamorous arrival of a steam locomotive.

And for the 200 or so gathered souls, it was truly evocative—a rekindling of that unique emotional bond which has for eons linked the human and equine spirits.

"They're all geldings. Over a ton each!" exclaims Howard Buck, 66, an "old farm boy" from Otterbein, just a stone's throw south of Goodland.

"We used to take big boys like this to the field," says another time-weathered bystander, gazing at the line of 10 massive Belgians, resting near the nearby diesel tractors of Mike Minniear's Case IH dealership.

"Say…do ya think they could out pull your tractors?" asks an idler, smile growing as he waits for an answer from the diesel tractor man.

"No," Minniear finally answers. Then pausing briefly as he glances at the damp ground, he adds with a smile, "Well they could probably outpull 'em in the mud, but I wouldn't want that to get out." Everyone laughs.

Laughter has been the point of this trip after all. "Smiles all around," says David Helmuth, the teamster whose sharp eye for spirited horseflesh and whose determination to build a national champion team ended with a hands-down victory at the "Super Bowl" of draft horse showmanship—the Ocala, Fla. equine *showdown*.

The event drew 236 teams of six or eight horses from across North America.

"I won every class that they had," says Helmuth.
—*Mike Lyon,*
The Daily Journal, Kankakee, Illinois.
*September 23, 199_*

CROWD-PLEASERS. In or out of harness, Belgians always captured—and enjoyed—the attention of admirers from all generations. Ralph Silver (above) visited hitch on his 101st birthday.

Once a Ford Man…WE RODE the wonderful hitch at Weston, Illinois near Interstate 55 and Chenoa.

Brad, my fiance, drove a semi for 35 years and could hardly pry himself away from looking inside, outside, under and all around. He is a Ford man and loved the semi.

He stated over and over that he'd never seen anything that nice and would love to drive it. Matter of fact, that's all I heard all the way home!
—*Norma Bradley, Chatham, Illinois*

Hitch Inspires Mad Dash

WE LIVE about 30 miles north of Chicago and yesterday, on a whim, I called the Hitch Hotline for the first time ever. Well, I couldn't have picked a more perfect time! They were straight south of us, about 3 hours away in Chenoa, Illinois.

We threw some clothes in a suitcase, drove to Chenoa and found the hitch after dark. We got a motel room in Pontiac and drove back the next morning to see horses being harnessed and giving seniors a ride, then stopping at a grade school to talk to the children.

My husband, Don, grew up on a farm, so he really loved seeing those big guys. He was also fascinated with their traveling stable—what a rig!

We really enjoyed our impromptu trip. Thanks!

—*Mrs. Donald Smith*
Buffalo Grove, Illinois

A HIT WITH THE KIDS! Schoolchildren, like those from Ulysses, Kansas (top) and the class of Amish students and their teacher in Monroe, Indiana (above), found the hitch an interesting "subject" for their study!

"MANY TIMES when we come up on a farm, a herd of cows will come to the fence, curious about just what is coming down the road. Then when they see these six big horses up close, they take off running with their tails up! We still laugh every time we see that—I'm afraid we may have cut milk production for a day or so for some of the dairy farmers along the route.

"Dogs haven't been a problem, either. Sometimes they come running toward the road, barking fiercely. But when this big team gets up close, most of the dogs just turn, put their tails down and head back toward the house!"

nice note after riding hitch. It said, "Wow! What a thrill; read about the hitch in your magazine but never dreamed I'd have the chance to actually ride!" Glad she could get aboard.

Jan. 23—Sunday, so we're taking it easy today here at the RV park. It's a very scenic area; beautiful cactus on the mountains all around us.

Lots of people visited us today, and they're still talking about yesterday's great barbecue!

Jan. 24—Mountains were hazy as we walked 11 miles to Stanfield. But in spite of the haze, we could see two crosses atop Maricopa Mountain—quite a sight!

A lot of campers are staying at Table Top RV Ranch, our stopover location for tonight. And before I forget, I want to add this charming note to my diary from a group who rode our hitch a couple of days ago: "We're five cousins who met in Arizona after 30 years apart. Little did we know we'd get to ride on the hitch. Congratulations! (signed) Shirley Thompson, Beth Evans and Kathy Stuhlmiller of Nebraska; Royeen Hein, Michigan, and Connie Tighe, California."

Jan. 25—Today we were visited by a group of 80-some folks from Reiman Publications Country Tours, led by Bob James. Gave them the "royal tour" of our semitrailer and rides on wagon as well.

Ashley rode on the wagon today, too, for the first time since she had her pups. (The puppies are about 3 weeks old now and mighty cute little rascals!)

Passed some beautiful alfalfa fields, my kind of country. About 2 hours into our trek, the sky turned gray and winds kicked up; thought we were gonna have a tornado! But it just rained for 2 hours.

We're staying in Casa Grande tonight, which marks the halfway point of our trip across Arizona!

Jan. 26—Left this morning at 8:30 for a 16-mile trek to Elroy. (People were already out to see us getting groomed at 7 a.m.!) Saw about 500 along route.

Local Department of Public Safety official stopped us on the Interstate and said we couldn't travel on it. So, we cut through some fields and circled out through the desert to get to our layover site at the Truck Stop of America on Toltec Road.

Jan. 27—Before we left Elroy this morning, a group of Elroy Elementary School pupils rode in the wagon. Then ♂

we continued 11 miles to Picacho, where we're staying at the 80-acre Youth Haven Ranch, owned by Dave and Francie Kipling.

Weather was very pleasant, in the mid-70s and sunny.

Jan. 28—Cooler today; 63° and breezy with light sprinkles. *Arizona Star* reporter came out to do a story on the hitch and shoot photos. David also conducted a seminar for the students at Picacho Elementary School.

If you're into nuts, you might already know that Picacho Peak (which we passed today) is known for its pecan trees. We also saw an ostrich farm along our 14-mile route.

Talk about a long neck—when an ostrich swallows, it has to listen for the echo to know when its food hits bottom! (Okay, I know that was a bad joke. Sorry, I was just horsing around!)

Jan. 29—Pulled into Marana after a 13-mile trek in brisk 50° (but sunny) weather. Can you believe it; there was frost on the ropes of our awning this morning!

People were excited to see us; about 600 greeted us along the way. Marana's mayor was also on hand to welcome us.

We're staying at the local fuel stop for the night.

Jan. 30—Super Bowl Sunday! A lazy day; no travel. The crew watched the game, and we also hosted about 500 people who dropped by before and after the game.

Jan. 31—Saw lots of cotton fields as we walked 10 miles along Highway 40. The interstate was very busy, so David drove us on the frontage road, which had little traffic on it.

Things got pretty dusty on the frontage road, so the crew rinsed us all off in afternoon—just in time, too, because a reporter from the *Tucson Citizen* newspaper came out and took pictures of us!

He also interviewed David and some of the 40 or so people who rode with us today. We're camping tonight near a McDonald's restaurant; wonder if they have Mac-falfa burgers?

"WE'RE definitely seeing a part of America that lots of folks never see. For example, we recently passed through the town of Plum Tree, Indiana. The whole town consists of two buildings side by side—our semi was longer than the entire town!"

HEY, THAT'S US! In photo above, visitors share a feature on the hitch with Vikki and David. At top right, youngsters discover that an offering of grass is the way to a Belgian's heart!

Thank you, thank you!

OUR HATS are off to David and Vikki for having to sit out in all kinds of weather. I just wish ours could have been better for them!

We just had to thank you for sending your beautiful horses through our area. When I first started reading about it in your magazines I didn't think it would come through our area, but I'm thankful it did.

We do apologize for our Illinois weather, but rain or shine, the people were there to see the hitch! And what a treat, listening to all the older people talking about when they farmed with horses, using the big boys to plow or for extra "pull".

My daughter, Denise, was really excited about all of this. She's 29, but listening to her, she sounded like she was 9 again!

I ordered a hitch program long before they got here for my granddaughter. She's only 2, but she likes horses.

To top off the weekend, my daughter and granddaughter got to ride with the hitch. (I would have, too, but someone had to drive the car to meet them a mile down the road!) My daughter bubbled for 2 days.

Also, I must tell you that I work at the K&H Truck Plaza in Gilman, one of the hitch's stops, and the crew is just super. They were never in the way, and they sure know their horses!

I know you will be getting thousands of letters, but I just had to write. Thank you again—you brought back many happy memories for the older folks, and made some new memories for the younger ones.

—*Ruth Schroeder*
Danforth, Illinois

CHAPTER THREE

CROSSING THE HEARTLAND

Feb. 1—Traveled 10-1/2 miles on a very curvy road today and crossed the Santa Cruz River. Cars were cautious when passing us. Temperature was 28° in the morning and warmed to 64°.

Tonight we got a soapy bath so we'd look handsome tomorrow at the Rodeo Grounds. Reminds me of the song *Gonna Rinse That Mane Right Outta My Ear*. Staying tonight at Bianchi's Pizza northwest of Tucson.

Feb. 2—A nippy 32° this morning. Went 8-1/2 miles to Tucson Rodeo Grounds, where about 1,000 people were waiting for us.

Someone brought a bag of doggy bones for Ashley and her pups and candy for the crew. No bales of alfalfa for us, though—too heavy, I guess.

David gave a seminar and answered questions, and Vikki gave rides on the wagon. Later, Vikki found homes for two of the pups. One will be named "Vikki", the other "Tiffany".

Feb. 3—Just before we left this morning, one of the Reiman Country Tour groups came by to see us. All 34 people, including tour director Mary Lynn Lemerond, got to ride on wagon.

Covered 9 miles to tonight's stop at Duffy's Diesel Truck Repair station, where Tim Carter and sons are proprietors. Passed Joe Garagiola's Rodeo Park along the way…I didn't know he'd gone from horsehair to horses!

Crew cleaned all vehicles, getting ready for a big weekend.

Feb. 4—Another 9 miles and we're at Pima County Fairgrounds, where Arabian, Quarter Horse and Jumper Show is taking place. We'll stay in barn stalls just like home and put on a show for other exhibitors tomorrow and Sunday.

Feb. 5—Saturday. Today's activities included a Hunter/Jumper event. More than 1,300 people stopped by to see us, too, including many of the Arabian horse exhibitors. We felt mighty proud to be here.

Feb. 6—Today was the finals for the Arabian Division at the show. I'm told many of the people at the show were wearing *Reminisce* T-shirts and hats. I'd wear them myself, but they don't come in my size.

Feb. 7—Felt good to be back in harness. We traveled 8-1/2 miles through desert filled with climbing cactus and other unusual vegetation (pretty fancy verbiage, huh?). Crew put up tent tonight in case it rains.

Feb. 8—Well, it rained all right—

Hitch Lifts Spirits in Flood Areas

WHAT A JOY to learn that the hitch will be passing within 25 miles of my home! I can hardly wait—the souvenir program has my whole family excited.

Rainy weather hit us hard here in Fulton County, Illinois. Haying has been a problem, as has combining wheat. The Spoon River overflowed, but, of course, nowhere nearly as bad as the Mississippi. Many cornfields were under water, and we hope the hitch doesn't encounter any problems coming through this area.

Thanks again for *our* horses. Truly an inspired idea!

—*Roberta Postin, Lewistown, Illinois*

"ONE OF OUR more amusing incidents occurred when we stopped at a convenience store that also had gas pumps. We were loading people onto the hitch when a lady ran up and asked excitedly if there was room for one more. There was, and she got on.

"After the ride ended about a mile down the road, the hitch stopped and everyone started getting off except this lady. She said, 'Why are you stopping?' I explained that each ride is about a mile long and then the riders get off and others get on. The lady exclaimed, 'You mean you're not taking me back?'

"I didn't have to answer; everybody else was talking for me, and kidding her, saying, 'This hitch is on its way to California; it's a one-way ride.' But I did arrange a ride for the lady back to the convenience store to get her car.

"The next day, as we were giving people hitch rides, a car whipped by and pulled over to the side, and a woman jumped out, nearly getting hit by another car as she ran over to us. I recognized her as the lady who needed the ride back to her car the day before.

"'Can I get another ride today?' she asked excitedly. 'That ride yesterday cost me $30.'

"I must have really looked surprised when I said, 'You're kidding me; our rides are free. Who charged you $30?'

"'Well, when I got back to the store, they'd towed my car away,' she said.

"'Where was your car parked?' I asked.

"She said, 'At the gas pump.'

"Of course, we gave her another ride. I didn't dare ask if she'd left the gas pump's nozzle in her car's gas tank!"

Hitch Reminds Folks of 'Real America'

MY HUSBAND, daughter and 9-month-old grandson rode the hitch between El Paso and Eureka, Illinois on October 2, 1993. My daughter, who has always enjoyed working with seniors, had just completed her nursing degree and ended up sitting next to an elderly gentleman on the wagon.

His wife was sitting across from them and asked my daughter if she would mind if she (the wife) took a picture of her husband and my daughter together. Ann, my daughter, said that she didn't mind at all, and put her arm around the gentleman, which brought a big smile to his face.

As they got off the wagon, the lady asked for my daughter's name and address, and about a week later, Ann received a complete set of photos in the mail, along with a very nice letter!

It seems like so much of the news you see on TV is always bad, but the day we visited the hitch, I thought, "How refreshing! This is the real America, the one we so seldom hear about!" Thank you, Reiman Publications, for helping to remind us of all the good things and good people we have in this country!

—*Nettie Creech, Charleston, Illinois*

Pamela Hoff

UPON REFLECTION... Midwest pond provided attractive mirror image of the hitch (above) for lucky photographer one morning. Below, crewman Dan Bisbee chats with visitors while polishing harness—almost a never-ending task while hitch was on the road.

Mae Stevens

Admiring Youngster Gets Special Thanks

SETH, MY SON, thinks David and Vikki are heroes, so when he received an autographed picture and letter from them a few days ago, thanking him for the wedding picture he'd drawn of them, he was elated. The autographed picture now stands on our piano in the dining room.

David also sent Seth an autographed T-shirt and he wears it constantly. He's very proud to tell everyone about David and Vikki!   —*Renee Lowe, Canton, Illinois*

all night long and until about 8 this morning.

After it cleared up, we covered 12 miles, crossing Cienega Creek, heading for Marsh Station Road. Saw snow on nearby mountain peaks.

Started raining again in afternoon, so hard that David decided to take us back in semi to fairgrounds where we could stay in box stalls rather than in mud. Also, crew's tent needed repairing after being damaged in high winds this morning.

Feb. 9—It rained cats, dogs and *horses* today and was very windy. David decided not to move the hitch. Instead, he left to scout out the route for the next 10 days. (Maybe he'll run into Kit Carson!)

We exercised for a while this afternoon. Crew was happy to have their tent repaired—no more singing *Raindrops Keep Fallin' on My Head.*

Feb. 10—Crossed into Cochise County, traveling 8 miles. Saw couple of llamas. (I hear they're good pack animals. Like to see *them* pull a rig like ours!)

Tonight David and Vikki got to visit a desert movie set and meet Gene Hackman and Sharon Stone. There weren't any horse stars for us to meet. Stayed tonight at 24-Hour Quick Pic Gas Mart.

Feb. 11—Big Crowds as we hitched 10 miles to Benson; 500 people this morning, another 750 this afternoon and 300 in evening. (Take that, Hackman and Stone!)

Saw lots of Iowa license plates on I-10; my, that's a busy highway. Maybe folks are checking us out for the big finale in Centerville this summer. Staying at Doc's "Big A" Auto Parts store tonight.

Feb. 12—Saturday. Moved only 4 miles over to Lions Park, where they're holding Territorial Days this weekend. That event brought out the crowds: 300 in morning, over 1,000 in afternoon and 700 in evening.

Also visited a very enthusiastic group of seniors at Quiburi Mission Center, where David gave a seminar about our cross-country trip.

Feb. 13—Sunday. Stayed put today, chinning with seniors who love us because they remember their younger days when they worked with Belgians.

Territorial Days events still drawing huge crowds. Old-fashioned dresses and ♂

hoop shirts are in style this weekend.

Feb. 14—Today was the 50th day of our trek east. Crossed San Pedro River as we headed 9 miles to Exit 312 on I-10. As we left, saw lots of motorhomes with Midwest license plates, particularly Iowa and Michigan, heading home after Territorial Days. People told us they'd heard about our trip on their way here.

Feb. 15—We did 10 miles today, hitching through Texas Canyon, one of the prettiest areas we've driven through so far on our trek east. A crowd was waiting for us there; gave rides to some 500 people.

My buddies earned their oats today on an uphill climb to an elevation of nearly 5,000 feet. (It was my day off, so I rode in the semi.)

We stayed on Johnson Road at—get this —"The Thing", a combination truck/bus station, restaurant and souvenir shop.

Feb. 16—Sunny but cool. The route leveled out, and we saw some wild cattle with huge horns running around in the open range area. Also spotted a large hawk sitting on a billboard beside her nest. Guess she figured it paid to advertise her presence.

Feb. 17—Another 12 miles, reaching Willcox, where local radio station did live interviews with David for morning and evening broadcasts.

More big crowds; 1,000 this morning, another 750 in afternoon and 500 in evening. We also thrilled 60 students at Cochise School with rides.

Spent night with nice people at Stouts Cider Mill. They gave me and my buddies tasty apple peelings; poor crew members only got pie and ice cream.

Feb. 18—Brought a bit of happiness to seniors at Northern Cochise Community Hospital. They asked David lots of questions as he entertained them with stories about our country-wide trek.

Windy today; tumbleweeds tumbling all along our 13-mile route. Crew won't put up tent tonight for fear of doing a Mary Poppins act.

Feb. 19—Saturday. On to Bowie, 12 miles down the road. Visited Fort Bowie National Historic Site, where Vikki chatted with about 350 people at

LOW CLEARANCE! Nursing home activity director didn't have much headroom while seated astride Tim (above left). Wagon steps are no obstacle for little guy wanting a ride at center right; sign shown in far right photo suggests they knew the hitch would pass that way!

Pearl Beckner

Country's Reminisce Hitch Evokes Memories of Better Times

HE WEIGHS as much as a Chevy pickup.

Stands taller than the lankiest NBA center ever to play the game.

And he's darned sure the biggest visitor ever to shoulder his way through these doors.

A groan of amazement issued from the dayroom of Piper City's Palmwood Health Care Center Monday night with the long-anticipated arrival of "Cody".

The purebred Belgian draft horse—at 10, the "old-timer" on Reiman Publications' *Country's Reminisce Hitch*—ducked beneath the doorway's lintel, then rounded a tight corner with surprising grace to emerge barely beneath the dayroom's 8-foot ceiling.

Inside, a crowd of a hundred or so Palmwood residents and other villagers stood awestruck by the seeming incongruity of it all. Such power and size. Such grace and gentility. Such a visitor!

Cody's presence here is emotional for many. Evocative. The elusive recollections of the dimming past made suddenly physical and solid and real again.

"He's warm," Helmuth recalls of the reaction of one of Cody's eldest admirers, a 109-year-old woman who stroked his flank some weeks ago during another nursing home visit.

Yes, he's warm.

And so is the memory of better times, rekindled, if only for the moment, by this hulking, gentle giant.

Stroke victim Carlton Gibson—himself a draft horse man in better days—moves forward in his wheelchair.

His hand sweeps down that familiar flank, hard-muscled from a decade in harness, alive with the soft scent of equine sweat and leather.

And he sobs.
—*Mike Lyons*
Daily Journal, Kankakee, Illinois

Photos: Hal Prey

Mike Bartel

From the Mouths of Babes...

WHEN editor Rick Van Etten visited the hitch at London Mills, Illinois, he heard this conversation between 9-year-old Krystine and her mother, Theresa Ball.

After intently studying the horses in their stalls for several minutes, Krystine ran up to her mom and announced loudly, "I checked out all of the horses and guess what—they're all boys except Magic!"

Everyone in the area immediately "tuned in" to hear Krystine's follow-up. With obvious concern and more than a little reluctance, her mom finally summoned the nerve to ask, "How do you *know* that Magic isn't a boy?"

"Well, Mom," Krystine replied smugly, "A boy horse wouldn't have such long eyelashes!" (For the record, Magic—like all the other hitch horses—*is* a boy.)

"ALL OF US on the crew have noticed what 'hams' these horses have become—whenever we get near a town or a group of people along the road, they perk up their ears, hold their heads high and swing them from side to side!

"They love all of the attention and seem to be enjoying this trip every bit as much as we are. And it appears to be mutual—these folks in the Midwest sure seem to get a kick out of seeing us coming!"

Chasin' the Clouds Away. OUR AREA was hit hard by the '93 floods, and having the hitch visit here brought a bit of sunshine to our day. Thanks to you country people for such a beautiful way of putting us in touch with America's past.
—*Ramona Myers, Stronghurst, Illinois*

open an house sponsored by the local Chamber of Commerce. I was proud of her; she handled herself real well.

Feb. 20—Sunday. David met Larry Mahan at an Arabian Horse Show over in Scottsdale, where he and Vikki spent the day. Larry and David were together at L.A. County Fair in 1991 when David won Six-Horse Hitch class. Now Larry is considering doing a movie about our trip.

We horses just relaxed in our stalls and dozed in the afternoon. (I don't say we cat-napped so as not to offend Ashley.)

Feb. 21—Heading for San Simon but won't get there until tomorrow. Made 9 miles today, passing field after field of pecan trees.

Spent the night in the desert next to railroad tracks, and surprise—an Amtrak train made an unscheduled stop right near us so passengers could get off and visit and snap pictures! Lots of campers and cars also stopped. We were surprised to have so many nice visitors in such a lonely spot.

Feb. 22—Made it to San Simon, 8 miles today. Stopping at 4-K Truck Stop, where lots of truckers pulled in to chat and take pictures. They've been keeping track of our progress on their CB radios…guess you could say we're the talk of the road.

Feb. 23—Our last day in Arizona. Traveled 12 miles on Interstate 10 along railroad tracks. Another train stopped to let passengers off to see us. The train was 78 cars long; I counted 'em while standing around letting folks take pictures.

Stopped at San Simon Unified School District 18, where we met Superintendent Michael Reed and 175 students. David gave driving exhibition on the school playground. Another desert stop tonight.

Feb. 24—Hello, New Mexico, "Land of Enchantment".

Crossed paths with a fellow from Jayco Industries who had helped David install propane tank on the motor home; he was delivering a fifth-wheel trailer west of here and stopped to say hi.

Tonight we got our feet checked and got new shoes when we stopped at Desert West Motel. Vet checked us out and said we're in great shape. I could have told him so if he'd asked.

Feb. 25—Some 300 cars passed us ↷

on our 10-mile trek to Gary Road, where we stopped for the night. Saw some bighorn cattle standing in the shade of a billboard sign; had horns about 5 feet from tip to tip. Wouldn't argue with one of those critters!

Feb. 26—Saturday. Created a stir as we drove into Lordsburg; folks in stores along West Motel Drive came out to wave and wish us luck.

We made 10 miles today through very dry land; I'm no weatherman, but I say we could use some rain.

Owners of Stouts Cider Mill came to see us again, brought another box of apples. Thoughtful of 'em. Got baths tonight before bedding down at Hidalgo County Fairgrounds.

Feb. 27—Sunday. With some time on my hands—er, hooves, I read over some of the notes many of our hitch riders have left behind.

I liked one from the Ferrier family, six brothers and sisters. They'd met at Silver City, New Mexico to celebrate the 60th birthdays of the two youngest, who are twins (the "babies", they call 'em). There was Doris, of Linchlup, N.Y.; Peg of Cameron, N.Y.; Agnes, Redding, Pa.; Warren and his wife, Helen, also of Reading; and twins Paul of Salisbury, Md. and Pauline and her husband, Ray, of Silver City, N.M. Quite a wagonload, huh?

Feb. 28—Lots of people visited today as we moved on 10 more miles, stopping at an abandoned gas station at Muir exit for night. (Good thing horses don't need gas; we'd be out of luck!)

Among riders was 67-year-old Homer Mays of Chesapeake, Ohio. Homer learned about us in *Farm & Ranch Living* and decided to catch up with us after visiting his daughter and son-in-law in Victorville, California. Said he thought riding the hitch is an excellent way to see the country. I agree, even though I'm on the pulling end!

March 1—Mighty quiet out here; our clip-clopping sounds loud as we mosey along on shoulder of Interstate 10. Only other sound is cars beeping at us as they pass—must have been about 300 of 'em as we traveled 10 miles to next stop, where crew rinsed the dust off us.

March 2—Here we are at the Con-

"IT'S GOTTEN downright chilly out here these past few weeks! But even though the weather's definitely turning colder, the reception we're getting from people in the towns we're passing through is just as warm as ever.

"It seems like everybody knows about the trip now that we've traveled over 1,100 miles across eight states since we left Maine, and have already given nearly 10,000 people a ride on the wagon.

"The teachers along the way are telling us that this is a 'living history' lesson about draft horses and how things used to be, and they don't want their kids to miss it. We think that's great, to know that this trip is helping to bridge the 'generation gap'."

No Obstacles in *Their* Way...

ON THE ROAD between London Mills and Roseville, Illinois, on October 11, 1993, a senior couple was very slowly making their way up the steps into the hitch wagon.

About halfway up, the man paused behind his wife to wave at the surrounding crowd and proclaim, "Please don't mind us; my wife and I each have an artificial leg, but we made up our minds that *nothing* was going to keep us from riding with the hitch!"

The crowd burst into applause.

From the Publisher's Pen...

THE FAST BREAK convenience store and gas station in Lomax (Illinois) is usually not as congested as it was Friday morning when *Country's Reminisce Hitch* rolled into town. Six large, beautiful Belgian horses were pulling the wagon with about a dozen happy riders aboard, waving to their friends and neighbors.

Driver David Helmuth and his bride of less than 2 months, Vikki, were on the driver's seat joined by Rod Brannen, a vice president of Reiman Publications.

HERE'S LOOKIN' AT YOU, KID!
Rod Brannen and grandson Ben visited the hitch in Lomax, Illinois.

Mrs. Brannen and their grandson were with some of the local people riding in the wagon.

Henderson County Sheriff Thompson and his deputy, Mike Bailey, helped line up the LaHarpe Junior High School band, under the direction of Jane Ford, as they led the parade to the Lomax Senior Center in downtown Lomax.

A new bunch of riders climbed eagerly into the wagon as the band led the procession to the west end of town. Another bunch of riders rode west to Dallas City, where the high school band was scheduled to meet them.

It is not often that a small junior high band and a team of Belgian horses brighten a small town like Lomax. This was rural America in action and the lump in your throat made you feel proud to be a part of it.

David Helmuth told the large crowd assembled at the Senior Citizens Center, "It's people like you that help make our trip worthwhile. The days could get awfully long without your cheery smiles and salutations. God bless you all!"

Thanks to Reiman Publications for creating an experience for a lot of us rural citizens! —*Jim Burling Sr.*
Hancock County Journal-Pilot
October 20, 1993

Norma McClure

Mary Brannen

HIGH IN THE SKY. Above photo shows wagon on hydraulic lift used to position it for placement during transport; space below wagon in rear of horses' semi is utilized for storage of harness and additional equipment.

CROSSING THE MIGHTY MISSISSIP'. On a blustery October day, the hitch crossed the Mississippi River from Niota, Illinois to Ft. Madison, Iowa. David whoa'ed the hitch halfway across the river and asked riders to join him in a prayer for the summer's flood victims.

tinental Divide, up about 4,600 feet. We moved 12 miles through lonely desert area, crossing into Luna County.

Saw only a few cars and semis; now I know why they wrote that song *Lonesome Cowboy*. I'd be one lonesome horse out here—this is a nice place to visit, but it ain't Belgian country.

March 3—Bobby got his picture taken today with David and Vikki when a newspaper reporter from Deming visited as we stopped at Butterfield Station. Lots of RVs out this way.

March 4—This evening a hobo stopped by to chat. David graciously offered him a meal, and he accepted.

Staying tonight in a field at Mile Marker 72 after 10-mile trip over sand and cactus. Some of crew is spending the night in hitch's trailer in parking lot alongside local NAPA Parts dealer's place.

March 5—Saturday. Traveled 12 ♂

miles into Deming. We're still the talk of the road—many cars and semis stopped along Interstate 10 to look us over.

Tim was man—er, horse—of the hour today when David and Vikki took him to Mimbres Nursing Home and to Willon Manor, where residents got to pet him. They also got rides on wagon. In all, some 350 people rode in the afternoon.

Some Mennonites stopped by, including Mervin Yoder, who chatted with David in Pennsylvania Dutch. I didn't know David could speak anything but English and horse!

March 6—Sunday. Spent the day at NAPA Parts store parking lot, where big crowds began arriving as early as 9 this morning. Recognized lots of people who'd also come yesterday.

Phone calls kept Deming Chamber of Commerce members busy answering questions about hitch and our route. David and Vikki drove 60 miles today, scouting out our route ahead.

March 7—Headed out of Deming On Hwy. 26 this morning, passing lots of trailers. Gave Deming one last look at our skills as David put us through our paces, doing a pinwheel in the middle of street; mighty fine driving exhibition, if I do say so myself. Covered 10 miles, crossing Mimbres River.

March 8—Still out in the middle of nowhere, yet people are coming from somewhere and waiting beside the road for us to pass. Gotta say we're happy for some company besides jackrabbits.

March 9—It's the 70th day of our cross-country trek, and we made 14 miles today to a desert area near Mile Marker 35—still in the middle of nowhere. In fact, that's the name of an eating place out here where crew stopped to take on water—the Middle of Nowhere Cafe.

It was very windy; saw the crew wearing coveralls and using umbrellas to block the wind.

March 10—Crossed into Sierra County, stopping at Hatch after 14 miles on the road.

Passed LAS YVAS Valley Dairy, a large dairy with Holsteins, along the way…and had to stop later while a road crew moved some heavy equipment out of our way. Those guys seemed to enjoy a look at *real* horsepower.

Stayed tonight at lot of Jerry Lackey, the Chevrolet dealer in town.

March 11—Drove along Ameri-

Dressed for the Occasion!

I'M WRITING on behalf of my mother, Zella Bonsall, who was fortunate enough to get a ride on the hitch wagon when it stopped at the Madrid Home in Madrid, Iowa.

I remember Mom telling me that someone asked her name and hometown, and mentioned that she would appear on the videotape being shot by one of the home's staff members. She responded, "Good thing I have on my new red hat—it matches the wagon!"

Mom was 90 years old and passed away in May. I'm so glad that she got to ride with the hitch when they visited Madrid—thanks for bringing her such happiness!

—*Bette Honeck, Ankeny, Iowa*

Made Their Day! WHAT A THRILL it was when the hitch came through Milton, Iowa. The principal of the school where I teach surprised us by letting us put together a small parade to welcome the hitch to town, with the band leading the hitch to its overnight stop. I don't know who was more excited—the students or the staff!

"AS WE crossed over the Mississippi River, Vikki and I decided to offer a tribute to all the people who had suffered in the floods last summer. We stopped right there in middle of the bridge and joined with the people on the hitch in a prayer.

"It was a very special moment. You can't believe how much you bond with people in a moment like that."

The hitch arrived at lunchtime, but all of us—even the cooks—decided that food could wait. We weren't about to miss the experience of a lifetime!

Milton may have seemed like just another tiny town along the route to the hitch folks, but it was really a big day for us. It was an event shared by our community that likely will never be forgotten. —*Sue Wolf, Memphis, Missouri*

A Six-Horse Birthday. WE RODE the hitch on November 11, 1993. It was my daughter Crystal's 8th birthday, and David and Vikki sang "Happy Birthday" to her as we rode along. It was a day she'll never forget!

—*Carol Djuren, Mason City, Iowa*

Rick Van Etten

"TAKE THIS RIG TO CENTERVILLE!" At least, that *appears* to be the command given by Marlene Thompson (on wagon seat) when the rest of the crew "stepped in" for the Belgians.

BUSY DAY (from top) includes cleaning harness, bathing and exercising the horses. Below: David shows how he holds the lines, one for each horse in the hitch.

Just Nothing Prettier...

"I DON'T THINK there's anything prettier or closer to nature than a team of draft horses. You go to parades and fairs, and if a new $150,000 tractor drives by, people will take a look. But you drive a nice team of horses like this by them, and people will always look twice or three times."

—*Charley Quinn, Bancroft, Iowa*

can Canal, which runs from Denver down to Mexico. Lots of farms out this way filled with pecan trees and ostriches. Also saw quite a few fields of both green and red chiles, and some nice alfalfa. I heard this was the only farmable area in New Mexico; it's about 300 miles long.

Staying tonight at Riggs Chile Company and Ostrich Farm. (Never did understand why some folks spell it "chili" and others "chile". Either way, it's hot stuff!)

March 12—Saturday. Still traveling through the chile capital of the world, doing 10 miles into Arrey, where we're staying at J.H. and Margaret Shares' place. Lots of Holstein dairy farms along way.

Crew stopped at Caballo Lake Trading Post run by Ron and Joyce McPherson in Caballo, where they took on water for our vehicles.

March 13—Sunday. Stayed put today, enjoying J.H. and Margaret's hospitality. David and Vikki flew back to their farm in Nashua, Iowa to get all their equipment ready for spring.

It rained all afternoon, but we still had *lots* of visitors—about 3,200.

March 14—Still staying in Arrey. Watched people boating on Caballo Lake. Would have joined them if they'd asked in a *neigh*borly way. Instead, I exercised in the pen along with my buddies.

March 15—Got under way at 8:30 and traveled 9 miles in the desert along I-25. Very scenic here with Caballo Mountains off to our left.

Staying overnight in the desert. Wow, it's lonely out here; could drive a horse to hay.

March 16—We drove into Truth or Consequences, named after Ralph Edwards' famous TV program where contestants had to do silly things if they couldn't give the right answers to questions. (Makes me wonder if there's a town somewhere renamed "Mr. Ed".)

The bank greeted us with a welcome sign. Crowds picked up; lots of people lined the route from Sierra County Fairgrounds to Williamsburg, many taking videos and snapshots.

March 17—Begorra! Today's St. Patrick's Day, and me name is O'Firestone.

About 300 people came at 8:30 this morning to watch us be groomed and ♂

see us put on a driving exhibition. As we headed out, we passed quite a few RV parks, the First Baptist Church and Our Lady of Perpetual Help Catholic Church.

Staying tonight at Elephant Butte Lake State Park.

March 18—Very dusty 10-mile trek today through lonely desert area, seeing nothing but cactus brush.

No place to hook up for water today, so a couple of crew members drove ahead to rest area to fill up. They sponged us down later to get rid of dust, then vacuumed and brushed us. Stayed tonight in an area called La Canada Alamesa.

March 19—Saturday. A mighty lonesome ride today. Lots of cars passed us in this desert area, but we had no riders. I'm beginning to feel like an Arab instead of a Belgian!

We'll sleep in the desert again tonight.

March 20—Sunday. Relaxed today in our stalls. Crew watched TV during a slight rain this afternoon.

Heavy traffic on Interstate 25, including many "snowbirds" from up north.

March 21—Lots of cars on the interstate have license plates from Rhode Island, Missouri, Iowa and North Dakota. (Scenery's so monotonous here that reading license plates seems like fun.)

Biggest excitement of the day was a nice soapy bath for me and my buddies. Spending night at truck stop and Mini Mart at Exit 115.

March 22—Traveled 10 miles to San Marcial Road, which is Exit 124 off I-325. Quite a few drivers stopped to take our pictures. Boy, we're going to end up in a lot of scrapbooks across this great country!

March 23—Covered 15 miles through a pretty area flanked by beautiful mountains and canyons.

Crowds picked up as we entered San Antonio. (Yep—there's a San Antonio in New Mexico, too, in case you're not up on your geography like I am.) Saw some 150 people in the morning along route; another 200 in afternoon as we relaxed at the town parking area.

Crew enjoyed cookout this evening. Somehow, hot dogs and potato salad don't excite me.

March 24—Stayed put here in San

Bobby a Hit with Her Dad

I CAN'T LET any more time expire before saying "Thank you!" for stopping at the Ft. Madison Health Center. My father, who is a resident there, will be 80 on November 30, and when David and Vikki brought "Bobby" to the center, Dad started sobbing uncontrollably.

David asked for someone to bring Dad up to Bobby so that he could pet the horse. An attendant wheeled Dad up to Bobby, and the transformation was remarkable. Dad stopped crying and actually smiled—the first time he's done so in many, many months.

Someone took a picture, and Dad is prouder of that photo than anything he's ever had. We enlarged it to a 5x7 and it now hangs on the wall of his room, along with the framed centerfold from the souvenir program and the profile photo of Bobby.

I should also mention that due to an accident with a semi, both of my parents were left totally incapacitated a few years ago. Prior to that, they were both active and completely independent, jetting all over the U.S. to see my children and me.

I just wanted to let you know how *much* you have meant in his life. I know that another one of the hitch horses is named "Magic", and that's certainly appropriate: The hitch seems to have a magical effect on anyone who sees them.

If you ever pass through Ft. Madison again, stop in at the health center and see the pictures on Dad's wall. God bless you on your continued journey!

—*Sandy Cornish, Donnellson, Iowa*

MAKING FRIENDS. Above, Vikki introduces a youngster from Camp Mitchell, sponsored by the Southwest Kansas Association for the Visually Impaired, to one of the horses. Below, she takes time out for a snack.

Cody Visits 'Good Sam'

NEARLY a ton and a half of Belgian horsepower visited the Van Buren Good Samaritan Center in Keosauqua (Iowa) last Wednesday. Cody, one of the horses from *Country's Reminisce Hitch*, was led into the building, where the residents had a wonderful hands-on experience petting his velvet nose and huge chest.

He filled the corridor and nearly touched the ceiling with the tips of his ears as he walked down the hall. Administrative Assistant Rochelle Scovel even volunteered to sit on his wide back, and she practically rubbed her head on the ceiling.

David Helmuth, the driver of the hitch, and his wife, Vikki, graciously brought this gentle giant to the center.

Staff Development Coordinator Phil Oliver videotaped the visit so that anyone in the community may watch it at any time.

The hitch left the state of Maine last April and is traveling across the United States in celebration of the 50th anniversary of senior centers.

—*Van Buren County Leader-Record*
October 28, 1993

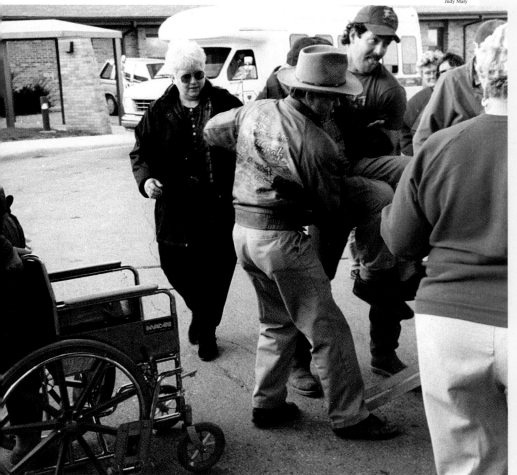

Judy Maly

GETTIN' A LIFT. David and crewman Ron Page help a senior from his wheelchair onto the wagon.

"THE CREW has been in good spirits throughout this whole trip, and they've been extremely busy. Each day, they must set up and take down the horse stalls, feed the horses, and do the hundreds of little jobs necessary to keep us rolling.

"There just isn't any time to fool around. And, fooling around where there are animals—especially animals that weigh more than a ton apiece—could cause big trouble. It's not the smart thing to do. And the crew agrees with that.

"So, we all tend to business and keep our focus on what we set out to do—to meet people all across this country, especially the seniors to whom we owe so much!"

Hitch Brings Out the Best

I GOT the first ride up to the grade school in Decorah—the kids really loved seeing the horses come clomping onto the playground! A couple from Cedar Rapids and I got off at school and realized we had no way to get back to our cars. I told them we could probably just ask someone for a ride, and then found the manager of a gas station who said he'd be happy to drive us back.

When he dropped us off, I told him I owed him a favor. He said he'd settle for some lefse. I'll be sure to drop some off for him next time I'm in town—it seems like seeing the hitch brings out the neighborliness in everybody!

—*Eunice Stoen, Decorah, Iowa*

Antonio today. Town is small: a gas station, cafe and a hardware store.

Crew cleaned our equipment during day while we relaxed in our stalls. When they got done with that chore, they started grooming us for tomorrow's trek.

March 25—Did 12 miles, mostly uphill. Had to leave the interstate because of construction; got off at Exit 147 and headed through the town of Socorro.

Stopped at Socorro Head Start Program School and gave some 75 students a treat, seeing us and hearing David tell about trip. Also visited town's senior center, where crew shared lunch with residents and David gave a short talk. Bobby and I gave rides to about 50 residents in center's parking lot. Bet they never thought they'd do something like that in their golden years.

March 26—Saturday. We're 8 miles up the road, stopped at Lemitar in an open parking lot. Was chilly this morning, only about 47°, but some 100 people turned out to watch us being groomed and prepped for today's trip.

By noon, the temperature had climbed to 68°. This area looks more like Belgian country—it's full of beautiful green alfalfa fields.

March 27—Sunday. Spent the day resting in Lemitar. Weather was downright *un*-desertlike; when we woke it was 20° degrees and snowing!

Me and my buddies wore our heavy blankets during the afternoon and kept our heads low to the ground. The crew parked all vehicles around our stalls to block out the wind and snow. Folks around here must be used to it, because about 150 came to see us throughout the day.

March 28—Not much warmer today—26° at 7; only up to 52° this afternoon. We made 14 miles, arriving at State Game Refuge, where we'll stay tonight.

Bosque Farms Senior Center brought a group of seniors who had the thrill of their lives riding on the hitch wagon.

David and Vikki were invited to dinner by Jordan Pareo, who owns a farm near Vequita. (No room for horses at the table, I guess.) Crew chatted around the bonfire.

March 29—We walked 8-1/2 miles, ↻

then rode the semi another 7 miles to Vequita and the Pareos' farm, where we're staying tonight.

Pretty mountains around here; can still see snow on peaks. Film crew got some great shots of us as we crossed the Rio Grande.

This evening David held a seminar at a dinner party attended by some 200 people. Gave away lots of prizes and souvenirs.

March 30—Really enjoying myself here at Pareo Farm. No travel today. Instead, crew prettied us up; groomed and vacuumed us, tied our tails and braided our manes, then decked us out with bows and rosettes.

We trotted into the farm arena and performed in high style, showing off with circles, figure eights and wagon docking. David was especially proud of us; called us the "mighty six" and said we pulled even harder than we usually do on the road. See what show biz can do to a horse?

Afterward, we were rewarded with apple treats. Yum!

March 31—Boy, did we get up early today—3:30 a.m. for grooming before being trucked back to where we stopped 2 days ago. Temp was 40° at this high elevation; you could see steam rolling off us as we trotted 10 miles through mountainous area.

Film crew filmed us as we cut off I-25 and headed northwest toward Mountainair.

Apr. 1—Just another trot in the desert today in sunny 70° weather. I'm not into counting cars, but would guess about 250 passed us, the drivers, as always, tooting their horns and leaning out of their windows to cheer us on.

And, there were some 40 people who didn't mind the desert heat and rode the hitch. We're still moving northeast along Hwy. 60, a straight road but slightly uphill.

Apr. 2—Pretty much the same routine today: lots of cars but almost no riders along our 8-mile route. Still hot; 75° and very sunny!

Apr. 3—Easter Sunday, and the 89th day on our trek east. David and Vikki did Easter Sunday proper: they attended Easter Services at the First Baptist Church back in Belen with the Pareo family.

The crew is also enjoying the holiday;

Belgian Bobby Born Near Rockwell

THE STOP in Britt on Thursday by the famous six-horse Belgian hitch brought one of the team's stars close to home.

"Bobby", a 2,400-pound gelding, is one of the horses used on the team and was born on the Paul Pruin farm just north of Rockwell (Iowa).

"When you raise them from a colt

and do the training like we did him, you don't forget," said Pruin, adding that he had called the horse "Sam" when he owned it.

Bobby made history in 1991 when he sold for $21,000 at auction, which is still the record auction price for a gelding. He has since won several awards, including being named the Grand Champion Gelding in the National Belgian Show in Davenport last summer.

David Helmuth, driver and trainer of the team, said Bobby has been "worth every dollar paid for him back there in 1991".

Some of the other horses raised on his farm are now geldings on other major hitches around the country, but none of them have had the amount of attention as the team Bobby is currently on, said Pruin.

Although the team receives the best care throughout the trip, it is not immune to tragedy. "Jack", an 8-year-old horse who was normally paired next to Bobby, died of a heart attack while the team performed at Audubon on Tuesday.

—Mason City Globe Gazette
November 11, 1993

HEADS UP! Even the Belgians had opportunities to do a little sight-seeing while they were en route to California.

"PROBABLY the most unusual—and saddest—experience of our entire trip occurred on our way to the senior center in Audubon, Iowa. The center's director had told me earlier that afternoon that there were seven residents who couldn't get outside to see the hitch, and asked if I could bring an extra horse and take him inside to meet these people. I agreed, and we had Magic tied to the rear of the wagon as we drove the hitch over to the senior center.

"As we came to an intersection, my left-hand wheel horse, Jack, suddenly collapsed. I immediately whoa'ed the team, and Vikki jumped down and ran to him. The vet told us later that Jack had died instantly of a heart attack.

"Everyone stayed calm, including the horses, and we quickly got Jack out of his harness. Then I turned to a policeman traveling behind us and asked him to radio for a veterinarian. The vet arrived almost immediately and removed Jack to his place for an autopsy.

"The question on everybody's lips was, 'What are you going to do now?' For one thing, we had all of those people at the senior center waiting for us. Suddenly, it seemed like there was a reason that we had an extra horse with the hitch that afternoon.

"We'd never done this before—Magic is a lead horse, but we put him at the wheel in Jack's position. He handled it like a real pro—talk about teamwork!

"We were only about 10 minutes late getting to the senior center. I'll admit that Vikki and I were pretty shaken, having just lost one of our great horses, but we made it.

"The vet confirmed that Jack died of a heart attack. He also said that Jack had a heart murmur, and that the steady exercise he'd been getting in the hitch had actually strengthened his heart and prolonged his life.

"Jack was born and raised in Ontario, Canada. He was a super horse and won many awards, just about everything he could ever win.

"When he was harnessed up that afternoon, he was pawing the ground and eager to get started. He was always like that, always willing to give his all and happy to be pulling with his teammates. That's how we're going to remember him!"

we spent the day relaxing in our stalls.

Apr. 4—Covered 13 miles along Hwy. 60 as we headed into the pretty town of Mountainair, New Mexico, founded in 1902 and known as "The Gateway to the Ancient Cities".

It's *really* up in the mountains, nearly 6,500 feet. I think I overheard David telling Vikki and the crew that this is the highest elevation of our entire cross-country trip. Some 1,170 people live here, and they greeted us with a sign that said "Welcome Belgians", complete with balloons!

Apr. 5—Treated 200 students of Mountainair Elementary School to a visit with hitch; David also told them all about our trip.

Lots of campers and RVs passed us along Hwy. 60; snowbirds heading back home, I guess, now that winter's over. I'd like to live like that when I retire…although I suspect I'm a little too large to be called a "snowbird"!

Apr. 6—Still heading northeast through New Mexico. Boy, this is rugged territory! I call it "the middle of nowhere", but, by gosh, some 400 cars filled with people came out to see us.

Other excitement was two Santa Fe trains passing us along the way. Staying in town of Willard tonight. After we got here, David and Vikki took Tim to nearby Estancia to give a seminar at the town park. Bet Tim could give that talk himself by now—it'd be right from the horse's mouth!

Apr. 7—Can't believe how chilly the desert is at daybreak—only 50° at 7. At noon, it was still only 60° plus cold and windy.

We're at a really lonesome stop tonight—an abandoned farmhouse on a ranch. I can see cattle in the fields, along with a pronghorn antelope or two. Makes me feel grateful to be part of this hitch family!

Apr. 8—Covered 10 more miles of desert. No riders but plenty of cars!

Arrived at the farm owned by Bob and June McLaughlin on Hwy. 60, in Encino. David ordered feed and alfalfa hay for us today, so our menu is set for the next couple of weeks.

The crew also cleaned our horse ♂

EARLY HORSEPOWER. Demonstrations of farming with draft horses, staged by local farmers along the route, drew many spectators, including crewman Steve Zbornik (in center of photo).

trailers; sure is nice to have such service!

Apr. 9—It was 53° and windy this morning, but by noon it was 70° and sunny, although still windy enough to muss my mane.

Hitched about 8 miles to RV park in Encino, where there were showers for the crew. Guess we'll have to wait for rain to get *our* showers, but we did enjoy relaxing after we got here.

Apr. 10—Sunday. Believe it or not, it *snowed* at 7 a.m.! No wonder; it was only in the 20s.

Not much better at noon, still only 43°, still snowing and still windy. Glad to spend the day holed up at this RV park—stayed cuddled under heavy blankets!

Apr. 11—There was snow on the ground as we started out at 8:30 this morning, and we could see lots of the white stuff on nearby mountain peaks.

Great for skiing, unless you're a horse. Can you imagine me whipping down a ski trail on two pairs of those hoof sleds? I'd rather hitch my fate to a wagon!

Apr. 12—Happy to reach Vaughn, elevation 5,964 feet and 7 miles down the road. Swung off Hwy. 60 onto Hwy. 54. Got to meet two busloads of kids from the town's elementary school.

Tim showed off while Vikki told them all about our trek. Students asked lots of good questions about the trip—and about us horses, naturally. After all, we're the *mane event*!

Apr. 13—Wow! Today it's 1 year since we dipped our hoofs in the Atlantic and started our cross-country trek, and what a year it's been!

We've met so many, many great people and seen so many wonderful sights along the way. Not many horses can brag about hoofing it every inch of the way across this great country of ours.

Crew toasted our anniversary by building a bonfire at our desert stop tonight and enjoying a steak cookout.

Apr. 14—It was an uphill trot today as we traveled about 10 miles along Hwy. 54. For company, we had rocks and open fields—not much else to see in this desert area!

I'm sure we won't have anyone dropping in on us as we park for the night alongside the highway. You've got to be a loner to like this desert life. Saw a few horses across the road; don't know if they're wild or not. At any rate, they didn't whinny "hello"!

Apr. 15—We finally reached a

Snow No Hindrance to Hitch!

WE ARE LOCATED just 9 miles from Centerville, where your famous hitch has been this past week. There just aren't enough superlatives to describe how much enjoyment has been derived from Reiman Publications' efforts.

Our library carries all your publications, and when some of our patrons finish with old issues, they bring them in and we put them on our free table for others to read.

We have ordered the video and souvenir program and will be eagerly awaiting the video of the remainder of the trip.

Personally, I drove over on Saturday, October 30, to watch the hitch and some local bands parade around Centerville's square. It was snowing and blowing so much I was sure the event would be canceled. Wrong! They all performed as scheduled.

My mother, who is 92 but not able to get out of the car, was absolutely thrilled. Please accept our thanks!
—Mary Lou Raymie
Moravia Public Library, Moravia, Iowa

CENTERVILLE is county seat of Appanoose County in south-central Iowa. Here, crowd gathers before courthouse in town square, near hitch sign and Golden Horseshoe.

Early Days in Centerville a Real 'Drag'!

CENTERVILLE—"America's Hometown"—is the largest city in Appanoose County, and its county seat. Appanoose is a Sac Indian name meaning "Chief When a Child". The county was formed shortly after Iowa became a state in 1846, and Centerville was founded a year later.

The city is located only 7 miles south of Rathbun Lake and a dozen miles north of Missouri on the historic Mormon Trail. Set in the midst of generally rolling topography, it is surrounded by rivers, creeks and watersheds.

The town was built around a square with two-block-long sides, believed to be the largest town square in the world. That claim has never been proven, but as a 1989 history of Centerville points out, no one has stepped forward to challenge it, either!

One early problem for the young business district was a simple one—mud. The unpaved streets around the square turned to a river of muck after each rainfall. When the streets dried out, they were badly rutted by horses and wagon wheels.

The town solved the problem with "Drag Days". Men and women from surrounding farms hitched up their best horses and dragged harrows in a "loop-the-loop" around the square. The streets were smoothed, the citizens had a day's entertainment and the top drivers took home prizes.

Some historians believe these drivers might also be responsible for creating the area's first farm-to-market roads, since they smoothed paths on their way to and from town!
—The Appanoose County Historical Society, Centerville, Iowa

Horsing Around

ONE OF the most famous draft horse hitches in the nation is coming to town with one of the most famous draft horse shows in the nation.

The six-horse team of Belgians known as *Country's Reminisce Hitch* will be on Main Street at 3 p.m. Thursday and will give rides between the downtown area and the fairgrounds between 3 and 5 p.m.

After the rides, a seminar about draft horses will be given at the fairgrounds, where the team and support groups will be staying for the night.

A nationally renowned draft horse show is held at the fairgrounds in Britt each Labor Day weekend.

Country's Reminisce Hitch is named after the magazines *Country* and *Reminisce*. The two magazines are sponsoring a coast-to-coast trip under the theme of "Pulling for Seniors" to honor the 50th anniversary of senior centers in America.

During the trip, the hitch has stopped at senior citizen centers and provided rides. The goal of the hitch is to "elevate concern, respect and service for seniors", according to a press release.

The team of six champion Belgians driven by Iowa native David Helmuth is expected to draw a lot of attention not only from Britt residents, but around the north Iowa area, said Marie Steenlage, director of the Britt Chamber of Commerce.

"We anticipate a lot of people coming from some distance to see the team. Some people who have talked to me said they have already gone down to southern Iowa to see the team," said Steenlage.

The stop in Britt was not part of the original route planned for the team's cross-country trek. Helmuth and the team actually started from Maine on Easter Sunday and have traveled across New Hampshire, Massachusetts, New York, Pennsylvania, Ohio, Indiana and Illinois, averaging about 10 miles a day.

The trip was originally planned to be nonstop to California, but this summer's unpredictable weather delayed the journey after logging 1,400 miles to Centerville.

The team is making a six-stop tour of Iowa before heading by truck to California. From there, the rest of the trip will be made in reverse, with plans to return to Centerville next summer.

—Kevin Baskins, Mason City
Globe Gazette, November 10, 1993

town, Santa Rosa, 14 miles down the road. We did better than Mark, one of our crew; while driving the semi pulling our horse trailer, he got stuck in soft desert sand and had to call for help.

Steve Tajia, from nearby Pastura, pulled him out with his Mack truck. I admire such horsepower…even if it isn't quite natural!

Apr. 16—This is our 100th day on the trek back east, and whatta day it's been!

As we set out for the senior center in Santa Rosa, a rabbit shot out of the crowd along our parade route down Main Street with a big black dog (called a Rottweiler, I heard someone say later) right behind it.

They both ran *right underneath* J.R., who was on the left in the swing team. J.R. spooked and reared up, nearly landing on top of Stoney to his right, who also spooked, and suddenly we were off to the races!

Bobby and I, in the wheel position right in front of the wagon, kept our heads, I must say, as we headed down Main Street at almost a full gallop. Chip and Magic at the lead also did their best to stop the runaway. David got J.R. and Stoney under control after a couple of blocks, and no one got hurt.

Everyone thought David did a great ♂

SIGN erected near Golden Horseshoe in Centerville's town square explains purpose of cross-country trip—honoring seniors— made by *Country's Reminisce Hitch*.

"ON ONE of the hottest days we experienced, 105°, a hitch rider asked a rather ironic question that ultimately led to a big change in our plans. He said, 'What are you going to do when it gets cold?'

"We realized he had a point. We were still in the Midwest, and we could see now that walking 10 miles a day wasn't going to get us through Iowa, Missouri, Nebraska and Kansas before it got cold. It even gets cold much farther south, in Oklahoma and Texas, by Thanksgiving.

"When we finally reached the Mississippi River, we hoped it wouldn't still be raining after the summer floods. But it was pouring for quite a few days, and had also turned very cold. Autumn was definitely upon us. We decided it was time to fall back on our 'contingency plan', something we'd been discussing ever since that fellow asked us the question on that extremely hot day.

"Although we were kind of reluctant to do it this way, we decided we were going to have to split the trip by stopping at a point in the Midwest, then truck the horses out to the West Coast. Once we got to San Diego, we'd start back, walking the rest of the distance from west to east until we got back to the place where we'd left off earlier.

"That way, we'd still be able to say we'd walked the entire distance across the country. It wasn't an easy decision, but we decided that it made the most sense in terms of what was safest and most comfortable for everyone involved, including the horses.

"It's funny, thinking back to the remark made by that one rider and how it led to such big changes in our plans!"

job handling us. (Personally, I think it was more a case of we veteran horses helping David to get things under control!) At any rate, it was definitely a "hare"-raising experience. By the way, we kept our date with the senior center!

Apr. 17—Sunday, and we're taking it easy at the Big Valley Ford parking lot in Santa Rosa after yesterday's excitement. New Mexico State Senator Peter Campos, incidentally, stopped by to welcome us officially to his state.

He was on the wagon yesterday with David when the runaway took place, and he complimented us again on our teamwork in bringing things under control.

Lots of people visited us today, taking pictures and riding the hitch. Gotta mention Everett Haglegate who owns Big Valley Ford; he's really promoted us here, lining up radio stations for interviews, alerting local businesses and inviting everyone to help us feel welcome. Thanks, Everett!

Apr. 18—After such a busy and exciting weekend, it was a bit tough to get back in the routine this morning!

There were quite a few people out early watching us get harnessed up. We made a short run today, only 8 miles.

Apr. 19—Made a quiet 16-mile run to-

"SINCE Centerville has the world's largest town square, we decided to stage the world's largest hayride while we were there. So, during our radio talk shows and interviews that week, we asked local farmers with flatbed hay wagons to bring them into town on Friday night, and Saturday we would give it a try.

"We ended up with 17 hay wagons. We hooked 'em up, put the whole shebang behind the hitch, loaded the hitch wagon with people and closed the tailgate. Then we piled people onto the hay wagons—about 450 people in all.

"With all that weight, the tires of the hay wagons were a little low, but the horses pulled all 17 of those wagons clear around the world's largest town square. They were pulling so hard to get started that there were sparks flying from under their hooves!

"Everything went perfectly except that one wagon near the back was a bit wider than the rest and it nicked the fender of a local man's car as we made the turn. We reimbursed the owner for the slight damage—he was very understanding about the whole thing—and now he can tell his kids and grandkids that he sacrificed a fender for an event that would make *The Guinness Book of World Records*!"

MINIATURE "Golden Horseshoe" (above), one of 18 provided by Centerville, was presented by David to each town the hitch stopped in during truck transport to California. In center photo, excited riders participate in "World's Largest Hayride".

Minnesotans Enjoy 'World's Largest Hayride'

ON OCTOBER 29, my brother, Bob Dwire, and his wife, Oda, of Arco, Minnesota and my husband, Gene, and I from Granite Falls, Minnesota were among the lucky people who rode the "World's Largest Hayride" in Centerville, Iowa.

Why was this so special to us? My brother had cancer and was very ill but badly wanted to see the hitch. The four of us traveled to Centerville in Bob and Oda's van so that he could rest as much as possible.

All four of us were able to ride the hitch during the hayride. Bob was very cold, so we wrapped him in a black quilt decorated with yellow flowers, and Oda jokingly referred to him as her "flower child". I took photos of him posing with the horse named Bobby.

He was very proud of those photos and showed them to everyone who came to visit him. On December 14, he passed away, and we know that the happy memories of his visit to the hitch made his last weeks easier.

—*Sharon Sannerud*
Granite Falls, Minnesota

Draft Horse Hitch Hails Seniors; Britt Stop Part of Cross-Country Trek

THEY TRAVEL across the country in a semi trailer custom built especially for them.

Their names—Chip, Magic, Firestone, Junior, Bobby, Jack, Stoney and Eddie—are proudly emblazoned on the side of the trailer and everywhere they go, they draw a crowd. Their stop in Britt (Iowa) during the middle of the afternoon on Thursday was testimony to their appeal, drawing several hundred people.

It's not a rock group creating the fanfare. Chip, Magic and the rest are Belgian horses, part of the *Country's Reminisce Hitch* team making a cross-country trek that started as a trip from Maine to California.

After leaving from Maine on Easter Sunday, the cross-country trek was delayed by this summer's bad weather. Although the journey was originally planned as a nonstop trip, the hitch was delayed enough that the team will now go to California and start the trip back to Iowa's Centerville.

The trip is expected to be completed next summer for the team, which travels about 10 miles a day.

Followers of the team tend to be more geriatric than teenyboppers, which is also by design. The theme of the journey by the champion six-horse hitch is "We're Pulling for Seniors", and is sponsored by two magazines, *Country* and *Reminisce*, as a way of marking 1993 as the 50th anniversary of senior citizen centers.

The driver and trainer of the team, David Helmuth of Waverly, said all money raised during the trip through the sale of souvenirs will be divided among the 15,000 senior citizen centers across the nation.

During the journey, stops are made at senior citizen centers and Helmuth has even taken one of the horses, standing over 7 feet tall, into the lobbies of the nursing homes when weather kept residents from coming out.

Rides are also provided during the stops. The wagon holds 12 passengers, and by the time the team had reached Centerville last month, Helmuth said 15,000 people had taken rides.

"People always ask me if this gets boring, but when you have that many people with you, it never gets boring," Helmuth said.

For many of the seniors that turn up at stops, horses represent fond memories of farming in the days before tractors.

"I don't think there's anything prettier or closer to nature than a team of draft horses," said 79-year-old Charley Quinn of Bancroft. —*Kevin Baskins*
Mason City Globe Gazette
November 12, 1993

STEPPIN' OUT. Belgians parade before enthusiastic crowd lining Centerville's town square, reputed to be world's largest.

Beverly Huffman

"A MAN approached the hitch in Centerville and exclaimed, 'I'm telling you, there's nobody farther away from home than I am. I flew in here just for this. I just landed at the airport in Des Moines, rented a car and drove down here to see the hitch.'

"I asked where he was from and he replied, 'Portland, Maine!' I told him he did indeed win the prize for being the farthest from home!

"It started to snow the last day the hitch was in Centerville, following our trip around the state of Iowa. We thought that snowfall was almost like an omen—it proved that we made the right decision to change our plans."

day, traveling through some beautiful canyons. Also saw cattle grazing on dried grass—the land is very dry and rain is badly needed.

Stopped tonight at the Fina Mini Mart in Newkirk, off Exit 300 of Interstate 40.

Apr. 20—Still on Interstate 40 as we traveled 11 miles into Montoya at Exit 311. Saw several herds of antelope grazing in fields that actually reminded us of some areas in the Midwest.

Apr. 21—Finally rained this evening! Crew covered our harnesses and the wagon because it came down pretty hard for about 2 hours.

After it stopped raining, a beautiful rainbow decorated the sky. I hear people believe there's a pot of gold at the end of each rainbow—you couldn't fool a horse into believing that!

Staying at Stuckey's Dairy Queen tonight. Ice cream cones for the crew; hay for us!

Apr. 22—Good thing we traveled only during the morning today because it thundered and rained in late afternoon, causing some flooding in our stalls. Crew dug ditches around edges of stalls to drain off the water. They even had to spread new shavings for our bedding.

Staying near a McDonald's restaurant in Tucumcari tonight. Hope I don't wake up smelling like hamburgers! Lots of people asking about big doin's this weekend...

Apr. 23—Mighty big crowds today, a total of nearly 2,000 visited us in our stalls during the day and another 700 in the evening! Some 670 people rode the hitch.

Many along our parade route through town later held up signs that read "Welcome *Reminisce Hitch*". Vikki and Ashley got to ride in a Mustang convertible. The Tucumcari High School Band performed a concert for 200 residents and workers at the Van Ark Senior Center.

The band also accompanied us to Everett Haglegate's Big Country Ford dealership, where we're bunking tonight in the parking lot. Incidentally, Everett, who rode on the wagon with David to parking lot, pledged $200 to the band for their concert there.

Apr. 24—Sunday. People here have really taken us to their ↷

hearts. Big crowds still turning out to visit with us—just between 1 and 3 this afternoon, we had nearly 300 riders.

There'll be lots of pictures in albums and videos recording this weekend. On top of that, the Big Country Ford people were giving beautiful balloons and free soda pop to the kids. It's really been a fun weekend in Tucumcari!

Apr. 25—I felt frisky this morning as we headed out of town at 8:30 with lots of happy memories of the weekend. Felt like I was still in that parade.

Not a very nice day, though; 33° and very windy. People didn't get out of their cars; just took camera shots from inside. When we stopped for the night, crew couldn't put up the tent because of the high wind. So we hunkered down in our stalls with our winter blankets.

Apr. 26—Highlights of the day were a stop at Logan Municipal School, where we entertained 300 pupils, and a visit to Logan Senior Center.

Apr. 27—This was no day to brag about, either: 29°, cold and windy at 7 a.m. About 150 cars, many with Oklahoma license plates and some with snow on their roofs, passed us as we headed east on Hwy. 54.

Only had about a dozen hardy hitch riders today. Vikki and Marlene visited the Country Ostrich Ranch owned by Gerald and Lisa Floeck. The Floecks have operated the ranch since 1980, one of the oldest and largest in New Mexico, they say.

Apr. 28—Getting close to the Texas border; arrived at the senior center in Nara Visa shortly after noon. Residents enjoyed petting us. (We horses need to be stroked, too, you know!)

Apr. 29—Brrr! This area was the coldest in the country today—26°, windy and about 4 inches of snow. Travel with the hitch was out of the question, so we stayed put with our winter blankets in our stalls.

Crew even had to enclose the tent around our stalls to keep snow from blowing in on us. Lots of lightning, too. Vikki says the storm blew out the microwave oven in their motor home!

Apr. 30—Woke up this morning to find it was 40° and sunny. The snow had melted and we were on our way into Texas—we were just 4 miles from the border when the storm hit and pinned us down yesterday.

Had about three dozen riders—business seems to be picking up!

"THE HITCH CARAVAN, including the special semi which houses the horses, traveled 100 miles a day on the way out to California. We left Centerville for the West Coast on Monday, November 22.

"We stopped in 18 towns along the way, and we had some pretty interesting experiences. For instance, we got into Auburn, Nebraska on the Wednesday afternoon before Thanksgiving Day, and that evening the entire area was clobbered by a sleet storm. On the news that night, there was footage of lots of cars and trucks that had spun out on the interstate we'd crossed just a few hours earlier—that made us very thankful we'd reached Auburn without a mishap!

"In each of these towns, we told the people who came out to see us that we were just passing through now, but that we would be back, with the horses pulling the hitch. We made a point of telling everyone that these horses were going to pull the hitch every inch of the way.

"Some folks asked us why we would bother hitching through the desert when there wouldn't be hardly anybody out there. They'd say, 'Why not just load up the horses and truck them?'

"My response to that was always the same: 'That's not driving across America. We are going to drive them coast to coast, walking all the way.'"

Zeph Earhart

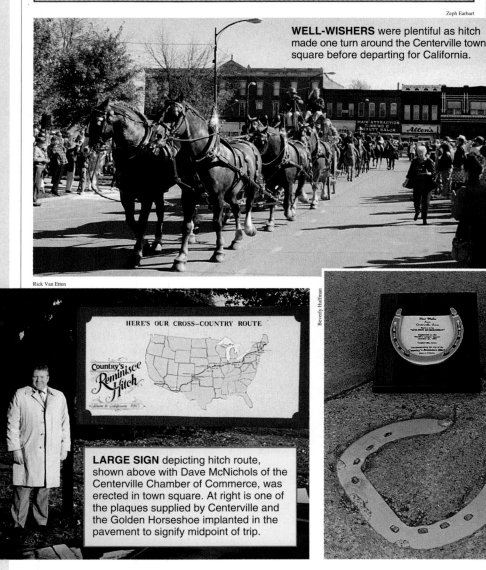

WELL-WISHERS were plentiful as hitch made one turn around the Centerville town square before departing for California.

Rick Van Etten

Beverly Huffman

HERE'S OUR CROSS-COUNTRY ROUTE

Country's Reminisce Hitch

LARGE SIGN depicting hitch route, shown above with Dave McNichols of the Centerville Chamber of Commerce, was erected in town square. At right is one of the plaques supplied by Centerville and the Golden Horseshoe implanted in the pavement to signify midpoint of trip.

CHAPTER FOUR

HEADING BACK

May 1—Sunday. Our first full day in Texas. Crew spent the day cleaning and polishing everything for our jaunt through the northwestern part of this great state.

We got prettied up, too—crew groomed us during the afternoon.

May 2—We're having some Texas weather today—62°, breezy and a bit humid. Some 200 cars passed us, including two semis from Kansas that stopped in the middle of the road and took pictures of us.

Saw plenty of feedlots with many head of beef cattle. Also starting to see lots of greenery—grass is very lush, leaves on trees turning green, a sure sign of spring!

Crew gave us a clipping today. Luckily they were finished by 6:30 because it started to rain.

May 3—Heard that Texas Governor Ann Richards declared yesterday "Senior Citizens Day" throughout the state in honor of our cross-country trip! Especially liked that part of her proclamation that read, "and its team of champion Belgian draft horses".

Sue Cunningham and Peggy Pippin of Hartley, Texas also wrote us a nice note after riding the hitch. "Glad you came through Texas. You will be talked about for a long time."

Staying tonight in giant XIT Feed Lot, which houses some 167,000 head of beef cattle. I heard the XIT ranch was the largest in Texas!

May 4—If I may say so myself, we looked marvelous today, all nice and shiny, with our manes and tails braided up and decked out in our show collars, as we rolled into Dalhart, Texas and were greeted by nearly 2,000 people.

The mayor presented David and Vikki with black felt hats and the Governor's proclamation. And all the crew members were officially made "Honorary Texans" in a ceremony conducted by Carol Artz, executive vice president of the Dalhart Chamber of Commerce. She's been a great help, setting up various events for our stay in town.

TV Channel 7, ABC from Amarillo, videotaped us coming into town. We gave rides to residents at Dalhart Senior Center. Towns of Dumas and Stratford also bused in seniors to see us.

When we got to the parking lot of Charles Langer's Ford dealership, it was

Dave Herrewig

David Hunter

AFTER SPLASHING in the Pacific, the hitch headed east out of San Diego (above). Shortly after leaving the city, it encountered the first of many winding mountain roads (below).

"ON DECEMBER 13, 1993, we splashed the horses in the Pacific Ocean to start the trip back east. We found the perfect place, a beach crowded with people. The horses just loved the water, and the people were treated to a sight they'll probably never see again.

"The highway out of San Diego was hilly and narrow, with hairpin curves. We discovered that was typical of what lay ahead. For several days, the hitch moved only about 6 miles a day, rather than 10 or 12, because of the steeper grades.

"We traveled through the desert, which was a pretty lonely ride until we reached Calexico, California. As we entered the town, we drove right along the U.S.-Mexican border, which practically goes down the middle of the road.

"Now, if we ever were to travel from Centerville, Iowa to Canada, we'd be able to say that the hitch traveled from coast to coast *and* border to border!"

Hitch Boosts Mother's Spirits

YOUR continued reports of the hitch's progress have given me the idea of taking my mother to see, and hopefully ride, the hitch when you arrive in San Diego. I am keeping abreast of your progress and plan to give my mother a special Christmas present the weekend of December 11 before the hitch leaves on its return journey to Centerville.

Sad to say, this has not been a very good year for us. My father passed away just before Father's Day, and this December would have marked my parents' 50th wedding anniversary, which my mother will greatly miss celebrating.

Just being able to see the hitch and pat the horses will add a bit of brightness to her life, which is devoted to rescuing injured and orphaned wildlife and working with her fellow seniors.

—*Laura Leifer, Buellton, California*

David Hunter

DOMESTIC DUTIES were ongoing during the hitch's journey, whether cleaning the wagon (above) or bathing the horses (at right). Regardless of the activity, visitors always enjoyed stopping for a look-see and conversation with crew.

Bath Day...WE WERE pleas-
antly surprised to have the hitch route go right through our town. We got to see the hitch's semi trucks and the huge horses. The horses were having their baths, and little children were petting their noses.

Very beautiful—the horses, the equipment, everything! We are so pleased to have been there!

—*Grace Harter*
Lemon Grove, California

Gail Edwards

filled with 500 people from seven states. Students from Dalhart Elementary School were also there to greet us.

May 5—Back to a quiet routine, walked 10 miles north along Hwy. 385, a two-lane road through some beautiful farm country. We're still knocked out from yesterday's festivities; snoozed in our stalls this afternoon.

Lois Ward and her husband visited from Tucson. Lois bought the first puppy from Ashley's litter and named her "Vikki". (Good thing they didn't take a male puppy; they might have named him "Firestone" and my heritage would've gone to the dogs!)

Crew is being very careful at our roadside stop; somebody mentioned *rattlesnakes*!

May 6—Still traveling through open country served by irrigation systems. Lots of cars on the road, as well as some Harley riders who stopped and took a picture of Cody standing beside their bikes—guess you could call that one "A Horse and a Hog".

Some of crew went bowling in Dalhart; I didn't have any time to spare. (Yet another one of my sterling puns!)

May 7—Reached Coldwater Canyon after a 10-mile walk in warm sunny weather. Saw lots of farmers working their fields.

David and Vikki were invited to attend a rodeo tonight in Guymon, Oklahoma, just across the state line. They got a big hand after the announcer informed the crowd that the couple driving the hitch team was in the audience.

May 8—Sunday, a great day of rest for us. Not many people here in the Coldwater Canyon area. They're still telling us this is rattlesnake country, so we're treading lightly...

May 9—Got a stormy weather welcome as we crossed into Cimarron County in the Oklahoma panhandle today. Started raining about 1:30 p.m., followed by hail, wind, lightning and thunder.

Then, around 7, a Boise City police officer stopped by to warn us of a tornado watch. We stayed calm through it all; it takes a mighty big ♂

wind to ruffle a Belgian. Crew ate dinner prepared for them by the Ron Overstreet family of Boise City.

May 10—Got a happier welcome today as we entered Boise City. Town's Wildcat Band performed a concert at the fairgrounds where we're staying tonight. (Saw that big dinosaur across the road again!)

Kids are trying to earn donations for local library. We also gave rides to people at Boise City Care Center; even some of the residents in wheelchairs got rides.

That hail yesterday caused lots of crop damage, I hear. Also heard something else: some 150 rattlesnakes have been killed recently in area. Got two kinds here: prairie and diamondbacks. All I can say is, Whoa! A snake's a snake in my book, and I dislike 'em all!

May 11—Made 11 Boise City Elementary School youngsters really happy; they got to ride with the hitch. Then we drove north on Hwys. 385 and 287, parts of it flat, others hilly.

Crew still being very careful because of those rattlesnake stories we've been hearing.

May 12—Good-bye, Oklahoma; hello, Colorado! Great welcome as we rolled into Campo in Baca County. Local school band riding on a red bandwagon drawn by a team of black Percherons played for us as we clip-clopped to our overnight stop in Wells Memorial Park.

David gave the band a $200 check for their performance. About 200 people greeted us, including one lady who said she drove 200 miles, from Rye, Colorado to ride the hitch. She was so happy, she was crying. I could have hugged her—well, nuzzled her anyway!

Crew was treated to dinner at the Campo Community Building.

May 13—We celebrated 13 months on the road today—Friday the 13th—by driving 13 miles to Jeff and Carla Deeds' farm, where they raise cattle and pigs.

The Deeds treated the crew to a cookout this evening, delicious hamburgers topped with huge sweet onions, Junior and Steve said.

May 14—Big crowds as we rolled into Springfield, Colorado; 800 in morning, 600 in afternoon, another 200 this evening. And more than 400 people rode the hitch—what a happy group; they sang *God Bless America* and *Jesus Loves Me* as they rode.

Spike and Cody drew extra duty,

"**DON'T TRY THIS AT HOME!**" was the message David often jokingly added when autographing this photo for souvenir buyers. Letter-writer below says she could have benefited from his methods!

From One Stunt Person to Another...I COULD HAVE

USED David's help 55 years ago when my friends and I tried Roman riding. If only we'd had sense enough to harness the two horses together like he does! We never thought of that!

Also, the horses we rode would have been terrified of the surf and we never could have boosted each other onto their backs while wearing a billowing long raincoat like the one David has on in his picture.
—*Barbara Duncan*
Carmel Valley, California

COMMUNITY ON WHEELS. Colorful hitch vehicles provided rather striking contrast to the surrounding terrain of Southwestern deserts. In some instances, overnight campsites were determined primarily by proximity to water supply.

"IN YUMA, Arizona, the hitch ran into huge crowds of people. An official at the local Chamber of Commerce said Yuma is a very popular winter spot and some 60,000 'snowbirds' come down here each year.

"I remembered that when we drove through Elkhart, Indiana earlier and saw all those trailers and motor home manufacturing plants, I wondered where all their vehicles would go. Well, believe me, many, if not most, come to Yuma.

"There's lots of sand and cactus in those RV parks, and it's quite a sight to see the long caravan of RV owners come into town to fill up their RV's with water!"

mingling with residents at Springfield Nursing Home and Springfield West Home. Radio station KLAR interviewed David, and the *Baca Weekly* did an article on our trip.

May 15—Sunday, so we're taking it easy at the park here in Springfield. Saw lots of people who came out yesterday; couldn't get enough of us, I guess. For working so hard during the past week, Vikki gave each of us an apple!

May 16—Kind of hated to move on, but we've still got a lot of miles to go. Walked to Vilas, where we met with local school kids. Vikki talked about the trip with them. A number of people from town of Lamar, north of here, also paid us a visit.

May 17—Pulled into Walsh, Colorado after walking 10 miles; arrived at noon just as the wind was kicking up to 50 miles an hour. As things quieted down, we visited both senior centers in town. Walsh Elementary School let students out of class to come see us.

May 18—Well, it finally happened —*snakes*! We were about 3 miles out of Walsh this morning when, all of a sudden, Bobby jumped sideways and bumped into Cody. A diamondback rattler at the side of the road had tried to strike at him!

Luckily, it missed. But then, within the next mile, we saw a second and a third, coiled and ferocious-looking, like they were mad enough to strike, too. And we saw four more dead ones that ♂⟶

David Hunter

EASY DOES IT! Due to numerous hairpin curves and steeper grades, mountain roads frequently reduced daily distance covered by the hitch.

Birthday Rendezvous

I'D FOLLOWED the hitch from the start, and was well aware it had left California for the return trip to Iowa. As we planned a car trip to celebrate my birthday, I thought of calling the 900 number to see where the hitch would be, but didn't. I figured we'd never find it, even if we knew for sure where it was.

The first day of our trip, I noticed a blinking light on a frontage road just south of Tucson. My husband took a closer look and said it was a truck following a six-horse hitch pulling a red wagon!

We got off at the next exit and I started taking pictures as soon as the hitch was in sight. It's a good thing no one was taking pictures of *me*—I was so excited that I was jumping up and down! By the time the hitch reached us, several other people had stopped, too, and we all climbed on for a ride.

I can't begin to tell you what a joyful experience this was. Thank you from the bottom of my heart for the most wonderful birthday I've ever had.
                                        —*Lois Newton*
                                        Scottsdale, Arizona

had been killed on the highway!

Gotta say, all things considered, we handled it pretty well. But we've all been very careful about watching our step this evening! We're spending the night at the state line between Colorado and Kansas.

May 19—Over the line and into Kansas, heading for the town of Manter. Vikki took Tim over to Tribune Senior Center to chum with residents. Also met with 35 Manter school kids and got our picture taken on the scales at the Bunge Grain Company.

Farmers working; huge tractors, disks, planters and irrigation machines are running constantly in surrounding wheat fields.

May 20—Reached Johnson City, 9 miles up the road. Saw a bull snake along the way, sunning himself on hot pavement. He ignored us and we ignored him.

Coachman, Ashley's remaining puppy (the one Vikki kept) caught a garter snake and tried to bring it into their motor home. (I bet you're thinking, enough about snakes, already!)

Manter Elementary School kids—42 of 'em and three teachers—followed us over to see the hitch. Local high schoolers also visited us. Reporter from Garden City interviewed David and Vikki.

May 21—Staying at Leonard Wilson's farm outside Ulysses, Kansas tonight. Leonard has one of the state's largest farms—3,600 acres of wheat and barley.

As we rested, David and Vikki got to

Hitch Takes Riders off the Beaten Path

THE HITCH'S cross-country journey reminds many of us of the trip made by our nation's pioneers. But our ride on the hitch came closer to that rugged adventure than most!

I set out with my secretaries, Tina and Chris, to catch up with the hitch at its planned destination near Eloy, Arizona. We expected it to be a fun day, but we had no idea what an adventure it would turn out to be.

We were driving down the freeway when we spotted the hitch just past Exit 198. We waved and moved on to an open space beside the freeway near Exit 199 so we could take some photos as the horses passed. Quite a few other people had the same idea, and before long a small crowd had gathered.

When the hitch reached us, it came off the freeway and onto the spot where we'd gathered. What a sight, seeing those beautiful horses walk into our midst! Some of the riders climbed down, and Chris and I climbed on for a ride. Tina would drive to the next stop to pick us up.

Just then, a highway patrolman noticed the crowd gathered at the side of the freeway and told David he was concerned it posed a traffic hazard. Soon four more patrol cars arrived. Most of the officers wanted to provide an escort along the freeway shoulder, since there were no frontage roads. But the first patrolman insisted the hitch proceed off the freeway—through the desert!

He helped David cut through a section of fence, and off we went! At first I was disappointed, but after spending some time behind those beautiful horses, I decided

ARIZONA ADVENTURE. At the request of state police (above), David made a real "cross country" detour while in Arizona. According to correspondent Edward Horkey, everyone aboard had a great time!

this was the *only* way to see the desert. It was easy to imagine what it felt like, smelled like and looked like a hundred years ago, when the pioneers first crossed this very land. We jostled over steep ridges, tilting and bumping along, enjoying every minute. Rabbits and hawks eyed us with suspicion, wondering what this strange sight could be.

After several miles, we pulled out of the desert and back to civilization near Exit 203. We were all tired, hungry and a little dusty, but no one was complaining. The scenery, conversation and camaraderie had been truly memorable.

The horses seemed happy to get back to their stalls, where they were watered, fed, and well cared for. Tina had brought along some apples, which the horses carefully took from our hands. David took off immediately to scout the next segment of the trip—*off* the interstate this time!

While our trip through the desert was totally unexpected, it was a priceless experience for which we're very grateful. I wouldn't trade it for *any* trip along the freeway! —*Edward Horkey Tempe, Arizona*

Photos: Edward Horkey

"OVER THE HILL" GANG, an organization of retired Arizona state troopers and other Department of Public Safety employees, treated the hitch crew to an old-fashioned barbecue.

"IN CASA GRANDE, Arizona we were guests at a huge pig roast hosted by Ed Short and the 'Over the Hill Gang'. Ex-Governor Rose Mofford was also there, and Roy and Bobbi Reiman attended, too. We appreciated the fine Southwestern hospitality!

"A few days later, after passing through Tucson, we stopped for the night out in the desert. The next morning, a high wind came up, a terrible wind, as I remember. It blew the tent covering the horses' stalls clear over the top of the semi, damaging it badly.

"David knew there was a tentmaker in Tucson, so we took the torn tent there. He worked until midnight to repair it.

"After that, the towns were few and far between in the desert. It felt good to have the workers on passing trains wave to us, and some even stopped for a few minutes to chat. They were some of the friendliest people we met.

"Some people drove their cars into the desert to find us, in places, I'm sure, they never would have otherwise driven their cars. Even in that desert, they would always find us. They didn't get lost. But then, neither did we!"

read our fan mail, including a nice note from Nancy Morgan, assistant to the director at the Stanton County Senior Center, which read, "What a treat for everyone—young and old alike. The waiting over the last few days only added to the pleasure of your arrival!"

May 22—Sunday, so we're still at the Wilson farm. Flies got to be a problem, so the crew had to put up "fly zappers" and fly tape. Pesky little critters. Maybe I should learn to use a flyswatter myself!

May 23—Police escorted us today on our 11-mile trek into Ulysses, Kansas, where the mayor presented David and Vikki with the key to the city. Seems like the whole town welcomed us as we rolled in.

Forty students from Big Bow School met us, too. We're staying at Black's Glass Company tonight.

May 24—Before we left Ulysses this morning, we visited with residents at the local senior center. Gave quite a few rides to the folks, including their director, LaVonne Michael.

Police blocked off traffic as we maneuvered through town on our way to the community of Hickok, 11 miles away.

May 25—This may be a small community, but we're seeing lots of people, some 700 today, with more than 200 hitch riders. Mennonite families in the area were especially excited at seeing us.

Huge wheat and alfalfa fields around ↷

Desert Adventure Kindles New Friendships

WE MET the hitch on a sparsely populated stretch between Casa Grande and Tucson, Arizona. Only half a dozen people were waiting for rides, and my husband knew how excited I was about the whole thing, so he didn't meet me at the first stop, enabling me to ride an extra mile.

Talk was nonstop with David, Vikki and the other riders, who represented not only Arizona, but also Minnesota, New Hampshire and one of the Dakotas.

When my husband finally claimed me, one of the other riders couldn't find hers, so we took her ahead to the crew's evening stop. It was such fun meeting new people and feeling that we all had a common bond!
—*Karen Nielsen*
Fountain Hills, Arizona

WAGONLOAD OF CAMARADERIE. Riders everywhere enjoyed visiting with passengers from other states.

here. Staying at the Mark McLain farm tonight. Got a note from Raymond and Ruth Junge, who said they traveled 290 miles to ride the hitch. "Your senior citizen project is marvelous," they wrote.

May 26—Despite on-again, off-again rain, about 250 people met hitch, including residents of Sublette Senior Center. One pickup point was the Hammond Hog Farm, which handles as many as 7,000 pigs. That ain't hogwash, as they say!

May 27—Highlight of day for me was Polaris & Country Feed dealer bringing out feed for us; he also dropped off an ATV for the crew to ride around in. Looks like fun—too bad I never learned to drive!

Staying at Junction of Hwys. 144 and 56, near old Santa Fe Trail.

May 28—Some 750 people were waiting for us as we rolled into Montezuma, Kansas. Close to 300 rode the hitch, including residents of Bethel Home. Many Mennonites live in this area. Staying at the Popy Farm overnight.

May 29—Sunday. A restful day in Montezuma. David and Vikki really liked the weekend here; plenty of family-oriented togetherness, they said. There are seven churches in this area.

About 98 percent of the families are Amish or Mennonite. While we were being photographed by visitors, crew was being honored at a dinner in the Community Building, hosted by Sherry Yost.

David was the guest speaker. A quartet entertained with songs like *Church in the Vale* and *How Great Thou Art*.

May 30—Memorial Day on the road, 12 miles to the town of Ensign, Kansas, where we're staying at an abandoned schoolhouse.

Lots of cars passed us, people on their way to family get-togethers, probably. Many stopped to ride and have their picture taken. I've got a feeling I'm going to be in a lot of family albums—I can just see future generations looking at the pictures and saying, "Who was that big brown horse in the family?"

May 31—At first, David stopped us at the lime rock quarry, 9 miles from last night's stop, but he was afraid we'd get stuck in the soft dirt of the open gravel pit with rain coming on. So we walked another 5 miles, into Dodge City, where we're spending the night at Cooper's Muffler Service.

June 1—Hundreds of people were

WIDE-OPEN SPACES and rugged terrain of the Southwest provided hitch crew with an interesting change of scenery…even if rattlesnakes were an occasional threat!

"SINCE LEAVING San Diego, we've traveled almost exclusively through mountains and desert. Of course, that means a real change in scenery from what we saw back east and in the Midwest—needless to say, you don't see many saguaro cactuses in Iowa!

"We've passed through areas that have been absolutely breathtaking, like Texas Canyon in Arizona, which has some of the most beautiful rock formations we've ever seen. Of course, we've also encountered some places you'd be tempted to call 'the middle of nowhere'. Many of the desert areas we traveled through were very sparsely populated; sometimes it seemed like the only signs of life you'd see for miles were range cattle and pronghorn antelope."

Close Encounter of the Surprising Kind

WE HAD been enjoying the articles about the hitch each time we received our new issue of *Reminisce*. Much to our surprise, on March 4, at 10:25 a.m., we saw the hitch on the frontage road alongside Interstate 10 west of Deming, New Mexico, just over the Continental Divide and about 70 miles east of the Arizona state line.

Farther down the highway, we saw the trucks at the hitch's camping spot. My husband and I and friends had been visiting other friends in Mesa, Arizona and were on our way to Austin, Texas to visit relatives.

We were thrilled and excited to see the hitch so far from our home in Grand Rapids, Michigan, and had fun telling our traveling companions all about it. Seeing those beautiful horses and the handsome young couple driving the wagon really made our day!
—*Robert and Thelma Shears, Grand Rapids, Michigan*

THE MANE EVENT

Hitch Provides Live History Lesson

ON FEBRUARY 2, while out for breakfast with guests from Wind Lake, Wisconsin, we noticed the hitch on the front page of the Tucson paper—which was a day old! They had been at the Tucson rodeo grounds the day before and were leaving this morning.

We literally gulped down our breakfast and were off to the rodeo grounds. They had left an hour before! We caught up with them on the road and passed them so we could videotape them coming down the street.

As they passed us, David yelled out, asking if anyone wanted a ride. Did we ever! Three of us rode with the hitch all the way to I-10 and Craycroft Road, their overnight stop. What a thrill!

I told my son about the hitch, and he and his wife and three children went over to I-10 the next morning to watch the horses being harnessed up. These children are home-schooled, so this day turned out to be an exciting field trip for them.

Because rain was threatening, many people left after taking pictures. So my son and his family got to ride all the way to the next night's stop at the Pima County Fairgrounds. Not only that, but David was given permission to cut the fence along the road so that he could get the hitch off the expressway and take us cross-country.

What a ride! The kids loved it. And what a history lesson, too! My son told the kids how America was settled by people coming from the east to the west by horse-drawn wagons. Of course, the wagons weren't nearly as "deluxe" as the one we were riding in!

My husband, Bob, and I went back to the Pima County Fairgrounds the next morning to see the horses again, take more photos and pet those velvet noses. It's surprising to see how many of the people around here have seen the hitch in other states. The Belgians must be the most photographed horses in the country—maybe the world! They are truly a sight to behold, and everyone on the crew is so gracious, kind and willing to talk and answer questions.

You are making millions of people happy across this country. Thank you so much for so abundantly sharing with others what the Lord has given you. You have blessed many!

P.S. Sad but glad the hitch is moving out of our reach—my house is getting mighty dusty as we chase them around the country!

—*Nancy Braun*
Tucson, Arizona

"NEAR BENSON, Arizona, as we were traveling through a desert area, I spotted what I thought was a short tree. As we drew closer, this 'tree' moved.

"It was a mule deer, and another one with beautiful antlers was standing next to him. As we got closer, they trotted off across the desert, but stopped again to watch us after they'd gone a little distance.

"In all, we've seen antelope, coyotes, jack rabbits, mule deer, owls and eagles along the way."

WINTER MONTHS proved a good time for desert travel, as conditions remained relatively mild and hitch "followed" spring northward.

waiting as we arrived at the Boot Hill Stage Stop in Dodge City—they were coming out of shops, the public library and homes to wave!

We were decked out in our show collars and had our manes and tails braided. (Mighty handsome, if I do say so myself.) Over 350 people, including residents of a number of senior centers here, rode the hitch, some groups entertaining us with songs.

Staying tonight in the parking lot of Manor of the Plains Nursing Center.

June 2—As we headed out of Dodge, were still busy giving rides, but once we hit the open country, we had the wagon all to ourselves.

Wheat fields around here are being worked by huge John Deere equipment. But the area needs rain; irrigation machines working overtime.

Bill Dean brought out chops and steaks for crew; no wonder they loved Dodge City!

June 3—Walked through town of Wright on way to Bellefont-Offerle area. On the way, we stopped at Spearville Senior Center, where the residents treated David and Vikki to snacks.

Sorry we couldn't stay in Spearville, but we needed to cover our usual day's miles. But David did hold a seminar and we gave rides.

June 4—Met up with group of 60 bikers pedaling from Los Angeles to Boston in a "Pedal For Power" bicycle tour for the League of American Wheelmen. They travel 80 to 100 miles a day ♂➔

—my buddies and I'd go through shoes and harnesses in a hurry at that pace!

Steve Zbornik's birthday today. Crew had a surprise for him, including a cake. Good thing he didn't ask me to help blow out the candles; there'd have been frosting all over the place!

June 5—Sunday at Midway Park in Kinsley. Nearly 500 people visited today. Humid, so the crew sprayed us down with the hose; they also used fly spray because those pesky flies are back.

There's a sign in the park, by the way, that Kinsley is the midway point in the USA—equally 1,561 miles from San Francisco and from New York. Put that in your geography book!

June 6—Crossed into Pawnee County today. Saw lots of cars from other states and from Canada; some stopped and people climbed aboard the wagon for a ride.

Wheat around here is starting to "golden up", as they say, and combines loaded on trailers are standing by to go into the fields.

June 7—Mighty quiet day today. Hardly any traffic on the road and few people as we walked 8 miles to Garfield, Kansas.

June 8—Walked 12 miles into Larned, Kansas, traveling the red brick road into town. (Found out they pave all their streets in town with red brick.)

Visited Meadowbrook Manor for seniors. Ron and Sharon Arnold of Larned told us about her father, Virgil Ault, who had seen us passing through Great Bend last fall on our way to San Diego.

In January, he suffered a stroke and could not make himself understood when he talked. But when Ron and Sharon brought him to see us, he gave a big smile and said clearly, "I remember them from Great Bend," and then, as Sharon said, "We couldn't understand the rest." Stuff like that kinda gets me choked up…

June 9—Another quiet day as we traveled 10 miles to Pawnee Rock. We're staying at Farmers Co-Op.

Rainy in the morning but cleared later, and some 200 people came out to see us.

June 10—Reached Dundee. TV Channel 2 of Great Bend came out and took pictures of people riding hitch. Passed

MANY FAMILIES came from far and wide to visit the hitch.

Horses Bring Smiles to Seniors

WE RODE the hitch wagon from the Sierra County Fairgrounds to the New Mexico Veterans' Center. When we arrived, most of the residents already were assembled outside, waiting to see the hitch. As David explained why the hitch was traveling across the country—Pulling for Seniors—many of the residents broke down and cried to think someone would do this for them.

Then David invited them to pet the horses. They moved forward slowly, some in wheelchairs, and reached out to touch the animals. Many probably grew up on farms where horses were used, and thought they would never get to touch horseflesh again in their lives. It was wonderful to see so many smiles on faces that had had no reason to smile recently.

—*Marilyn Bullard*
Truth or Consequences, New Mexico

Jack Sauder

"THE BIGGEST adjustment we've had to make is having the horses shod more frequently; their shoes are getting a lot more wear crossing this rugged desert landscape. We've also had to replace the rubber on our wagon wheels more often.

"Probably our biggest challenge has been to make sure that we always have plenty of water. The tank in the semi holds 200 gallons, but we've encountered one or two areas where we had to go a good distance between refills.

"One benefit of being out here in the Southwest is that the horses have had the opportunity to enjoy the wide-open spaces. On several occasions, ranchers have invited us to camp on their land, where the horses could be turned out in a good-sized corral. They made the most of the opportunity to kick up their heels!"

Hitch Helps Reunite Family

WHEN we rode the hitch outside Silver City, New Mexico on February 28, it was the "frosting" on the week-long birthday celebration for the "babies" of our family, Paul and Pauline, twins who turned 60 on February 25.

This was their first birthday together since their 18th, and the first time all of my brothers and sisters have been together since our mom's funeral in December of 1989.

Riding the hitch from our family were: Paul Ferrier and his wife, Wanda; Pauline (Ferrier) Yount Smidt and her husband, Ray; Margaret (Ferrier) Molton; Agnes (Ferrier) Crawford; and Doris Ferrier. Our brother Warren Ferrier and his wife, Helen, also attended our party but had to leave before getting a ride.

Thanks so much for the wonderful experience…and for bringing us all together again!

—*Agnes Crawford*
Redding, California

'The Hitch' Rolls Through the Valley

WHAT HAS a total of 24 legs and a combined weight of 12,650 pounds?

Would you believe a Belgian draft horse team, now muscling its way at a stately walk through the Ancient Cities area? The six-horse team, driven and trained by David and Vikki Helmuth and assisted by a crew of enthusiasts, is now 11 states into a cross-country journey, the goal of which is to benefit the senior citizens of America.

David Helmuth commented that the high point of the journey was his marriage to Vikki in Sugarcreek, Ohio on August 14 of last year.

"This trip has been our honeymoon," he said. Helmuth trained each of the hitch's horses and is a champion on the show circuit as is his wife and partner, Vikki.

As the horses were being fed in their stalls at Mountainair on Monday, they exhibited gentle, cheerful and curious dispositions. It was obvious to all that these gigantic creatures are the product of diligent, dedicated attention, worthy of top-drawer professionals.

Originally, draft horses were bred in Europe to work the fields. This team seemed just as happy pulling the wagon, custom-built in Bayfield, Ontario, as they would have been pulling a plow in the 19th century.

During rests, the Helmuths often visit senior citizen centers with one of the horses as a guest, and have so far offered free rides to almost 25,000 people.

On Wednesday afternoon, while the team rested near Willard, the Helmuths brought one of their horses to Arthur Park in Estancia.　*—Jack Pressly*
The Estancia Valley Citizen
April 7, 1994, Estancia, New Mexico

ROCKY ROAD! Hitch riders never seemed to mind if the trail got a bit bumpy as shown below. At right, Vikki, David and the Belgians enjoy a relaxing moment after day's travel.

many more combines getting ready for wheat harvest.

June 11—Busy day as the police escorted us into Great Bend. Visited with some 1,500 people today, including a couple who had gotten married in the afternoon and posed on the wagon for their wedding group photo!

Stopped at Cherry Village Nursing Center and Great Bend Manor, where David held seminars and gave rides to residents.

June 12—Sunday, so we're still at Brit Spaugh Park & Zoo, where we stayed last night. Just a lazy day, rolling in the grass and grazing in our lots.

This park is great for the crew also, with swimming pool, basketball courts, tennis courts and, of course, wildlife at the zoo.

There was a horseshoe tournament in the park. I didn't enter; didn't want to take advantage of amateurs.

June 13—Whew! Hot and humid this morning. Got up to 100° by noon, and very windy.

Gotta thank Janet Siebert of the Great Bend Chamber of Commerce for all of her help today. More snakes around here, they tell us. Yipes!

June 14—More hot, windy, sticky weather as we put in 10 more miles. Crew ate dinner at Great Food Restaurant, where we're staying tonight. So windy all day (up to 60 mph) that they decided not to put up our tent for the night.

June 15—Can't believe this weather—more of the same! Knocked off at 1 after going 12 miles to Junction 156 and County Road 10.

David's considering starting at 4 a.m. and traveling during the early-morning hours if this hot weather keeps up. He's got my vote!

June 16—Covered 8 miles, arriving at Villa Grace Center and Good Samaritan Home, where we gave rides. Cody really made out; he got to visit inside the centers...where they have air-conditioning!

June 17—Arrived in Ellsworth to a warm welcome after 13-mile walk. Lots of salespeople came out of shops and businesses to greet us.

In one passing car, the driver was ♂➜

using sign language to describe us to his passenger—must have been steering the car with his knees!

June 18—Despite humid 93° weather, more than 1,000 people visited us after we arrived in Brookville. Big doin's here this weekend—a flea market in the town park.

Crew ate dinner at restaurant in Brookville Hotel, best around this area for fried chicken, I hear.

June 19—Sunday. Nearly 800 people came around throughout the day, some as early as 8 this morning. Many, I found out, had reservations for that restaurant with the great fried chicken. (Don't know if I'd like that fowl taste!)

June 20—Not as humid and there's a breeze—pretty refreshing! On to Bavaria, 11 miles away.

Busy road, as trucks are hauling away wheat being harvested in adjoining fields. Beautiful corn and alfalfa fields here, too.

Seeing lots of out-of-state license plates, like Oklahoma, Texas and Louisiana. The Wilson Senior Center brought out a group of seniors for rides.

June 21—Pulled into Bicentennial Park in Salina—it was swamped with people waiting to greet us! Crowd totaled nearly 1,200; we gave nearly 400 rides.

Big media day, too. Salina radio station interviewed David, and reporters from Wichita and Topeka also came out, along with the *Salina Journal*, to do stories and take pictures.

Jack and Jean Dayhoff of Boulder, Colorado paid us a nice compliment: "It's a real honor for the seniors to have this hitch. You are all so cooperative with everybody."

June 22—Left Salina at 8, traveled 14 miles on old Hwy. 40 into Solomon, Kansas. Schowalter Villa of Hesston brought a group of seniors 50 miles in a van and met us on the road.

Dwight Lockhart of New Cambria

Where There's a Will...

WHEN WE LEFT Iowa to see the hitch in New Mexico, we had all the information we needed to find it—or so we thought!

We tried calling towns along the hitch's planned route, but no one we reached knew anything. One person even asked what a six-horse hitch was!

Then we decided to try the 900 number to find out the hitch's exact location. But we couldn't do that with our cellular phone, and couldn't find a single motel or pay phone that would let us call a 900 number. Disaster!

Finally my husband said, "Call the kids back home, have *them* call the 900 number and then call them back for the report." Good idea!

We finally caught up with the hitch and crew near Lordsburg, New Mexico. We were especially impressed with a young crewman who we're sure missed a hot supper so he could talk to us and show us the trailer. We had such a good time that we came back for another visit the next morning!   —*Gene and Ruth Ann Dischler*
Rockwell City, Iowa

"**YOU WON'T BELIEVE** what's coming up behind us!" certainly would have been an understandable reaction by the driver who happened to catch this glimpse of the hitch in his car's rearview mirror.

A Perfect Match... YOU COULD HAVE searched the world over and never found two people more suited for what they are doing than David and Vikki Helmuth. The kindness they show to seniors is outstanding!

—*Virginia Sauls*
Quemada, New Mexico

OSTRICH FARM in New Mexico had David and Vikki doing a double take as they approached while driving the hitch. The area is becoming increasingly popular for raising the giant birds.

"AS WE WERE traveling northeast along Highway 26 toward Hatch, New Mexico, we suddenly found ourselves wondering if we'd been out in the desert too long and were seeing a mirage.

"There was a good-sized ranch up ahead, and we expected to see cattle as we got a little closer. But instead, what we saw was an entire flock of ostriches!

"As it turned out, that whole area of southwestern New Mexico is becoming an ostrich 'hotbed'. The climate and conditions are similar to those of southern Africa, where ostriches come from originally, and quite a few ranchers are experimenting with raising them.

"We were invited to dinner at one of those ranches, and the owner explained that there's a growing market for ostrich meat and eggs. In fact, we had one couple take a ride with us who had come to New Mexico to buy a pair of ostriches for their farm in Illinois!"

SMILES ALL AROUND. Hitch visitors and riders were always willing to put on a happy face for photographers. Many said seeing the Belgians and riding in the wagon gave a real boost to their spirits!

also met us on road; said he had just come out of the hospital after a 3-month stay for pneumonia. "Calling the Hitch Hotline and reading *Reminisce* helped me pass the long days just lying there in bed," he said.

Stopped for the night alongside railroad tracks adjoining the town park. People visited us in the evening until 10; very interested in seeing us horses get new shoes.

June 23—On to Abilene, 10 miles away. Staying at beautiful fairgrounds here. David took Tim to Senior Citizens Center, Highland Care Home and Frontier Estates for retirees.

Tim wowed Dona Myers, the manager. David dared her to climb onto Tim's back. She did, her head nearly touching the lobby ceiling, to the delight of watching residents.

TV Channel 12 from Wichita interviewed David and took pictures. Our oldest rider today was 80-year-old Georgia Noble of Stockton.

June 24—Rolled into Chapman, covering 13 miles by 1 p.m. Still lots of riders along way, about 200.

Crew got chance to read their mail this evening. Got a nice note from Ray and Velva DeBaere of Marshall, Minnesota, who said they'd driven to Salina to help their son with the wheat harvest. "We can't believe we got the chance to ride with you folks," they wrote.

June 25—Staying put for a quiet weekend in the park at Chapman.

Crew is still catching up on notes from hitch riders, like Ann Smith of Abilene, who wrote, "A beautiful team. Thank you for doing this for the people of America's beautiful country. God bless you!"

June 26—Sunday, and still relaxing in Chapman. Before I forget, want to remember to talk to David about ↻

meeting Wilbur and Iona Schrock of Hesston. Wilbur's mother's maiden name is Helmuth; Iona thinks David and Wilbur might be related!

June 27—Very hot today as we traveled 10 miles on a hilly road leading into Junction City, Kansas. I haven't looked at a map recently, but I think I heard someone say we're about two-thirds of the way through the state.

David, Vikki and Cody visited Good Samaritan and Valley View Centers. David also did TV interviews with Channels 6 and 13.

June 28—Whew! A very hot 94° as we did 11 miles in an area of corn-fields and rolling hills. We're staying along the side of the road tonight in Geary County.

June 29—Another scorcher today. Felt great to get a soap bath this afternoon, with that refreshing cold water rinse.

Land around here is U.S. military installation so we're seeing lots of out-of-state car licenses. The army uses the land here for target practice; I sure hope their aim is good!

June 30—Pulled into Leonardville after a hot 14-mile trek. David, Vikki and Tim visited the senior center in Riley, and later the Leonardville Center.

Mr. and Mrs. Lloyd Kraft of Gridley dropped us a note, saying they and five of their grandchildren—Stacie, Kristiana, Angela, Heidi and Bryden—drove 140 miles to ride the hitch. We appreciate them thinking enough of us to do that!

"WHEN YOU consider that New Mexico is the country's fifth largest state, you begin to understand why it took us 9 full weeks to walk across it! It's an especially long trip when you take the diagonal route that we did.

"We crossed the state line from Arizona into New Mexico on Thursday, February 24. By maintaining our pace of 10 miles a day, 6 days a week, we finally made it into Texas on Saturday, April 30—but only *after* being pinned down by an unexpected 12-hour blizzard on our second-to-last day in the state!"

HEADING DOWN a desert highway, the hitch sets forth on another day's travels. Even in sparsely populated areas, people continued to show up along the route for a ride in the wagon.

SCENIC RIDE. Desert mountain ranges provided interesting change of scenery for the hitch crew.

"NOW THAT we've made it through the Manzano Mountains—where, by the way, we passed the highest elevation of our entire trip, 6,500 feet at Mountainair, New Mexico—it's all downhill from here!

"We'll be getting back to the flatlands soon, and to warm spring weather. It got a little cool in some of those mountain regions. But even if the weather wasn't always agreeable while we were in the mountains, the scenery more than made up for it!"

James Panetta

CHAPTER FIVE

THE HOME
STRETCH

Harry Hinkle

TIME OUT. Lunch break gives crew (above) a chance to "take five". Below, happy youngster enjoys getting personally acquainted with his favorite hitch horse, Firestone.

Marilyn Wilmes

July 1—Whew! Today was the hottest day of the trip—102° by noon. We took it slow and switched places so each of us pulled for a while, then rode in the semi.

Tonight at 7, a big storm came through with lightning and 70-mph winds. Vikki said afterward she felt like Dorothy in *The Wizard of Oz* because the wind actually lifted her into the air!

David had circled the motor vehicles around the tents to provide as much windbreak as possible. Still, the howling winds ripped tent panels and snapped poles and braces. It was pretty scary there for a while!

July 2—Still hot, but not as bad as yesterday. The crew hosed us down before we got rolling toward Blue Rapids because we were caked with mud from the storm last night.

Along the way, we stopped at Blue

Scott Anderson

OFFICIAL MEMORANDUM
STATE OF TEXAS
OFFICE OF THE GOVERNOR

Since our days as an independent republic, Texans have possessed a singular confidence in our ability to unite behind shared visions and to take decisive action to transform them into reality. Thus, the energies of millions of determined individualists are focused through the lens of consensus and concentrated with enough force to accomplish virtually anything we set out to do.

Texans share few convictions more universally than their resolve to help their older friends, neighbors and family members live with independence and dignity in their own homes for as long as possible. These seniors, after all, have given us everything: life, encouragement, guidance, discipline, personal and spiritual values and a distinctive cultural heritage.

Every Texan can name many other examples of people they know--family, friends, teachers, coworkers--who have saved their most remarkable accomplishments for late in life. This is the rule, not the exception, when people have the opportunity to maintain health, meaningful activity and social usefulness as long as realistically possible.

Quite often, discussions of aging focus on what we lose with the passage of time. To some extent, this simply acknowledges the truth of our own mortality. Even so, there are many good reasons to focus, whenever possible, on the mental and physical abilities we can maintain throughout life--and on the gifts time bestows only on those who have lived long.

Since April 13, 1993, the Country's Reminisce Hitch wagon and its team of champion Belgian draft horses, driven by David Helmuth, has headed west from Maine with the slogan "We're Pulling for Seniors." The year 1993 marked the 50th anniversary of the founding of the first senior center in the United States, and the hitch undertook its cross-country trip to celebrate and generate awareness for this very important milestone.

The hitch, with its crew of David and Vikki Helmuth and seven other people, will travel through Texas for approximately 10 days in late April and early May. They will be in Dalhart on May 2, 1994. It is fitting that on this date Texans of every age should be encouraged to direct a more generous share of their volunteer time, financial support, creative energy, and--most of all--their love and attention toward the prior generations to whom we owe so much.

Therefore, I, Ann W. Richards, Governor of Texas, do hereby proclaim Monday, May 2, 1994, as:

SENIOR CITIZENS DAY

in Texas and urge the appropriate recognition thereof.

In official recognition whereof, I hereby affix my signature

21st day of April, 19 94.

Governor of Texas

BY PROCLAMATION... In honor of the hitch's "We're Pulling for Seniors" theme, Texas Governor Ann Richards proclaimed May 2 "Senior Citizens Day" in the Lone Star State.

Going the Extra Mile...

Going the Extra Mile...IT IS SO refreshing to see folks having fun and at the same time considering the older folks, whose fun might be limited.

It seems even the horses have gotten into the spirit of bringing joy and remembrances to folks along the way—they step so proudly and look so alert!

The whole crew is to be congratulated on the good job they're doing despite the long hours required of them. —*Mr. and Mrs. J.G. Picone, Galveston, Texas*

"WE'RE SEEING and giving rides to quite a few 'snowbirds' on their way home back north— many of them are following the same route we are!

"We've had riders from as far away as Ontario and Alberta, Canada, many Midwestern states like Illinois, Iowa, Minnesota and Ohio, and even a busload of kids from a school in North Carolina!"

VISITING with hitch enthusiasts from around the country provided crew with variety each day. Below, David discusses route with state trooper.

Rapids Nursing Center. We also saw lots of fireworks booths being set up... looks like it'll be another bang-up Fourth of July.

July 3—Sunday. The Blue Rapids Fire Dept. will be holding a July Fourth pork roast in the park where we're staying, and they invited our crew.

Quite a few people from Topeka, Kansas City and Wichita visited today. A surprise visitor was Marge Grieves of Topeka, who rode the hitch with grandsons Ryan and Cole. She wrote a note saying, "This hitch is very special to me as my brother-in-law Roy Reiman is married to my baby sister, Bobbi. God bless you all!" This hitch gets to be more a family affair every day.

July 4—Highway officials asked David not to travel today because of ex- ↪

pected heavy holiday traffic. We didn't mind—it was a grand family picnic here, with families and grandmas and grandpas all sitting on lawn chairs while kids ran all around playing "fetch" with their dogs.

Tonight, what else? Big fireworks lit up the skies. (We horses can't "ooh" and "aah" the way people do, but we nickered our approval.)

July 5—Crossed the Big Blue River as we headed into Marysville along

"AFTER a full year on the road, we're still really enjoying ourselves. That says a lot for the crew and the horses, and especially about all the tremendous people we're meeting.

"That's what makes each day exciting and interesting —meeting new people all along the way who genuinely appreciate what we're doing for seniors. We've now walked over 2,800 miles and have given rides to nearly 30,000 people, and every day still seems like a new adventure!"

HELPING HAND. At left, Vikki gives a young horsewoman a hands-on lesson in braiding a mane, using a style known as the "Aberdeen Plait".

the famous Oregon Trail. Halfway there, David hosed us down because of the heat. That sure felt good!

David, Vikki and Cody visited the Nursing Center. And the Marysville Senior Center brought out a busload of seniors to ride the hitch. In turn, the center provided a noon meal for our crew.

July 6—Before we left Marysville, we stopped at the Valley Vet Center, where some friendly folks wanted to snap a photo of us.

Covered 12 miles into Home City. We're staying tonight at Blaine Smith's place.

July 7—Woke to a storm alert, which ended at 9:30 a.m. Today's weather was a bit rainy but much cooler and breezier. About 80 people rode on the wagon even though they had to use umbrellas.

July 8—Passed through Baileyville on way to Seneca, where we're camping tonight in a wheat field owned by Jim and Susie Enneking. We had a police escort through town.

Joyce Hotthers of Seneca jotted a kind note which read, "This hitch has

XIT RANCH
SITE OF HITCH STOPOVER HAS COLORFUL HISTORY

IN THE 1880s, the XIT Ranch was the largest range in the world under fence and it all lay in the Texas Panhandle. It covered portions of 10 counties: Dallam, Hartley, Oldham, Deaf Smith, Parmer, Castro, Bailey, Lamb, Cochran and Hockley, which contributed to the erroneous belief that XIT stands for "Ten in Texas".

The brand was actually designed to circumvent rustlers. It could be run with a straight iron and prevent rustlers from successfully burning over the XIT brand.

The ranch's 3 million acres sprawled over what is now Lubbock, Texas, northwest to the Oklahoma Panhandle, in an irregular strip that was roughly 30 miles wide.

The ranch resulted from the state's need to pay for a new state capitol. On November 9, 1881, the Texas state capitol was destroyed by fire. An agreement was reached with Charles B. and John V. Farwell of Chicago to build a $3 million capitol, payment for which was to be 3 million acres of Panhandle land.

The Farwell brothers borrowed money in England to develop the ranch, and in 1885, the first cattle—Texas longhorns—were moved onto the XIT. At one time, the XIT Ranch ran 150,000 head of cattle.

Eventually the cattle were sold off and the land was sold in small parcels, although 350,000 acres still remain. A reunion, featuring a rodeo and barbecue, to honor the cowhands who worked the XIT Ranch is now held every August in Dalhart, Texas.
—*Chamber of Commerce, Dalhart, Texas*

SIGN LANGUAGE. The message came through loud and clear: Folks were glad to see the hitch when it passed through their part of the country! Relief sculpture of hitch (above) was carved from a single piece of butternut wood by John Vanderstappen, who presented the piece to David and Vikki as a wedding gift.

"WE DECIDED that Oklahoma was the 'Lucky 13' of our trip—it was the 13th state we walked through, and we crossed it during the 13th month we'd been on the road. Even more incredible (and not that we're superstitious, of course), we came very close to leaving this 13th state on Friday the 13th!

"We crossed the state line from Oklahoma into Colorado on Thursday, May 12. After we set up camp in the town of Campo, Colorado that afternoon, a couple of folks who'd stopped to see us asked if we were planning to travel the next day. I said, 'Sure, unless the weather prevents it," then asked if there was some reason we shouldn't move on.

"They both grinned kind of sheepishly and one of them finally said, 'Well, tomorrow *is* Friday the 13th!' Then we all laughed and I told them that we couldn't let that stand in our way because the people in Springfield, Colorado were expecting us on Saturday, and they'd be mighty disappointed if we didn't come."

given so many senior citizens in care homes a bright day and brought back so many memories for them. Thanks for all you've done."

July 9—A quiet 12-mile trek today. Staying at a park at junction of Hwys. 36 and 75.

Pearl Dearing and Sheila Waltke of Colleyville, Texas said they crossed Texas to see us but got caught in sleet storms and had to keep going until they met up with us in Kansas.

July 10—Sunday. We're staying put in our stalls under beautiful shade trees. This evening, people from the Apostolic Christian Church brought out dinner for the crew.

July 11—Rode on Blue Star Memorial Highway into Sabetha. Seniors from Sabetha Manor came out to pet ♂

us and ride the wagon. Around noon, David stopped under a shade tree in town and cooled us with a water hose.

July 12—Crossed into Nebraska this morning and went through Dawson, town of "The Good Life". Lots of road construction along 10-mile stretch, but road crews were very cooperative.

July 13—Traveled north on I-75, passing corn, bean and hay fields. Saw lots of young people detasseling corn.

July 14—Rolled into Auburn, population 3,443, and lots of them came out to see us—about 1,000 during the day and another 300 in evening. Detoured

Hitch, Square Dancers in Tune with Simpler Times

OUR SQUARE DANCING group, the Fun Finders, had a wonderful time dancing and sharing our hobby with the hitch crew in Springfield, Colorado!

When that wonderful wagon rolled into town, we recalled the days we'd spent growing up on farms, when wagons and *real* horsepower were a way of life.

We visualized prairie schooners circling the campfires. We remembered stories of times when, after a long journey, a barn raising or a hard day's work in the fields, all the country folk gathered to share a bite to eat, sing a song, swap a tale or two…and dance. There was no generation gap then—children and old folks alike shared the joy of dancing as they bid the day's cares farewell. Tired kids fell asleep on the sidelines as the dancers waltzed or two-stepped the night away.

My mother always said she'd rather dance than eat; today, at 86, she still would. As we danced on cobblestone streets with David, Vikki and the crew, we could almost hear those fiddles of long ago.

Our dancers, like the hitch crew, help us step back into America's past and keep our traditions alive. Dancing with the crew was the opportunity of a lifetime, an experience we'll never forget.—*Marjorie Swearingen Colorado Springs, Colorado*

HITCH HOEDOWN. The Fun Finders square dance troupe (shown at left and above right) performed for the hitch when it passed through their state, and David, Vikki and the crew joined in on the fun.

MAINE TO CALIFORNIA!

Bobby   Jack   Stoney   Eddie

Dean Edwards

over to Good Samaritan Center to give residents there rides. Staying in barns at Auburn Fairgrounds.

July 15—Swung over to Brownville, about 11 miles east, and crossed the Little Nemaha River. Town sign says 148 people live here. Also spotted a Lewis & Clark Trail marker along our route. Wonder if *anybody* lived here when they came through.

July 16—Had a full menu of weather early this morning—rain, small hail, lightning and wind. Still, we managed to get under way about 8 o'clock.

Crossed the Missouri River bridge into the "Show Me" state of Missouri. Staying tonight at fairgrounds in the town of Rock Port, which has 1,400 people. Town's slogan is "Proud Past and a Bold Future".

July 17—Sunday. We've spent a lazy day in the fairgrounds barns. Lots of

"WHILE we were heading east along the shoulder of Highway 160 in Colorado, we suddenly heard something we all recognized immediately—anyone who's ever seen a rattlesnake in a movie or on TV would know that sound immediately!

"Just as I heard the rattle, Bobby—who was at the right wheel position—suddenly lunged forward. I looked down and saw a rattler recoiling itself just a few feet off the shoulder of the road—it apparently had struck at us but missed as we passed by!

"I 'whoa-ed' the hitch just a little ways beyond, and we checked to make doubly sure Bobby hadn't been struck. Luckily, he hadn't—the snake was apparently too far off the road to have reached him, but the incident really put all of us on our guard.

"Before we reached our stopover location that day, we saw *six more rattlers*, two live ones and four that had been killed on the highway. Evidently, the warm weather had brought them out of hiding and we just happened to be passing by as they were on the move.

"I don't have to tell you, we were extra careful when we set up camp that afternoon!"

Dean Edwards

The Reiman Hitch Arrives in Baca County

EXCITEMENT filled the air as the Reiman Hitch made its entrance into the first town in the state of Colorado on Thursday, May 12. In conjunction with the residents of Campo, the Campo High School Band welcomed the hitch by playing several songs while riding in a band wagon built by Mr. James Nidey. Two Percheron horses owned by Mr. Delbert Jones of La Junta, Colorado pulled the Campo Band Wagon.

The hitch was led to the school where several area schools were participating in a junior high track meet. Camp was set up by the hitch crew at the Campo Community Building. That evening approximately 150 people enjoyed a potluck dinner with the hitch crew.

Saturday, the hitch was escorted into Springfield by Sheriff Goff, dressed in his old cavalry outfit and riding a horse. He was accompanied by Kaylea Means and Rebecca Rutherford.

The town had a fair-like atmosphere with music in the air—the kitchen band and the Springfield Junior High Band performed for the crowd's entertainment.

Later in the day, Vikki Helmuth gave rides to those wishing the experience of riding in a horse-drawn wagon. Two of the three spare horses pulled this wagon.

Around 3 p.m., the hitch made its way to the nursing home; while there, Annie Dukes, the administrator of the hospital, and David Helmuth did a live interview about the hitch on KVAY.

Then the horses made their way to Springfield West housing for the residents there to enjoy seeing the horses. In the meantime, the Fun Finders square dancing group from Colorado Springs entertained the crowd back at the park. After their presentation, the crowd was encouraged to participate with the Fun Finders; many of the audience plus David Helmuth joined in the dancing.

There were several visitors in town, some of them coming after they had called the 900 number to find out when the hitch would be in Springfield. Everyone enjoyed the horses and the activities planned by the members of the Springfield Chamber.

Monday dawned with blowing wind and partly cloudy skies. Many well-wishers came to say good-bye to the hitch. The horses pranced with pride as they pulled the wagon loaded with enthusiastic riders out of the parking lot.

Monday night the hitch set up in Vilas and Tuesday night Walsh entertained them. Wednesday will be our last day to have the hitch in our wonderful state before they head into Kansas.

We in Baca County wish the team a safe trip as they continue their travels!

—*The Baca Weekly*
Springfield, Colorado, May 18, 1994

people came out to see us today.

July 18—David decided to spend another day here in Rock Port since it's still hot and humid. We horses got hosed down twice to keep us cool.

Overheard the crew talking about the countdown they're starting of the remaining days. I'll let them do that—without any fingers or toes to count on, it's hard for me to keep track!

July 19—Pulled into Tarkio amid more hot, humid weather. Crew even hosed down the semi trailer; they must think the heat will peel the paint right off it!

Seniors from Pleasant View Center in Rock Port followed us here to get their rides on the hitch.

In the evening, members of Tarkio's Chamber of Commerce treated crew to watermelon. Wouldn't mind chomping on a piece myself.

July 20—Crossed the Tarkio River today on our 13-mile trek along Hwy. 136. Did a lot of visiting, giving rides to residents of the Bethesda Care Center, Northern Manor and the Convalescent Center.

July 21—Rolled along on Hwy. 136, flanked by corn and bean fields, arriving in Burlington Junction at noon. It's a lively little town of 634 people. As we entered town, people poured out of shops and stores to say "Welcome"!

July 22—As we headed north on I-71, we saw cattle grazing in beautiful green pastures.

A breezy day as we traveled 10 miles, passing through Clearmont—really small, just 175 people living there—and into Braddyville right on the Iowa state line. Stopped at senior center there.

July 23—We crossed into Iowa this ♂↱

James Panetta

Jim Hommel

Phyllis Eckert

morning. We're in the home stretch now, and I can smell the finish line.

Vikki says she saw our ears perk up as we passed the beautiful border sign that read "Iowa—Come Explore the Heartland". Thanks, we will!

Passed through Shambaugh and on to Clarinda, where a fellow riding a half Percheron/half mule behind the hitch helped direct traffic. Gave rides to residents of Goldenrod Manor, Regency Retirement Residence and Bethesda Care Center.

July 24—Sunday. A lovely, lazy day in Clarinda. Some 400 people visited us in our stalls throughout the day.

David met with Dave McNichols from the Centerville Chamber of Commerce to talk about the big doin's planned when we get to Centerville. Got me thinking again about the end of our trip...starting to feel a little sad to realize it's ending.

July 25—Another lazy day in Clarinda. David and Vikki went home to Nashua to prepare for our homecoming in a few weeks. They put our nameplates on the stalls in the barn that will be our home. Lots to think about.

July 26—Well, we made our last turn east, heading out on Hwy. 2 for the final leg of our historic journey. Traveled 9 miles to New Market, a small but very friendly community. Mayor Loren Dailey welcomed us officially.

July 27—Arrived in Bedford, where hundreds of people were waiting for rides on the wagon.

The oldest rider today was 101-year-old Ralph Silver. He said he remembers riding across America in a covered wagon and recalls when Indians stopped ↷

Just Passin' By... WE'D SPENT THE morning picking gooseberries. When we came up out of the creek banks to stow our brimming pails in the pickup, what did we see but six beautiful Belgians pulling the hitch right in front of us!

Later, we learned the hitch parked for the night only 3 miles from our farm. We put off the job of stemming gooseberries and hurriedly piled into the pickup to see those horses and drivers again.

We were impressed with how well the horses were cared for, enjoyed visiting with friends who'd come to see the animals, and learned one horse had been taken into the local nursing home so residents could see and touch him.

Thanks for brightening our gooseberry-picking day!

—*Ina Hurley*
Kanopolis, Kansas

"WHILE WE'VE BEEN crossing the Kansas plains, temperatures have been in the upper 90s, with very high humidity.

"After just a couple of days of this, we decided to start leaving earlier in the morning to try to 'beat the heat'. Some mornings we'd be on the road before 7, and this worked out well because we'd get to our campsite well before noon—usually the hottest part of the day.

"On most days the horses were already unhitched and cooling off in the shade under the awning by 12."

Ada Miller

Elaine Pitts

Julie Barrette

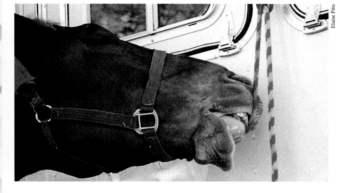

Tina Thompson

WE WERE TEMPTED to ask, "Can you 'spot' the Dalmatians among all of the horses on these two pages?" But we decided just to let the Belgians, like the one shown at bottom right, have the last laugh.

Julie Barrette

Ethelene Henzy

Ellen Morin

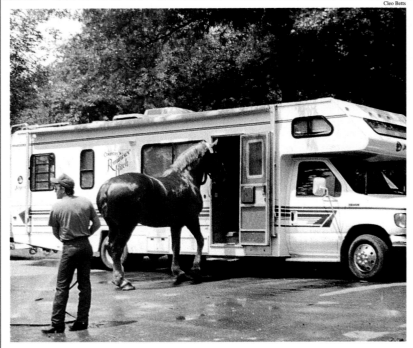
Cleo Betts

WHOA! One of the Belgians seems to have taken a wrong turn on the way to his stall!

The Horses Are Coming!

CHRISTOPHER and Amanda Hagan, ages 7 and 10, didn't seem to care that they were jumping around in the middle of Hwy. 40 just east of Abilene.

All the Hagan children cared about—along with about 35 other people waiting along the roadside, including their mother, Debbie—was that the horses were coming.

First spotted about a half mile away, a team of six Belgian draft horses could be seen sauntering down the highway, dwarfing the hitched wagon they pulled.

"This is one of those once-in-a-lifetime things," said Debbie Hagan as the group eagerly inched its way toward the approaching horses and wagon. "It's not going to be too often that the kids get to see animals this magnificent and impressive."

—Brian James, The Topeka Capital-Journal
Topeka, Kansas, June 25, 1994

them and wanted to trade spoiled fish for flour. When Ralph refused, one Indian poked him in the nose and took his flour anyway.

July 28—Before leaving town, we visited Bedford Manor Nursing Home. Then we traveled 12 miles to the farm owned by Dale, Wayne, Janet and Dave Danielski, where we're staying tonight. Understand their farm is a no-till research and demonstration facility.

July 29—Traffic was busy on the highway as we covered 12 more miles. Lots of people along the way, many with Texas and even Florida license plates on their cars, are telling us they're planning to be in Centerville for the wind-up ceremonies.

July 30—Another 10 miles on a curvy and hilly road, and we're in the town of Mt. Ayr. Saw a number of signs on the road that read "Welcome *Reminisce Hitch*" and "Congratulations, *Reminisce Hitch*". Nice to be appreciated. Visited with residents of Clearview Nursing Home.

July 31—Spending Sunday in Mt. Ayr. Good thing, because lots of people wanted a ride. Some 150 people visited us in the morning, another 500 this afternoon and 350 in the evening.

Aug. 1—Staying here another day to give people in Mt. Ayr every opportunity to see us before we push on to our big finish in Centerville. And, boy, ♂➤

Hitch Wagon Hits Town

LESS than a hundred yards away, a yellow spray plane flitted and droned back and forth over a farm field like an oversized, overworked bumblebee. But it didn't merit more than a quick glance from the clusters of men, women and kids scattered along Hwy. 160.

Their eyes were fixed on something far more fascinating: six magnificently muscled Belgian draft horses pulling a bright red old-fashioned wagon with gold-spoked wheels. Harness leather squeaked and chains jangled as the hitch jostled along on its continental crossing, evoking memories of long-ago journeys in the days when horses and wagons were a common sight on the Plains.

Lucky onlookers got to share in the experience, riding along with David and Vikki Helmuth for a mile or two.

"It's kind of bumpy…but it's fun, especially when they get to trotting a little," said David Unruh, who brought his young family to experience their first-ever horse-drawn wagon ride.

"Our oldest girl (Erica, age 3), that's all she could think about the last 2 days …that she was bigger now and she could ride with the horses," Unruh said. Erica

and others in the area had seen the hitch last December, when the horses and wagon passed through aboard transport trucks.

David Helmuth was reveling in the lush green countryside, which had been an austere brown when the hitch last passed through.

Truck drivers and even train engineers have stopped their vehicles to visit with members of the hitch and snap a few photographs. Maurice Norton of Liberal was one of those shadowing the hitch with a camera as it passed through Hickok, just east of Ulysses in the southwest corner of Kansas.

"I have kind of a passion for this," he said. "I try to take pretty pictures, and I've been waiting for them to come back through." He liked his subject matter, clicking off frame after frame, getting the team and wagon from every angle.

The closest the hitch has come to a mishap was when a rattlesnake—one of several spotted during the desert portion of the crossing—struck at one of the horses but missed.

—Mike Berry, The Wichita Eagle
Wichita, Kansas, May 25, 1994

"I HAVE NEVER in all my life been through a storm like the one that blasted through Blue Rapids, Kansas on the evening of Friday, July 1! We sure found out for ourselves that what they say about Kansas weather is true.

"I was making a presentation to a good-sized group of people when I got word that severe storm warnings had been issued. I told the folks that they'd better head for shelter.

"We could see the storm building up to the north. Less than 45 minutes later, it hit us. We already had the horses' stalls set up under the awning, and all of us worked like crazy to get the side panels up all the way around, converting the horses' area into a fully enclosed tent.

"Then we circled the rest of the vehicles around the outside of the tent to provide as much windbreak as possible. When the wind hit, it was really howling!

"Vikki, her mom, Marlene, our four crew members and I were all under the tent at different spots, each hanging on to a tent pole and struggling to hold it down. The awning and side panels were snapping and popping—it sounded like gunfire! We could hear the rain hammering like hail on the vehicles.

"At one point, we saw that the wind was causing the tent's main rafter to bow in almost 3 feet! I was afraid it was going to bend and snap in half, so I climbed up on Magic and braced it with my arms. I was really praying hard then.

"We were all getting scared and I knew everyone wanted to take shelter, but we all hung in there. All of the horses stayed pretty calm, but we weren't. The storm lasted an hour and 10 minutes.

"The next morning, we heard that the wind gusts had exceeded 85 miles an hour, and we didn't have any trouble believing it—the wind blew over our harness rack, and we found pieces of harness scattered all over the big park where we were camping."

HOME, SWEET HOME. Erecting the tent over the horses' stalls was a daily task for the crew. Huge awning was nearly destroyed by storm near Blue Rapids, Kansas.

are they taking advantage of it—about 600 came out to see us at the sale barn, another 450 in the evening.

Aug. 2—On the way out of town this morning, stopped at Mt. Ayr Health Center to say "hi" to residents and give many of them rides.

Lots of visitors again today—450 during the day, and nearly 500 in the evening before it started to rain. We put in 11 miles to get to Kellerton, where we're going to camp for the night at the County Highway Department barn.

Aug. 3—Crossed over I-35, our last interstate of the trip, as we moved 11 miles to the Decatur County line.

Lots of memories of all the highways and byways we've traveled the last 16 months. Gotta tell you, the police in Mt. Ayr were among the nicest we've met up with on this entire trip. If I wore a hat, I'd tip it to 'em.

Saw cars with license plates from Missouri, Minnesota, Illinois and even Maryland along the route. Staying tonight at the Texaco station owned by Don Richards.

Aug. 4—We're in Leon after a nice

EARLY START. Hot weather encountered while crossing the Great Plains necessitated some sunrise departures.

Ruby Brown

PLEASE SIGN HERE! David and Vikki happily autographed programs, photos and magazines for hundreds of visitors.

"PASSING BACK THROUGH those communities we drove through last fall on our way to San Diego has been very nice—we've enjoyed the spring and summer weather, and visiting again with many of the same folks we met last year when we were all bundled up against the cold!

"We all remembered the sleet storm we ran into in Auburn, Nebraska the night before Thanksgiving, and the blustery days in northwest Missouri and southwest Iowa just prior to that. Needless to say, it was nice to be driving the hitch in our shirtsleeves this time around!"

Signature Tells All...

I AM A VERY HAPPY 83-year-old who has been watching the travels of the wonderful hitch for the past year and a half. What a thrill it was to be able to see them when they came to Auburn, Nebraska!

I had showed my souvenir program and video to my friend, Eunice Naviaux of Omaha, when I visited her last fall, and she said we'd go see them when they came back to Auburn.

Sure enough, I returned to Nebraska and we traveled to Auburn and Brownville and found the hitch! David and Vikki were both very gracious and I'll never forget them.

David noticed I had my camera and he took a couple of pictures of me with Vikki and Stoney. What a thrill!

Next morning I rode the wagon for the first mile out of Auburn. Then Eunice and I passed the hitch and drove on to Brownville, where we watched the crew set up camp. We hadn't realized before what a big undertaking that must have been every day!

After the hitch reached Brownville, Eunice asked David to autograph her program. She has been teaching handwriting analysis classes for several years so she was able to tell him all the nice things she found out about him through his writing. She finished by saying, "But it also looks like you're stubborn!" He had a good laugh but didn't deny it, and Vikki added, "You got that right!"

I'm delighted Eunice and I got to spend so much time with the hitch—what a wonderful way to help seniors have fun!
—*Louise Blowers, Ridgecrest, California*

Linda Cookson

Rita Boyd

"WE'VE BEEN on the road for about 15 months now, and as we look ahead to the end of the trip, all of us are feeling pretty excited but also a little sad.

"Even though the trip hasn't ended yet, we're already starting to reminisce about the people we've met and the things we've seen—as we sit around talking after dinner each evening, one of us will usually say something like, 'Remember that guy back in Pennsylvania?' or 'Remember that one lady at the senior center in Indiana who hadn't been out of her room for 3 years?'

"There's no question about it; this has definitely been a once-in-a-lifetime experience, one that none of us will ever forget."

warm day in the 80s. Visited a number of senior centers along the way—the Leon Senior Center, the Community Center and Westview Acres. Also, Osceola Care Center bused some residents down to see us.

Gotta say "thank you" to Mrs. Webster for arranging our welcome in the town square. She certainly alerted lots of people to our coming—300 visited in the morning, 400 in the afternoon and 300 more in the evening. Crew was treated to dinner by people from the local Citizens Bank.

Aug. 5—Cool and breezy as we covered 11 miles to junction of Hwys. 2 and 65 on the Wayne County line. Didn't even break a sweat.

Aug. 6—More delightful, cool weather as we trotted 12 miles to Corydon. Heard that the outlaw Jesse James got here ahead of us—way back in 1871—because he had plans to rob the local bank. Wonder who his "getaway horse" was…

Aug. 7—Sunday. We're staying at the fairgrounds here in Corydon. Heard that we're going to get an extra day off ↻

RIDIN' HIGH. Youngster from Camp Mitchell, sponsored by the Southwest Kansas Association for the Visually Impaired, enjoys his "high altitude" seat atop Cody.

tomorrow before we travel to Centerville.

Saw about 700 people today. The crew's very busy cleaning all the equipment. It's nice to relax and watch *them* work! All we have to do is look pretty.

Aug. 8—Yep. I heard right—we've got an extra day to relax here in Corydon.

Aug. 9—Spent much of the morning getting gussied up for the big parade in Corydon this afternoon. Our manes and tails are braided; we're get-

Missourian Shares Memories

PICTURES OF FIRESTONE in your magazines remind me of a horse named Charlie we had when I was a child. He was a beautiful animal, very spirited and always pleasant to work with. My father kept about 14 horses for working our 400 acres, and sometimes we had a pair of good but "ornery" mules as well.

I myself kept two teams until about 1952, and especially enjoyed working with a team of well-trained black mares. Many times I used them to pull out stuck loads that other teams had given up on.

I finally sold them because I just couldn't work them every day, which is necessary to maintain good communications between man and animal. Your hitch has brought back many pleasant memories! —*Harry Breerman, Tarkio, Missouri*

Photos: Rick Van Etten

LOOKING BACK..."Early horsepower" demonstrations of various farming methods, such as plowing (above and at right) and mowing hay (below), were staged at the Faris Farm just west of Centerville, Iowa in conjunction with the hitch's return. Area farmers brought out their favorite teams and antique equipment to give visitors a firsthand look at how things were done in the days before tractors. The demonstrations drew lots of interested spectators, including many who enjoyed reminiscing about "the good ol' days".

Dave Herrewig

It's All in the Name...ALL

MY LIFE (I'm 78 years old) I'd heard of the Iowa town named Clarinda. I've met many people from Iowa and have asked them about it, but none of them had ever heard of the town.

Then, as I was reading the story of the cross-country journey made by the hitch, I saw "Clarinda" right in *Reminisce* magazine! So there really is such a place, just like my mother told me!

You see, Clarinda, Iowa was named for my great-great-grandmother, who was (according to my mother) the first female child born to the settlers in that area. Her name was Calista-Clarinda—how could anyone forget that!

If I were a bit younger, I'd make the trip to Iowa to meet up with the hitch. Who knows, I might even discover some long-lost relatives! —*Margaret Sams Chicago Park, California*

146

THE MANE EVENT

GIFTS GALORE! Vikki and David received hundreds of presents from well-wishers along the hitch route, including everything from the handcrafted oak shelf shown at left to the Belgian Christmas wreath below. The Helmuths extend a hearty "thank you" to everyone for their generosity!

Susan Feasel

Loren Schlipf

"ON THURSDAY evening, August 11, our crew had its last meal together as a team. Relatives and friends of crew members were there, too. My aunt and uncle, Marge and Roy Bridges, came all the way from Maysville, Kentucky to see us. I've not seen them since our wedding a year ago. Mom's sister, Margie, and my father also came from Ohio.

"It was a wonderful experience for all of us to have that one last meal as a crew, because we'll probably never be that way again. We've lived on the road as one great family, sharing thoughts and sorrows and memories. We've been like brothers and sisters to each other.

"It was just a great evening, and a very fitting way to conclude our trip. And I have to admit, there were a few tears, too!"

ting new shoes and we'll be wearing our show collars. How's that for dressing formal?

Lots and lots of excited people lined parade route. Various hitches, some single driven, others in pairs, also took part, plus a number of marching bands from various town organizations. Afterward, public was invited to fairgrounds for free food. Must have been more than 1,000 people there.

Aug. 10—Left at 8 o'clock, and as we traveled through town we saw a sign identifying the bank that Jesse James robbed back in 1871. Tough way to make a living; he should have tried honest work like ours!

Started to rain while we were on the road. Riders used umbrellas; said they were determined to ride, rain or shine.

Aug. 11—Final day of travel. Covered nearly 12 miles, reaching Appanoose County. Hard to believe this unique adventure is coming to an end. No more getting up in the morning and traveling to a new town…I think I'm gonna miss all that.

Today so many people wanted to get on the hitch we changed riders every half mile, making it possible for everyone to get their memorable ride. Spent the rest of the day getting spiffed up for tomorrow.

Staying at McClintock's Vet Clinic just outside Centerville tonight. Crew shared their last dinner of the trip.

Tomorrow, we return to the Golden Horseshoe!

Aug. 12—Boy, talk about a day filled with excitement! Lots of people visited us throughout the day at the vet's barn, then about mid-afternoon the crew began grooming and harnessing us for our final walk into town.

At 4, we left the vet's with a load of riders and walked about a mile to the Centerville Law Center. There we picked up our last load of riders, including Mayor Bucky Henderson and Roy and Bobbi Reiman, for the final walk into town.

The Centerville High School Band preceded us into the town square, playing the theme from *The Magnificent* ↻

We Did It!

Sixteen months after beginning its epic cross-country journey, *Country's Reminisce Hitch* completed the 3,800-mile trip by returning to the "Golden Horseshoe"!

"GIVE 'EM a little room, please—these horses want to *see* that horseshoe! They've walked a long, *long* way to get here!"

These were the words jokingly called out to the excited crowd by hitch driver David Helmuth on Friday afternoon, Aug. 12, as he "whoa'ed" the six champion Belgians of *Country's Reminisce Hitch* and faced them right at the "Golden Horseshoe" in Centerville, Iowa's town square.

The enthusiastic onlookers, numbering around 5,000 individuals and representing at least 20 states (including the four corners of the country—Maine, California, Florida and Washington) responded with laughter and a rousing cheer.

David handed the lines to his wife, Vikki, stood up in the wagon seat, swung his hat overhead and let out a loud yell. Then he bowed to the crowd as they applauded.

"We're absolutely delighted to be here," David said. "I have to admit there were some days when we wondered if we'd actually make it. But these horses *proved* they're the champions we've said they were, and with your support and the grace of God, we did it!"

The return to the "Golden Horseshoe" on Aug. 12 marked the end of the coast-to-coast trip that began almost exactly *16 months* earlier—on April 13, 1993—in Kennebunkport, Maine. The hitch walked all the way across New England, Pennsylvania, Ohio, Indiana and Illinois before last fall's cold, rainy weather finally forced the crew to call a halt in Centerville, Iowa.

To mark the official stopping point, a Golden Horseshoe was implanted in Centerville's town square. Then the horses were trucked to San Diego, California (originally planned as the hitch's final destination), where they splashed

5,000 PEOPLE from 20 states crowded the town square in sunny Centerville, Iowa to welcome the hitch upon its return to the "Golden Horseshoe" at the conclusion of 16-month journey.

in the Pacific before heading back east.

When the champion Belgians got back to Centerville on Aug. 12, it culminated the *first-ever* cross-country trip completed by a six-horse hitch.

Divine Intervention?

The afternoon of their return to Centerville was sunny and hot, providing those hitch enthusiasts who crowded the

town square with an ideal opportunity to "welcome home" the Belgians and crew. Interestingly, however, most of the rest of Iowa experienced heavy rain throughout the day.

"On our way there that day, we drove through rain coming down so hard the wipers couldn't keep the windshield clear," reported publisher Roy

ROY AND BOBBI REIMAN joined the Helmuths on the wagon as David addressed the crowd.

Reiman, who, with his wife, Bobbi, traveled to Centerville to join in the homecoming celebration.

"We were both really concerned that the final lap of the trip that afternoon might have to be postponed because of the weather. But, almost miraculously, the skies cleared and the sun came out when we were less than 40 miles from Centerville. It seems God smiled on this hitch all along the way, and did so again right to the very end of this trip."

After Roy and several Centerville dignitaries appeared on stage to welcome the hitch home, a second Golden Horseshoe was implanted in the pavement.

The first horseshoe placed last October faces west, indicating the East Coast-to-Centerville portion of the trek, while the second one faces east, reflecting the return from the West Coast portion of the trip. The Golden Horseshoes are reminiscent of the famous "Golden Spike" driven to mark the completion of the first transcontinental railroad in 1869.

Home to "Paradise"

After the ceremony at the town square, David and Vikki drove the hitch to the Appanoose County Fairgrounds in Centerville, where they greeted well-wishers, celebrated their first wedding anniversary on Aug. 14 and gave a driving demonstration each evening through Aug. 17.

The horses spent the following weekend making appearances at the Iowa State Fair in Des Moines, then headed home for some well-deserved rest in the pasture at David and Vikki's farm, "Paradise Acres", at Nashua, Iowa.

Nashua is a charming and famous little town—it's the home of "The Little Brown Church in the Vale". Many of you may remember the song that was written about that tiny church, which is the site of over 700 weddings a year and is now visited by more than 150,000 people annually.

So, if and when you visit the hitch at Paradise Acres on the west edge of Nashua, you can visit this famous little church on the east side of town. Likewise, those who come to see the church will now have something else to see in this community—six beautiful Belgians who walked across America!

> *"These horses proved they're the champions we've said they were..."*

Seven—only in our case, it was the Magnificent Six! Nearly 5,000 people were waiting for us as David drove us up to the Golden Horseshoe, and the cheering and applause were tremendous!

After we arrived, David thanked everyone for their support during the past year and a half, then he introduced each of us. Roy Reiman also thanked everyone, and some of the Centerville dignitaries made speeches, too. It was quite an occasion!

After they implanted another one of *my* golden horseshoes in the pavement, facing the one that was implanted last October, David drove us on out to the Appanoose County Fairgrounds, where we'll be staying for the next 5 nights. More big doings are planned, but I for one plan to start sleeping late these next few mornings!

Our hitch has now ended its cross-country odyssey. On behalf of my buddies—Bobby, Cody, Chip, J.R., Eddie, Magic, Spike, Stoney, Tim—and the crew, I'd like to say "thank you" to the thousands of friendly, generous and down-to-earth people whom we've met along the way.

You are all the backbone of this great land. Our adventure has provided us with the opportunity to see the very finest part of America—*its people*—and for that, we're truly thankful.

THE MANE EVENT

Firestone

Rick Van Etten

All Aboard...
One Last Time!

RIDING THE HITCH for the final mile to the Golden Horseshoe in the Centerville town square were "Senior Queen" Edna Burgher, 97; 2-year-old twins Ashley and Megan Sharp, acommpanied by their parents, Joe and Jackie Sharp, and 2-month-old brother, Spencer; Centerville Mayor Marlin "Bucky" Henderson; John Broshar of the Appanoose County Board of Supervisors; Larry Wilkinson of the Centerville Chamber of Commerce; and Roy and Bobbi Reiman.

Dave Herrewig

TRAIL'S END. David Helmuth and Roy Reiman implanted the second horseshoe to signify completion of trip.

Long-Distance Accolades

(The following arrived by fax at Reiman Publications on the evening of Friday, August 12.)

CONGRATULATIONS! You made it! We have followed you all the way by the 900 Hotline number and have the videotape and souvenir program as well.

We were particularly interested in your celebration in Centerville, Iowa as we lived in Centerville, Washington for 20 years. Both of us were raised on farms and my husband, Vern, began driving a team at a very young age. We both are very fond of horses and the six-horse hitch is "the top of the line" for us.

I was born and raised in Ohio just a short distance from Sugarcreek, where David and Vikki were married. We wished mightily that we could be there, but the distance was too great.

We especially admire what you have done to pull the country closer together, and the boost you have given senior citizens cannot be measured. Your determination to see the gigantic project to its end is very admirable.

We know it took a lot of dedication on the part of all the participants, as well as the horses. Again, we congratulate and praise your tremendous efforts!　　—*Vern and Edie Hinshaw*
Yamhill, Oregon

Roster of Riders

Here they are! Listed below and on the following pages are the names of many of the people—representing *all 50 states*—who shared in the historic cross-country journey made by *Country's Reminisce Hitch.*

Although we estimate nearly *50,000* people rode with the hitch during its 16-month trek, the following list totals about 12,000 names. This is because we included only those folks whose names and hometowns we were able to verify from the rider-signed release forms or from letters and postcards sent to us at Reiman Publications.

Unfortunately, we were unable to "decipher" many of the handwritten names and addresses on the release forms. We certainly didn't want to offend anyone by making a "best guess" at the spelling of his or her name and getting it incorrect.

Also, in order to get this book published as quickly as possible after the completion of the journey, we had to determine a cutoff date for the entry of all names. The names from any letters or cards received prior to that date, and from all legible release forms, are included in this roster.

For simplicity, names are arranged alphabetically by each rider's state and hometown. You'll notice that the states and towns listed weren't all on the official hitch route. Many folks traveled long distances from their hometowns just to be part of this once-in-a-lifetime experience—in fact, as we mentioned above, after completing this roster we discovered we had riders from all 50 states…and several other countries as well!

To *everyone* who rode or visited the hitch during its journey, we say thanks again for your interest and support!

Alabama
Birmingham—Rev. Renae V. Kochla;
Browns—Jennifer Koehn;
Huntsville—Jim Quinn, Angela Ryan;
Luverne—Cristy L. White;
Mobile—Ray Grazian;
Tuscaloosa—Wanda Hennings.

Alaska
Anchorage—Rodney & Beth Beetch, Kailyn & Chelsea Keetch;
Eagle River—Ryan Woodard;
Fairbanks—Dorothy More;
Ninilchik—Foster Leng.

Arizona
Apache Junction—Donald & Pearl Lowstuen;
Arizona City—Barbara L. Warren, Bill & Barbara Warren, Loyal J. Wiese, Elmer Worl;
Bellemont—Betty Hovey;
Benson—Winnie Barrett, Joyce Hules, Ralph & Sharon Knop, Jim & Audrey Luedke, Merle Lukens, Helen Miller, Peg Plant, Elizabeth Weimer, Joyce Wenz;
Bowie—Sharleen Benham, Janice Grizzle, Connie Holmes, Rev. Joy Light, Manen Roberts, Thelzelria Wade, Zelma Wade;
Buckeye—Lee & Virginia Hunter, Marion & Margie Ratlief;
Casa Grande—Ila Carpenter, Winn Glass, Bernice Hawkins, Mert & Bev Kohrs, Audrey & Leon Patterson, Denise Schoeneweis, Alana & Kristyn Smith, Bekki Smith;
Cave Creek—Kathleen A. Johnson;
Chandler—David & Peter Guth;
Cochise—Pat French;
Dateland—Mary Estep;
Eagar—Elnora Lund;
Eloy—David Aguirre, A. Shaki Babbaar, Lillian B. Carr, Juan Flores, Chris Garcia, Shirley Legate, Debra Ohara, James Ohara, Detrick Thomas;
Florence—Betty Fornshell, Cathy Foster, Maurine Gladish, Helen H. Pohlman, Miriam Reed;
Fountain Hills—Karen Nielsen;
Glendale—Dick & Linda Davis, Keri Pepper;
Globe—Vic Owen;
Gold Canyon—Walt & Nyla Satchwill;
Green Valley—Ken & K.C. Peters, Dan & Anne Piedmont;
Hereford—Pamela Sue Waters;
Kingman—Bonnie & Edward Craven;
Maricopa—Phyllis Langlois;
Mesa—Kathie Bauer, Mildred Clawson, Mr. & Mrs. Dale Coffin, Robert Leigh, Margaret Mentzer, Bradford & Kyle Milbrandt, Laura Olson, Bonnie Schuckert, Edna Weed, Jared Wessels;
Payson—Betty West;
Pearce—Marie Burgess, Mr. & Mrs. Don Emmons;
Peoria—Ruth Grannis, Ed Moore;
Phoenix—Eula Brown, Brandon & Cody Duncan, Allen Freed, Nancy & Al Hume, Sophie Lebler, Mr. & Mrs. E.E. McDonald, Enrique Medina, Junior & Ruby Miller, Edie Resler, Clarabelle Smelser, Tio A. Tachias, Jim & Ila Vankilsdonk, Mr. & Mrs. Jonas P. Yoder;
Portal—Charles Jensen Sr.;
Safford—Richard C. Moore;
San Simon—Althea & Ray Mitchell;
Scottsdale—Charles & Lois Newton, Lois R. Newton, Betty Phillips, Kenneth E. Welch;
Sun City—Harrell & Ann Richmond, Lena & Cyril Winkelbauer;
Sun City West—Betty A. Norman;
Sun Lakes—R.O. & Verona Anderson, Malcolm & Leah Wissler;
Tempe—Dorothy A. Smith;
Tucson—Patty A. Bostian, David & Gina Braun, Matt Cale &

Hanna Braun, Nancy & Bob Braun, Stefan L. Dekraker, Neil & Joyce Everingham, Gene & Marg Fehr, Paul Hanover, Etheline Henze, Barbie Howland, Carol Humphrey, Audrey Lainson, Shay Lane, Tyrell & Cole Lane, D. Lavergne, John & Alice Lynn, Truman & Dorothy Mayer, Shawna McCoy, Elizabeth Morrison, Mr. & Mrs. Harold L. Nuhn, Mallory Olmsted, Edna Phelps, Ray & Margaret Redmer, Carol Reece, Lena Schielke, Dorothy Shaffer, Jim & Dorothy Speer, Kay Stark, Floyd Summers, Julia Kaduk Tarczali, Mason & Misty Walker, September Walker, J.R. & Ryan Ward, Lois Ward, Gerrie Warren, Noreen Werthmann, Rane Lynn & Lacey Widman, Rex & Lori Widman;
Willcox—Margaret Davidson, Betty Leithead, Corinne M. Stoud, Robert Watson, Carol Wien;
Yuma—Frank & Rolla Becker, Marlyss Bradshaw, Mrs. Donald Danielson, Mr. & Mrs. William D. Doty, Tom & Joyce Gehring, Charles & Reba Holland, Ernest Huber, Ilse Johnson, Donald Kruger, Travis Mitchell, Nikki & Adam & Amy Murray, Lillian Ogden, Jay Wilkens.

Arkansas
Dardanelle—Irl & Ruby Sheely;
Gentry—Sharla Nightengale;
Gillett—Debbi Reed;
Hiwasse—Shirley Hofmann;
Lakeside—Russ & Bonnie Clark;
Ravenden—Henry & Pearly Hirsch;
Rogers—Irma Neujahr;
Springdale—Mary J. McCaffery.

California
Anaheim—Gary W. Rudd;
Bakersfield—Rebecca Whipple;
Big Bear City—Gerald Hellickson;
Boulevard—Norma Jean Barber;
Brawley—Janet Rutherford;
Brea—Jim & Beverly Meek;
Buellton—Laura Leifer;
Burney—Doris & Raymond Huffman;
Burson—A. Musil;
Calexico—Antonio P. Tirado, Danikla Tirado;
Carlsbad—Robert J. Winslow;
Carmel Valley—Barbara P. Duncan;
Carpinteria—Sharon Brouse;
Chino—Jake Dejong, Julie Williams;
Chula Vista—Cliff Markin;
Cohasset—Al & Charlotte Newell;
Concord—Kim & Nathan & Luke Harmon, Nancy Marshall;
Cudahy—Lail Elder, Loraine Harris;
Dalhart—Wanda Robertson;
Daly City—David R. Canada;
Diamond Bar—David & Joan Little;
Dulzura—Dolores Cardenas, Char Gruenwald, Robert, Diane & Manie Gruenwald, Sally Pechota;
East Sparta—Stephen Reidl;
El Cajon—Bonnie Hofmann, Bob & Fran Medaris, Geraldine Mentior, Harce & Annie Rice, Debbie Walker, Jack & Virginia Walker, Harold K. Wilson;
El Centro—John L. Dantice;
El Dorado Hills—The Forlines Family;
Encinitas—Eugene P. Walsdorf, Mary Ann Wood;
Encino—Caroline Perry;
Escondido—Lawrence A. Onan;
Fall River Mills—W.L. Johnson Jr.;
Fort Bragg—Carl & Doris Force;
Fullerton—Edward & Helen Fornwalt;
Garden Grove—Lisa Riske;
Glendora—Miran & Betty Sivcovich;
Hemet—Bernadine Bradley;
Hesperia—Jodie Williams;
Holtville—Don Dantcve;
Huntington Beach—Larry & Janey Cooper, Rebecca Cooper;
Irvine—Pamela Schneider;
Jacumba—Floyd Alexander, Mary Robinson;
Jamul—Greg & Colleen Beck, Lynn Dobson, Tom Rouse;
Lakeside—Christine Manzella;
Lemon Grove—Naomi Gerdts, Grace Harter, Richard Seaney;
Livingston—Robert Leatherman Family;
Los Angeles—Ruth Carver;
Midway City—Elizabeth & Eilen Cooper;
Moorpark—Shelly & Chrissy McCin;
Moreno Valley—Devin McLaughlin;
Newbury Park—Nancy Harvey;
Ocotillo—Sally A. Bly, Doris Daugherty, Chestyne Qualey, Dolores R. Rittenhouse, Angie Sienko;
Paramount—Mr. & Mrs. Cleo Pierson;
Pasadena—Bob Hoback;
Pleasant Hill—Jere Conzalez;
Pomona—Glenn & Beverly Cris;
Potrero—Sharon & Vanessa Arnold;
Rancho Dominguez—Adrian & Sue Whitaker;
Red Bluff—Paul & Donna Schoelen, Edna Wright;
Redding—Agnes Crawford;
Rescue—Mr. & Mrs. Robert Caskey;
Ridgecrest—L. Blowers;
Ripon—Jeanne Rudd;
Roseville—Carl & Helen Rick;
San Clemente—Frank E. Hoban;
San Diego—William F. Carter, Katherine Dannevik, Roxanna Faust, James F. Graves, Michael Hrenko, Amber Kingsley, Betty J. Leverenz, Mary Ruth Miller, Minnir Miller, Pamela & Logan Piburn, Elaine Pitts, Virginia R. Pollock;

Marilyn Strickland

San Francisco—Gloria Silver;
San Rafael—Ginny Anderson;
San Ramon—Mr. & Mrs. L. Ashworth;
Santa Barbara—Mr. & Mrs. Tony Gamberdella;
Saratoga—Doris Ball;
Sky Valley—Lloyd Hartman;
Sonora—Bob & Gloria Silver, Connie Tighe;
South Gate—Kenneth Hein;
Templeton—Marjorie Burke;
Trabuco Canyon—Kathy & Alex Whalen, Tyler & Cheslea Whalen;
Valley Center—Donald L. Thomas;
Ventura—Sharon Reeves;
Walnut Creek—C.P. Daane, Jane Fraim;
Whittier—Stan Ainslie, Roxanna Randall;
Yucaipa—Rose Hammond.

Colorado
Aurora—Ardis England, Lee Grof, Linda Hidsalek, Carlyle Skogen, Linda T. Stuart, Matthew & Andy Stuart, Annie Lee Taylor-Rox, Tim Yoder;
Bennett—Kathy L. Root;
Boulder—Jean A. Dayhoff, Bill & Margaret Jones;
Broomfield—Margaret Wagner;
Campo—Kendra Alton, Karen Berryman, Phyllis Dixon, Celest England, Leroy England, Helen Harvert, Nila Houser, Marshall Lowder, Mr. & Mrs. Allen McCarty, Tammy Newman, Shirley Nidey, Kenneth Shaw, Opal Smith, Michala Wait, Doug & Anne Wray, Paul Wray;
Canon City—Frank Hopkins, Walter Stahlecker;
Castle Rock—Mae J. Smith;
Center—Ernest & Mary Bloxson, Brian Lewis, Bill Worker, Evelyn Worker;
Colorado Springs—Mary Adair, Freda & Bill Chase, Herb & Dawn Hoover, Larry Miller, Jack & Marilyn Moldenauer, Naomi Reynolds, Julie & Jennie Speidel, Stephanie Speidel;
Como—Gertrude L. Daley;
Denver—Norma Blakley, Cindy Capen, Pauline Cavanaugh, Harold A. Nelson, Royallene Presott, Patty Stulp;
Englewood—Carnie Shrader, Darlis Weinreich;
Erie—Kay Love;
Evergreen—Monte M. Adams;
Fort Collins—Jesse & Viola Alumbaugh, Jan Cipra;
Fruita—Phyllis Ford;
Golden—Paul & Loraine Ritchlin, Al & Nan & Chris Vorhies, Catie Vorhies;
Grand Junction—Mary Huffine;
Granada—John R. Schulz;
Greeley—Rose Tapia;
Holly—Robert Kirmer;
Hugo—Jordan & Diana Jolly, Louise Webb;
Jefferson—Bettylou & Thomas Schiebel;
Kim—Cecila Moody;
La Junta—Verlin Huhns, Lloyd King, Alma Kuhns, Charley Sommerfeld, Stella Sommerfeld;
Lakewood—Russ Bromby, Wade Manley;
Lamar—Bill Blazek;
Laporte—Edward & Marion Reish;
Las Animas—Dawn Kunan;
Littleton—Susan Brooks, Cory & Amy Marner;
Loveland—Cindy Capes, Louis W. Ward;
Meeker—Wendy Graham;
Monte Vista—Marvin & Maryann Mitchell, Mary Ann Mitchell, Bill & Evelyn Worker;
Nathrop—Bob Estep;
Olathe—Dennis Becker, Jeremy & Tyler Becker;
Otis—Melainie D. Rime;
Palmer Lake—Albert E. Miller, Ken Smith;
Parker—Mr. & Mrs. Harvey Chubb;
Pritchett—Kelly & Bridget Abbott;
Pueblo West—Dick & Jean Larkin;
Rocky Ford—Anita Beadles, Claude & Viola Bender, Karl & Mabel Enns, Franklin & Esther Heatwole, Magnar & Doris Hjelmstad, Paul Isaak, Henry T. Klein;
Rye—Edith Robinson;
Snyder—Linda Scott;
South Fork—Wilbur H. Harris;
Springfield—Nancy Aguilar, Sheila Aldrich, Robyn Bitner, Frac Brown, Vickie Burk, Cassandra Buttermiller, Nicky Buttermuller, Gladys M. Cave, Clarence Chapman, Shelby Chapman, Elizabeth & Paul Chatham, Mary Chatham, Zinda Chatham, Bethany Cooper, Marty Cooper, Ben Cox, Nellie Deweese, Jerry & Ammie Dukes, Debbie Dunlap, Eva Dunlap, J.J. Eden, Ross & Leila Ellis, Kylea & Kaleb Eskew, Jennifer Gale, Rhian Gonzales, Britany & Brianna Gragan, Brenda & Beau Grogan, Bill & Vicki Hall, Pam Hartley, Carmen Homsher Family, Lary E. Houser, Pat Howard, Marla Humphrey, Cathy & Mike Irwin, Duane Larson, Joseph & Maxine

Lenart, Mary Ann Levalley, Helinda Mackey, Susie Mackey, Harbert O. Mann, Gina Martin, Kelly Mason, Lew Mathews, J.B. McElroy, Janice Means, Sue Merrill, Mona Millican, Debbie Moody, Arlene Owens, Melissa Packard, Dorothy Porter, Cheryl Rutherford, Malle Shaperd, Aimee Shepherd, Bryan Spetts, Doris Steinbrueck, Mary Kay Thompson, Casey Velson, Shana Wade, Terry Wallace, Wayne Workman, Amanda Young;
Sterling—Les & Grace Schroeder;
Superior—Charles F. Woods;
Thornton—Shirley Crouse Family;
Vilas—Eldonng Houser, Cynthia Hulman, Glen & Islip Hutchen, Idrys Hutches, Quayde Thompson;
Walsenburg—Tom & Vicki Farrell;
Walsh—Barb Barson, Hattie Darity, Brenda Forgey Whitney, Van & Beverly Freeman, Vera Lois Fulbright, Sherry & Sharalee Hancock, Tera & Tead Hancock, Rhonda Hebberd, Lynzea Hetrich, Andrea & Sarah Hume, Rod Hume, Edna Litke, J.P. Marion, Sally Mindell, Shanda Proehl, Milton Ross, Melissa Sharpe, Patricia Tate, Judy Trahen;
Windsor—Lester & Thelma Kuenning;
Yuma—Cindy Stolp, Tim Stulp.

Connecticut
Canaan—Douglas J. Carlson Sr.;
Durham—Jane K. Lafountain, Matt & Jane Lafountain;
East Canaan—Isabelle Carlson;
East Haven—Tony & Anne Gambardela;
Enfield—Shirley Clark;
Kensington—Don & Carole Cross, Carole Grass;
Kent—Florence Jones, Patrick Redmond;
North Granby—Herbert Dewey;
Rockville—Mrs. David Hangartner;
Shelton—Bill & Babe Peters;
Trumbull—Ann Katrinak;
Wallingford—Helen Coty.

Delaware
Dover—George F. Wiltshire;
Hartly—Henrey E. Swartzentruber.

Florida
Anna Maria—Heidi Short;
Bartow—Edwin S. Wilson;
Bradenton—Nora Brahler;
Brooksville—Hazel Smith;
Clearwater—Esther Woodard;
Davenport—Norman E. Harris;
Deerfield Beach—Jeannie Anderson;
Englewood—Doris Reiser;
Fern Park—Jane P. Millen;
Fort Lauderdale—Shirley Lovejoy;
Fort Myers—Al & Maebelle Pinkoski;
Fort Pierce—Bertha E. Gerard, Karen Main;
Fruitland Park—Mr. & Mrs. Robert Schultz;
Haines City—Kathryn Reising;
Hobe Sound—Jane Hannold;
Lake City—George & Ruth Hollingsuoth;
Lakeland—Rhonda Miller;
Largo—Arthur R. Miller;

Lehigh Acres—Gladys Hartle;
Lutz—Mrs. M.S. Smith;
Miami—Lisa Smith;
Milton—John R. Hoff;
Nokomis—Archie Hostetler;
North Fort Myers—John & Margaret Krugh;
Orlando—Vern Abbott;
Palm City—Mr. & Mrs. D.N. Luce;
Palm Springs—Doris M. Reel;
Pompano Beach—Patricia Kelsey;
Saint Petersburg—Virgil & Carolyn Feltner;
Sarasota—Ray Beachy, Jack Driscoll, Jane Driscoll, Mrs. Walter Noffinger;
Sorrento—Larry & Nancy Peetis, Nancy Pettis;
Tampa—Richard & Janet Cressy, Esther Tuttle, Suzette Wehust;
West Palm Beach—Chuck Heckman;
Winter Haven—Marcia Ann Marlin;
Zephyrhills—Sheila Seme;
Zolfo Springs—Ralph Leonard.

Georgia
Brunswick—Beth Jackson;
Columbus—Rex & June Ellis;
Fayetteville—Sylvia Marie Hitchell;
Jonesboro—Helen Murtha;
Valdosta—Lauranell & Nick Westberry.

Hawaii
Honolulu—Clara & Christine Locher, Julie Locher, Carl Spear.

Idaho
Aberdeen—Clint & Marge Krehbiel;
Kamiah—Debbie Simler, Verla Simler;
Morral—Kate Hunsicker;
Moscow—Floyd & Louise Trail;
Priest River—Mary Alma Laird;
Saint Anthony—Rose Kubal.

Illinois
Abingdon—Kenneth Davies, Dorlene Green, Farrell Hallbick, Wilma Hallbick, Mrs. Paul Hummell, Bertha Kilburn, Lorraine Shoner, Edith Shugart, Shirley Simkins;
Aledo—Helen Bopp, Helen E. Bopp, Bessie Castor, Zella Docherty, Betty Hofer, Sara Jones, Juanita McKinney, Freda Mitchell, Susan Sutton;
Altamont—Ann Zacha;
Alton—Eva McDonald;
Amboy—Russell L. Hopkins, Russell Horkimer;
Anchor—Kay L. Bose, Martie Eyer;
Arrowsmith—Roy Brent, Elaine Franzen;
Arthur—Irene Farmwald Family;
Ashkum—Mary M. Ducat, Betty Krueger;
Ashton—Janice Patterson;
Astoria—Ron Burtz, Tammy & Matthew Burtz, Danny Caldwell, Katie & Heidi Caldwell, Anna Danner, Anna Dannu, Orley Shaw;
Atlanta—Phyllis Rankin, Dennis W. Smith, Helen M. Smith;
Aurora—Loraine Thomas;
Avon—Beverly Blunt, Cleona Chase, Marlene Chatterton, Laurie Chick, Kathleen Eatherton, Kathy Effland, Jean Frankhauser, Margaret Hickerson, Rosetto Holloway,

Barbie Howland

Della Steffer

We're Pulling for Seniors!

Kenneth M. Howard, Cassie John, Betty Kepple, Dean Lock, Mike Lock, Doris Marshall, Beverly McGrew, Larry & Marilyn Melhouse, Miss Michelle Melhouse, Max Phelps, Connie Pool, Karen Schmalshof, Lois Schmalshof, Betty M. Shaw, J. Marvin Staggs, Mrs. Greg Stonebraker, Curt & Ginny Westfall, Julia Williamson;
Bardolph—Kay Easley;
Bartonville—Hazel Ditto, Pauline Stevenson;
Basco—Murle Kill;
Baylis—Norman & Anna Mae Dean;
Belleville—Mrs. Verlan Kamper, C.E. Oliver Jr.;
Bement—Duane & Martha Medaris;
Benson—Anna Oltman;
Berwick—Debbie Farris, Darrell Page;
Big Rock—Pete & Betty Wolsfeld;
Biggsville—Robert W. Gibb, Jerry Weibel;
Blandinsville—William & Rosalyn Meriwether;
Bloomington—Karen Allen, Kathy Bachman, Barbara Green, Melvin Holt, Mr. & Mrs. L.B. Manahan, Ed Payne, Lyle D. Stoller, Ann Marie & Brian Tap;
Bonfield—Stanley Voigt;
Bourbonnais—Kenneth Ponton;
Bradford—Jean Henley;
Brimfield—Walter Herrmann, Kathy Maher, Vivian Moody;
Buckingham—Genevieve Berger;
Buckley—Sharon Kinzinger;
Buffalo Grove—Mrs. Donald Smith;
Burlington—Lewis Miles;
Burnside—Delbert & Vada Bergman, Phyllis Housewright, Patricia Lacroix;
Bushnell—Marcia Hart, M. Hollis, Lewis & Irene Hutchins, Almalee Johnson, Ronald & Deloris Kepple, Alan & Carole A. Lochmiller, Tammy & Adam McKee, Freida Seward, M. Sheckler, Linda Spangler, George A. Suter;
Cabery—Donna Masching;
Calumet City—Lois Riley;
Cambridge—Margie Martin, Alice J. Reed, Jim Reed, Vernon Steffen;
Camp Point—Jessica & Jared Bean, Justin & Janelle Bean, Ulfert H. Ideus;
Canton—Vilda Berry, Carroll Dearing, Kyle Dearing, Melba Dearing, Colleen Hubbert, Beverly Liddle, Carolyn K. Long, Renee Lowe, Ruth White, Don Wolf;
Cantrall—Margaret Oliver;
Carlinville—Josephine Remling;
Carpentersville—Wayne & Terry Fitzsimmons;
Carthage—Harriet & Robert Bright, Lucille Coffman, Dianne Jackson, Richard Jones, Iola Shipman, Richard Souder, Frank Urton;
Catlin—Donald H. Fleming;
Champaign—Dee Laird;
Charleston—Thomas & Nettie Creech;
Chatham—Norma Bradley;
Chatsworth—Chris Cain, Dorothy Hubly, Harlan Kahle, Mary Kerians, Evie Ortlepp;

Chebanse—E. Allen;
Chenoa—Delmar G. Augspurger, Kay Birch, Karen Heins Family, Russell Jolly, Brenda Kuntz, Shirley L. Lorance, Wayne Raber, Mrs. Lorene K. Reimer, David Schmid, Cora Sechrest, Mildred Weber, Glen & Elizabeth Wilkins, Liz Wilkins;
Cherry Valley—Ruth Baxter, Betty Carlson;
Chillicothe—Dona Heston;
Christopher—Pete & Frances Furlin;
Cissna Park—Charles A. Allen, Elmer W. Kaeb, Lucille Knapp, Marilyn Knapp;
Clinton—Marie Campbell, Andrea R. Spencer, Paul A. Sprague, Dorothy M. Wantland;
Coal City—Doris Bottens, Jean Vilt;
Colchester—Mrs. Leona Dixon;
Colfax—Shirley Schleeter;
Colona—Ed Mayhew;
Congerville—Rachel Fogle, Jacob & Abby Hartman, Lisa Hartman, Amanda Herget, Edward Leman, Gail Leman, Kary & Kelsey Leman, Karlita Sloter, David Steffen, Linda Wilson;
Cornell—Sherry Goggin, Irene Gregory;
Cortland—Mary Aldis, Boots Ewing, Marian Huffman;
Cowden—Roger & Naomi Corley, Eileen Smith, Peggy Teuker, Floyd Tuekee;
Crescent City—Kathleen Post;
Crete—Evelyn Duncan, Jackie & Amanda Wiersma, Lisamarie Wiersma, Phillip & Stephan Wiersma;
Cropsey—Leota Brucker, Margery Pratt;
Crystal Lake—Glen & Belva Goldbeck;
Cuba—Barbara E. Marshall, Marilyn Thompson;
Cullom—Edna & Emory Hayslette, Ruth Remmers;
Dallas City—D. Eckhardt, Darlene McGaw, Julie Pence, Margaret K. Rice;
Danforth—Ruth Schroeder, Diane Smyser;
Danville—Martha Burton, Charles Hawkins;
Decatur—Mary Oliver, Gale Quick;
Deer Creek—Lyle Bridges, Mary Compton, Floyd Hofmann, Raymond & Viola Wagner, Emil Wurmnest;
Deerfield—Dorothy & Bill Bixby;
Des Plaines—Deanna Willer;
Dewey—Russell & Fern Massanari;
Dixon—Warren & Alice Friedrichs, Marilyn Schultz;
Donovan—Victoria Marquis, Wilbur Munson;
Dunlap—Rorke Pauli, Christine Whalen;
Dwight—Neil Bennett, Nora Hemenover;
Earlville—David Englehart;
East Dundee—Ina Ahrens;
East Lynn—Mary L. Hatfield;
East Peoria—Melody Bennett, Ruth Lewis, Casy Miller, Sara A. Shinn, Irene J. Weldrop;
Easton—Linda Powley;
Edwardsville—Nancy Sullivan, Marian Utechtt;
Effingham—Mary C. Hoelscher, Edgar Tucker, Pauline Tucker, Brenda Zerrusen;

Egan—John Mailand;
El Paso—Carolyn Buck, Karol Enright, Kenneth & Mary Lovings, Mary E. Lovings, Keith Martin, Tim Matzke, Lori Miller, Barney & Vera Reeves, Bernard J. Reeves, James Reeves, Norman & Rose Robeson, Mr. & Mrs. Loren W. Schlipf, Spring Amanda Uphoff, Helen Zimmerman;
Elburn—Mary M. Richtman;
Elkhart—Joseph K. Jones;
Ellisville—Ralph Wilcoxen;
Ellsworth—Lincoln Buella, Lincoln Builta;
Elmwood—John C. Potter, Norman Streitmatter;
Elvaston—Mrs. Glenn Lunt;
Eureka—Carol Anliker, Gloria Barrich, Henry O. Blunier, Mary Lou Guth, Eva Harvey, Norm Hoerr, Jack A. Lewis, Eva Limkeman, Carol Martin, Sylvia Martin, Wilhelm Puzich, Mildred Reeb, Sam Schmidgall, Jerry Schumacker, Viola Schweigert, Ida Sluga, Ruth Stalter, Archie Unzicker;
Fairbury—Mary Bachtold, Arthur Bahler, Edna Feller, Ezra Feller, Marcia & Caleb Grosshans, Perry Honegger, Mrs. Wayne Honegger, Betty Hussbaum, Casey Hussbaum, Clarence Koehl, Marie & Stephen Koehl, Grace Lawrence, Helen Leman, Louis Martens, Curtis Meiss, Janice Meiss, Harold Metz, Ruth & Roberta Meyer, Mrs. Ross Mowery, Tom & Lois Simpson, Luella Sohn, Karla Steidinger, Trish & Leann Steidinger, Dorothy Tollensdorf, Renae Waldbeser, Amy Zehr, Joan Zehr;
Fairview—Clark Burnett, Norma St. Clair, Mrs. Obil Myers, Melba Schleich;
Farmer City—Brandon Merle Reynolds, Fred E. Reynolds;
Farmington—Roy E. Allen, Pat Bowen, Marilyn Doubet, Delbert & Irma Heape, Jay Jacobus, James Leuzi, Mickie Ulm, Pat Vawter;
Fiatt—Cheryl Bradshaw;
Fisher—Leonard Unzicker;
Foosland—Nathan Beachey;
Forest City—Otto Dierker;
Forrest—Mrs. Elmer Bailey, Janet Farney, Andrew Fisher, Earl & Esther Gerber, Marcia & Timothy Gerber, Rochelle Gerber, Melinda & Jenna Harms, Cynthia Kaisner, Leona & Valerie Kaisner, Phyllis Krippel, Jerry & Kathy Leman, Jonathan Leman, Rosie Maurer, Lois Nance, Harvey Rieger, Kenneth Steffen, Elmer Stoller, Mr. & Mrs. Ed Stork, Ben & Irene Traub, LaRae Walter, Janet Weakman, Peggy Young;
Freeport—Susan E. Bacon, Robert Fishburn, Edwin Mantzke Jr., Clarence Riemer;
Galesburg—Betty Anderson, Velma Brown, Alice Davis, Martha Erickson, Marion Griffith, Jasper Jones, M. Nylander, Jean Nyman, Earl & Carolyn Park Jr., Helen Peterson, Ruth Pruett, Rena M. Reager, Rena Rengor, Dorothy Selander, Beverly White;
Galva—Reuben Anderson;
Gardner—Alta Clark;
Geneseo—Rene & Anez Emmerson, Dona Wexell, Alice Wiese;
Geneva—Jane E. Wiemerslage;

Gibson City—Vickie Miller, Hubert & Alma Stipp, Paul Stipp, Stephen & Julie Stipp, Eugene Swearingen;
Gifford—Hilda Schluter;
Gilman—Carol A. Bargmann, Mollie Reighel, Gloria Reitz, Brittany Ann Schmid;
Gilson—Guy Bates, Bridgit Schwarz;
Gladstone—Gail H. Babcock, Virginia Ross;
Glasford—Andrea Hill, Melinda Melhouse;
Glendale Heights—Jim Wheatley;
Golden—Albertus & Dorthy Ufkes;
Good Hope—Angie Haffner, Mary McFarland, Guynne Worthington;
Goodfield—Rod & Lynda Hinrichsen, Wilma Rediger;
Grand Ridge—Lemuel R. Rees Sr.;
Grayslake—Armita Mabie;
Green Valley—Diane Million;
Greenup—Sheila Green;
Gridley—Sean Carpenter, Margaret Cleary, Marie Dodson, Lillian Fleming, Joe & Irma Grusy, Avis S. Hall, Evelyn Hardman, Joseph Hayes, William Helbling, Elsie M. Kinsella, Litta Kinsella, Clyde & Wilma Kuntz, Jeanette Lavallier, Virgil & Genevive Reeves, Josephine Theissen, Bev Wells, Neal Wettstein, Doug & Darla Wilson, Marissa Witzig, Norma Witzig, Margaret Zangerle, Keith & Linda Zimmerman;
Gurnee—Axel Erickson, Helen Ostman;
Hamilton—Katie Martin;
Hanna City—W.O. Culver, Mrs. John Hartmann, Cara Holmes, Berniece Stevens;
Harvard—John L. Weter;
Havana—Norma J. Tackman;
Herscher—Mrs. Elmer E. Berger, Melvin & Opal Earing, Bonnie K. Jordan, Robert W. Nesbitt, Mrs. Laverne Schultz;
Highland Park—Burton Tillman;
Hinckley—Bob Willrett;
Hoopeston—David Sturm;
Hudson—Glenn A. Miller;
Illiopolis—Alvin & Nancy Dial;
Industry—Pat Garthaus, Edward Skiles, Neil & Karen Skiles;
Iuka—Billy & Elsie Finn, Freida Purdue;
Joliet—Cindy Parks;
Kankakee—Joan Butz, Marge Jefferson, Gerald Legan, Denise Schiel, Hilda Yung;
Keithsburg—Beulah L. Sheriff;
Knoxville—Meredith Mattson, Marge Reynolds;
La Grange—Carol A. Comstock;
La Harpe—Dianne Blythe, Roger D. Comstock, Laura Gittings, Jan Gutting, Robert Mapes, Leta Shumaker, Darline Stout;
Lake Zurich—Richard & Karen Brooks;
Lakewood—Jennifer & Ashley Jones;
Lanark—Mr. & Mrs. Quin Kosmecki, Richard Sweitzer;
Lansing—Ruby Brown;
Laura—Florence Lacost, Sharon Larner, Helen L. Lumberry;
Lebanon—Vernon & Iona Wolf;
Lewistown—Irene Beadles, Jerry O. Lillie, Susan McAdams, Roberta Postin Family, Judy Willcoxen;
Lexington—Karen Brown, Mrs. John L. Fischer, Jan Freed;
Lincoln—Fred Kavelman, Louise Wiebers;
Little York—Mrs. William Livingston;
Lockport—Edgar Kirkham;
Loda—Kristin Lemenager;
Lomax—Kathryn Horton, Lloyd M. Martin, Randy & Ellen May, Martha Reed, Brad & Andy Webster, Gregory Webster, Kenneth M. Webster;
Lombard—Edna Miller, Ruth Mueller;
London Mills—Daphne Blankers, Heather Cook, Shirley Cook, Kenneth Daley, Stanley A. Davis, Stanley & Jane Davis, Wrenn R. Grice, Malcolm Shortness, Glenda Waterfield;
Long Point—Jade Stimpert, Linda Zavada, Ryan Zavada;
Macomb—Harriet Bricker, Mary Luan Clark, Howard Culson, Esther Heaton, Ken Hutchins, Geneva Keithley, Beth Miller, Lana Myers, Margaret VanEtten;
Manteno—William Grimes;
Mapleton—Mary Bontz;
Marengo—Pam Lee, Diana Petersen;
Marissa—Homer Wayland;
Marseilles—Dorothy D. Harden;
Marshall—Marion & Loie McConchie, Nina Stogsdill, Harold Stosdill;
Martinton—Duane C. Boudreau;
Mason City—Marie Fouts;
Mattoon—Hulda Couch;
Media—Sue Bride, Lisa & Abby Corzatt, Brandon Rothzen, Kayla & Susan Rothzen, Ron Rothzen, Earl & Mary Taylor, Duane Torrance, Douglas & Robin Watson;
Melvin—Emerson Muehlenpfort;
Metamora—Phil Fischer, Richard & Marilyn Jennings, Steve Johnson, Ferne Jones, JoAnn Kreider, Iona Schaidle, Carl Schaidle Jr., Mr. & Mrs. Melvin Weyeneth;
Milford—August Anderson, Marie Lockhart, Jennifer Morgeson, Dorothy Slife, Maryann & Robert Sloan, Robert O. Sloan, Claire Smith, Harry Tammen;
Milledgeville—Gail & Betty Deets;

Millstadt—Leona Beil, Richard Masching;
Mineral—John Cessna;
Minonk—Ron Seggerman, Betty Steinhilfer, Esther Uphoff;
Minooka—Walter Friant;
Monmouth—Joyce Anderson, Max Anderson, Charlene Caldwell, Weona & John Erickson Sr., Mae Fredrickson, Joyce Johnson, Robert D. Lantz, Grace McCrery, Marilyn Perrin, Diana L. Price, Susie Mae Shoemate, Mr. & Mrs. Frank Wallace Family, Norma Watson, Martha Whiteman;
Montgomery—Marvin Bush;
Monticello—Gary A. Briggs;
Morris—Ruth Jackman;
Morrison—Virginia Weekley;
Morton—Jane Hoffmire, Ruth & Levi Kaiser, Susan & Jared Powley, Stacy Roberts, Elizabeth Schick, Esther Sitton, Diane Tanner, Arthur Zehr, Donna Zimmerman;
Mount Auburn—Harry & Merl Cook;
Mount Carroll—Warner Hartman;
Mount Morris—Betty Hare;
Mount Pulaski—Dean & Doris Cates, Robert & Joellen Maske;
Mount Sterling—Wilma Bordenkircher, Dwight Kerley;
Murrayville—Saddie Piggott;
Naperville—Elizabeth A. Buckley, Phil & Kathryn Holler;
Nauvoo—Jane Little, Willis Marshall;
New Athens—Elvera Mahan;
New Berlin—Barbara Bodine;
New Boston—Betty Sedam;
Niota—Lynn Barritt, Grace Bertschi, Janet Gregory, Jackie Johnson, Patricia Lacroix, Josh & Rebecca Pence, Glen Rea, Sasha Rea, Polly Reed;
Normal—Sherrie Taylor, Kathryn Vitek;
Oak Forest—Dean V. Lilly;
Odell—Roy Clark, Amy K. Davis, Bonnie A. Davis, James Davis, Betty Kennedy, Charles Muir;
Onarga—Delores Butzow, Brice & Brandt Breymeyer;
Oquawka—Pauline W. Bigger, Charles M. Kraft;
Orion—Laura Morris;
Orland Park—William Hoffman, Alma Stellwagen;
Osco—Kim White;
Ottawa—Wesley J. Freebairn, Luke Hennenfent, Charlene Wilkins, Wayne Wilkins;
Owaneco—Carl & Marge Satterle;
Palestine—Vera Knoblett, Ruth Reinbold;
Palmyra—Mrs. Allen Cole;
Paxton—Richard Anderson;
Pearl—Laura Vaster;
Pecatonica—John Eaton;
Pekin—A. Berchtold, C. & Mourine Hagen, Cameron Robert Hill, Mary Alice Hill;
Penfield—Ruth Basham, Christopher Buhr, John Buhr;
Peoria—Lucille & Robert Beyer, Cheryl Buhr, Beverly Campbell, Janeen Campbell, Linda Frazer, Mildred Lear, Mary Meyer, Stacy Negley, Jo Anne Richardson, Dorothy Sestedt, Grace Shoemaker, L.C. & Alberta Smith, Susan Streitmatter, Jacqueline Tamplin, Donna Trail, Laura Vaster, Jim Wagand, Phyllis Wenzel;
Peotone—Lila Jacobs, Mr. & Mrs. Robert Norman;
Perry—Elmer L. Bradbury, Norm & Donna Rieger;
Peru—Dorothy Boers, Irma & Joseph Gallagher;
Pinckneyville—Vern & Vivian Gielow;

Piper City—Christine Boma, Florence Ficklin, Merle Harford, Joe & Mary Kratz, Jeri & Chris Manhart, Jerry & Evelyn Rebholz, Beverly J. Richardson, Tark Sterrenberg, Marie Wahls, Sally Wahls, Lloyd Woodward, H. Wycoff, Roger & Benjamin Wycoff;
Plymouth—Mrs. Carroll Moose;
Polo—Velva Chriss, B.E. Horton;
Pontiac—Lisa Brill, Sandra Degenhart, Marie Koltveit, Joyce Post, Carol M. Studebaker;
Prairie City—Betty Chase;
Princeton—Chester M. Grafft, Dorothy Grafft, Sharron Klingel;
Prophetstown—Gail & Janet Goodell;
Quincy—Rose Burling, Mr. & Mrs. J.C. Newkirk, Pat & Shirley Styles, Miss Jane Wittler;
Rankin—Elsie Hofbauer, Marvin Lewis;
Rantoul—Carl & Ann Albers;
Raritan—Daisy Gibb, Pauline Overstreet;
Reddick—Mrs. Dale Anderson;
Reynolds—Donald & Clarice Docherty, Edmund & Leona Swanson;
Rio—Don Fritz, Dale L. Johnson;
Roanoke—Jenny Christner, Sue Garber, Brett Hodel, Curt Hodel, Jenell Hodel, Cathryn Hostetler, Lavina Hostetler, Marilyn Hostetler, Winifred Martin, Lois McCauley, Erby & Anna Belle McGhee, Bill Schumacher, Roy Wiegand, Marvin Yordy;
Robinson—Eugene Richart;
Rochelle—Rhodora Hagemeyer;
Rock Island—Beulah Spaulding;
Rockford—Mrs. William Pell;
Rockton—Linda Blunck;
Roscoe—Robin Byrne, Viola A. Cuff;
Roseville—Danielle Beard, Louise Beaty, David Bellinger, Ann & Vic Corman, Mrs. Max B. Galbraith, M. Hawkin, Sheri Hedburg, Janis Johnson, Orma Jean Kirkpatrick, Rex Lozier, Martha Martin, Dorothy Massingill, Maude Mithcell, George & Loretta Mueller, Bob Nicoli, Lawrence E. Pepper, Leland Rodgers, Judy Russell, Evelyn Shook, Polly Swanson, Bud Thompson, Lucille Twomey, Norman Watson, Dorothy Wilson, Agatha Zimmerman;
Rushville—Fern Cox;
Rutland—Rosemary Oldenburg, Adam & Collin Seggerman, Linda & Wade Seggerman;
Saint Anne—Carol E. Cyrier;
Saint Augustine—George Coursey, Kay Jockisch, Ted Murk, Lewis Powell;
Saint Charles—Shirley Whisnant;
Saint Joseph—Karen E. Erdman-Reitmeier;
Salem—Eugene Bookhout;
San Jose—John Bockwitz, Henry & Shirley Imig;
Sandwich—Charlotte Buyers;
Saunemin—Delores Schulz, Helen Spafford;
Savanna—Leroy Getz, James & Ethel Hendrick;
Sciota—Kathy Waldinger;
Seaton—Mrs. Wendell Dillavou;
Secor—Barbara Allen, Michael Detweiler, Nelma Eastman;
Serena—Derrick & Brett Dziekonski, Paula M. Dziekonski;
Sheldon—Kim Bithos, Robert Buck, Marilyn K. Busick, Madeline Conrad, Mrs. Harold E. Light, William & Bette Schoolman;

Jack McCool

Silvis—Betty Edmunds;
Smithfield—Verle Henderson;
Smithshire—Margaret Hilten;
South Beloit—Carolyn Kalk, Darlene Peterson;
South Pekin—Mary Ellen Parker;
Springfield—Homer Bradley;
Stanford—Linda Lubke;
Sterling—Harold Kreider, R.L. Mellendorf;
Steward—Andrew Barkei;
Stillman Valley—Doris R. Harrar, C.L. Hillers;
Strawn—Verla Davis;
Stronghurst—Dale Anderson, Chatherine Corzatt, Teresa Fox, Mrs. W.H. Pence, Robert Pollock, Roy E. Swanson;
Sutter—Carl Beeler, Raymond & Naomi Klingler;
Sycamore—Doris Bolander;
Taylor Ridge—Shirley Bush;
Taylorville—Hazel F. Ealey;
Tennessee—Juanita Briggs, Margaret Lewis;
Teutopolis—Mardell Weis;
Thawville—Charles & Bernice Hildenbrand, John & Marcia Hildenbrand, Betty Schmidt, Mr. & Mrs. Orvil Stiegman;
Toluca—Russell Litchfield;
Tonica—Bernice Barr, Art & Edna Johnson, Joyce Marshall, Esther Winner;
Toulon—Philip & Ruthe Anderson;
Towanda—Joellen Evans;
Tremont—Mrs. Robert Frank, Michelene Koch, Mrs. Paul S. Koch, Peg Sauder, Marge Schaefer, Kelly Stuber;
Trivoli—Don Allen, Shirley Harman, Beta & Charlene Ricca, Earl Stalter;
Victoria—Tyler & John Johnston, Willard Johnston;
Warsaw—Mrs. Dan Kropp;
Washburn—Mrs. Paul Zook;
Washington—Bertha Burnett, Don Clark, Josie Cooper, Fern Crist, Mr. & Mrs. Doss, Carol Doss, Jerry Fleener, Hank Grebner, Doris Higgins, Kimberly Horton, Margie Kerry, Bob & Nancy Lake, Ruth Lehman, Velma Leman, Rosemary Martin, John Medill, Laura Walwer;
Watseka—Shannon Clement, Dellas Fortin, Marla J. Frye, Bob Green, Alice Jones, Jeni Madison, Eldor Meyer, Maxine Thompson, Gerald Ward, Cheryl Wessels, Lula Wood;
Wauconda—Eleanor H. Adams;
Waukegan—Sandra Cullifer, Jim, Jerry & Amber Santo;
Weldon—Wilma Goble, R.A. Marsh, George Tool;
Wellington—Mrs. Franklyn Lee;
Wenona—Fay Cook;
Westchester—Christine Altrichter;
Westville—Sandy Schulz;
Wheaton—Martha Carson, Geri Smith;
White Hall—Emily Esarey;
Wilmington—Lorraine Cunnings;
Winchester—William Coats, Mary Ellen Jameson;
Winfield—Lucille P. Doughterty;
Winnebago—Lee & Sue Fulrath, Richard D. Whitney;
Winnegabo—Dick & Grace Whitney;
Woodhull—Art Nelson, Jacqueline Nelson;
Wyoming—Eileen Cree, Sam Kieser, Martha Rachel, Mrs. Charles Stewart, Helen Stewart, Eldon & Donzella Wheeler;
Yates City—Carl Bowman;
Yorkville—R. Cottingham, Ruth & Gordon Schobert.

Indiana

Akron—Mrs. Harvey L. Arthur, Alice Balmer, Mrs. Jim Ross, Jason Smith;
Albany—Sue Bowdell, Doris Fowler, Robert Lewis;
Albion—Patricia Dyson, Barbara Robertson;
Alexandria—Nettie Hollies;
Amboy—Mr. & Mrs. Lloyd Ellars;
Anderson—William Gates;
Attica—Earl Taylor, Marilyn A. Taylor;
Auburn—Glenna Brown, Linda Coughlin, Beth Crilly;
Aurora—James Brittain;
Avilla—Timothy Deal, Gail Olson;
Battle Ground—Donna Peterson;
Berne—Dean A. Bahre, Marilyn Bahre, Jeanette Baumgartner, Ron & Julie Becher, Margaret Beitler, Deloris & Bryce Christy, Viola Dennison, Florine Fluckiger, Marguerite Gaiser, Ruth Gottschalk, Helen Habegger, Mr. & Mrs. Sylvan Habegger, Mrs. Earl Lehman, Susie Lehman, Berniece Lehmann, Ernest Liechty, Gorman McKean, Conrad Nagel, Brent & Marie Neuenschwander, Elise & Shana Neuenschwander, Jeanene Neuenschwander, R. Neuenschwander, Shirley Neuenschwander, Virginia Nussbaum, Berdella Priechty, Betty Roussey, Gloria & Lance Sommer, Irena Sprunger, Sam Yager, Kenneth E. Yoder;
Bloomfield—Beverly J. Peaper;
Bloomingdale—Sheila Grover;
Bluffton—Jim Barbieri, Angie Baumgartner, Lula Baumgartner, Nathan & Philip Bertsch, Brenda Cochran, Colin O. Cummins, Loretta Dahl, Kenneth Elliott, Evalyn Fate, Mark & Barb Gerbe, Alvin Gerber, Ann Gerber, Barb

Gerber, Betty L. Gerber, Mrs. Jean Gerber, Margaret Gerber, Kenneth Gilliom, Ralph Ginn, Dorothy Gottschalk, Jane Gregg, Pat Harris, James Higgins, Marlene Huffman, Marlene Isch, James & Mary A. Jackson, Phyllis Johnson, Lucille Kaehr, Betty Kain, Cindy Lambert, Nellie Miller, Jenny Monroe, Sheila Myers, Drew Neuenschwander, Jacki Ortiz, Floyd E. Priser, Marilyn F. Schwartz, Deb & Eric Springer, Nedra Steary, Della Steffen, Jeanne & Josiah Steffen, Sarah Steffen, Barbara J. Stobbe, Karen Stultz, Marlene Vanhorn, Denise Wall, Sylvia Wann, Doris Williams;
Bourbon—Abigail & Laura Miller, Galen Miller, Janice Miller, Kendra & Vancen Miller;
Bremen—Mary E. Karstedt, Wayne & Margaret Smith, Mrs. Earl Yarian;
Bringhurst—Marianne Garber, Marlene Peters;
Bristol—Nathan Nussbaum;
Brook—Everett Moline;
Brookston—Eleanor J. Biddle;
Brookville—Amy Michelle Reddig, Wayne & Diana Reddig;
Bryant—Anna Wolford;
Bunker Hill—Rod & Marty Fenimore, Roderick L. Fenimore, Eugene Spangler, Travis Spargler;
Burnettsville—John & Vivian Alma, Janice & Brayson Hoover, Amy L. Kendall, Jimmy Paul, Marcia Summers, Ruby E. Tam, Amy Wilson;
Butler—Barb Graham;
Cambridge City—Gertrude Wissler;
Camby—Grace Whittington;
Camden—Jason & Sheila Brubaker, Reuben Brubaker, Mrs. Max Eikenberry, Darwin Fisher, Wanye Fisher, Doris Harter, Dennis Kuns, Mrs. Eugene Wolf, Faye Wolf;
Carbon—Lureue Merca;
Carthage—Betty Abbott;
Cedar Lake—Timothy Greene;
Centerville—Pat & Kelli Bowers;
Chalmers—Cathy Klopfenstein, Harold Shell, Bethel Sickler;
Churubusco—Mrs. Robert Gaff;
Cicero—Mr. & Mrs. Bill Starr;
Claypool—Lloyd Tillman;
Columbia City—Argyle & Betty Beard, Marion & Elaine Beard, Ivan & Mary Blaugh, Geraldine Dailey, Sarah Hollenbaugh, Louise Luderman, Dorothy M. Miller, Luella Myers, E. Schilling, Marilyn Wright;
Columbus—Martha Shaffer;
Connersville—Marvin & Henrieta Rose;
Converse—Barbara Landers;
Corydon—Ralph D. Wiseman;
Covington—Dorothy H. Bodine;
Craigville—Arthur Gahman, Barbara Reimer;
Crawfordsville—Mrs. Chester Campfield;
Crown Point—I.B. Richardson Gerlach, Barbara Gerlach Hudson, Joan & Edward Schmitt Jr.;
Decatur—Imogene Abbott, Lola Abbott, Jerod Adler, Marguerite L. Baker, Carolyn Barger, Wanda Bieberich, Barbara J. Blume, Dustin Bollinger, Haley M. Byerly, Maxine Caffee, Judy Collins, Carol Dailey, Raymond & Dorothy Eichenauer, Cynthia Everett, Aden & Erin Feasel, Susan Feasel, Tyler & Lucas Feasel, Richard Franz, Elbert Fuhrmann, Lindsay & Alyssa Funk, Pat Gerber, Dustin Girod, Julie Jahn, Jon Kaehr, Marla Manley, M.M. Marbach, Jevalyn McCullough, Linda McMillen, Rex

McMillen, Russel & Delores Mitchel, V. Nyffeler, Rena
 Reynolds Family, Todd Selweyer, Anna Spangler, Marlene
 & Elise Vanhorn;
Delphi—Daniel & Michael Carbaugh, Lois M. Mears;
Demotte—Kenneth & Martha Sekema;
Denver—Mrs. Robert Judy;
Dunkirk—Billie Myers, Betty Powers;
Earl Park—Kim Donohue, Fay Fuller Family, Gale & Marty
 Gordon, Mrs. Galen Shultz;
Elkhart—Jerry Krull, Erma Reynolds, Mark Ross;
Elnora—Marjorie & Robert Dunn;
Elwood—Ray Miller, Barbara Peeper;
Etna Green—Andy & Nancy Hostetler, Janette Hostetler;
Fair Oaks—Sara King;
Fairmount—Jim & Leketta Giselbach, Mr. & Mrs. Raymond
 Giselbach, Doretta Harter;
Flora—Dorothy Flora, Mrs. Jesse Hufford, Levi Hufford, Helen
 Kinzie, Steve Kuns, Robert W. Peterson, Courtney &
 Weston Rinehart, Jim Yost;
Fort Wayne—Cliff Campbell, Sandi Champion, Dolores Crilly,
 Miriam Crouch, Marilyn Culbertson, Cyndi Detrich, Darrel
 Hitzemann, Beth Howell, Janet Howell, Marilyn G.
 Klopfenstein, Alvin Linnemeier, Steve Linnemeier, Jean
 McClelland, Trent McGregor, Loretta W. McLaughlin,
 Allegra North, Patricia Paisley, Maxine Roussey, Shari
 Roy, Audrey Saum, Judy Senger;
Fowler—Sheryl & Ashlee Richert;
Francesville—Ruth Rohloff;
Galveston—Junior & Sharon Ault, Lois Bowman, Mary Jeffries,
 Beverly Noel, Neil Robertson, Darrell & Carmen
 Thompson;
Gas City—Ruby Foster;
Gaston—Leland T. Glass;
Geneva—Mrs. C.S. Blowers, Emiley Gaskill, Patricia Haffner,
 Miriam E. Hilty, Shelly Hough, Pauline Minnich, Earl J.
 Moser, Jason Mosser, Todd Myers, Roger & Treva
 Schaffter;
Goodland—The Burtons, Avalynne Cooper, Frances Dubea,
 Mrs. James English, Mary V. English, Michael Keith
 English, Leo & Mattie Marion, Elizabeth Schneider,
 Clarence Schuette, William F. Small, Joseph D. Ziegler;
Goshen—Jeanette Barden, Robert & Rachel Barden, Harvey E.
 Beachy, Elizabeth Bontrager, Esther Bontrager, Bill
 Breckbill, Donita Brookmeyer, Crista Mishler, Yvonne &
 Sherri Mishler, Paul W. Shank, Grace Shaum, Paul Shaum,
 Catherine Stump, Mrs. Raymond J. Thomas, Eugene
 Yoder, Virginia Yoder;
Grabill—Abner F. & Janneth Gerig;
Greencastle—Nancy Allen;
Greenfield—Carl Beeson;
Greensburg—Carol Scheibler, Ruth Ann Shake;
Greentown—Leelia Cornell, S. Eikenberry, R. Kring;
Griffith—Sarah Selander;
Grissom AFB—Lynn Arrington;
Hagerstown—Mrs. Frances Hanen;
Hanna—Mrs. Elmer Heiniger;
Harlan—Linda Gouell;
Hebron—Sue Bell, Dorothy Sorensen;
Hoagland—George Saalfrank;
Hobart—Carl E. Park, John Randle, Herb Sonntak;
Huntington—Sue Blair, Georgiana P. Carl, Mary L. Eberhart,
 Gale Eller, Bob & Millie Hedrick, Ruth Jackson, Mr. &
 Mrs. Paul Johnson, Mary K. Lamont, Becky Lyons, Earl
 Lyons, Toni Rae Mayo, Alfred Meyed, Judy Pennock,
 Marjorie Readinger, Caleb Richardson, Lela Sale, Janice
 Shipbaugh, Mrs. Edwin Sieberns, Robert Troyer, Frieda
 Ulm, Mrs. Guy Wiley, Maxine Wiley;
Idaville—Vicki Arvin, Jaime Carman, John Gooding, Cheryl K.
 Hunt, Rick Morehouse, Sara Sickler;
Indianapolis—The Archers, Mr. & Mrs. C.R. Dobbins, Althea
 McKenzie, William C. McKenzie, Norma Moxley;
Kendallville—Margie Deal;
Kentland—Don & Teri Hartman, Pat Knepp, Verna Marcum,
 Dan & Deb Stoller Family, Mrs. Harold Stonecipher, Alice
 Terrell, Jenny Washburn;
Kewanna—Lois Kumler, Mildred McColley, Beth Weller;
Keystone—Judy Herring, Kendra Moser, Jerrod & Jade Sisler,
 Rebecca Sisler, Mr. & Mrs. Jerry Sleppy;
Kingman—Mitchell Simmons;
Knox—Harvey Hammerlund;
Kokomo—Ernie Beachey, Gerrie St. Calir, Jay & Helen
 Mathcett, Ferol Stahl, Trina Yager;
La Fontaine—Noel Dillon, Bonnie Ramey, Diana Snodgrass,
 Carl Steele, Martha Tirus;
La Porte—Sharon Dietz, Cherie Fuller, Pamela Griffin, Pamela
 Anne Griggin, R. Harder, Zachary Shott;
La Crosse—Ed & Lea Frank;
Lafayette—Rachel Kallik, Bob McCabe;
Lagro—Richard & Joyce Speelman;
Lake Village—Donna Kingdollar;
Lebanon—Mrs. Joel R. Hancock;
Leo—Devon A. Phillips;
Liberty Center—Doris Inskeep, Tammy Morris;
Ligonier—Woodward Hawk, Bernice Mullet;
Linn Grove—Steve Bauman;
Logansport—Buella Aswalt, Elizabeth Barton, Marilyn
 Berkshire, Carolyn Byers, Howard Carbaugh, Joanna
 Chapman, Hughel & Mary A. Cree, Tom Crowe, Jim &
 Barb Delaplane, Gwen Eagan, Norma Flohr, Richard J.
 Flory, Don Forgey, Eileen & Debbie Frey, Charles & May

Gill, Pat Gray, Lorabelle Hiatt,
 Martha M. Huff, Eugene Koch,
 Leonard Lewis, Betty J.
 McQuinn, Jesse H. Morgan, John
 Peterson, Barth A. Risher, Glenda
 Schwanke, Amy Scott, Don
 Shelhart, Rich Wild, Kenneth L.
 Worman;
Lucerne—Harold L. Remley;
Macy—Irene Fitzpatrick, Marsha Neff,
 Edith Tilden;
Marion—Rita Debard, Catherine
 Doretta, Lois Killey, Linda
 Knight, R.N. Knight, Catherine
 Richey, Vera Sanders, Bonnie
 Stevens;
Markle—Phyllis Confer, Mona
 Gearheart, Opal Smith, Mike
 Thomas;
Marshall—Oral & Ruth Simmons;
Martinsville—Maurice Canatsey,
 Warren Crohn, Hayley D. Isom,
 Mr. & Mrs. Dale Maxwell,
 Melvin Maxwell;
Medaryville—Connie Christensen;
Merrillville—Jeane Smith;
Mexico—Karla Wolfe;
Michigan City—Mrs. J.M. Perschke,
 Ida Puschke, Vaughn Rebbeck,
 Leon E. Tuttle;
Middlebury—Craig Bontrager, Mervin
 Bontrager, Mose & Katie
 Gingerich, Wilbur S. Miller,
 Noble W. Nusbaum;
Mishawaka—Robert & Mary Lemon;
Mitchell—Elmo Chastain;
Monon—Cindy Griffin, Mary
 Sandberg, Helen F. Wilson;
Monroe—Dustin Girod, Laura Arnold,
 Shelbi Barger, Mrs. Ralph Bluhm,
 Mr. & Mrs. Melvin Bontrager, F.
 Clair Carver, Bonnie Ehrsam,
 Tammy Fennig & Family,
 Lucille Freels, Sam J. Hilty, Inez
 Hirschy, Devone Johnson, Shirley
 Johnson, Cindy Kauffman, Greg
 & Candy Landis, Mrs. Jeff
 Lehman, Sondra & Patrick
 Leman, Diana McCullough,
 Barbara Rydall, Marilyn Mae Schaadt, Elaine Schug, Patty
 Schug, William Schwartz, Wanda Smith, Deloris Sprunger,
 Tara Steffen Family, Elizabeth Strahm, Glen Stucky, Jill
 Yoder, Joel & John Yoder;
Monroeville—Gerald V. Smith;
Monticello—E. Rita Blederwolf, Clara Bowen, Stacy Foulks,
 Ralph Hall, Mrs. Larry Hunt, The Kilmers, Carol Knight,
 Luis Lindquist, Tom & Doris Maddox, Jean Monnett,
 Martha E. Rice, Mrs. Jerry Ruch, Lola Sellers, Mr. & Mrs.
 Allen Stotler;
Montpelier—Cathy Brook, Gloria S. Ray, Cathy Shaffer, Becky
 Sisler;
Mooresville—C. Ola Brown;
Muncie—Jason Heritage, Joey Heritage, Marvin G. Miller;
Nappanee—Steve Burkholder Family, Fern Helmuth, Dean &
 Edna Hochstetler, Dawn Huff, Eldon Miller;
New Castle—Jane Burke, Janet Evans, Violet Pierce;
New Paris—Cindy Yoder;
New Ross—Lowell & Lois McMullen;
New Whiteland—Doug & Courtney Skaggs;
North Judson—Betty Kalinke, Jeanne Schacht;
North Manchester—Lavon Behny, Mr. & Mrs. Jared Blocher,
 Maribeth Cook, Don Driver, Leona Fetters, Helen Fingerle,
 Matt Fitzpatrick, Leon & Opal Frantz, Violet R. Hartsough,
 Audrey Henderson, Eldon H. Knecht, Richard Laver,
 Rachel Metzger, Fern Miller, Angela Myers, Don Mylin,
 Ruth Ann Mylin, Jeremy Rockwell, H. W. Zahler;
North Vernon—Lee & Dee Banguess, Nila C. Morrison;
Onward—Lindsay Morris;
Ossian—Bill & Julie Allen, Joyce Schaper, Richard & Rita
 Snider, Delight Springer, Betty & Bill Yaney;
Otterbein—Marguerite Waber;
Pekin—Lee Marino;
Peru—Vennie Dillman, Sherry Gehring, Pauline Horner, Connie
 Hunt, Jean Johnson, Randy C. Prokop, Angela Myers &
 Residents, Nancy Spradley, Suann Stoner, Dora May
 Tumblin, Sandra Walker;
Petroleum—Jessie Nash;
Pittsboro—Kay Bollinger;
Plain City—Gary Zerkle;
Plainfield—Susan K. Darnell;
Plymouth—Donna Anderson, Therald Grossman, Ralph
 Lamborn, Ben & Margaret Smith;
Poneto—Pat Holloway, Pam Meeks;
Portage—Don Sharpe;
Porter—Fern Tavernier;
Portland—Herbert C. Bye, Fred & Virginia Conkling, Arvin
 Jones, Peter Metz, Earl Pusey, William Pyle;
Preble—Louise Bieberich;
Redkey—Greg Champ, Mandy Champ, Kristy Rogers;
Remington—Harold Clark, Michael Keith English, Carolyn

Lola Abbott

Herre, Kathy Herre, Leon L. Kaeb, Louise Shelmon,
 Delores Wilder;
Rensselaer—Beverly Dunlap, Bill & Mary Holbrook, Shawn &
 Erin Holbrook, Lucille Hubeny, Calvin Miller, Marvin
 Miller, Virginia Lyn Salyer, Jeryld & Tina Torbet, Mary &
 Milo Ulrich, Mike & Mary Ulrich;
Reynolds—Lori A. Allen, Dustin & Tyler Hileman, Phyllis
 Hoover, Julie & Robbie Salomon, The Snyders, Eleanor
 Williams;
Richmond—Harry & Mabel Schweizer;
Roanoke—Theda Hollenbaugh, John Klingenberger, Phyllis
 Mills, Dave Wilson;
Rossville—Philip Brubaker, Sarah Flora, Paul Rinehart;
Royal Center—Forest E. Davis, Larry Dodt;
Rushville—Darlene Fry, Agnes Koontz;
Saint John—Mrs. Louis Krown;
Salem—Jessie Garber;
San Pierre—Mr. & Mrs. Robert J. Janotta, Keith Kalinke
 Family;
Sellersburg—Helen Graf, Paul & Diane Graf;
Shelbyville—Joann Ragsdale;
Silver Lake—Ivan & Marla Brovont, Ruby Metzger, The Reavis
 Family;
South Bend—Lorraine Havens, Dolly Hersom, George Sellers,
 Harley & Marilyn Sellers, Marilyn & George Sellers;
Speedway—Herman E. Price;
Spiceland—Mary E. Coffman, Helen Miller;
Star City—Florence Gunter;
Swayzee—Marion Boswell, Rita Debard, R.R. Motchett, Karen
 Wilkins;
Sweetser—The Chandlers;
Syracuse—Theo Thomas;
Tipton—Larry F. Whitesell;
Twelve Mile—Jonathan Denlinger, Sylvia K. Miller;
Uniondale—Julie Bradley;
Urbana—Kevin Baer, Mrs. Clyde Dawson;
Valparaiso—Lisa Clemans, Louis L. Cumings, Patrick K. Hill,
 Nancy Hughes, Linda Layman, Paul McKenzie;
Wabash—Brittni Airgood, Max Bechtold, Wilma J. Bever,
 Sandra Calvin, Hazel Cecil, Linda Collins, Betty Cooper,
 Louise Dawson, Beverly Denney, The Drudges, Betty
 Ellars, C. Robert Elrod, Helen Elrod, Barry & Joe Eppley,
 Ethel Fogel, Pauline Fogel, Ruth A. Truss-Gardner,
 Carolyn L. Gilbert, Bob & Ines Gillespie, Don Gillespie,
 Fran Gillespie, Robert E. Gillespie, Jerry Gorne, Belva
 Gray, Estel Harman, Terrie Hay, Carole Hiner, Linda
 Knight, Calvin Lawyer, Mrs. Don McDaniel, Mrs. E.
 Woodrow Miller, Mrs. John W. Miller, Marilyn Miller,
 Melissa Neil, Chester Perigo, Cindy Renbarger, Mary
 Louise Ridenour, Bryon Schdemmer, Mrs. Robert H.
 Stauffer, Gene Stout, Glen Summers, Susan K. Taylor, Ida

May Watson, Jenny Yentes;
Wakarusa—Frank Williams;
Walkerton—Retha Hostetler, Ed & Martha Keeling, Carlene
  Simpson;
Walton—Duane Downhour, Ron Lane Family, L. Robertson,
  Ross Robertson, Elizabeth Sprinkle;
Warren—Kari & Krysta Brubaker, Richard Brubaker, Shelbia
  Deakyne, Mildred S. Elam, Pat & Ralph Eltzrath, Helen L.
  Freck, Karen Hunnicutt, Marjorie Jones, Helen Lafreck,
  Virginia Lievrance, Judy Mauger, Jane Park, Harold
  Poulson, Kenneth Poulson;
Warsaw—Dorotha Binkley, Bob & Helen Moyer, Tom
  Robinson;
Waterloo—Charles Freed;
West Lafayette—Rachel Kallick;
Westport—Joan Whitten;
Wheatfield—Stanley Deboer;
Whiteland—J.D. Skaggs;
Whitestown—Mr. & Mrs. John E. Hancock;
Winamac—Mrs. Patt Axley;
Wingate—Tonya Coon;
Wolcott—Heidi Bahler, Lowell Bahler, Jodie & Troy Clark,
  Joshua & Michelle Furrer, Melissa Furrer, Troy Furrer,
  Mrs. Lloyd Kyburz, Laurie Miller, Gordon Palmer, Mr. &
  Mrs. James L. Rector, Debra & Jon Woodbrey, Hazel
  Wright;
Wolcottville—Karl & Joellen Housholder;
Woodburn—Steve Breit.

Iowa
Ackley—Donald & Verjean Arends, Irwin & Frances Flessner,
  Arnold & Nancy Knipfel, Dorothy M. Meyer;
Adel—Ryan & Heath Lewis;
Afton—Mollie Kruse, Cheri Lilly;
Ainsworth—Harold & Gladys Carson;
Albia—Loyd & Anna Landgebs, Patricia Ryan, Donna Walsh;
Alburnett—Bryan Stonerook;
Allerton—Cody Hackney, Cheri & Clell Moore, Chris &
  Lindsey Moore, Leighton & Betty Moore, Darlene Roberts;
Alta Vista—Melvin & Avis Johnson;
Alton—Martha Jochum;
Altoona—Coral Jones, Louella Speck;
Anamosa—George & Marie Brown, Roy & Gertrude Folkerts;
Anderson—Eric & Elva Nyren;
Ankeny—Bette Honeck;
Aplington—Calvin Kannegieter;
Arispe—Dorothy Eyberg, Oliver Eyberg;
Atlantic—Charles & Mavis Bailey, Helen Ferguson, Mrs. Leon
  Hoegh;
Audubon—Esther Aagaard, Ethel Elsberry, Anna Krottinger,
  Floyd Lacy, Mr. & Mrs. Dale D. Levis, Dorothy Mountain;
Avoca—Oliver & Donna Felker;
Ayrshire—Margaret Rumin;
Batavia—Jack & Pat Glasgau, Alice Hagans, Delna Heston,
  Leonard Heston;
Beaconsfield—Irene Crigler;
Bedford—Jerry & Dale Beemer, Zonette Beemer, Cecil Beery,
  Elizabeth Benson, Maggie & Susan Benson, Willie Black,
  Mariella Blake, Bernice M. Bonar, Avis Bowens, O. Doris
  Brooks, Bryan Cross, Wayne & Dale Danibski, Alicia &
  Luke Davison, Sandy Davison, Rob Dawson, Patricia &
  Katy Dukes, Christie Eagan, Pauline Ehlers, Glenda Fluke,
  Stella Freemyer, Nellie Gold, Norma Gold, Louise
  Goodson, Kim Gordie, Cathy Hardee, Jessica & Justin
  Hardee, Doris Harglee, Emory Heree, Karen Heusley, Ruby

Heyle, Mike Hipsley, Brandi Jo &
Chris Irvin, Jennifer Irvin,
Michael & Jessica Irvin, Evonne
& Ken Jennett, Shanda Jensen,
George John, Leslie Lee, Ellen
Lemke, Alleen Longfellow, Judy
McCall, Marge Mellott, Kathy
Nelson, Robert Odell, Marie Park,
Connie Parrish, Hollie Peckham,
Mrs. Olin Perdew, Bradley Riley,
Dawn & Brooke Riley, Roscoe
Schooling, James Schrodt, R.
Sleep, Gary Spencer, Bruce
Sprague, Bud Sprague, Vickie
Sprague, Marvin Stevens, Chloe
Stewart, Connie Townsend, Gary
& Amy Wackernagle, Thelma
Walston, Patty Weese, Guy &
Louise Weit, Marjorie Wheeler,
Alisha Wilat, Myrna Wilson;
Belle Plaine—John & Mildred Schild;
Bellevue—Bob & Carol Sears;
Benton—Jerri Graham, Norma
  Stringham;
Bettendorf—Warren & Veneta Ewen,
  Dick Golly;
Birmingham—Steve Nunkrich;
Blakesburg—Gary Chidester, Phil & Eunice Valentine;
Blanchard—Paul Klute;
Blockton—Joyce Brown, Lyle & Mary Cavin, Debbie & Tracy
  Davenport, Heather Davenport, Louise Dukes, Candice &
  Matt Faubion, Alva Johnson, Dave Johnson, Lenore King,
  Limsey Lincoln, Dorothy Newkirk, Mary Schuster, Lewis
  & Doris Shiflett, Judy Wilt;
Bloomfield—Pearl E. Garbati, Nancy Armstrong, Lyle
  Augspurger, Matrson Cary, Nick Cramer, Jane Dearborn,
  Roberta Gravitt, Herb & Ione Haffner, Patty Hainline, Amy
  Harbour, Nancy Harbour, Sandra Harvey, Hope Hewitt,
  Edward Hutchcroft, Joy Johnson, Ashley & Kim Levda,
  Cleo Lunsford, Harry McMains, Twyla Miller, Shelby
  Morton, Donald Myers, Norma Myers, Donald G. Smith,
  Zac Sprouse, Mary Stufflebeam, Dova Sutton, Ryan Ward,
  Sonya Ward, Alva C. White, Ken Wuthrich, Russell
  Wuthrich;
Bode—Grant & June Olson;
Bonaparte—Lucille Adam, Alice Meek, June Rice, Kay
  Wingate;
Bondurant—Dorothy Hayes, Donna Speas;
Boone—Evar M. Anderson, Myron Johnson, Rita Kindahl, Amy
  McBirnie, Ivan & Fran Nelson, Mary Ellen Siler, Gary
  Silver, Dean Wirtz, Esther Zeigler;
Braddyville—Jesse Adams, Delores Bragg, Mr. & Mrs. Gilbert
  Burett, Larry & Joyce Clark, Mr. & Mrs. Lowell Clayton,
  Sarah Davison, Jeanene Drennen, Jeremy & Jayne Dunn,
  Brneda Gauke, Sandy Hamilton, Pat Hanson, Kris
  Hennema, Dustin & Kyle Henry, Loyalea & Rodney
  Henry, Kate & Emily Hoft, Bettie Hull, Blair & Bailey
  Humphrey, Seth & Jessica Humphrey, Joyce Kirchner
  Family, Donna Marriott, Ashley & Tyler McKenzie,
  Zachary McKenzie, Scott Murphy, Vicki Nally, Karly
  Parker, Connie Stevens, Janiece Vandaman Family;
Brayton—Mr. & Mrs. Dalton Thompson;
Bridgewater—Sindra Jensen, Warren Johnston;
Brighton—Vera A. Jarvis;
Britt—Jane E. Hilton, Dorothy Hiscocks, Joe Keiderling, Esther

Genevieve Reeve

  Ziegler;
Burlington—Donald Beckman, Roger & Margo Droz, Helen
  Gerdes, Edwin & Merle Holmes, Shirley Klopp, Jerry &
  Tudy Knauss, Gerald D. Smith, Jerry & Helen Smith,
  Wilma Stafford, Roland L. Wiemann, Marjorie Workman,
  Orville Young;
Bussey—Mary E. Frost, Merlyn Peters;
Camanche—Ila Bergersen, Dorothy Bolte;
Carlisle—Martin & Betty Gardner;
Carnarvon—Albert Ohden;
Casey—Leora & Neil Kingery, Donald & Lottie Kinney,
  Nicolas Newbury;
Cedar—Colleen Ashman Family;
Cedar Falls—Dora Howard, Gabe & Ann Leutzinger, Allen
  Malon, Marvin V. Messerschmidt;
Cedar Rapids—Donald & Barb Boesenberg, Gerald & Cathy
  Carter, Dorothy Dostal, Lewis L. Howard, Margaret &
  Gerald Probasco, Cal & Lil Thompson, Marie Wilhelm;
Centerville—Elsie Albertson, Blake Bailey, Alfred & Carolyn
  Bauman, Carolyn Bills, Janie & Benjamin Brennan,
  Michael Brennecke, Alisha Briggs, Burrel L. Browns,
  Frank & Helen Bubenyak, Mary Burkhiser, Jewell
  Davenport, Donald M. Dudley, Mildred Earhart, Mary A.
  Eckiss, Felva D. Farnsworth, Bruce & Darla Fuller, D.
  Fuller, William & Jenny Fuller, Mrs. R.W. Hamlin, Brandi
  Hindley, Cameron Hindley, D.J. Hindley, Ginger Hindley,
  Janet G. Houser, Mike & Mabel Huffman, Dale G. Jones,
  Carol Keener, Edith Kendall, Courtney Kottman, Beverly
  & Dennis Laurson, Kelly & Kevin Laurson, Lori A.
  Logsdon, Eva Martin, Louese McCully, Clyde McGee, Fr.
  Joe Miller, Sam & Barbara Montegna, Mary Morson, Edna
  & Virginia Padovan, Carol & Jacob Phillips, Jay & Linda
  Phillips, Norris & Evalyn Price, Aaron & Alicia Purdum,
  Mr. & Mrs. Thomas P. Reynolds, Mrs. Lois Reynolds
  Family, Mary Roby, Brenda Royer, Richard & Sue
  Ruckman, Ryannan Ruckman, Tony L. Sheston, Wayne L.
  Sheston, Delores Sisul, Mary Laura Strunk, Bernard Terry,
  Leroy & Thelma Thamke, Matey Weist, Roy Witraw;
Central City—Lester Schatzle, Leo & Natalie Smith;
Chariton—Freeda Faust, Alice Glassinger, Cynthia Byers-
  Layug, Opal Longley, George & Maxine Murray, Reva
  Rimkus, Veda Soms, Dale Turnquist;
Charles City—Mr. & Mrs. Ivan Lokenvitz, Thomas W. Oliver;
Charter Oak—Jim & Lois Hart;
Cincinnati—Ted Corder, Laurie Oden, Mr. & Mrs. Elvin
  Thomasson;
Clarence—Melvin Hasselbusch;
Clarinda—Diane Adams, Elaine Armstrong, Lois Baker, M.
  Bates, Rhonda & Courtney Brown, Amanda & Jacob
  Bryant, Dee Bryant, Julia Cavin, James Chrouser, Ceciel N.
  Davidson, Lillie Dillon, Amy Driftmier, Alisa Eason,
  Amanda & Sara Eason, Martin & Melodie Fairman, Mrs.
  Rudy Falk, Dick Johnson, Grace Johnson, Homer Karg,
  Ardis Kearney, Kathy King, Verne King, Diane Kort, Jay
  D. McCall, Karen McClarnon, Megan & Luke McClernon,
  Marcella McKay, Mary McKinley, Phyllis J. Miles, Jason
  & Brent & Sam Minor, Shirley & Jessica Mondero, Jan
  Moses, Karmen Moses, Debbie Murren, Deb Nelson,
  Rosalie Neumeyer, Neil Ohden, Wayne Otte, Zack &
  Whitney Peterson, Norma Phuffer, Jennifer Plagge, Dwight
  Pratt, Janet L. Ross, Valerie & Daniel Spinler, J.
  Sunderman, Margaret Taylor, Marena Vihorio, Jean
  Wagoner, Becky Walker, Cindy & Jeremie Wichman,
  Leone Winger, Ethel Woldruff;
Clarion—Bernice Weld;
Clear Lake—George C. Lunn Jr.;
Clearfield—Helen Lyddon, Lisa Wilson;
Clermont—Marlene Durscher;
Clinton—Elizabeth J. Dahm, Pat Harbron, Donald & Marian
  Paasch, Cassandra & Adam Young;
Coin—Jenny Armstrong, Katie & Jeff Armstrong, Marcia
  Armstrong, Shirley Baker, Ivan & Esther Runyan, Jamie
  Stevens;
College Springs—Darlene Larabee;

Susan Darnell

Colo—Carl & Pauline Gleason;

Columbus Junction—Fran & Jim Morrison, Gary & Denise Schieffer, David & Ruth Seitz;

Conesville—Mr. & Mrs. Bob Manley;

Confidence—Carole & Nathan Schultz, Melissa Schultz, Stephanie Schultz;

Corning—Marney Beemer, Shierlee Deahl, Veldon Deahl, John P. Fees, Chelsey & Debbie Hogan, John Holbrook, Diane Johnson, Anita Thomas;

Corydon—Jeff Austin, Colleen Bay, Joyce Bryan, Hallie Carlson, Wilda Dodson, Debbie Evitt Family, David Foster, Josh Fry, Kathy Gotheridge, Bill Grode, Alicia & Minnette Harvey, Talton Hogue, Dusty Hysall, Bryan & Sue Johnson, Ashlee & Jennifer Middlebrook, Beth & Doris Pollock, Mary Jo Riekens, Julie Rouse, Janett Rush;

Council Bluffs—Elinor Hamilton, H. Franklin Hemmingsen, Coleen Jensen, Gerald D. Turk, Eileen S. Viele;

Cresco—F. Nast;

Creston—Wayne & Maryalice Abel, Harold Black, O. Bowers, Dorothy Brown, Mary & Slim Burg, Shirley Buxton, Helen Caldwell, Evelyn Chapman, Louise Duskin, Ray & Betty Fogle, Ann Heacock, Wilma Johnson, Betty Jungat, M. W. Jiggs Klindt, Jeffrey Kruse, Connie Little, Shirley Little, Evelyn Looney, Bonita McCay, Maxine McElroy, Alzoa McNichols, Diana L. Miller, Matthew & Eric Miller, Randy Miller, Sheryl & Justin Miller, Tiffany & Ruth Miller, Claudie Moore, Christina Morse, Ethylene Ray, Florence Roberts, J.E. & Vivian Schwab, Cindy & Cara Shelby, Mr. & Mrs. Weldon Swigart, M.J. & W.M. Tichnor;

Dallas Center—David & Dena McGlothin;

Danville—Mrs. Robert Gerdes;

Davenport—Don Schneckloth;

Davis City—Cathy Henderson;

Dawson—Dale Grow;

Dayton—Esther Porter;

Decatur—Max Albaugh, Lamar Bontrager, Aaron Harbeson, John & David Harseson, Christopher Hollis, Verlin Miller, Amy Norman, Lisa Porter, Karen Yoder Family;

Decorah—Margaret Koch, Donna Koenig, Eunice C. Stoen, Karen V. Westby;

Denison—Martin & Mary Lally;

Denver—Marilyn & Harold Wente;

Derby—Howard Cattell;

Des Moines—Betty Caswell, Lyllis & Roger Friest, Beth & Kenneth Massey, Marylouise & Ray McElroy, Bill Miller, Ervin Miller, Louise Renes, Donald & Jeanette Roam, Ruth Robinson, Lois & Dorothy Schooling, Janet Sheets, Grace Sickels, Lori Soloman, Bernita M. Swanson, Charles Thomas, Verl M. Weber, Donna Whitman, Alice & Mary Wisner;

Diagonal—Martha Hammond, Ryan & Tashia Hammond, Retha Herold, Hubert Herralet, Doris Hood, Oren & Mara Lou Jeter, Claire Newton, Danielle Newton, Judy Newton, Nola Newton, David & Liz Wiley;

Donnellson—Alverda Blankenburg, Mrs. Howard Hennies, Shirley Hirschler, Dolores Koller, Patricia Koller, Linda Kont, Reuben Neff, Ann Penrod, Jessica Penrod, John & Janet Pletscher, Wanda L. Reu, Darrell Seyb, Howard & Sheila Vorwaldt, Shirley West, Carla Yoder, Mildred Yoder, Judy Young;

Douds—Roy & Donna Copeland, Mrs. Keith Smith, Dorothy Tedrow;

Dows—Mrs. Allen Boyington, Bernard & Norma Russell;

Drakesville—Jacquline Bolin, Mary Stocker, Lyold & Helen Thompson;

Dubuque—Le Ann Keller, Les Pautsch, Linda Schultz, Keith A. Shaw;

Dunkerton—Chancel L. Mixdorf;

Durango—Marilyn Frederick;

Earlham—Dale Stanley;

Early—Milt & Nera Zimmer;

Eddyville—Grace & Ronald Francis;

Eldora—Hazel Hollingworth;

Eldridge—Harold & Bethany Syring;

Elgin—Paul Butikofer;

Elk Horn—Esther Andersen, Jason Lantz, Milie Mortensen, Julletta Petersen, Esther Scott;

Ellston—Mr. & Mrs. Vaughn Case, Al & Jane Christopherson, Arden Espeland, Carol Espeland, Jason Hinz, Shirley & Barry Waters;

Emerson—Don & Ruby Godfrey;

Essex—Jenny & Jill Freed, Lisa & Megan Slater;

Exline—Farrah Lancaster, Curt & Jolene Oden, Donald & Julia Oden, Larry Sedgwick, Ernest & Alfreda Wolver;

Fairfield—Lloyd Buch, John Davis, Justin Harvey, S.M. Richardson, Connie Robertson, Glenn & Arlene Tedrow;

Farmington—Cleta Cocherell, Guy Ann Eastin, Bonnie Ekle, Lois Harland, S. Janeba, Lloyd Meinhardt, Jim & Donnie Moline, Heidi Shriver;

Farnhamville—Ruth Fredrickson;

Farragut—Lola May Ossian, Marilyn Troxel;

Floris—Mr. & Mrs. Lowell Carroll, Vesta Howk, Leama Tallman;

Fontanelle—Elizabeth Jensen, George Jensen, Mary L. Livingston, Dale & Violet Luhrs, Verlea Stiva;

Fort Madison—Floyd Faeth, Paul J. Holtkamp, Dorothy Kenel, John Knox, Megan Mohrfeld, Robert Olson, Harold Piatt, Mrs. Arnold Riedl, Virgil Schumaker;

Fremont—Douglas Lappin, Mary Ellen Moore;

Galva—Lloyd Babcock, Roland Stahl;

Garden Grove—Dave Douglass, Ruth Thomas;

Garwin—Elwood Siernen;

Gladbrook—Loraine Otto;

Glenwood—Mrs. Max Stonebraker;

Gowrie—Eric Fredrickson;

Grand River—Freda Adams, Norma Becker, Lucille Lippold, Tammy Thomas;

Gravity—Bonnie Akers, Jeremy Blake, Richard Christie, Melva Churchill, Ruthy Keyt, The Nickells;

Greeley—Joann Fitzpatrick;

Greene—Richard Merfeld, Dale & Vena Gail Poppe;

Greenfield—Cliff & Phyllis Bax, Pearl M. Hailey, Betty Handley, Robert Handley, Dean Miner, Le Vern & Rita Reis, Earl & Thelma Shinn;

Grinnell—Verleen Eggman, Ross & Betty Ratcliff, Katherine White;

Griswold—Chester Larson;

Grundy Center—Virgil & Bernice Abels, Henry Bockes, Barbara Brown, Cletus Decker, Phyllis Decker, Irma M. Delfs, Bob Johnson, Susie Johnson, Lois Saylor;

Guthrie Center—Janice Walston;

Hamburg—William H. Herndon, Roger Horets;

Hampton—Delores Bender, Erla Eastabrooks;

Hedrick—Floy Jones;

Hiawatha—Vernon & Irene Fay;

Holand—Herman Balher;

Hospers—Dale Stover;

Hubbard—Dwain J. King;

Humboldt—Lucas & Janelle Wigans;

Humeston—Mildred Bright, D. Carter, Eileen Funk Family, Dale E. Hull, Anne Norris, Katie Norris, Marty J. Norris, Glendene Paugh, Patsy Porterfield, Don Richard, Dean Scheeter, Jayma Smith, Mr. & Mrs. Ernest Sponsler, Mary Ellen Stanley, Merle Stanley;

Imogene—Marie Murphy Family;

Independence—Phyllis Murdock, Jay I. Partridge;

Indianola—F.K. Freeman, Wilbur Holcomb, Dorine Westerly;

Ionia—Louie B. Hugh;

Iowa City—Dave & Betty Brenneman, Gary & Sharon Lust;

Jefferson—Ross W. Hansen;

Johnston—Dorothy Miller;

Joice—Maryon E. Holtan;

Kalona—Kelli Ferguson, Louis & Lois Gugel, Daniel & Nita Miller, Dorothy Ropp, Lorena Ropp, Ralph Schlabaugh, Paul Swartzentruber, Chris Troyer, Frank Yoder, Ila Jane Yoder;

Kanawha—Cecil & Maxine Eliason, Willis & Arlene Engh, Leona Freerksen;

Kellerton—Mitchell Adams, Christine Barton, Bonnie Brown, Jeff Brown, Richard Derscheid, Chelby & Ashleigh Durbin, Dee Euritt, Cela Fugate, Linda Gibson, Rosella Greimann, Barbara Hall, J. E. Highton, Helen Laird, Taxanne Larson, Sandy & Sam Lowery, Jane McDaniel, Eileen Miller, Kylee & Nici Minnick, Forest & Darlene Overholser, Billie Smith, Brad & Jess Smith, Brian Smith, Chrissy Smith, Staci Tull, Nicole Vanderflught, Tanya & Cody Vanderflught, Rick Webb;

Kellogg—Berdena Vas;

Keosauqua—Hubert E. Jones, Maxine Shagsta;

Keota—Gayle Brinning, Mr. & Mrs. John H. Copper, Junior & Lorene Henry;

Keswick—Raechel H. Axmear;

Kimballton—Vera Bennett;

Knoxville—Cal & Em Ball, Riccardo & Nelly Campero, Florence Cronbaugh, Beverly Jones, Wava Jean Meyer, Bryan Michelsen, Durl & Isola Schletzbaum, Kyle Shilling, Jack & Bev Sterling;

La Porte City—Duane & Kris Dauth, Marilyn Lee;

Lacona—Sandra Perry;

Lamoni—Bill Ballantyne, Basil Barth, R. Barth, Carina Bruner, Donna G. Campbell, Harvey Campbell, Rose Ericson, Jackelyn Flowers, Amy Green, Paul Griffith, Kermit Harrington, Tonita Helton, Maurita Jeanis, Margaret Landis, Susan Mendenhall, Marvin Parkhurst, Nellie Parkhurst, Brenda Phelps, Donetta Phelps, Ralph Silver, Eugene & Betty Tabor, Toby Yates;

Laurel—Cheryl Anderson, Irene Weir;

Le Mars—Harold & Janice Albert, Goldie Denniston, Margie Hodgson, Lu Vois & Maryann Schmidt, Herman & Helen Schulz;

Lenox—Nettie Cordell, Aileen Dickerson, Bernadine Ecklin, Carolyn K. Gray, Rita Miller, Frances Moyle, Robert Rhoades;

Leon—Diane & Lanita Beachy, Loretta Beachy, Ron Braby, Ken Byler, Mark Dorr, Donna Flummer, Betty Flynn, Homer Hemery, Lewis Hicks, Dustin Hill, Helen Hooney, Melody & Kara Jeffery, Dina Jones, Donald & Shirlie

CROSS-COUNTRY

Chip   Magic

for Seniors!

Shirley Johnson

Mary Stufflebeam

Woodward;

Morning Sun—Laura Fortune;

Moulton—Thelma Ballanger, Krystynah Cooper, Brydon & Rodganna Kaster, Rodger & Byranna Kaster, Tailyn & Sharena Kaster, Tiffany & Zachary Mason, Mary Philby, Bev Saner, Karen Smith, Lloyd Wettstein;

Mount Ayr—Berneeta Austin, Mekenze & Kegan Bishop, Shane Bishop, Dale Black, Emma Borrusch, Mildred H. Cannon, Betty Cole, Justin Cole, Betty Conley, Bernard & Jordan Crawford, Pauline Creveling, Vera M. Deemer, Mr. & Mrs. Kenneth Driftmier, Chris Eason, J.M. Elliott, Alan Force, Jerry Forkner, Cleola Geist, Kelsey Geist, Carol Glendenning, Sharon & Duane Glick, Denise Golliday, Kim Greenland, Joe Haley, Josh Haley, Ralph Hampton, Bob Hinz, Matt & Jacob Hubbard, Kay Keller, Michelle Lawrence, Vicki Loomis, Mary Ann & Eric Mathany, Kay Nelson, R. Nieman, Pam & Callie Poore, Joanne & Mary Sue Pritchard, Dan Reynolds, Sharon Reynolds, Joe Rough, Joan Routh, Duane Schafer, Gerald Smith, Louise Stamper, John & Josh Standerford, Marcia Thonalter, Anne Townsend, Linda Trenkle, Brian & Adam & Amy Triggs, Lynda Triggs, Shane & Sheldon Triggs, Sondra & Ashley Triggs, Roxie Vanderjogt, Dorothy Waller, Amy Weeda, Matthew Weeds, Peggy Worthington;

Mount Pleasant—Matthew Barton, Rex Brown, Kenneth Crile, Mr. & Mrs. Lawrence Moore, Karol Ross, Joy Schlatter, David & Joy Schldlter, Jeanette Trueblood, Mrs. Paul Willite, Ruth Willits;

Mount Union—Stephen Burden, Mildred Crocker;

Mount Vernon—Ella Mae Fricke, V.E. Lauer;

Murray—Cindy Hamer;

Muscatine—Betty Crawford;

Mystic—Alex & Morgan Burch, Bill & Sharon Burch, Norene & Andrew Hancox, Justin Hudson, Dean & Marilyn Perkins;

Nashua—Lyle & Myrna Jepson;

Neola—Erwin & Alice Zarestky;

New Hampton—Mag Wieling;

New London—Carol Berner, Jill McCabe;

New Market—Melva Bix, Marie Campbell, Levi Derry, Kerry Graham, Alex Hansen, Sam & Sabrina Hargis, Madylene J. Huntsman, Angie & Cody McKay, Brian Moore, Diane & Wesley Mullen, Zachary Mullen, Kristine Scott, John Robert Sederburg, Rozann Seela, Jay Sunderman, Darrell Teetens, Elizabeth Thompson, Shalaey & Jessie Varkies, Mat & Tim Vorhies, Connie & Megan Wallace, Marilyn Williams;

New Sharon—Robert Burggraaf, Mary Stewart, Darnell Stout;

New Virginia—Andy Guzman, Jim Morris, Liona Vanden;

Newton—Carol Brain, Tammy & Nikki Brain, Mrs. Roy W. Couch, Wilma Kirkman, Wayne Vandalein;

Nodaway—Bonnie & Nicholas Berggren, Lilly Berggren;

North Liberty—Mary Jo Ogden;

Northboro—Danny & Courney Apperson, Sandy Apperson, Beth Christensen, Ruby Scotton;

Numa—Irene Arbogast, Bill & Mary Bostwick, Gary & Larry Clark, Gayle Davenport, Martha Furlin, Lee Schmell;

Oakville—Helen Hamilton;

Ocheyedan—Clarence Dirks;

Oelwein—John Holtz, Bob & Betty Smith;

Ollie—Maxine Northup, Charles Wonderlich;

Onawa—Doris Ashburn;

Orange City—Abby & Bekah Ahrenholz, Curt Ahrenholz, Pat & Hanna Ahrenholz, Doug Calsbekk, Nancy Jansen, Bernie Reinders, Sharon Rowenhorst, Harold Vandekieft, Dorothea Vanderloon, Kim & Julie Vanpeursem, Mr. & Mrs. Russell Vanpeursem, Williard & June Vanpeursem, R. Visser, Barney Ziztema;

Osceola—Mr. & Mrs. Oral L. Eddy, Christine & David Frohling, Nancy & Elizabeth Lohr, Dean Powell, Faye C. Powell, Eugene Rumley, Mrs. Donald Stamper, Lenore & Stan Stickler, Allen & Marjorie Weeda;

Oskaloosa—Mescha & Tanner Craver, Cecil & Ione Hulbert, Robyn McCrea, Edward Veldhuizen, William A. Veldhuizen;

Otley—Jo Ann Schroeder, Mary Lou Vanroekel, Tunnet Vanwyk;

Ottumwa—Bonnie Beadle, Rachel Beadle, Mildred Burkhiser, Leila Carlo, Roberta Cunningham, Dorothy Engle, Bert Giltner, Darlene Goodman, Lucille Hart, Beverly Huffman, John Maring, Bill & Gladys McDowell, Dolores Miley, Robert S. Miley, Mildred Stevens, Elrella Wagner, Mary Lou Woollums;

Oxford Junction—Jeff & Darla Field;

Jones, Pattie Keller, Harold Lamphier, Florence Leahy, Jason & Michael Miller, Fannie Miller Family, Ken Mingler, Donna Nall, Ruby Owens, Marla Petty, Becky Puhrey, Bob Putney, Andy & Dorris Redman, Ivan Stoltzfus Family, Clara Stout, Virgil & Lynda Wagler, Charles Warren, Lewis Webster, Myron Yoder;

Libertyville—Jessie Hanna, Mrs. Lenora Johnson;

Lineville—Nathan Brenecke, Edna Euffield, Harold Quick, Judy Shields, Justin Shields, M. Shields, Sarah Shields, Sierra Shriver, Ardon Williams;

Little Rock—Ned J. Deboer;

Lockridge—Mrs. William Watson;

Logan—Lyle & Betty Oloff, Mrs. Rosalie Redding;

Lone Tree—Carl & Wilma Ogren;

Lorimor—Lena Fizer, Gerdon Kirk, Ronald & Norma Woodley;

Lucas—Mary Ann Irving, Elara White;

Luton—Dorothy Scudder;

Madrid—Zella Bonsall, Elizabeth Cronk, A.J. Guigli, Wayne & Vera Hick, John Knox, Kathy & Kaitlyn Romitti, Esther Shearer;

Manchester—Berneice Carpenter;

Manly—Amy Grady, Jesse Tomlinson;

Maquoketa—Brett Mitchell, Joyce Mitchell, Virginia Powelka;

Marion—Mr. & Mrs. Don Fairchild, Bernard & Bertha Stoecker;

Marne—Kenny Viether;

Marshalltown—Kevin Jungst, Ted & Beverly Schultz, Paul & Maxine Speas;

Mason City—Carol & Travis Djuren, Jason & Crystal Djuren, Donna Hejna, Karen Olthoff;

Masonville—Robert & Helen Clemen;

Massena—Leroy Hansen, Delmer McElfish;

Maurice—Dennis Vanroekel, Janie & Monty Vanroekel;

Maxwell—James Beal;

Mediapolis—Erna Centner, Charles Earnest, Julie Schmidgall;

Melcher—Eddie Langebartels;

Melrose—Pat Knowles, Hope Tuttle;

Menlo—Virginia Vanduzer;

Middletown—Heather Cousins;

Milton—Gladys Bachmann, Hale Conlee, Evelyn & Wayne Humphrey, Neal E. Kinsinger, Denise Moore, Linda Ruberg, Mrs. Adam Snyder, Bonnie Whitmill;

Minden—Shirley Kahler, Harley & Becky Lund;

Mitchellville—Bailey Andrews, Beth Douglas, Joann Fry, Herman Settje, Normajean & James Warnock, Larry Welch, Linda Winton;

Monmouth—Mr. & Mrs. Forrest Miller;

Monroe—Dick Dehaai, George Timmins, Ramona Vanbaale, Hugo & Jean Vandervelden, John Vanroekel;

Montezuma—Orva J. Bender, Clyde Griffin, Floyd & Marjorie Little, Russell & Jeanete Wiley;

Montrose—Kay Jenkans, Dottie Traver;

Moravia—Richard & Leona Davis, Virginia Hollinger, David Horn, Mary Lou Raymie, Phil Prate, Teresa Strunk, Ron & Cassie & Tyrl Welch, Grace Whitehead, Marion

Packwood—Everett & Loriene Spanier;

Pella—Wendell & Janella Anderson, William Mathes, Henry Monster, Bobert & Johanna Roorda, The Roorda Res., Ernest Steenhoek;

Piagone—Jared & Kathy Eklin;

Plano—Thelma Close, Kathryn Darrah, Wayne Darrah, Michelle Egbert, Becky Green, Harriet & Marcus Green, R.L. Joiwer, Dale Jones, Eleanor Jones, M. Long, Thelma Young;

Pleasantville—Eva Hampton, Kathryn & Harvey Rees;

Pocahontas—Elwood Mayberry;

Portsmouth—Mrs. Stan Martens, Zachary Martens;

Prairie City—Wayne & Marge Chambers;

Prescott—Jaenne Birt, Carol Boraird, Don R. Douglas, Joe & Cheryl Holbrook, Glenn Laird, Pam & Jeremy Mitchell, Howard & Eana Vorties;

Promise City—Mr. & Mrs. Paul Alexander, Brenda Benson, Merle & Ada Cadwell, Lisa Carter, Mr. & Mrs. Eston Curtis, Nathan Devore, Mary Johnson, Audrey Kinser, A. McMurry, Geri Poole, Rhonda Rockwood, Glorile Swan, Leck & Pat Tuttle, Jay Williams, Charles Woodyard;

Pulaski—Pat Altheide, Joann Avis, Janice Batterson, Dorothy Goldizen, Kim Sample;

Red Oak—Louise Deen, Daniel Fisher, Lyn Gibson, Beth Nissen, Lena Purcell, Darrell W. Stevens;

Redding—Alison & Rhonda Quick, Brian Quick, Tawnya Still;

Rippey—Carl King;

Riverside—Mary Troyer;

Rockford—Jerald Montag;

Rockwell—Carrol Rice, Mary C. Smith;

Rockwell City—Wilbur Acklin, Gene & Ruth Ann Dischler;

Rose Hill—William Goodman;

Rowan—Robert Avery, Luelda Tudor;

Rowley—Gerald & Gladys Main;

Russell—Lucille Pohlenz;

Sac City—Bud Owens;

Saint Charles—Louisa & Kate Bedwell, Bonnie Downs;

Salem—Sharon Davis;

Seymour—Justin Boggs, Alister Cash, Gary Elliott, Jamie & Karen Elliott, Joyce Masaoay, Dean Smaniotto, Jimmy Steele;

Shambaugh—L. Lefeber;

Shannon City—Sandy Arnold, Shirley Arnold, Tom & Clay Arnold, Ruby Stephens, Donald L. Vorhies;

Sheffield—Ednabelle Smith;

Shenandoah—Dorothy Boylan, Wilda Brown, Kendra & Kenny Crum, Leona & Spencer Harris, Roy C. Hopkins, Darlene Kowalke, Twyla McQueen, Tiffany Mick, Lois Rolf, L. Vanbuskirk, Marvin Warnemunde;

Sibley—Margaret Attig, George & Dolorys Helmers, Nancy Suchy;

Sidney—Forrest Driever, Roger A. Rasmussen;

Sigourney—Russell A. Aldinger, Ellene Clarahan, Everett & Betty Derby, Eugene Snakenberg;

Sioux Center—Greta Dezeeuw, Alice Dooyema, Mary Hubers, Nel Wissink;

Sioux City—Wilbur Bennett, Dolores Engle;

Slater—Susan Skei;

Sperry—Mrs. Warren Hohmbraker, Ashley & Lauren Walker, Michael Walker;

Stockport—Buena Hendricks, Ed & Helen Niederhuth;

Storm Lake—Mrs. R.E. Mailliard;

Stuart—Judy Linn;

Sully—Henry Rolffs, Russ Vanderweerdt;

Sumner—Aaron Kinne, Wayne & Loraine Priebe;

Swan—Joyce Lockey, Harry W. White;

Swedesburg—Lavern Hult;

Tama—Arnold Veleta;

Teeds Grove—Wilbert & Leola Behrens;

Thornton—Jessie Oilkers;

Tipton—Maxine Ehlers, Elmer & Ina Hack, Earl Howe, Alice Whitlatch;

Toledo—Colleen Hoskey;

Udell—Byron & Felva Tait, Jelva Tait;

University Park—Amy Light;

Van Meter—Robert H. Feldman;

Van Wert—Johanna M. Draper, Margaret Watson;

Villisca—Donna Patton, Anita Wardenburg, Willard White;

Walcott—Jean Engler, Earl Meyer, Ray Moldenschardt;

Wapello—Rose Mary Hayes, Forrest & Peggy Hunt, Mary M. Wallace;

Washington—Herb Hammen, Maxine Jarrard, Celine McMurry Noll, Bernard Reed, Connie Reed;

Waterloo—Rosemarie Deruiter, Lewis E. Hanna, Ruth Hudson, Anna L. Leisinger, Paulette Sewell;

Waverly—W Albrecht, Bill Dean, Evelyn M. Duwe, Carl Eggleston, Ardith Fox, Erwin & Opal Lampe, Lillian Liebers, Lowell Mabon;

Wayland—Roger & Mary Lou Farmer, Kay McGuire, Matthew & Monte McGuire;

Webster City—Patricia Ludwig, Pat & Don Nokes;

Weldon—Helen R. Boggs, Joan R. Boggs, Jan Jackson, Marvin Kauffman, Virginia Reynolds, Mr. & Mrs. Harley Sponsler, Duane & Shaun Troyer, Merlin & Eric Troyer, B. Truman Yoder;

Wellman—Eugene & Elsie Blosser, Cecil & Elda Shettler;

West Bend—Rex Brown;

West Branch—Frank & Marge Floerchinger;

West Grove—Joan Scott;

West Point—Carroll Fraige;

West Union—Gloria Schatz;
Westside—Gail Luft;
Winfield—Lois Everett, Mrs. Wendell Helphrey;
Winterset—Don & Kay Ham, Donald & Karen Ham, Lawrence Hooper, Lois Stuart;
Winthrop—Barb Holtz;
Viota—Aletha Miller, Kelly & Spencer Miller;
Woodburn—Peggy Frizzell, Harley Pippin;
Woodward—John & Lora Stidolph;
Woolstock—Henry & Dorotha Powgnas;
Worthington—Susan Wolfe;
Yale—Ivan A. Rynearson.

Kansas

Abilene—Margaret Abel, Heidi Anderson, Kim Baier Family, Amber Book, Cindy Borchardt, Daniel & Jesse Brinker, Sheryl Brown Family, Joanne Burgos, Joan Christner Family, Matthew & Ben Cook, Justin Crocker, Sandy & Ed Dresser, Karen Elliott Family, Jeanne Freeman, Mrs. Clarence Garten, Tierra Gentry, Kim Goering Family, Amanda Hagan, Chris & Deborah Hagan, Sheryl Hale Family, Savannah Hand, Linda & Jessie Hasselman, Jacque Havice, Neva & David Heck, Lavonna Helvey, Helen Hettenbach, Judy Hettenbach Family, Earl & Ethel Higgins, Leo Hocker, Alicia Holaday, Kenton Howard, Pat Howard, Shirley M. Howard, Eva Katzenmeier, Hilary Katzenmeier, Rein & Heather Katzenmeier, Carol Kenney Family, Megan & Millary Knitter, Cindy Krizek, Harry Kuntz, Redella Lay, Barbara Leckron, Virginia L. Lessenden, Jeanne Livingston, Candi & Jandi Loader, Chester & Evelyn Long, David & Sam McClain, Leta Meats, Jim Mikesell, Wayne & Erma Mills, Jacque Mitzger, B. Monton, Terri Mosburg, Becky & Jessie Polzella, Glenda Renz, Nathaniel Robinson, Mary L. Rosproy, Katie Schenck, Chris Schwab, Edith Scripter, Ann Smith, Sharon Smith, Jim Stalder, Jacob Suskey, Mildred Sybert, Patty Wilson Family, Ada M. Wood;
Almena—Elizabeth Combs;
Alta Vista—Olga Blum, Clarence Horne;
Anthony—Eric Smart, John L. Smart;
Argonia—Bill Holden, Maxine Holden;
Arkansas City—Lloyd Bills, Neda Jo Bills, Bonnie Fair, Joanna Gilliland, Bonnie Gilmore, Elda J. Haradeb;
Assaria—Lester & Ione Johnson, Rena Rundquist, Louanne Short Family;
Atchison—Margaret Adcock;
Athol—Norma L. Larson;
Augusta—Mary E. Walker;
Axtell—Twyla Gaston, Chelsie & Corey Koelzer, Courtney Koelzer, Amy & Ryan Mathewson, Lisa & Daniel Mathewson, Justin Person, Brenda Peschel, Marla Porting, Giles Schmitz, Jamie Smith, Laverne Strathman;
Baileyville—Jena & Megan Deters, Nancy & Kristen Deters, Ross Deters, Richard Feldkamp, Shirley Hasenkamp, Mildred Haug, Vernie Haug, Jolene Heiman, Nick & Jeanne Holthaus, Rita Strathman;

Dean Lilly

Baldwin City—Lola Ford, Lila & Dale McMillen, Darlene Taylor;
Barnes—Edgar & Gertrude Behrens, Nik & Melodie Sediv, Heidi & Danelle Sedivy;
Basehor—Gail Grilly, Clayton B. Smith;
Bazine—Sonya Foos, Susan Kuehn;
Beattie—Rachel Carleen, Sam Dunlap, Ben Gurtler, John Hawkins, Becky Jasko, Lori & Greg Jasko, Ryan Johnson, Steve Koch, Dana Oneil, Irish Oneil, Michael Roesch, Minnie Rueger, Brenda Schneider, Jennifer Schneider, Melissa Schneider, Chris Skalla, Blane & Terri Smith, Ann Studer, Jim Wapp, Lynn Wassenberg, T.J. & Caleb Wilson;
Belle Plaine—Lori L. Mead;
Belleville—Anthony Seaman;
Beloit—M.E. Leidig;
Belpre—The Gales Family, Karen Skalsky, Tonnette Steckman;
Bennington—Kris & Alison Pilcher;
Bern—Jocelyn Dunmire, Rod & Joleen Edelman, Heather & Lana Edeman, Marge Edeman, Esslinger Gerty, Lora & Leslie Heiniger, Marie Heiniger, Duane Meyer, Helen Meyer, Joyce Meyer, Kaye L. Meyer, Eleanor Mosteller, Willene Nusbaum, Hazel Strahm, Wilfred Strahm;
Berryton—Leona Fultz, Rita Renyer;
Beverly—J.M. Haeh;
Blaine—Alice & Laurence Krohn;
Blue Rapids—Mary Alice Baker, Phillip E. Bigham, Margaret Blaske, Becky Clark, Will Clark, Shelly & Chantele Constable, Warren & Farren Constable, Susie & Jimmy Davis, Tiffany & Kim Davis, Tim Downand, Rachael Gray, Erick & Mathew Hofmann, Tim Holliday, Ashley Johnston, Amanda Lockhart, Raechel & Daniell Lockhart, Esther Musil, Edgar H. Pralle, Pansy Rudolph, Jennifer Sownard, Lowell Spedt, John & Leona Stauffer, Amanda & Kim Wessel, Jim Wessel, Kevin Wessel, Colleen Wienck;
Bremen—Debra Kruse, Howard Moehlenbrink;
Brookville—Delbert L. Armbrust, Ethel Diehl, Jeremy Diehl, Cindy Lindsay Family, I. Martin, Florence Mullen, Virginia Pillar, Opal Schulz, Joyce Sheridan, Gayle Wilkins, Linda Zachary;
Buhler—Clara Ediger, Roland & Sarah Froese, Robert & Bertha Janzen, Wilbur Resier, Alvin & Lois Scheel Family, Irvin & Ester Schroeder, Kelly Wolfer, Lane & Kay Wolfer;
Bunker Hill—Dorothia Anderson, Juli Reiss, T. Steckman;
Burdett—Howard & Ginger Barfield, Ann Lynam, Donna Stejskal, John Todd;
Burlingame—Lewis Miles;
Burns—Trint Ellert;
Burr Oak—Rich & Cam Gates;
Burrton—Calvin Troyer, Eileen Umholtz;
Bushton—Deena Bolz Family, Edith Corn, Virgil & Geri Habiger, Margie John, Sandra C. Johnson, May K. Radenbery, Kelli Stevens Family, Lorain Sturn, Geri Wilkens;
Canton—Betty Koehn, Brenda & Janette Koehn, Lanita Unruh, Mitch & Pat Unruh;
Carbondale—Dennis & Vera Brinkman, J.G. Grindal;
Carlton—Mary Reel;
Cedar Point—Ralph Linnens;
Centralia—Elizabeth Bonjour, Ester Ennekins;
Chanute—Delhert Uden, Gene & Cleo Webber;
Chapman—Sandra Acker, Theresa Acker, Kathy Albers, Misty Anderson, Patricia Austin, Kaye Burgett, James Caldwell, Rebecca & Zackary Caldwell, Heather Corbett, Glenda Dixson, Collette Erickson, Gwenn Espeseth, Melissa & Shane Fisher, Adam & Andy Gobber, Elizabeth & Julie Hamel, Sheila Harris, J.D. Iszac Haynes, Janet L. Hoskins, Diana D. Irvine, Rebecca D. Kelly, Pete Krier, Glen Livingston, Colleen Miller, Geri Neumbauer Family, James & Kyle Owen, Susan & Tom Owen, J.D. & Tommy Pelfrey, A.W. Rausch, Alaina & Alan Reed, Aaron Rickley, Lindsay Roskens, Cassie & Brett Salsbury, Ella M. Settgast, Viola Strauss, Marilyn Weishaar, Debra Wood, Matthew & Kristin Wood, Alexia & Ashley Zeigler, Shawn & Heather Zimmerman;
Chase—K. Bryant, Colleen Hawley;
Cheney—Dorothy & Martin Kohler;
Cimarrol—Frank Fight;
Cimarron—Hannah Bartel, Kenny Cossman, Carl Davis, Charles Ebersole, Marva Jantzen, Mike Jantzen, Dale Kirby Family, Curtis Koeh, David Koehn, Merle Koehn, Tony Koehn, Valoree Koehn, Martin Nichols, Clyde Powell, Brenda Russell, L. Tinker, Nellie Toews;
Claflin—Bonnie Buehler, Lori Farmer, Glenna Miller, Deidre Moran, Jeremy & Tim Pflughoeft, Ann Schaffer;
Clay Center—Judy Bauer, Ashley & Whitney Bohnenblust, Jay Bohnenblust, Don Close, John Deetjen, Ileen Ehrsam, Mark Friedrich, Eddie & Verena Haden, Cheryl B. Kline, Allen & Courtney Lang, Lavone Lang, Shelly McClure, Leon B. Mugler, Mary G. Osthoff, Lloyd Swenson, Lucille Wohler, Esther Yarrow;
Clearwater—Larry C. Clark;

Hertha Levis

We're Pulling for Seniors!
MAINE TO CALIFORNIA... 1993

Clifton—Catherine Newell, Laverne Peterson;
Collyer—Eric L. Emig;
Colony—Wilma & Weldon Goodell;
Concordia—Ralph J. Chubbuck, Ruth Cozine, Neva Demanett, Betty L. Everitt, Margaret Graham, Erna & Herb Hedstrom, Pat & Joseph Ostrom, Ruby Stpierre, Wayne & Eleanor Switzer;
Copeland—Jeanette Becker, Vern Becker, Arlene Bunnell, Barbara Casey, Kenneth & Mary A. Derks, Michael & Janae Esau, Annette & Lorena Frank, Jackie Gibson Family, Ray Johnson, Kandra, Bernice & Sandy Koehn, Carol Koehn, Jana Koehn, Jenny Koehn, Marsha Koehn, Myron & Tyson Koehn, Nolan Koehn, Randy Koehn, Tam Koehn, Loretta Loewen, Lorene Nichols, Kenneth & Audrey Nickel, Shirley Nickel, Evangelyn Nightengale, Jan Schafer, Ann Schmidt, Dale E. Schmidt, Merriann Schmidt, Gail Schmidt Family, Kara Smith, Jane Tyler, Carl & Shari Unruh, Cheryl Unruh, Lana Unruh, Norma & Brian Unruh, Phyllis Unruh, Shirley Unruh, Victoria Ward Family, Tillie Wedel, Fran Wedel Family, Vicki Wedel Family, Margaret Weidner, Betty Whitaker, Eva Wiebe, Myrna Wilson, Esther Withers Family;
Council Grove—Gail Edwards, Andy & Anna May Olson, Jo Ann Stiver, Alan Young;
Delia—Richard Lewman;
Delphos—Raymond & Edna Hoffhines, Rex McKain;
Denton—Vanetta Geiger, Mr. & Mrs. Phil Harrison;
Derby—Tom & Lynn Muskus, Jane Pomeroy, Margie Smith;
De Soto—Becky & Robert Klingler, Ben Klinler;
Dighton—Joyce Ellis, Lavone Richards;
Dodge City—Penny Alger, Kim Ashlock, Loren Ashlock, Travis Bailey, Andrew Barkhart, Lynn Bartel, Twila Beck, Mike Berg, Maggie Bilboy, Wayne Blauvelt, Suzanne Bondurant, Margaret Brennan, Leota Brown, R. Brumit, Judi Buckley, Carrol Burnett, Ona Lee Burton, Jacob Busch, Seth Bush, Ashley Chapman, Pat Childress, Elise Clark, Wendy & Amanda Clouse, Mark Cochran, Andy Coffin, Ramona Cole, Dane Conant, Dona Cragg, Douglas Cummins, Charree Donley, Steanie Donley, Janae Dons, Mary Duffield, Nicole Eaton, Nellie Evans, Velma Faulds, Erlene Flowers, Johnny Flowers, Jerrod Frederking, Karen Gat, Missy Giersch, Lindsay Gogolski, Melissa Goldsberry, Teri Green, Ron Greenley, Lodema Gumm, Don Hahn, Agnes Hall, D. Hamilton, Mrs. Dean Hamilton, Sarah Hampton, Dennis Hanes, Allison Hatfield, Connie Hatfield, Marissa Herbert, Michael Herbert, Tyler Herman, Eddie & Catherine Hertel, Molly Heyer, Maxine Hohrmann, Sheri Holtfeich, Serria Hostetler, Glenda Hutchcraft, Jessica Ingram, Carol Jean Jackson, Wayne Jackson, Sharli Jefferson, The Kaley Family, Cecil Karleigh, J. Kephart, Ethel Knobbe, Katrina Konrade, Debbie Lloyd, The Lukebogolski Family, J. Markus, Cathy McBee, Hugh McLaughlin, Tony Merle, Kala Miller, S. M. Million, The Millions Family, Jonathan Mills, Martha Mink, Vicki Mirt, Jim Musick, Pam Neeley, Chad Niles, Fred Offenle, M. Ogden, Alyssa Ontiborug, Lyman & Lucille Parnell, Rod Perkins, Tom & Crystal Perry, Sue Powell, Kathy Rees, Lucille Richard, Madison Riley, Isaac Roehm, Sharlene Roesener, Deiedra Rogers, Earl Roney, Dee Dee Royle, K. Royle, Ryan Royle, Tyler Royle, Jeff & Blake Rumbaugh, The Rumbaugh Family, Connie Salmans, C. Sanchez, Katie Schminke, Melora Schriner, Janice Scott, Kayla Scott, Roxanne Scott, Evie Seybert, Tim Shea, Pauline Skaggs,

Arnold Riedel

Bettye Sloan, Fred Smith, Dana & Kara Sparks, Connie Stein, Kady & Ryan Stein, Viola Steinkuehla, Martha Strecker, E. Subert, D. Thomas, Chase Tiemeyer, Jeramie Torrez, Susie Tracy, Marlene Underwood, Dustin Volz, Nicole Webb, Dana Weber, Mr. & Mrs. Leon Weigner, Linda Wellbrock, Bernice Whittaker, Linda Wilson, Krystal Woodring, Katie Yoder;

Douglass—Deborah Suntheimer;

El Dorado—Polly Grubb;

Elkhart—Kay Coen, Elsa Ferne Durkee, Susan Kern, Janis Smith;

Ellinwood—Ruth Banks, Carol Happin, Floyd Hopkins, Normalee Isern, Brandon Kaiser;

Ellis—Carol Pinney;

Ellsworth—Sue Arensman Family, Patricia L. Benda, Glennys Bruning, Leroy Bruning, Connie Diaz, Alice Dowley, Teresa Froese Family, Emily Green, Sandra Green, Karen & Kassie Grothusen, Zach & Kassie Grothusen, Ed Hoffhines, Loren Hopkins, Laverna Hunter, Daryl & Marilyn Huslig, Viola Jiricek, Linda & Andrew Kohls, Sharon Lindman, Susan Manes, Justin Paden, Clearance Peterman, Christian Scherling, Cheryl Schneider, Jean Soukup, Roxanne Stevenson, Niki Sutty, Paula & Eli Svaty, Julie Thompson, Connie Warta, Jewel Wheeler;

Emporia—Linda Cookson, Ed & Lorena Eisenhauer, Barbara Gerriets, Erma Mae Jones, Joyce K. Smith, Louise Snook;

Ensign—Tyler Beggs, Craig Dohrman, Velda Holsten, Jeff Reinert, Shirley Richardson, Lindsay Underwood, Robin Underwood, Ryan Vandergiesen, Kim Wilson;

Enterprise—Vicky Chamberlin, Janie Dolton, Gary Patterson, Wyoming Snyder;

Erie—Linda Lolla;

Eudora—Mary Lou Hamlin;

Eureka—Marlene Moreland, Gyneth Munsell;

Fairview—Barbara Kleitz, Alvin Kruse, Elmer & Paul & Tom Middendorf;

Ford—Desiree Raines, Kim Stout, Michelle Stout;

Fort Dodge—Larry Cecil, Donald Lavigne, Don Roges, Velma Seroghame;

Fort Riley—The Osborne Family, Lindsey & Lacey Singleton, Maria Singleton;

Fort Scott—Harold Craft, Marie Myers, Priscilla Sellers;

Fostoria—Genoa Benedick;

Fowler—Ruth J. Grubb, Rose Lee;

Frankfort—Ashley Howell, Rachel Jones, Everett Shearer, Les Shearer, Cameron Winslow;

Galva—Mr. & Mrs. Roy Becker, Patricia Fells, Mr. & Mrs. Gavin Johnson, Mr. & Mrs. Elmer Koehn, Mr. & Mrs. Henry Koehn, Karen Koehn Family, Leah Nightingale, Clarence Russell Family, Jack & Eleanor Smith, Daryl Unruh, Karen Unruh, Marlin Unruh, Vernald M. Walline;

Garden City—Carol N. Anderson, Ed Berg, Brian & Stephanie Coleman, Steve & Karla Coleman, Inez Dew, Vicki Dye, Marisha Eck, Steven Eck, Lela Hendrick, Bernard Killer, Dale Marine, Maxine Marine, Jennifer Norman, John & Audra Noyes, Esther Sculley, Stanley C. Smith, Verda Thomas, Tim Unruh, Art Wiebe;

Garfield—Corrine Brack, Kent Converse, Tamara Dipman, Brenda Froetschner, Lorelee Froetschner, Christina Holaday, Lisa Hulsey, Barbara McFann, Fay Murphy, Dorothy Novotny, Brenda Reed Family;

Garnett—Mr. & Mrs. Cleo Betts, Carl & Lila Graybill;

Geneseo—Bobbie Boye, Patti Gustus, Steven Janssen;

Glasco—Marilyn & Reed Griest, Benton & Maxine Jones, Orwan Mann;

Glen Elder—Howard & Patty Cooper;

Goddard—Leslie & Eleanore Greenwood Family;

Goessel—Arlene Asmussen, John Dick;

Goff—Martin G. Butrick, Carol Lueger, Carmen & Wilma Thompson, Darryl Thompson, Eugene Visser;

Great Bend—Nancy Baxter, Justin Belt, Grella Berscheidt, Melvin Brach Family, Ashlea & Andrea Brack, Phyllis Brack, Velda Brittain, Jessica Champ, Virginia Champ, Nick Christiansen, Jeff Claphan, Steve Clarke Family, Lynne Curran, Florence Curtis Family, Earl H. Davis, Shirley Degenhardt, Melissa Doherty, Peggy Faris, James Garner, J.T. & Joann Gaunt Family, Chris Geer, Jenny Glen, Elda Glynn, Garrett & Gregory Glynn, Jennifer Glynn, Annette Goering, Helen Green, Lebrina Halsup, Ronnie Hambry, James & Lavina Hanks, Edna Harbaugh, Destiny Hayward, Kristi Heinz, Luke Helmuth, Brenda Herrman, Gary & Pat Hinson, Bobbie Hughes, Debbie Hupher, Owen & Mary Jones, Diana Kaeberle Family, Bertha Kahn, Connie Karlin, K.L. Kerr, Tom Klug, Jesse Kruger, Jennifer Lee, Wendy Lockhart, Linda Mai Family, Judy Manning, Mindi E. Mattocks, Deborah McLaughlin, Sally Medlock, Erma Meyer, Roy Milford, Kenny Miller, Julie Mitchell, Lorrie Moyers, Karen Neuforth, Mary Newman, Sally Odell, Abby Olson Family, Beth Paden, Jacklyn Payne, L.E. Peterson, Sonya Petrik, Kristin Potter Family, Donald Powers, Laura L. Reddig, Connie Remmert Family, Edna Rice, Betty Riggs, Bob Robbins, Willa Ruth, Nicole Schartz, Dorothy Scheideman, Jeannie Schrader, Karen & Kaley Schrader, Janet Siebert, Don Smith, Shirley Smith, Bobby Stark, Mary Graves Thorson, Sylvia Triplette, Wayne Unruh, Sarah Untereiner, Deanne Weathers, Cathy Weber, C. Welch, Ed & Helen Wetzel, Mr. & Mrs. Leonard White, Ann Wiens Family, R. Wiley, Bob Younger;

Green—Lois Asp, Michelle & Matt Fry, Jayne Lund;

Greenleaf—Lori Pralle;

Greensburg—Clara Colclazier, Effie Miller, Dale Murray, Milton Sparke, Daryl Unruh, Donald Unruh, Charley Wadel, Eunice Wadel, John Yohn;

Grinnell—Walter Dohm, David & Alma Lubbers;

Gypsum—Jesse Becker, Elisha Carter, Harold Grainger, Leona & Jennifer Mutschler, Luke Mutschler, Richard H. Mutschler, Harlen W. Prater, Michael Redden;

Halstead—Wayne Smith, Raeletta Unruh;

Hamilton—Beulah Grilliot;

Hanover—Crystal Bahe, M. Clark, Esther Dixon, Mr. & Mrs. Harold Dixon, Buff Stohs;

Harper—Kathy Zimmerman, Vern Zimmerman;

Harveyville—Marjorie Baxter;

Haven—Harry & Mary Bontrager, Ervin & Alice Eash, Perry & Ada Eash, Atlee & Wilma Keim, Lonnie & Rachael McGee, Enos & Vera Miller, Enos & Clara Mae Yoder, Thomas & Vera Yoder;

Haviland—Kyndra Eck, George Yohn, Nadine York;

Hays—Ruth Ann Aschwege Family, Kristy Bieberle, Susan Corn, William S. Dreiling, Karla Stecklein, Kelton & Kassidy Stecklein, Shayne & Vanessa Wilson;

Haysville—Mable Clark;

Herington—Lucille Heiser, Ann Roehrman;

Hesston—Eli M. Bontrager, Perry Burkey, Bonnie Carlton, John Detweiler, Oren Detwiler, Ralph Detwiler, Enola Dreier, Karen & Ben Fulk, Ben Fulk Family, Lena Good, Adella Jantz, Roma Jantz Family, Melva Kauffman, Leonard Lichti, Max Marner, Wanda Marner, Raymond C. Novak, Harold D. Schmidt, Wilbur & Iona Schrock;

Hiawatha—Jerry C. Aller, Lillie Bindel, Mavis Geiger, Doug Grimm, Leslie Grimm, Louise Jacobs, Micki Meenen, Ashli & Kyle Meenon, Emma L. Middendorf, Alyssa & Brittney Monaghan, Coleen Monaghan, Kennedy & Esther Olds, Nancy Prawl, Stephen M. Spare, Elizabeth A. Wagner;

Highland—Jack B. Dillon, Helen Lewis;

Hillsboro—H.E. Heiser, Harold B. Jost, Cody Penner, Chester & Bernice Unruh;

Hoisington—Teri Doze, Diane Henry, Richard McGinnis, Steven Ritter, Lenore Steiner, Delilah Winkler;

Holton—Margaret Gardiner, Raymond Gardiner, Mistie Rhynhe;

Holyrood—Betty Boye, Marilyn Etchison, Tisa Pulin, Keith & Louise Ryan, Elaine Willt;

Home—Jane Haltman, Tamar Haller, Karen Johnson, Wes Johnson, Donna Haver Kamp, Tereas McMillan, Jessica & Jacey Rumbeck, Justin Rumbeck, Pat Seematta, Dustin & Devin Seematter, Joann Shum, Virgil & Lacey Stock;

Hope—Dan & Marcia Falen, Zola & Casey Morgan, John West;

Horton—Karen & David Beams;

Hoyt—Carolyn Golden, Lois Keller;

Hugoton—Chip Broaddus, Erma Heger, Chelle Leininger, Bill & Tina Leonard, Billy Leonard;

Huron—Frances R. Scholz;

Hutchinson—Rhea Brunner, Pat Bruns, Harold C. Cash, Harry Eshelman, Abe Friesen, Pauline Garcia, Charlotte Green, Esther Harder, John Headings, Eli Helmuth, Randall & Mary Lantz, Juanita Lemen, Clarice Mathews, Phil Mathews, Lamoine McEntarfer, Trenton Robinson, Robert & Sue Rue, Doran Schlabach, Karen Stickley, Glenn W. Stutzman, Linda Tegethoff Family, Marvin & Clare Ward, Gloria Yoder, Jonas & Lydia Yoder;

Independence—Lawrence & Rita Gillman, Althea Rector, Joan Shepherd;

Ingalls—Andy Friesen, Harley & Karen Friesen, Lorinda Friesen, Doreen Mininger, Frank Mininger, Sara Schultz, Ray Smith, Keith & Beverly Smith Family;

Inman—Dave R. Balzer, Fran Fast, LaVerne Newfeld, Mr. & Mrs. Arnold Regehr Family;

Iola—Harold Osborn;

Isabel—Carolyn Armstrong, Beverly Hewitt, Quentin Hirt, Leo & Fern House;

Jamestown—Eldon Larson;

Jetmore—Jason Cole, Lester Sager, Mildred Sager, Tanner Sager, Jeremy Whiteside;

Jewell—Janet Birdsell, Adam Butts, June Butts, Jim Dooley, Don & Shirley Simmelink, Vic Tullar;

Johnson—James & Wanda Banning, Nancy Banning, Blake Bexona, Patsy Bitner, Holly Brooks, Milton Burnett, Sharon Dimitt, Rachez Finley, Gail Jorgensen, Leon & Grace Kilgore, Helga Leininger, Jim Lenz, Rhita Mangels, Marjorie Millington, Jean Morris, Sharon Nelson, Gerald Nickell, Geneva Persanger, Marylee Ramsay, Tina Rodriguez, Virginia Snell, Dorothy Sponsel, Emma Walker, Lea Ann Zahnter;

Junction City—Teresa Archer, Shirley A. Carroll, James Davis, Karen Erichsen, Luke & Pam Erichsen, Leona Garrison, Ryan Garrison, Laura Mae Goad, Emily Heldstab, Jaimie & Sarah Heldstab, Michael & Brian Heldstab, Peggy Heldstab, Pauline Jennings, Irma R. Keffer, Gloria Lansbury, Erika G. Losonszky, Dottie McKinney, Margie & Emily Pinaire, Nancy Sampson, Brooke & Paige Shumaker, Jolene Shumaker, Lynn Sitton, Blanche Stiffler, Rusty Taylor, Billy Upham Iii, Heather Wahle;

Kanopolis—L. Fortman, Shirley McCary, Connie Svaty, Mr. & Mrs. Delorn Zahradnik, Leann Zahrasnik;

Kansas City—Grace Bixler, Britney & Betany Blomberg, A. Mullins;

Kinsley—Mary Carlson, Cindy Davidson, Nancy & R.G. Dimmick, Edward & Ruth Domme, Karen Garcia, Albert Hall, Gerald Herrmann, Nichole Janzen, Alice Katz, Mrs. Wayne Kese, Carol Naber, Marge Schmidt, Sharon Seibel, Mindy Stegman, Mary Strong, Kyler Vanmahmen, Jerad & Jesse Zink;

La Crosse—Charles & Frances Bankston;

Lakin—Betsy & Sharon Koons, Danny Koons, Harold & Berniece Loeppk, Michele Nightingale, Carrie Petersen;

Larned—Ron & Sharon Arnold, Leonard Aufdemberge, Krystal Beckwith, Lila Beltz, Libby Best, Marilyn Buchanan, Alice Callahan, June Callaway, Suzan Caro, Sarah & Abbie Collins, Olsen & Jordan Creighton, Pam Darling, Lloyd Davis, Leslie & Phyllis Deckert, Cathy Eaves, Glenda Eye, Margie Flickner, Kay Fox, Sharon Fox, Darlene Fox Family, Roland Froetschner, Shawna & Miranda Gilliland, Jean & Mystel Graver, Dena Haremza, Sheli Haremza, Michelle Hopkins Family, Janet L. Horner Family, Alice Howard, Louise Hunter, Lindsey Johnson, Ron Johnson, Jerry Johnson Family, Cassie & Bryce Keast, Alene Kirch, Jessica Love, Emma Marlett, Melissa Martin, Megan McDonald, Cynthia Mead, Valeta Milhon, Vicki Ostrander, Kay Parks, Dylan Penka, Charles Pfenninger, Noble Reeves, Helen Roberts, Jill Robinson, Dorothy Rose, Rosalee Roth, Jamie Ruehlen, Vera Schmidt, Melba Schneider, Mr. & Mrs. Leonard Seba, Marti Smith, Michele Smith, Wayne H. Ward, Cherie Weber, M. Webster, Edith White, Justin White, Jan White Family, Elizabeth Wilcox, Tiffan Williams, Josh & Justin Woods;

Lawrence—Betsy & Rae Redd, Randy & Joe & Jerry Redd;

Le Roy—Dana Meyer Family, Gregory K. Meyer, Justin & Kaitlin Meyer, Louis & Maydene Meyer;

Lebanon—Frances Hill;

Lenexa—Leland & Carol Bartel, Howard & Jerry Boehm;

Lenora—Judy & Darold Arnold;

Leon—Renee Lile;

Leona—Beverly Holder;

Leonardville—Joshua & Sarah Beall, Franklin Bulk, Carol Foveaux, Carla Hageman, Fern Hageman, Amber & Heather Hopper, Kenny Hopper, Elnora Jones, Kerry Jordan, Irene Klocke, Mildred Kunze, Evelyn Lawson, Luann Lund, Don Nannuga, E.J. Olson, Lilyan Oman, Dorrene & Ethan Peterson, Wava Peterson, Tina Pixler, Kelsey & Kyle Rothsberger, Royce Rothlisberger, Ashley Ruthston, Bonita Sprecker, Crystal & Tyson Strauss, Julie Strauss;

Lewis—Mandy Blevins, Lenice & Jill Divis, Marcile King, Harold Newsom, Jay Mee Peterson, T. Roenbaugh, Sage Sandelin, Alvin Wheaton;

Liberal—Bess Lofland, Amanda Naigle, Ford Nik Family,

Jennifer Vanley;

Lincoln—Deb Breneman, Leigh & Dennis Kasey, Linda Rosebrook Family;

Lindsborg—Emeline Brunsell, Jane Brunsell, Leonard Carlson, Judy Ellis, Barbara Kissick, Joyce Kurtz, Anita M. Nelson, K. Peterson;

Linn—Jody Richter, Jo & Christian Rippe;

Linwood—Teresa Aitken, Jane Harris;

Little River—Wayne Lowmaster;

Long Island—John & Evelyn Ponstein;

Longford—Ann Bergmeier, Christine Wolf;

Lorraine—Brock Alexander, Betty Rolfs, Mrs. Delmar Williamson;

Lucas—Toya Kasiska;

Lyons—Crystal Behnke, Margaret Harding;

Macksville—Katty Evans, Janet & James Hudson, Dan & Alyssa Renfro;

Madison—Barbara Ann Zimmerman;

Manhattan—Alice Adams, Terry Bakelman, Adam Bonewitz, Anna Mae Brenner, Jami Colley, Stacy Deetjen, Frances Ellis, Ruth Elliston, Kathy Elser, Ragnar Emrich, Donna Flahr, Freda Edie Hadle, Sue Hageman, Marie Henn, Ivy Hoffman, Denae & Dixie Jones, Margaret Leonard, Susan Mintert, Shane Montgomery, Virginia Morris, Yathika Perera, Lacy & Valerie Peterson, V. Phillips, April & Kandyce Reddig, Virgie Redding Family, Chester R. Unruh, Ken Visser, Eric Weddle, Dorothy Westervelt, Brenda Wienck, Wanda Wienck, Edna Williams;

Manter—Elizabeth Allison, Manter Elem, Tina Loader, Jenny Marshall, Pauline Wilkerson, Robert Wilkerson;

Marienthal—Lillie Schusindt;

Marion—Dick McLinden;

Marquette—Eldora Busby;

Marysville—Fred Bargmann, Brent Boyle, Bill Cain, Brooke Clelland, Ann & Scotti Cloeys, Lila Cockeriff, Alice Cottrell, Emma Eden, Cecil Glick, Marshall Griffin, Dale Hadorn, Susan & Bonnis Hale, Ruth Hawkins, Connie Heidebrecht, Tom Jogelsberg, Frank Johnson, Scott & Brian Kramer, Sharon Kramer, Karen Ladner, Frank Linden, Lisa Miller, Heather Norman, Robert Oconnor, Dorothy Peschel, Dr. Edward Steichen, Emily Sutton, Jamie Sweet, Mary Louise Thomas, Henry Vogelsberg, Elaine Wecher, Cerry Williams, E. Williams;

Mayetta—Jo Fenske, Josh Michael;

Mc Donald—Jay & Laura Poore;

Mc Pherson—Shirley Ade, James L. Aitkens, Beverly Alstatt, Raymond & Marie Chambers, Helen Louise Cheesman, Ruth Davis, Galen W. Fields, Geneva & Arlo Flickner, Valerie Frazier, Lillian Holler, Denise Koehn, Terry L. Koehn, Burdette & Beulah Larson, Joanna Mason, Shawna McAllister, Dale McSpadden, Duane & Opal Myers, Bernita Richards, Cindy Scott Family, Shirley Unruh, Rebecca Yoder Family;

Meade—Mr. & Mrs. Fred Alley, Ben & Alvina Bartel, Nick & Helen Ediger, Elmer Friesen, Jake & Viola Friesen, William & Allison Friesen, Fran Glen, Lisa Harshberger, Abe Isaac, Henry K. Reimer, Leon Toews, Eldo & Esther Wiens;

Medicine Lodge—Robert Witchey Family;

Mentor—Joyce & Jamie Hitchcock;

Meriden—Marla Rice;

Milford—Danny & Scotty Breidenstein, Elizabeth Frink, David & Jacqui Handlos, Susan McCleary, Evelyn Miller;

Miltonvale—Dorothy Carver, Clarence Ming, Hazel Ming;

Minneapolis—Holly Bickford, Rita Carpenter Family, Easter & David Clark, Darrel Hubbard, Leona Lott, Dorothy Muller, Nonie Nicklas, Mildred Smith;

Minneola—Jill Leis, Katie Mashak;

Montezuma—Laverne Billie, Jill & Todd Buller, Heidi Classen, Kevin & Carolyn Classen, Carolyn Classen Family, Alma Dirks, Daniel & Chad Dirks, Sandra & Matthew Dirks, Taylor Giesbrecht, Scott Glasscow, Fred Goossen, Beth & Hannah Harms, Dalen & Tina Harms, Jason Harms, Justin & Sean Hayden, June Hendrickson, Tracey & Tyler Hogie, Elizabeth Hollingsworth, Paul Host, Deanna Isaac, Lisa Isaac, Cassandra Jantz, Jerry Jantz, Ryan Jantz, Savannah Jantz, Nancy Kee, Troylene & Kale Keohn, Craig Koch, M. Koch, Sheila Koch, Andrea Koehn, Calvin Koehn, Chad Koehn, Charles Koehn, Diann Koehn, Gregory & Kendra Koehn, Janice Koehn, John & Kendall Koehn, Karen Koehn, Melani Koehn, Preston Koehn, Robert & Betty Koehn, Ross & Sherry Koehn, Russell Koehn, Sarah Koehn, Sheri & Sheldon Koehn, Sophia Koehn, Sueann Koehn, T. Koehn, Tanya Koehn, Tona Koehn, Janet Kohen, Mario Lozano, Jessica McConnell, Amy Nichols, Barbara Nichols, Brett Nichols, Jeri Nichols, Jerrell Nichols, Yvonne Nightingale, Tara Poppe, Velda Ratzlaff, Hank & Sharon Redger, Lisa Redger, Autumn Rhodes, Mona Rhodes, Gloria A. Schmidt, Jacki Schmidt, Lisa Schmidt, Nita Schmidt, Rosalita Schmidt, Tina Schmidt, Todd Schmidt, Wilma Schmidt, Bryce Sidebottom, Charity Smith, Stephanie Smith, Tyson Smith, Brenda Thomas, Cate Unruh, Janette Unruh, Teryl Unruh, Vadalene Unruh, Harry & Mary Ann Wedel, Christopher Yost, Florence Yost, Jed Yost;

Morganville—Jan Germann;

Morland—Georgann Meier;

Morrill—Bernard Chadwell, The Grubers, Gale Kellenberger, Selena Manche, Amy McKim, Don McKim, Jim Scoby, Anna & Leisha Tennal;

Moscow—Ralph White;

Moundridge—Dorothy Bates, Mark & Kara Classen, Andrew Dyck, Helen Flickner, Robert Jantz, Pearl Johnston, Chris & Colleen Koehn, Dora Koehn, Ethel Koehn;

Mount Hope—A.J. & Bernice Eisenhauer;

Mullinville—Sibyl McKinley;

Neodesha—Joe Behrskens;

Ness City—Jackie Misner, Joanne Stenzel;

Netawaka—Geraldine Sarensen;

New Cambria—Iva Base Family, Rose & Trevor Davis, Dorothy C. Day, Joyce Hardisty, Dewight Lockhart, Tom & Donna McAllister, Robert McCall Sr.;

Newton—Harold Andres, Mrs. Duane Bair, Janet Bair, Mr. & Mrs. A. Becker, Rodney Berg, Albert & Agnes Budde, Jerry Butcher, Velma & Ruddie Claassen, Leland & Neva Coester, Heather Cooper, Lorraine Cummings, Evelyn Dombrosky, Anita Houdek, Frank & Mary Kessler, John Lohrentz, Don & Kathryn Penner, Robert & Ruth Suderman, E. Ralph Titus, Albert Voth, Don & Gloria Webber, Jim West, Laveta Williams, Ryan Williams, Melvin & Ramona Yorgensen;

Nickerson—Jeanie Neujahr;

Frances Hill

North Newton—Larry R. Baer, Patrice Claassen, Orlando & Maxine Fast;

Norton—Karla Anderson, Mary Goldsby, Elbert Goldsy;

Oakhill—Mr. & Mrs. Leonard McIntosh;

Oakley—Alicia Albers, Della & Jenny Beamer, Sarah Beamer, Landen Halbleib, Myrna G. Heskett, Bernard & Sandra Huesluckamp, Sandra Muehlenkamp, Paula Rumback;

Odin—Shelley Demel;

Offerle—Albert Birzer, Carol J. Burhart, Janet Fowler, The Hattrup Family, Eletha McCollum, Peggy Molitor, K. Repiri, Terri Stegman, Kim Vannahmen;

Ogden—Janet Estes, Jon & Nick Estes;

Oketo—Bradley Heiman, Rhonda & Tony Heiman;

Olathe—Laura Markby, Angie & Kirsten Samuelson;

Olmitz—The Frieb Family;

Olsburg—Harold D. Callahan, Bob Edwards, Mary Lou Gibbs, Diana & Jacob Nelson, Nita Pope, Russell & Marie Pope;

Onaga—Merle Bonjar, Orville & Vera Marten, Winona Oswalt, Pat Ratcliff;

Oneida—Linda Feldkamp, Lyle Feldkamp, Robert Feldkamp, Betty & Marilyn Metzger;

Opolis—Sharon Harmon;

Osage City—Jessica Pullum;

Osborne—Berta Bleam, Marvin & Ila Knoll, Eva Lockhart, Doris M. Palmer, Barbara J. Wilson;

Oskaloose—Ruby Hale, Lowella Honeywell;

Otis—Hank & Emma Highfill, Rosemary Highfill;

Ottawa—Elsie Flory, Max W. Floyd, Juaneta Heckman, Beverly Hughes, Nellie Lederer, Margaret Shaughnessy, Russell & Wilma Shipps, Bertha Sylvester, Gale Woodrome;

Overland Park—Billie Bopp, Elverda Carlock, David Rinae;

Oxford—Wallace D. Martin Family;

Ozawkie—Leona & Kyle Tyler;

Palmer—Trudy & Jacob & Tim Ohlde;

Paola—Clyde Brewer, Fay Woodrome;

Partridge—M. Wagler;

Pawnee Rock—Geoffery Adams Family, Vivian Bright, Marvin Causey, Gabrielle & Shay Guesnier, Alice Ingram, Joyce Link Family, Kristin Loving, Jill Milhon Family, Steve Murphy Family, Robert & Mark Neeland, Jo Ann Quinn, Janice Schmidt, Mike & Joseph Stafford, Leanna Unruh, Jenny Wilson;

Peabody—Carol Gillet, Pauline McPheeters, Vada Ann McPheeters, Elfrieda Schmidt, Raymond Schmidt;

Penokee—Carol Larcom;

Plains—Debbie Eakes, Sharla & Darlene Kohn, Kimberly Shinogle;

Plainville—E.L. Glendenning, Norma Jean Glendenning;

Pomona—Geraldine Horne, Mollie Jo Worthington;

Portis—Leo & Irene Macy;

Powhattan—Jonathan Pollock, Luke Pollock, Sharilyn Pollock;

We're Pulling for Seniors!

MAINE TO CALIFORNIA...

Country's Reminisce Hitch

Nancy Dole

Alfreda Wolver

Pratt—Chuck & Daniel Buchmueller, Nathan Buchmueller, Mr. & Mrs. Willard Claassen, Donna Estes;
Protection—Wanda Ashlock, Esther Herman, Roy Herman, Adam Maloney;
Quinter—Jill Eikenberry, Trent A. Eikenberry, Donna Jamison, Katie Wise, Keri Wise, Emily & Nancy Wolf, Suzanne Yost;
Randolph—Jodi Anderson, Peggy Carlson, Greg Clark, Dale & Barbara Hanson, Derrick Hargrave, Gary & Diana Hargrave, Vicky Jacobson, Alpha Johnson, Arlene Kaump, Kristi Kaump, Janet Neilson, Ron & Ruby Peter, Emily Peterson, Russell Peterson, Cuma Rolfs, Carla & Hannah Schroller, Judy Shultz, David & Aj Specht, Alyce & Davis Specnt, Eldon L. Vandahl, Lindsey Zimmer;
Rice—Lila M. Briggs;
Richfield—Cristan McKinley, Alecia & Logan Smith, Theresa Smith;
Riley—Lewis Browder Family, Lela Brown, Sherry & Cody Brown, Sarah Buseman, Earl Dornberger, Lenice Frey, Sue Garver, Susan & Sarah Goff, Eileen Hageman, Doris Hoikes, Michele Lambert, Randall & Miranda Lindstrom, Terry McCormick, Rebecca L. Monihen, Angela Morgan, Cindy Ochoa, Ella Peterson, Jessica Renton, Jayson & William Sharp, Norma Sharp, Donna Sullivan, Ernest Sylvester, Cheryl Vanbebber, Lance & Justin Visser, Evelyn Williams;
Roeland Park—Lois Reagan;
Rolla—Harriet & Debbie Krey, Harrison Krey;
Rossville—Mrs. Leona Faulk;
Rozel—April McIntyre, Sarah Melia;
Rush Center—M. Maresch, Maxine Marsh;
Russell—Veta Landis;
Sabetha—Eldon & Katie Askoen, Todd Askoen, Virginia Bailey, Brenda Barrett, Deann M. Buser, Fred Edelman, Quentin Edelman, Sheri Nancy Eisnbise, Marla Estle, Gayleen Frederick, Lafe & Lyle Grimm, Ryan & Keith Grimm, Sandy Harter, Charleen Hartter, Jean P. Kyle, Leonard L. Liuengood, Lee & Kody & Abby Livengood, Alan W. Meyer, Hogan Popkess, Caitlin Riley, Joe E. Rokey, Shoni Rokey, Elaine Ronnebaum, Robert Rowland, Art Sanner, Jacob Scoby, Alice Sperfslge, Curt Strahm, Elmer & Phyllis Strahm, Kathy & Evan Strahm, Todd & Sharon Strahm, Alphia & Mamie Strahn, Esther & Charles Terry, Alan K. Thompson, Tracy Thompson, Wilma Tyler, Pam Wenger, Mrs. Lee White;
Saint John—Paul Enyeart, Mr. & Mrs. Wldon Howell, Grant Miller, Joel & Dustin Miller, Larry & Carolyn Mix, Virginia Snyder;
Saint Marys—Andrew Latham;
Salem—Leland Jones;
Salina—Justin & Carl Ade, Alycin Anderson, Ed & Shirley Andrla, Jean Armstrong, John Augustine, Nancy Axtell, Kelsey Becker, Rita Becker, Debbie Beckman, Nora Bengtson, Christine Berndt, Anna & Pam Bethe, Kassandra Bethe, Ron Bowman, Jessica Boyle, Michael & Jody Britt, Miranda Britt, Barry & Blake Brittendall, Ann Buchman, Ivanell Bulleigh, Hazel M. Burkle, Chris Cardinal, Connie Christy, William D. Clark, Catherine & Harry Cline, Therese Davis, Gladys E. Denny, Lucille Dibble, Margy & Aaron Duell, Lorrine Elm, Para Finch, June Fisher, Edyth Garcia, Marilyn Graham, Melissia Gregg, Vernon & Jean Hamilton, Allison Hammock, Carly Hansen, Erma Henrichs, Sonya & Justin Hernandez, Kelley Hulteen,

David Hummel, Dustin & Cammy Jacobsen, Stuart Johannes, Jean Johnson, Dorothy Katuin, Jen Kinnard, Lewis Kollhoff, Letty Lamer, Michael & Amy Landis, Linda Lecklider, Mary Leclair, Esther Loy, Joshua Macey, Marlene Mallon, Regina Marcotte, Lois McClaskey, Suzanne Morey, Alma D. Morgan, Marjorie Mugler, Barb Nelson, Charlotte Nemachen, Amanda Norgard, Karrie & Kimberly Norgard, Joni Parsons Family, Andy Pinnell, Bea Plott, Mary Plott Family, Clyde & Betty Robey, Charles Rogers, Wayne A. Ross, Terri Ross Family, Scott Seiler, Jeanne Sherman, Harriette Smith, Agnes Stemm, Marcia Stock, Thelma Sundgren, Doris & Sara Swenson, Lucille Symon, Susan Thornburg Family, Tyler & Kala Vancoevern, Merle Walker, Joanne G. Watson, Norman Waymarter, Harold Weis, Marianne Welch, Maxine Wilson, Gary W. Yates;
Satanta—Debby Barker, Stephine Blundell, Allison Ewing, Cindy & Allison Ewing, L. Froelich, Ashley Henderson, Robert Jost, Joe Kehns, Linda Kennedy, Mark McLain, Jonathan & Adam Oneal, Keith & Katrona Oneal, Seth Schlegel, Christopher Small, Gary & Karen Taton;
Sawyer—Melvin Reece;
Scandia—Cathy Wienck;
Scott City—Luann Buehler, Daisy McDaniel, Erma McDaniel, Ruth Schmied;

Seneca—Angie Bennett, Jonathan Bennett, Diane Bergman, Joey Biedemeier, Melvin Bredmeire, Jennifer Calderwood, Margie Caldwood, Waylon Enneking, Jim Enneling, Myka Feldkamp, Brenda & Tyler Haug, Jordan Haug, Connie Heiman, Randy Heiman, Linda Heinen, Colette Hermesch, Margie Hernen, Kara Holtchaus, Arlene Holthaus, Edwin Holthaus, Joyce Holthaus, Ryan Holthaus, Patricia Koch, Betty Kohake, Matt Laeger, Janet Linden, Tracy Linden, Kylee & Lindsay Luckeroth, Mike Lueb, Kurt & Carl & Elmer Melcher, Craig Noland, Elaine Osterhaus, Dustin & Daren Ronnehaum, Darin Strathman, Jamie Streit, Eric & Katie & Jeff Tanking, Jane Tanking, Alicia & Michael Zinke, Eric Zinke;
Sharon Springs—Verna Ritter;
Shasta—Anita Brown;
Shawnee—Betty & Katie Crane, Carol Mundy;
Smith Center—Bernetta Bose, Mrs. Chris N. Frydendall, Margaret Hahn;
Smolan—Karas & Chase Fairchild;
Soldier—Cedric Durst;
Solomon—Jill Curran, Joyce Divelbiss, Kim Gase, Donald Hargreaves, Jessica Nelson, Brenda Nusbaum, Barbara Peterson, Pat & Elizabeth Ryan, Marc Stephens, Diane Wilson;
South Haven—Wayne Greenlee;
Spearville—Jill Ackerman, M. Churning, Shari Diehl, Kathy Doussa, Fannie Hubbell, Mrs. Robb Issinghoff, Margaret Klenke, Urban Klenke, Maggie Knoeber, Cory Lampe, Dean Nasu, Beth & Felicia Sappington, Cindy Schmidt Family, Elizabeth Squibb, Kristi Strong, Tony Trenkamp, Bruce Vierthaler, Jill Vierthaler, Greg & Ginny Werner, Virginia Werner;
Stafford—Joyce Curtis, Vicky Harris, Mrs. August Hildebrand;
Sterling—Melissa Bucher, Margaret Reed, Mary Ellen Tippin;
Stockton—Sue Lesage, Georgia Noble, Paul & Florence Roelfs, Clifford & Jo Ann Roy;
Sublette—Evelyn & Eli Brown, Jordan Brown, Michelle D. Hamm, Renee & Connie Hamm, Vern Hibbard, Ruby Hockett Family, Dixie Hooper, Molly & Jessica Kail, Pat Kail, Mrs. Jonas Koehn, Stacey Koehn, Jeanette Koehn Family, Vaughn Lower, Tom McLain Family, L.G. Meairs Christy Nichols, Jerry Nichols, Maebelle Pelnar, Arella Roth, Ed Stoppel, Gina Timmons Family, Ardis Wait, Merle Wright, Darwin Yost;
Summerfield—Betty Bowhay, Terri Gee, Whitney & Seth Gee, Andy Koch, Abby Nemechek, Katie Nemechek, Mrs. Allen Schwarz, Patty Stueve;
Susank—Tina Gregg;
Syracuse—Karla Dionitt;
Tampa—Edwin & Elora Jantz, Elva Jantz;
Tecumseh—Kenneth & Betty Baker, John Davis, Mary Davis, Nora Iwing, Todd E. McMillen, Allen & Gladys Neuhaus;
Tescott—Duane & Cathy King;
Topeka—Janice Ashby, Dave Barnett, Carl Baron, Alan & Patty Barth, Phil Beurskens, Don & Marie Boaz, Emery Brinkman, Martha Brown, Margaret Corwin, Rachel & Betty Eddy, Gordon & Wilma Ensley, Edith Frisbie, Sandy & Mary Gragg, Alex & Marge Grieves, Ryan & Cole Grieves, Lucille Harold, Don & Mary Harrison, Betty Ingwerson, Alice Kaufman, Brandy Mann, Raqual & Tyler Mann, Dorothy Parman, Francis Perkins, Gloria Ruddy, Mark Sanchez, Angela Schneider, Verno & Ruth Shorthill,

We're Pulling for Seniors!
MAINE TO CALIFORNIA...
Country's Reminisce Hitch
Mary Mahon

Harold L. Wilch, Brock J. Winans, Alicia Wright;
Tribune—Melvin D. Ruder;
Ulysses—Josie Adams Family, Paula Alexander, Susan
    Alexander, Debra & Angela Barbo, Katrina Benyshek,
    Susan Biggs, Anita Bryant, Nancy Burgess, Mark &
    Wendy Calderwood, Linda Carpenter, Ramona
    Catherwood, Gail Dale Family, Carol Dalke, Janet Damon,
    Jerry Deckert, Diana Dick Family, Floice Dixon, Marie
    Dowell, Travis & Lisa Downs, Tammy Eberhart, Marge
    Ewing, Linda Ferrell, Cindy & Jennifer Finch, Ludi Franco
    Family, Jack Freeman, Loretta Goossen, Marita & Lonnie
    Goossen, Kristy Gregory, Geraldine Harp, Maurina
    Hartless, Karen Haskell, Tiffany Heckel, Ernest & Ruby
    Higgins, Mr. & Mrs. Hileman, Sy Hileman, Kim Hilger,
    Mrs. Harold Isaac, Greta Jantzen, John Jantzen, Judith &
    Rachel Jantzen, Bradley & Marilyn Jones, Anita Kehn,
    Ruth Kehn, Tomas Kehn, Ray R. Kepley, Denise Kinsey,
    Julie Knode, Barb Koehn, Letha Koehn, Micheline Koehn,
    Norma Jean Koehn, Randall Koehn, Sara Koehn, Yolanda
    Koehn, Denton Koehn Family, Robert Koehn Family,
    Marissa Konda, Louise Koop, Becky Langley, Lloyd
    Martin, Michelle Martin, Angela McCauley, Norma
    McCauley, Kim McGaughey, Lila McGaughey, James &
    Cathy Medlin, La Vonne Michael, Delbert J. Miller, Phyllis
    Miller, Darla Neidert, Lorie Nichols, Lisa Nightingale,
    Rhonda Nightingale, Robyn Nordyke, Kathleen Porter,
    Debra Richter, Dana Riley, Naoma Rundell, Angela
    Schmidt, Carolyn & Nolan Schmidt, Oren Schmidt, Pat
    Schmidt, Preston & Cameron Schmidt, S. Schmidt, Amy
    Scott, Evelyn Smith, Lisa Smith, Shawna & Kipp Smith,
    Marsha Smith Family, Leona Smyth Family, Alison
    Soelter, Kris Spearman, Shirley Stevenson, Vicki
    Stevenson, Marcy Stringham Family, David & Kimberly
    Unruh, Erica & Tressa Unruh, Karla Waechter, Teresa
    Weber, Shannon Wichman, Becky & Katie Wilson,
    Leonard Wilson, Jamie Yost, Ginny & Danielle Young;
Valley Center—Kathy & Johnny Vogt;
Valley Falls—Ted Montgomery;
Vermillion—W.B. Kramer;
Vliets—Joleen Ekstrum;
Wakarusa—Evelyn Davis;
Wakefield—Steve Braden, Matt G. Feller, Jan Keim, Kaitlyn
    Koralek, Charlotte Lambert, Rudy Oard, Luella Schmutz,
    Mina Shaw, Elwin Todd, Paul Visser Family, Hazel
    Yarrow, Helen Yarrow;
Washington—Florence Alwin, Velma Mereith, Eslie Moser,
    Jean Moser, Henry & Blanche Nagel, Charles Parks;
Waterville—Marjorie Anderson, Barbara Cramer, Susan Daniel,
    Brant Deraer, T.C. Frohberg, Don & Norma Hirt, Keri &
    Jami Hull, Dorothy Lindquist, Jennifer Pishny, Caleb &
    Peter Specht, Esther Ruth Specht, Jeremiah Specht, Janice
    Sweet, Lynn & Thelma Walker, Dave & Jessica Whitnell,
    Selene Youneberg;
Waverly—Jeanette Wiederkehr;
Westmoreland—Lois Kraushaar;
Wheaton—Verneda Valburg;
White City—Lorena Estes;
Wichita—Leo L. Bean, Laura Bickel, Gladys & Neil Cross,
    Glenn V. Dorr, Arlo E. Garrett, Beth M. Grainger, Martin
    Gray, Ivar Hanson, Chance & David Henderson, Debby
    Henderson, Kenneth Higeon, Edgar & Loeta Higeons,
    Doug Janssen, Wayne Kaup, Norma Litke, Dr. Bonnie
    Lynch, Virginia Maddox, Kathy McGinnis, Hermina
    Medlock, Twila J. Medlock, B.A. Mevey, Darrell Michael,
    Albert A. Miller, Pat Murphy, Wm. & Patricia Murphy,
    Forrest W. Newlin, George & Phyllis Preheim, Evelyn
    Ramsey, Berlin Raymond, Cathy Rodgers, Faye & Charlie
    Safarik, Ginger Schneider, Allen Schroeder, Greg & Ann
    Semrad, Justin Titus, June Westerfield;
Wilmore—Betty & Shane Yost;
Wilson—Virginia Florian, Kathleen Macer, Blaine & Garrett
    Urbanek, Sandra A. Urbanek;
Windom—Greg Mikkel;
Windsor Park—Stanley Nilhel;
Winfield—Lloyd Dowler, Gary Hunt, Sheryl Hunt, John & Ruth
    Thomson;
Woodston—Maxine Dibble;
Wright—Katie Eddy, Megan Eddy, Alan Hilmes;
Yates Center—Glen & Marilyn Shoar.

Kentucky
Ashland—William Abbey;
Campbellsburg—Morene Maiden Perry;
Columbus—Carmen Ellen;
Elizabethtown—Shannon Gutierrez;
Henderson—Gerald Schmidt;
Leitchfield—Jennifer Martin;
Louisville—Herb Buchart;
Maysville—Roy & Marjorie Bridges;
Murray—Kevin & Shannon Penne;
Radcliff—Cheryl Belfiore.

Louisiana
Cameron—Gene Tanner;
New Orleans—Daniel & Jason Miers;
Sulphur—George & Maxine Gamble;
Transylvania—Tracy Bennet Family.

Maine
Acton—Rhea Neal;

Sheila Seme

Alfred—Richard H. Johnson;
Berwick—Susan Burke, Priscilla Bushway, Jane & Robert
    Hilton, Harold Oulton Jr., Jenn Siudut;
Cape Porpoise—Edwina Davis;
Colder—Susan Stachewiez;
East Lebanon—Aaron Colby, Linda Desrochers, Robert O.
    White;
Kennebunk—Veronica Benya, Elizabeth Bernard, Helen Clark,
    Frances Coote, June Cummings, Deb Fitts, Clarrie
    Nickerson, Peggy Welch, Andrea Whitmer;
Kennebunkport—Lila Doe, Litton Dowson, Ruth Driscoll, Fran
    Hayes, Mildred & Peter Valeska;
Mars Hill—Hazel Sisco, Hope Sisco;
North Berwick—Eric Baron, Patsy Bragdon, Dayna Emmons,
    Kenneth Goodwin, Judy Ouellette, Pat Rohm;
Ocean Park—Frances M. Coote;
Sabattus—Tommie P. Jewell;
Stockton Springs—Alfred & Marilyn Deredin;
Stonington—Sandra Wiberg;
Union—Nancy Dewilde;
Wells—Elizabeth Ashworth, Margaret Kent;
York Beach—Larry & Christine Bowen.

Maryland
Accident—Rachel Mulea;
Annapolis—Molly J. Boron;
Bowie—Beth Lingg;
Elkridge—David C. Bravo;
Gambrills—Don & Joanne Walker;
Grantsville—Esther Beachy, Rachel Miller;
Lanham—Brandon Blanchard;
Rockville—Marilyn Hemmig;
Salisbury—Paul Ferrier.

Massachusetts
Agawam—Jim Fenton;
Amherst—Edith L. Sprague;
Ashburnham—Richard Chapman, Nancy White, Seth Wright;
Ashfield—Janna Clark;
Barre—S. Adenia Keenan;
Becket—Pam Trag;
Belchertown—Heidi Dufresne;
Bolton—Beverly Edwards;
Brookfield—Lorraine & Neal Lane;
Chelmsford—Alice E. Wheeler;
Cheshire—Robert H. Johnson Jr.;
Clarksburg—Dorothy Beebe;
Colrain—Patty Roberts;
Cummington—Anne & Kasey Emerson, Jane Emerson, Mae V.
    Emerson, Jeanette A. Horton, Eva Howes, Cynthia Joyner,
    Jean S. Joyner, Terry Robbins, June K. Whiteman, Kellie
    Wilcox;
Dalton—Betty & Ed Larkin, Dorothy Smith;
Drury—Harold Williams;
Easthampton—Irma & Dick Warnock;
Florence—Marian E. Conant, George W. Scheel;
Gardner—Sally Moussette;
Gill—Kathy Augustine;
Goshen—Carolyn & Ernest Carver;
Grafton—Nancy Deschenec;
Greenfield—Carol L. Skrabis;
Haydenville—Sylvia T. Clark;
Leeds—Edward P. Malinoski;

Medford—Arthur & Carolyn Dinsmoor;
Northfield—Vernon & Ruth Gillett, Patricia Wheeler;
Oakham—Barbara Wentzell;
Orange—Colleen Ward;
Pelham—Ruth E. Seitz;
Peru—Beverly Ballee, Debbie Burke, Beverly Waller;
Phillipston—Michael Flye, Vicki Levasseur;
Pittsfield—Pam Mennis, Ruth & Albert Morrissey, Anne
    Tenneson;
Plainfield—Betty E. Smith, Ruth Thatcher;
Rehoboth—Beverly & Carl Gobin, Carlton Gobin;
Russell—Jean Walther;
Savoy—Isabelle Harwood, Tami Hoag;
Sheffield—Sandra Boardman, Sheri & Rene Boardman;
Shelburne—Karen Gould & Children, Linda Herrera, Launie
    York;
Shelburne Falls—Cathy & Shelley Roberts;
South Falls—Nancy L. Dole;
South Lancaster—Frank & Lois Ponte;
Sudbury—Eleanor Morgan, Brian Sanders;
Templeton—Christine Curtis;
Turner Falls—Darlene Kellogg, Ora Prue, Charles & Gertrud
    Woodard;
Westminster—Mary Dugas;
Whately—Barbara Mario;
Williamsburg—Dorothy T. Beebe, Russell Clark, Dora E.
    Emerson, Wilma Hatch, Norma P. Kellogg, Brenda
    Lessard, Mr. & Mrs. Robert Tilley;
Windsor—Tracy Hall;
Worthington—Jean M. Eddings, G. Ruth McIntosh.

Michigan
Adrian—Wayne W. Lipp;
Ann Arbor—Gladys Schlenker, George & Jan Schnierle;
Athens—Phyllis A. Pifer;
Avon Lake—Mary A. Deahl;
Bad Axe—Sadie Steiner;
Battle Creek—Ann Edgell, Larry & Dora Sonicksen;
Bay City—Charles Bauman, Pat Cook, Alice Krueger, Bonnie
    Schlatter, Mabelle Wackerle;
Bay Port—Mark Stalter;
Belleville—Thelma Griffin, Maggie Jaster;
Bellevue—Pat Kent;
Berlin Center—The Myers;
Berrien Springs—Sandra & Rhonda Covell, Marjorie Gadway,
    Helen Root;
Blissfield—Earl & Cora Mae Phillips;
Buchanan—Bob & Katie Macklin, Robert Macklin;
Canton—Wava Hanna;
Cassopolis—Kay Erie;
Clawson—Jeff Gasiorowski;
Coldwater—Mrs. Arther Gibbs, Lawrence Smith;
Coleman—Lillian Aultman, Mildred Bauman;
Concord—Jean Pickell;
Davisburg—David Brown;
De Witt—Donna Balderson, Mrs. Arthur Newman, Sheral R.
    Tingay;
Farmdale—Ivan Rae;
Farmington Hills—Clara Griffin, Leona Hurd;
Fenton—Julie Schaub, Donald & Elaine Teggerdine;
Fowlerville—Dora Glover, Marjorie Rocker;
Frankenmuth—Fred Kern, John & Carol Schreiner;
Freeland—Lyle Lecronor;

Fulton—Mildred Mitchell;
Galesburg—Lynn Roe;
Gladwin—Royeen Heins;
Goodells—Glenn Schade;
Goodrich—Leta Gordon;
Grand Rapids—Joyce Altena, G. Donald Chisnall, Juanita A.
    Condon, Robert & Thelma Shears, Evelyn Versluis;
Grandville—Mrs. Lewis Elders, Jack Minthorn;
Greenville—Gloria Adams;
Harbor Springs—Roxann Arman, James Arman, Don & Ruth
    Arman Family, Winslo & Virginia Ash;
Hastings—Harold C. Anderson, Leo & Nyla Fifelski;
Holland—Judy Aalderink;
Holt—Laurence & Ruth Hammar;
Homer—Don Holmes;
Howell—Mr. & Mrs. Bruce Love;
Hudson—Grace Fish;
Hudsonville—Betty Hassevoort, Don Hassevoort, Chet &
    Sharon Haveman;
Ionia—Jerry & Joe Singerland;
Iron Mountian—Mary Ann Dain;
Ishpeming—Gene Foster;
Jackson—Phyllis Bungart, Phillip Smith;
Johannesburg—Leona Campbell;
Johnson—Julie Harrill;
Jonesville—Vernon & Mary Lou Feeney, The Hawkes Family,
    Theo Kintigh;
Kalamazoo—Harold & Donna Kitsmiller, Myrland & Norma
    Shutes, Arlene Simmons, Richard Simmons;
Kalkaska—Walter & Joanne Green;
Lake—Charles & Hazel Tryon;
Lake City—Ruth Williams;
Lansing—Caroll & Ruby Samuelson;
Linden—Juanita Smith;
Linwood—Helen Meylan, David Schlatter;
Livonia—Darlene Maginley, Larry Paden;
Manistee—Mrs. Harvey Lindeman;
Marcellus—Ruth Heath, Susan Kit Stewart;
Marlette—Jack & Karen Allan, Rev. John & Karen Allan, Lorna
    Caister;
Marshall—Owen Betz, Wayne A. Gleason, Pauline Reddick;
Mason—Ludell Cheney, Loren Everett;
Mendon—Mr. & Mrs. Lindsay Keeler;
Metamora—Relda Benscoter;
Milan—Robert Witcombe;
Milton—Wilbert D. Hupp;
Morrice—Lucille Jansen;
Muir—Quint & Agnes Cusack;
Muskegon—Catherine Berry;
Niles—Lee Frame, Helen Thompson;
North Adams—Ernest & Marjorie Griffiths;
Okemos—Albert Cook, Edward Obryant;
Otsego—Mrs. Bernard Brown;
Palmyra—Hugh & Lee Ellen Driggs;

Petersburg—Dale Eisenmann;
Pewamo—Marian Brown;
Pigeon—Tim Stalter;
Pittsford—Vernon Crandall, Billie & Chuck Deal, C.P. Deal;
Plainwell—Mrs. Lyle Champion;
Portage—Lanny H. Wilde;
Prudenville—Patti Goldsmith;
Reading—Al & Ina Carpenter, Marvin McClelland;
Rives Junction—Bill & Judy James;
Rochester—Bob & Sally Wagner;
Saline—Jean & Joseph Ferris, Mr. & Mrs. John Voorhees;
Shelby Township—Joseph & Margaret Hessell;
Sodus—Julie Wright;
Sturgis—Helen Gascho;
Sunfield—Jack Smith, Wayne E. Steward;
Temperance—Otto Miller;
Three Oaks—Zoe Ann Noble, Bill Schirk;
Twin Lake—Marie Lehmoine;
Vassar—Roy & Erna Maurer;
Vestaburg—Harry Brown;
Waldron—Shirley Williams;
Warren—F.W. Axthelm, Lizzetta & Jack Belz, Ray & Glenna
    Carr, Joan & Frank Sucaet, Frank Sycret, Cecila & Andy
    Wiegand;
Weidman—Walter Kaufman Jr.;
Westland—Lisa Dowgiallo;
Whitmore Lake—Conny Melchi;
Whittemore—George Erickson, Elwood Ruckle;
Wyoming—Gerrit Kortman, Gale Vandermoore;
Ypsilanti—Robert & Lelanel Malick;
Zeeland—Alma Hamelink, Bea & Julius Haveman, Gil
    Wedever.

Minnesota
Amboy—Cliff Anderson;
Arco—Mr. & Mrs. Robert Dwire, Luella Madsen, Harvey &
    Wilma Noble, Ernest Richmond, Leona Richmond;
Beaver Bay—Marjorie Johansen;
Belview—Floyd A. Schmidt;
Bemidji—Marion Husmann, Paula Schuessler;
Bloomington—Flossie Marxen;
Canyon—Carol Watts;
Cass Lake—Cliff & Clarinda Husft;
Chisholm—Cora Mae Perry;
Cohasset—Helen Nohr;
Darfur—Kenneth Rupp;
Fairmont—Karen Whitaker;
Foley—Leona Crook, Rolland Madden;
Forest Lake—Lilly Samson;
Fountain—Harvey Dohrmann;
Franklin—Randy Kvam;
Goodhue—Mr. & Mrs. Wayne Frederixon, Sidney A.
    Ronningen;
Granite Falls—Bob Dwire, Sharon Sannerud;

Greenbush—Arvid & Lois Dvergsten;
Hardwick—John Hubbling;
Hastings—Wally & Josie Lavalla;
Jordan—Loren Whipps;
Lakefield—Loren & Ethelyn Cuperus;
Le Sueur—Ray Schwarz, Maurice Thelemann;
Lewisville—Marilyn Hall, Vernon Schultz;
Mabel—Rita Forde, Mark Peitzmeier;
Madelia—Donald & Marge Gens;
Madison Lake—Lucille Dauk;
Mahnomen—Helen Simon;
Mankato—Orville Anderson;
Maple Grove—Theresa & Kahlh Halek;
Marshall—Velva Debaere;
Mc Grath—Marlene Simonson;
Milaca—Ruth Lindell;
Minneapolis—Roger Paulson, Arthur R. Thelemann;
Morris—Kenneth & Audrey Evink;
Nerstrand—Mr. & Mrs. Manford L. Isaacson;
New Hope—Rick & Doris Hagford;
New Richland—Vyonne Kabage, Reuben Nelson;
Osakis—DeWayne Zabel;
Park Rapids—Carl & Cathy Hammer;
Pillager—Tom Nuesse;
Plymouth—Mrs. Jon Lavasseur, Kathy Lavassuer;
Ray—Winnie & Russ Barrett;
Red Wing—Arlan Ashbaugh;
Redwood Falls—Marjorie Hewett, Melvin Hewett;
Rollingstone—Leonard Kreidermacher, Marcella
    Kreidermacher;
Saint Cloud—Lil Schwitalla;
Saint James—Ray & Janice Haler, Lyle & Harriet Wright;
Saint Paul—Jack L. Martinson;
Spring Grove—O.A. Fossum;
Stewartville—Marilyn Lansing;
Stillwater—Lloyd & Kathy Hubert;
Swanville—Blanche & Ivan Schultz;
Truman—Paul & Lorrain Ottomoeller, Eldor & Delores Pfeil;
Walker—Gladys Norgard;
Waseca—Sharon & Kassie Colbenson;
Wells—James & Jnaet Yokiel;
Whalan—Duane Tweten;
Winnebago—Harold Golly;
Worthington—Ken Hansberger.

Mississippi
Ellisville—Carl Maneil;
Gulfport—Harold Nall;
Ocean Sprigns—Martha Martin;
Okolona—Krystal Benner, Tracy & Kristy Benner, Darla Smith,
    Misty & Mikayla Smith, Heather Toews, Starla Unruh;
Vancleave—Lindsey & Gabriel Thomas, Lula Thomas.

Missouri
Albany—Lillian Lovitt, Janet Parsons, Joshua & Leslie Parsons;
Arbela—Joanne Aylward, Mary Howell, Lyle Livingston;
Arnold—Annett S. Graves;
Barnard—Margaret Linville;
Blue Springs—Kelly Wiles;
Bolchow—Roger & Marilyn Wilmes, Tim & Tyler Wilmes,
    Tristen Wilmes;
Bolivar—Arlene & Jack Palmer;
Bosworth—Kenneth Standley;
Branson—Tom & Virginia Martin;
Brookfield—Kenneth Holloway;
Burlington Junction—Lisa Adkins, Marianne Adkins, Mary
    Bowman, Olive Brown, Terri Carver, Bobbi Clark, Sharon
    Cowden, Janice Cummings, Helen Daughtery, Lary
    Dawson, Martha Dawson, Jeanette Denniston, Lacy &
    Lindsey Derr, Sonny Derr, James Downing, Jerry & Jolene
    Downing, F. Gray, Steve Hayes, Judy Hunt, Beulay Kelley,
    Bridget Larabee, Sara Larabee, Betty Jean Mires, Angela
    Ogle, Mary Parter, Kaylene Reed, Wanda Reed, Eric &
    Janessa Reeves, Carrie Ross, Carol Sherlock, Marjorie
    Sloan, M. Staples, Amber Stevens, Doris Stevens, Georgia
    Vanpelt, Cynthia Whitney, Stephen Wilmes;
Cainsville—Kerre Keith;
California—Tara Hartman;
Canton—Lester & Leta Hoffman, Leta F. Hoffman, Kenneth C.
    Krueger Sr.;
Clearmont—Anna Bears, Melissa Christiansen, Katy Danner,
    Katrina A. Dolin, Faye Gray, Jason Guthrie, Nathan &
    Brandon Guthrie, Bernice Hamilton, Amie Hutchinson,
    Charlene Kelley, Reva Kelley, Rosalyn Kinder, Dianna
    Logan, Jesse Logan, Janice McElroy, Alma Jean Morris,
    Chris Roger, Therese Teuscher, Katie Ulmer, Bruce & Ky
    White;
Clifton Hill—Orville Lindeman;
Clinton—Leroy Boden;
Darlington—Beverly Cummins, Garrett Merea;
Downing—Sue Jane Brewer, Bob Nicoli;
Eagleville—Charles Cluh, Laura Hamilton, Denise Tull;
Edwards—Vickie Cline;
Elmo—Izetta Castello, Diana Hunt, Shane Hunt, Steve
    Hutchison, Karen Riley, Suede Sanders, Judy Snodderly,
    Micah Wood;
Elsberry—Ruth A. Roam;
Essex—Juanita Farquhar;
Ewing—Betty Daggs, Mary Prigge;
Fairfax—Gale Ball, H. Beyer, Tammy Grossman, Dru & Mario

Cross-Country Hitch...
MAINE TO CALIFORNIA!

Burmita Ewing

THE MANE EVEN

Richard Hughes

We're Pulling for Seniors!
1993 MAINE TO CALIFORNIA...
Country's Reminisce Hitch

Oswald, Jennifer Rader, Bessie M. Tiemeyer, Mary Wasserfallen;
Fenton—Joanne Little;
Flemington—Wanda Peck;
Florissant—Beverly Gum, Aaron & Amber Hill, Emilee & Jackee Hill, Nancy & Carrie Hill;
Frankford—Tammy Tewes;
Garden City—Elda Claunch, James Clawnch;
Glencoe—Yolanda M. Palmer;
Gower—Hope Wilkinson;
Grain Valley—Dolores Sciolaro;
Grandview—Nadine Weldon;
Grant City—Doris McGinnis;
Guilford—Beverly Gillespie;
Hatfield—Joel Saling;
Helena—Garnet Mead;
Hermann—Ray & June Gregerson;
Higginsville—Kerri Romesburg;
Hopkins—Larry Davison, Pam Davison;
Hurdland—Harry & Virginia Holman, Victor & Betty Peterson;
Independence—Nancy Axton, Alfred Lefman, Tim Lefman, Ruby Morgan;
Jefferson City—Dorothy & James Gieck, Dorothy & Jim Gieck;
Johnstown—Nancy Morgan;
Kahoka—Doris Anderson, Bethany Bourgeois, Wilma St. Clair, Ashton Krueger, Debbie Lagsdon, Baxter & Helen Macomber, Helen Macomber, O.L. Spees;
Kansas City—Mr. & Mrs. W. Crim, Geri Hawkins, Donna Lockhard, Helen McKinley, Kathy Monson, Ryan & Katie Monson, W. Victor Morse, Amanda Riggs, D. & L. Riggs, Jeff & Nathan Sickeb, Irene Worley;
Kearney—Carolyn Krueger, Linda Merritt;
King City—Oren & Judy Steinman;
Kirksville—Barbara B. Dunscomb, Glenna Foster, Rollie Mathes, Jill Stoffer, Vicky Wehner;
Knob Noster—Ruby Beardsley;
La Plata—Robert & Theda Smithson;
Laquey—John West;
Lathrop—George McCorkle, Jeremiah Joe Saling;
Lees Summit—Lowell North;
Liberty—Joann Ortiz;
Luray—Lila Seaver;
Madison—James D. Brown, Connie Holder, Hazel & Larry Johnston;
Marthasville—Earl Eichmeyer;
Maryville—Gail Poppa, Paul Stiens, Rosalee Wilmes;
Maysville—Gary Hanna;
Memphis—Mrs. Jewell Coffrin, Eva Dye, Rick Fischer, Ida May Folk, Donna Miller, Garnet Schleeter, Donna Shoop, Myrtle Speagh, Brenda & Justin Winn, Sue Wolf;
Milan—Vic Cochran, Zella Fetterly, Ray F. Johnson, Cynthia Leslie;
Monroe City—Richard Adam, Richard & Rusty Adam;
Mooresville—Stanley Garr;
New Hampton—Kathleen Fastad;
Norborne—Orville & Lois Ramthun;
Oak Grove—Jerry & Lorraine Hatfield;
Oakland—Norman & Nancy Wallerstedt;
O'Fallon—Rosie Wilmes;
Old Monroe—Louise E. Sommer;
Parnell—Erma Berg, Francis Berg, Elaine Mitchell;
Pattonsburg—Vern R. Hellyard;

Pickering—Sandra Smith, Dagmar Whipple;
Plattsburg—Betty & Maurice Shoemaker;
Pleasant Valley—Lucie & Amanda Riggs;
Princeton—Ruth Ann Knutson;
Ravenwood—Charles Goodsom;
Rich Hill—Wayne Blevins;
Ridgeway—Justin Parkhurst, Rene Wilson;
Rock Port—Brenda Clemens, Darlene & Cody Joesberg, Kenneth Joesberg, Allen Richards, Mrs. Lavona Stalup Reid, Richard Zach;
Rolla—Traci & Aaron Brechnacher;
Rushville—Marlene Woolston;
Rutledge—Irwin Zimmerman;
Saint Catharine—Raymond & Leota Nickerson;
Saint Charles—Eileen Klohr, Lee A. Klohr;
Saint Joseph—Judy Jacobs, Sandy Little;
Saint Louis—Vera Babb, Thelma & Sherri Christy, R. Owens, Hazel Treanor, Edward & Helen Walsh;
Saint Paul—Mrs. Russell Schmidt;
Salem—S. Paul Wingfield;
Salisbury—Phyllis & Dusty Huds;
Seneca—L. Rese;
Sheridan—Kathryn Frueh, Fern Parman;
Sibley—Linda Morgan;
Springfield—Jack & Louise Buckley;
Stanberry—Sheila Curry;
Sturgeon—James Holder, Ray & Alamta Silver;
Tarkio—Harry Breermann, Eunice Brown, Richie Comstocl, Bryon Fosbirder, Ashley & Rita Knierim, Mary Ruth Koch, Merylan Lowrey, Mary McIntosh, G. Mehaffey, Shane Mitchell, Karla Murphy, Deloris Reeves, Carol Riley, Jeanie Schmidt, Amanda Smith, Travis Smith, Dorothy Turner, Annie Wakefield, Janet Wennihan;
Trenton—Charles Collins, Twila M. Collins;
Troy—Karen Reese Family;
Unionville—Carroll Bradshaw, Raymond Dole, Barbara Gome, Teresa Kinzler, Judy & Jeffery Pauley, Quentin Sayre, Louise Smith, Nancy Summers, Pearl Summers, Vicki Tipton LPN;
Urich—Lee & Emma Ewing;
Warrenton—Ruth Becker;
Watson—Donna Whelan;
Westboro—Mrs. J.H. Ohrt, Beth Pearson, Katherine Strauch;
Winfield—Adam Sommer;
Worth—Janet & Claudis Gladstone, Ruth S. Gladstone;
Wyaconda—Jesse Forquer;

Montana
Butte—Oleta E. King, Earline K. Sheff;
Manhattan—John Kuipers.

Nebraska
Adams—Eloise Tenners;
Alma—John & Edith Hogeland Family;
Ansley—Misty Ogle;
Arapahoe—Delbert Weatherwax Family;
Ashland—Carolyn Watson, L. Watson;
Auburn—Marilyn Behre, Marvin Biere, Kellie

Bogan, Dale & Matthew Bohling, Derek Bohling, Eva & Agnes Caultery, Judy Coe, Cindy Cole, Chandra Cooney, Dee Cooney, Chris Debuhn, Alvin Debuhr, Kathryn Ganger, Janyce Heywood, Brett & Jarod Ketter, Brooke & Jene Ketter, Nathan & John Klotz, Doug & Seth Kubick, Deb & Micaela Kubik, Adeline Matschutlat, Wilma McConnell, Kelli & Ryan Mertes, Helen Moody, Marlene North, Patrick W. Reich, Helen Remmers, Sharon Reynolds, Edris Rippe, Edus Rippe, Margie Shaffer, Laya Smith, Ruth Smith, Cortney Sommerhelder, Sydney Zaruda, Jessica & Alyson Zarula;
Aurora—Robert Dudley;
Beatrice—Larry & Heather Brennes, Frank Jurgens;
Bellevue—Betty Hovey, April Snider, Clayton Snider, Dean B. Thornbury;
Blair—Rollie Cape;
Brock—David Guhdy;
Brownville—Erna Blount, Elizabeth Bratcher, Ann Brewer, Harold Davis, Sandra Dorn, R.L. Gentert, Kelly Kempston, Bob Lutz, Pat Maley, Betty Mann, Daryl J. Obermeyer, Colleen Rinkleff, Vicki Stewart, Joyce Vice, Marty W. Wessels;
Burchard—Harriet & Dean Clark;
Cedar Bluffs—James & Linda Wirka;
Ceresco—Leroy Adams, Clifford Hughes;
Clatonia—Alma Essman;
Clyde—Kathleen & Eli Brown;
Columbus—Janell Anderson, Duane & Mary Behrens, Dorothy Courtier, Marjorie Koch, Mrs. David McNair, Sara & Joyce McNair, Sandy Wright;
Crab Orchard—Ken & Janet Trout;
Dawson—Janice Fischer, Vernell Hogue, Joyce Huppert, Ariel & Andrew Linville, Mary Linville, Judy & Justin Mueller, Katie Mueller, Starlyn Ramsey, Mari Skiler, Barbara Stuckmeyer, Mrs. Joe Williams, Janet Wittwer;
Dixon—Sterling Borg;
Elk Creek—Jodelle Janssen, Henry Watermann, Leona Watermann;
Elwood—Gene Baer;
Fairbury—Nadine & Walter Kriesel;
Fairfield—Helen Cook, Myral Cook;
Falls City—Carrie Dunn, Sania Eirkhoff, Connie Feek, Carole Gerdes, Elizabeth Janko, Virginia Jones, Connie Marrs, Janice Moore, Charles Rowland, Connie Rowland, Vicki Rowland, Ray Simon, Mary Walker, Cordean Wisdom, Clarence Yoesel, Steve & Doris Yoesel;
Fremont—Richare Arett, The Brands, J.L. Doksansky, Patricia M. Harris;
Fullerton—Marilyn McIntyre;
Geneva—Luke & Shana Shroyer;
Grand Island—Dorothy Semm;
Halmesville—Ernest Claassen;
Henderson—Willard Friesen;
Holdrege—Delores Dellapiero;
Holmesville—Marvin Steele;
Hoyt—Grace Rickel;
Humboldt—Angela Alexander, Judie Arms, Ann Berggren, Dixie L. Coggin, Jennifer Lynn Dejonge, Carleen Dettmann, Gary Hestermann, Regina Hitzeman, Rose & Carissa Hitzeman, Erik Kappel, Louis Luthy, Helen Moritz, Jeanne Standerford, Colleen Uhri, Denette Wheeler, Elta Whitney;

Howard Wisenburn

Johnson—Julie Buchmeier, Jeanette & Shelby Palmer, Charles Weichert;
Kennard—Jack & Susan Lorsch, John & Irene Lorsch;
Lewellen—Mr. & Mrs. Howard Newkirk, Ola Mae Swan;
Lewiston—Dean & Harriet Clark;
Liberty—Heather & Colten Bowhay, Tanner Bowhay;
Lincoln—Bonnie Clough, Bill & Harold Essman, Joann Essman, Mae Belle Haight, Hazel Howbett, Velree Lilja, Galen K. Madsen, The Madsens, Jane Stubbendick, Fern Waters;
Louisville—Ruth F. Persinger;
Mead—Clara Vavak, William T. Vavak;
Milford—Ron Vosta;
Monroe—Charlotte Morton;
Murdock—Mrs. Wallace Richert;
Nebraska City—Ruby Eschen;
Neligh—Mr. & Mrs. Clayton Ober;
Nemaha—Linda Hopper, Lois Smith, Paul & Faye Whitewell;
North Platte—Linda Herndon;
Omaha—Martin Dunklau, Tamara Hanks, Jerry & Mary Mahoney, James Nervig, Joyce Oloff, Elna Oltman, John P. Raymond, Jean Seffron, Carolyn Spitler, Carol Wall;
Palmyra—Lori Arett;
Papillion—Ruby Hahn;
Pawnee City—Mr. & Mrs. Louis H. Geweke, Linna Mort, Mary Alice Thiemann;
Peru—Loretta Kruse, Teresa Monnette;
Pickrell—Katie & Laura Higgins, Kristen Higgins, Michael & Jimmy Higgins;
Plattsmouth—Delphine Glup, Jack & Veva Sauder, Doris Slufter;
Ponca—Mariah & Francis Church;
Prague—Karen Houfek;
Rising City—Elietta Glock;
Saint Edward—Beth Evans, Kathy Stulmiller, Shirley Thompson;
Saint Mary—Florence Lempka;
Salem—Ann Baker, Linda Davis, Leslie Inks, Dwight L. Thompson, Satin Windles, Felicia & Orrin Zeigler;
Shubert—Jan Alexander, Edna Colglazier;
Spalding—Arlin Smith;
Steinauer—Kathy Speers;
Stella—Jolleen Hilgenfeld, Darlene Lockard, Julie & Jessica Lockard, Mona Williams;
Sterling—Dorlen Hier;
Table Rock—Vicki Bursovsky, Ed Flider, Bobbie Kunze, Ardyce Manro;
Talmage—Betty Hurst;
Tecumseh—Lester Baum, Susan & Tiffany Goracke, Tasha & Molly Goracke, Velda V. Koehler;
Verdigre—Helen Franek;
Verdon—Lois Miller;
Waco—Daniel Pralle;
Wakefield—Paul Burman, Glee Gustafson, Kenneth Gustafson, Maurice Johnson, Florence Van;
Waterloo—Ann Wachsmann, Justin & Libbie Wachsmann;
Wisnur—Betty & Jennifer Wiese;
York—Ray & Ruth Junge, Boyd & Rose Tietmeyer.

Nevada
Boulder City—Dorothy Holloway;

Reta Zody

Henderson—Dr. Daniel Schears;
Las Vegas—C.D. Hertig, Jen & Kath Perrah.

New Hampshire
Amherst—Martha Brown, Charles W. Stickney;
Antrim—Edward Boucher, Geraldine Rabideau;
Barnstead—Lorraine Jones;
Barrington—Carolyn Bedford, Sam Bergeron, Alice Brown, Dorothy Cogswell, Charlene Domingles, Charlene Domingue, Christina Morrison, Janet Varney;
Bennington—Phillip Traxler;
Bow—Christopher Andrew, Warren Bowden, Mary Moss;
Canaan—Mr. & Mrs. Edward Lary;
Candia—Gladys Baker, Anita Blackburn, George Lincoln, Jo Steele;
Canterbury—Kathie Fife, Elaine Hatch;
Chester—Barbara Hutchinson;
Claremont—Deb Desmarais, Mrs. Paul Gendell;
Concord—Elizabeth & Neal Andrew, Beverly Edwards, Lena Flanders, Helen S. Frary, Cheryl Haydon Family, Carrie Jenovese, Debra Mosholder, Debra Skaff;
Contoocook—Agnes Lux;
Deerfield—Anlene Clark, Diana Decota, Jason Decota, Robin Engel, Dawn Jodoin, Patience Lapierre, Kori Marquis, Delores Oneil, Dee Rollins Putnam, Bud Rollins, Willis Rollins Jr.;
Derry—Eliana Levine;
Dover—Hazel Demambro, Kay Demro, D. Kelley, Mr. & Mrs. Fred Riley;
Dunbarton—Laverne Mannion, Steven Merrill;
East Swanzey—Kyle & Levy Smith;
Elkins—Carla & Devon Marshall, Katelyn McCormick;
Epsom—Etta & Joyce Yeaton;
Gilmanton Iron Wks—Olive Tibbetts;
Grantham—Jill Barton;
Hancock—Elizabeth Price;
Henniker—Joshua Bourassa, Jaime Bumford, Judith Cox, Janet Higginson;
Hillsboro—J. Avery, Aubrey Mae Ciol, Barbara Ciol, Amy Cote, Ethel Crane, Ann Ford, Elizabeth Garland, Tracy Houghton;
Hopkinton—Beth Harlow, Megan Harlow;
Jaffrey—Pauline Halfpenny, Ann Niskala;
Keene—Tina Thompson;
Lancaster—Jean Hilliard;
Lee—Sheila Bennion;
Londonderry—Diane Dyer;
Lyndeborough—Roger Reynolds, Sally Reynolds;
Manchester—Sheila Fosher, Violet Poltak;
Marlow—Marion Chadwick;
Mason—Joy D. Bassett;
Merrimack—Rupert E. Sims, Debra Walter;
Milford—Barbara Cilley;
New Durham—Joanna Jackson;
New Ipswich—Mark & Shari Aho, Roy Coponen, Rachel Estola, Karen Kangas, G. Lynn, Lora Traffic;
Northwood—Lynda Barnes, Jane Bell, Davideen Isley, Kate McNally, Dot Pike;
Pembroke—Jaci Gagne, Susan Poulin;
Peterborough—Cathy & Courtney Duerig, Jeanne Gatcombe, Georgie Jurva, Debbie Rodenhiser, Judy Traffie;
Pittsfield—Dana Barton, Elist Fernald, Phyllis Murdough;
Raymond—Claire Fauth;
Rindge—Ruth Curran, Justin Goddard, Douglas H. Gutteridge, Art McNees, Anita Reini, Bryce Reini, Joyce Webster;

Rochester—Erma Bailey, Denise Lemieux, Rita Rial, Frank Scruton;
Somersworth—Sister Mary Judith, Francis Ward;
Suncook—Jessie A. Emerson, Linda Rollins;
Washington—J.L. Gaskell;
West Chesterfield—Mr. & Mrs. Bob Chamberlin;
Winchester—Warren H. Pettitt.

New Jersey
Belle Mead—Janette Shorey;
Bridgeton—Jere Davis, William H. Delbaugh, Laurena Thomas, Marilyn Wilson;
Cherry Hill—Mary K. Foglebach;
Great Meadows—Sue Colvenback;
Paramus—Bonnie Winters;
Pleasantville—Shirley Demill, June M. Driscoll;
Vineland—Myrtle & Russell Kempa;
Washington—Ruth Hoser.

New Mexico
Albert—John Bolton, Ben & Mary Morrison;
Albuquerque—Archie Bussell, Evelyn & William Cernousek, Tricia Geery, Tera Girard, Frank Halsted, Joann Hammett, Barbara Hawley, Anna Hindi, Gene & Lucille Hughes, Al Kiefer, Mary Kiefer, G.L. Lang, Mr. & Mrs. Joseph B. Losinski, Freda Mantei, Lezlie Montarya, Kim Peterson, Lloyd G. Spohr, Bill & Leila Straw;
Amistad—Marguerite Kimber, Yuriko One;
Artesia—Dorothy Gustin;
Belen—Vera Fagan, Miss Candy Kroenig, Cynthia & Bert Robison;
Caballo—Carolyn Nicole, Shirley Walker;
Cedar Crest—Mr. & Mrs. Scott Peterson;
Clayton—Winifred Blakely;
Cloudcroft—C. Richard Mitchell;
Clovis—Debbie & Raina Tillman;
Corazon—Carl Field, Elmer Reed;
Corona—Joyce J. Winchester;
Corrales—Ruth Kho;
Crystal—Louise Mark;
Deming—Angela Corrini, Cathy Cramer, Sheri Hamel, Alice Hanson, Rosetta Keeling, David & Ellie Loughborough, Eleanor & Brandy Loughborough, Esther Roppers, Paul Scott, Leatha Shebester, Donna M. Unger, Billy & Esther Wycoff;
Dora—Mary & Carl Fields, Hunter Hays, Ivy Wall;
Duran—Anna Hindi, Mary Lee;
Edgewood—Jon & Susan Bryau;
Elephant Butte—Daniel P. Fromer, Leona Duffy;
Fort Sumner—Edwin Lott;
Gallup—Tieneka Bulthuis, Mary Husband;
Glorieta—Kristy & Jeff Hanus;
Hatch—Abbey Dale Turner;
Hillsboro—Paul & Mary Hubert;
Las Cruces—Marylou Kersey, William & Wanda McNeil, Dolores & Harry Volkmer;
Las Vegas—Sue Scott, Eddie Sims, Elizabeth B. Sims;
Lemitar—Brian Durkin, Dawn Durkin, Lisa Fernandz;
Logan—Janet Bradshaw, Lacy & Russell Bruhn, Wilma Carpenter, Janette Lee Family, Denette Madrid, Wyle & Mary Belle Mason, Nancy Lee Morgan, T.J. Sutt;
Los Alamos—Helen Cake;
Los Lunas—Vernon R. Highland;
Mc Alister—Paul Sours;
Mountainair—Harriette Bayuski, Marie Campbell, Doris Jaquess, Pauline Swope, Arna Isabel Taylor;
Mountianair—Bernadette Rochette;
Nara Visa—Darin Bell, Lois Girard, Rose Mary Girard, James Judd, Van Robertson, Cleo Rock;

Crist Kurl

Navajo—Grace Begay, Pauline Clark, Effie Curtis, Grace Denetso, Marie Ford, Leonora Francisco, Elsie Mark, Mary Moore, Rose Wilson;
Newkirk—Terri L. Clark;
Pep—Grace & J.B. Bates;
Portales—Mary Brown, William M. Joy, Mr. & Mrs. Billy Prater, John W. Russell;
Quay—Jerry & Nealene Bradley, Phillip & Brad Griggs;
Quemado—Virginia Sauls;
Rincon—Shawna Kuenslter;
Rio Rancho—Ella & Gale Adams, John & Flo Stapleton;
Rogers—Kenneth Victor;
Roswell—Glynn & Nancy Turner;
San Antonio—Cindy Lam, Eddie Velasquez;
San Jon—A.R. & Elda Priest;
Santa Cruz—Cicilio Martinez Family;
Santa Fe—Sammie Hayes, Mr. & Mrs. Craig B. Zander;
Santa Rosa—Leroy E. Gutierrez, Loren Scott;
Silver City—John & Ora Scheibley, Pauline Yount Smidt;
Socorro—Shirley Bailey, Catherine Blythe, Anna Chavez, Samuel Chavez, Sherr Degil, Toni Edgington, Jean Frarssinet, Will & Wes Hazlett, Raymond Kameeso, Sandra Lucedu, Tony Medramo, Rosemarie Murray, Cheryl Peterlin, R. Alan Roes, Dolores Saullsberry, Alexander Stringer, Dottie Weed, Clinton Wilkerson, Mae Willden;
Torreon—Raymond Chemey, Ben Chenney;
Truth Or Consequences—Marvin Alburg, Marilyn Brinkmann, Marilyn J. Bullard, Irene Devereaux, Gloria Early, Lois Morrison, Gladys & Ted Norgard, Frances Smith, Nona Thomas, Marcia Ward & Family;
Tucumcari—Amanda Adams, Anita Aragon, Yolanda Arugen, Lena Barrett, Vicky Bemmington, Dutsy Bennett, Christina Benvidez, Janet Bios, Bliss Blair, Trina Brashear, Calyton L. Brown, John L. Brown, Robert Brown, M. Budd, Lucas Bugg, John Calbert, Helen Caldwell, Irene Callam, Judith Cartwright, Charlie Chavez, G. Chavez, Rita Coates, Linna Lou Coffin, Ruby A. Cooper, Mary Crespin, Cindy Dodd, Cora Donnell, Larry Dunaway, Lydia Encinias, Susan Gallegus, Sophie Garcia, Sybria Garcia, R. M. Gordon, Evette Grisco, Angela Griego, Jane M. Haase, Cathey Hockett, Mark Hodge, Rod Howard, Joseph Hurley, Anders Jensen, Mr. & Mrs. Oosay Jmez, Brandi Johnson, Juanita Kirkpatric, Jovita Laredo, Rosalia Littell, Ryan Livingston, Frank Lopez, Jerry Lopez, Gary P. Lowman, Denise Madricd, Karen Manning, Jose Marez, Max Mata, Veronica Mata, Carcelina Mawstas, Sharon McCauley, Cheryl McElroy, Irene Montano, James Z. Mowler, Cindy Newman, Glenda Northrup, Christine Noteware, Brandi Nucamendi, Valarie Ortega, Angolica Ortiz, The Ortiz Family, Audra & Krista Osteen, Stephanie Parks, Theresa S. Parr, Chandra Peterson, Candy Pownell, Melinda Quintana, Kim Roberts, Patrick & Donna Romo, Andi Sanchez, Grace Sanchez, Susan Schmidt, Chris Scioli, Ginger Sevarns, Peggy Shipley, Vicki Sieglen, Clarence Smith, Amanda Stephenson, Cindy Strickland; James Szaloy, Jeff Talbritie, Larry & Cathy Thomas, Fran Tollett, Chanee Unurh, Darlene Vasquez, Virginia Velasquez, Betty White, Audry & Nickolaus Wiegel, Alicea C. Ysco, Diana Ysco;
Vanderwagen—Carolyn Sautter;
Vaughn—Rebecca Gaana, Dulcie Sultemeier;
Veguita—Bonnie Doran;
Waterflow—Christene A. Hampton;
Willard—Joyce A. Hodgin, Pat Toennies;
Williamsburg—J. Gurnsey, John & Josephine Gutnsey, Teresa Hilty.

New York
Addison—Betty Emig, Harold Sison;
Akron—John & Merne Yousey;
Albany—Theresa M. Colburn, Patricia House, Ruth E. Lawlor, Gerald Shaye;
Albion—David Armer, Lois Higgins, Marlys Jones, Norm & Marge Lafferty, Jean Larnder, Franklyn Neal;
Alden—Ed & Ann Mosman;
Alexander—Carol A. Britton, Gary & Abby Diegelman Family, Rita McVay;
Allegany—Bertha Bucher;
Almond—Marilynn Kenyon;
Altamont—Shirley Gage, Jason Knaggs, Nancy & George Knaggs, John Pikcilingis;
Amherst—Esther Woodward;
Amityville—Janet Martin;
Amsterdam—Mrs. Laverne Francisco, Robert & Marcy Korona;
Andover—Fred Sisson;
Angelica—Betty Lou Shifley, Clyde Shifley;
Angola—Carol Sager, Elaine & Sharon Sager, Sandy Sager;
Arcade—Carol Abel, Gloria Arnold, Amie Bishoff, Marian Bookmiller, Nell S. Clark, Jane Haley, Mary Hulton, Yolanda Jakerbowski, Theresa Keen, Kathryn Landahl, Helen P. Landphain, Justin & Sarah Marks, Lisa Marks, Elaine Matthews, Betty Maynard, Loretta M. Payne, Bryan Zielenieski, Mary Zielenieski, Scott Zielenieski;
Argyle—Stanley J. Liddle;
Arkport—R. Demon, Mark & Emma Loree, Dave Smith, Rosemary Smith;
Attica—Gwendolyn Willey;
Auburn—Marina All, Ann Bradley, Helen Clark, Kathy R. Dalrymple, Eleanor M. Holmes, Cindy Jessie, Marion Jessie, Sue Meyer, Amy E. Murphy, Paul E. Newman,

Sandra Odell, Joy Pamplun, Kate Perry, Mary Simkulet, Mrs. Curtis R. Smith, Kyle Snook, Mr. & Mrs. Cameron Stuart, Francis Taylor, Dorothy Webster, Shirley Weldon, Barbara Young;
Aurora—Winifred C. Jones, Athena & Larue St Clair;
Avon—Matt Berger, Barb Clese, Audrey Cole, J.R. Coyne, Martha Goodberlet, Lynne Helmbold, Lillian Johnson, Mrs. Hoyt R. Mason, Vicki Rose, Joan Wright, Evelyn & Harry Zea;
Bainbridge—Lauren Bryden, Betty Hulbert;
Baldwin—Margaret Kaiser;
Baldwinsville—Mark & Ginny Collins, Betty Sue Dejohn, Dorothy Dickinson;
Ballston Lake—Bonnie Myers;
Barneveld—Ruth G. Kuchler;
Batavia—Henry & Jane Bartz, S.T. Langdon, Velma A. Prented, Marlin Prentice, Mary C. Vanalstyne, June E. Wood;
Bath—Gerald A. Button;
Battenville—Mr. & Mrs. Gerald Button;
Belfast—Ryan Edwards;
Belmont—Charles G. Austin, S. Wigent Family;
Bemus Point—Taye J. Colvin;
Bergen—Deanne, Lanni, Joe & Harriet Young;
Bernhards Bay—Max Whipple;
Binghamton—Carl & Beverly Stone;
Blasdell—Robert & Kristen Haier;
Bliss—Polly Biscaro, Helen Cross, Ashley Drew, Sue Fuller, Olivia Haxton, O. Horton, Janet Lawall, Carol Martin, Elisha Meeder, Erin Meeder, Sheila Newton, Tim Putman, Mr. & Mrs. Robert Quackenbush, Pamela Sampson, Jerry & Lyn Seewaldt Family, Eleanor Ann Smith, Sue Walton;
Bolivar—Willard Moser, A. L. Weimer;
Bombay—Bert & Janet Oesterling;
Boston—Clarence Kader;
Branchport—Sandy Hullings;
Breesport—Richard & Pat Roark;
Brewster—Donna & Ron Stephan;
Bridgeport—Tim & Khristyn Ostrowski;
Brocton—Olive Becker, Mary Burnett, Beverly H. Burton, Cindy Freay, Dorothy Post, Patty Robins, Kathleen Webber, Louise Young, Joyce Zirke;
Brookfield—Ruth Johnson, Nathan Rogers;
Brooklyn—Tony Canales;
Buffalo—Sue Freshour, G.C. Johnson, Linda L. Palmer, Catherine Steeves;
Burlington Flats—Stanley Shillieto;
Caledonia—Mary Thomas, The Webster Family;
Cambridge—Richard & Ruth Hooker, Marian Meyer;
Camden—David & Thelma Loveland, Kathy Morey, Mr. & Mrs. James Suits;
Cameron—Margaret Molton;
Canajoharie—Robert Fredenborg, Jennifer Moyer;
Canandaigua—Jean Bucher, June N. Ellis, William & Judy Gifford;
Cananoagua—Rose Cornish;
Canaseraga—Ruth Kenyon, Lois Phillips;
Canastota—Gail Blowers;
Caneadea—Francis Hull;
Canisteo—Dean Stewart, Clyde Zeltwanger;
Cassadaga—Mrs. H.T. Hilton, George Kaltenbach, Irene Lesch, Virginia Vanpootvliet, Norman Waterman;
Castile—Becky Broughton, Jazmin Cassady, Mr. & Mrs. Henry Cichocki, Harlene Daud, Christopher Edwards, The Eleaz Family, Cindy A. Feroleto, Helen P. Landphair, Linda Little, Tamara O'Connor, Diane A. Pond, Dolores Quigley, Laurinda Wallace;
Castle—Lisa Corklin;
Cattaraugus—Patricia Crandall, Elaine Deckhow, Dorothy Harvey, Marian Harvey, Judy Kennedy, Michelle Williams;
Cayuga—Kathleen Hultz, Carlene Kriegelstein;
Cazenovia—Sally M. Craner, Sharon Larkin, Marilyn Ramsden, Julie Sears;
Centerville—Ken Covet;
Central Bridge—Karl & Gladys Erikson, Jenine Forsthoffer, Frank & Elsie Hill, Ingrid & Arlton Lamont, Mrs. D. Schuttig;
Ceres—Ann Deschler;
Chadwicks—Patrick T. Kress;
Chaffee—Karen Czesak, Mildred Hittle, Joshua D. Holts, Sam Keraldi, Earl Northup, Earl & Martha Pfarmer, Norman & Marie White;
Cheektowaga—Joan Vallone, Linda Worthington;
Cherry Creek—Joyce Chase;
Cherry Valley—Karen Muratore;
Chittenango—Beverly Brownell, Mrs. Robert Hughes;
Churchville—Stephen Burkart, Richard Frew, Dwight Vail;

Cincinnatus—Mary Davis;
Clarence—Sandra Bennett;
Clifton Springs—Alice Brewer, E.M. Dennis, Marilyn Frost, Charles Snyder;
Clinton—Lynne Mosher, Marge Saddlemire;
Clyde—Ruth & Rhoda Gehman, Sandra Martin, Allen Nolt, Regina Z. Nolt, Agnes Wigfield;
Clymer—Betsy Bayle, Mark & Beatrice Ives, Becky Linton, Charles Smith, Robert Swanson, Becky Titon;
Collins—Ann Becker, Katie Botsfield, Patty Botsford, Edna G. Buckley, Frank Butzer, Deb Gabel, Jessica Gernatt, Sandi & Michael Johnson, Elinor Mesch, Kristine Rogers, Ida Rothfuss, Doris Smith, Karen Wallschlaeger, Betty Waltschlayer, Paul Willover, Kathy Young;
Collins Center—Justin Fyock, Brian Kader, Mr. & Mrs. Stuart Spencer;
Conesus—Mrs. William Greene, Joan Oakey;
Conklin—Diane Harder;
Constantia—Alice Williams;
Corfu—Carol Acquard, Jerome W. Arguard;
Cortland—Al Hauck, Linda J. Homer, Bion Manning, S. Marguerite Mulvihill, Nelson & Irene Searls, James & Norma Tanner, Betty J. Tinker, Helen Walker, Roberta Wilson;
Cuba—Harley J. Poore, Shirley Rambuski, Donald Raub;
Dale—Mildred Smith;
Dalton—Linda Clarke, Ronnalee Maker, Theresa Wood;
Dansville—Doris McMaster, George Bancroft, Shawn Davidson, Marylin Derrenblacher;
Darien—Tambra Johnson;
Deansboro—Kurt & Jacqueline Chapmann, Mary Lloyd;
Delevan—Deanna Ekroth, Kathy Hagerdon, Danel Hallock, Karne Idauock;
Delhi—Beulah Francisco, Cecil Francisco, Karen Rasmussen;
Depew—J. Palaszewski;
De Ruyter—Connie Skeele, Scott Skeele;
Dewittville—Mose W. Byler, Betty Stage;
Duanesburg—Frank Berical;
Dundee—Josh Beiler, N.R. Clancey, Newell & Joanne Clancey, Thomas & Myra Disbrow, Michael Glick, R. Hallenbeck, Cynthia & Arnold Mast, Kenneth Mast, Marj & Milford Mast;
Dunkirk—Michele Abendsclein, Alton A. Bonhoff, Minnie Butts, Mary S. Catalario, Penny Kalfas, Tracy Leikam, Debbie Lore, Harry MacCubbon, Jean Mekus, Carol A. Pacos, Kevin Schunk, Towne;
Earlville—Tina Ingraham, Mary Vanauken, Roxanne Waldruff;
East Aurora—Benny & Sally Bender, Marguerite Zeiner;
East Bethany—Dan & Clara Galliford;

East Bloomfield—Jean A. Mason, Amelia McWilliams;
East Concord—Sharon Shencer;
East Freetown—Mrs. Elna R. Stafford;
East Greenbush—Bill & Elaine Green;
East Meadow—Karen Schmitt;
East Nassau—Ed & Mary Ellen Carabis;
East Otto—Lillian Bowen, Sharon Wolf;
East Randolph—Helen Day, Glaydes Paisley;
East Springfield—Nola Cook;
Eaton—Cheryl Nettleton;
Eden—Betty Geiger, Gladys Rice, Karen Schmitt, Phyllis & Geo Slaughenhaupt;
Elba—Dolores Coughlin;
Elbridge—Sylvia Belzner, Marie F. Wise;
Ellicottville—Dean Morton;
Elma—Elsie Krieger;
Endicott—Frank Bauerle, Carolyn Bennett, Richard & Barbara Brooks, Mr. & Mrs. R.J. Brooks Sr.;
Erieville—Allen & Sue Clark, Mr. & Mrs. David Jones;
Esperance—Cecelia & Bernard Crandall, Erica Downes, Dorothy R. Edwards, Joe & Melanie Largeteau, Melanie Largeteau, Alice Markle, Kathleen Page;
Fabius—Marie Prindle, Edna Skeele, Pat Woodruff;
Fairport—Barbara Hunt, Jason M. Jacobs;
Falconer—Inez M. Allen, Phillip Allen;
Farmington—Colleen Ewing, Mandy Weigert;
Fayette—Lew & Millie Sorrentino, Mildred Sorrentino;
Feura Bush—Howard E. Wisenburn;
Fillmore—Leora J. Arnold, Jacqueline M. Bailey, S. Bailey, Chris Schulz, Jim Talbott, Audrey Zilker;
Findley Lake—Alicia & Brittany Bauer, Florence Boozel, Matthew Deist, June Mobilia, Edith Robinson, Rosalie Sensenig, Ruth & Conrad Stover & Family;
Fonda—Julie Morey;
Forestville—Lee H. Aldingell, Ella Brown, Pat Carpenter, Mrs. Pat Franklin, Tammy Franklin, Judy Hahn, Kimberly Ivett, Florabel Majeski, Evelyn McGuire, Lynda Pleszewski, Catherine Tyler, Pat Webb, Sue Wilson, Peggy Youngberry;
Fort Plain—Lorraine Marks;
Franklin—Ruth B. Laing, Konkle Ogden;
Franklinville—Shirley Lane;
Fredonia—Emily Bennett, Jennie Bielat, Carl Burt, Christina Cohvenback, Julie Davis, Heather Gould, Doreen Hall, Lois M. Hall, Kellee Nixon, Emily Saned, Margaret Skinner, Emily Volk, Karen Wahl, Mr. & Mrs. Lynn Watrous, Mr. & Mrs. Edward Waxhum, Merel E. West;
Freedom—Laurie Merrill, Laurie Merrill Family;
Frewsburg—Lee Songster;
Friendship—Donald Edwards, Nellie Edwards;
Fulton—Dennis & Rita Norton, Rita Norton, Rita F. Norton;
Gainesville—Annette Anderson, Wanda Andrews, Jenny Marley, Jerome & Nancy L. Marley, Ken & Kelly Marley, Leighanne & Lee Marley, Mike & Leighanne Marley, Amanda Olcott, Francis Reding, The Roberts Family, Gina Wetmore;
Garrattsville—Robert & Bertha George;
Geneseo—The Banker Family, Evelyn & Linda Farley, Evelyn & Shirley Farley, Shirley Farley, Bette Gove, Don & Ruth Hartnett, Ryan Louvain, Myrtle Merritt, Mrs. Robert Monroe, Bud Scully, Eleanor Vandeweert, Garry Vandeweert;
Geneva—Jan Bailey, Mrs. Robert Eakins, Terri & Bob Eakins, Mr. & Mrs. Harold Edington, Elsie L. Freier, Mary G. Hay,

Alton P. Kingsbury, Jeanne Leonard, Marlene Madin, Janet Martin Family, Landis & Janet Martin Family, James Minns, James Minns, Shirley Minns, Debbi Oswald, Carl & Ann Radder, Karen Rasmussen, Karl & Pennie Russ Family, Paula Tindale, Chad Walker, Bud Woodley, Charles Zeck;
Glenfield—Richard & Lucy Kapfer;
Gloversville—Mrs. Jean Persch, Harry J. Smith, Krista Vanvalkenburgh;
Gowanda—Jean Anni, Nancy Bowers, Jane Kuntz, Kelly McDonald, Jennifer Nicholson, Barb Tessmer;
Great Valley—Donald Potter, Donald & Joyce Potter, Kathie Potter, Wesley Potter, Susan Weaver, Tim Weaver;
Greene—Margaret Stiles;
Greenwich—Ronald Hunt;
Greenwood—Lola L. Lewis;
Guilderland—Bernice Parks, Anne T. Rose, Michelle Tillapaugh;
Guilderland Center—Mrs. John Nitsky;
Guilford—Esther Ward;
Hall—Duane Blowers;
Hamburg—Gloria Abbott, Harold & Joyce Meyer, Joyce Meyer, Geri Rosiek, Linda A. Schoenfeld, Linda Winter;
Hamilton—Carol Dunham, Dick Knabb, Richard & Shirley Knapp, Cynthia Kulak, Dorothy & Del Lehman;
Hamlin—Mr. & Mrs. Roger Banker, Rev. Liz Meacham;
Harpursville—Jim & Lynn Vanpelt, Marilyn J. Vanpelt;
Hartwick—Dorothy Manley;
Hemlock—Mildred Boback;
Herkimer—Mildred Boback;
Hilton—Sherry Bernreuther, Jacob & Jackie Swanson;
Himrod—Patricia L. Ellwanger, Andrea Stoltzfus, Sam Stoltzfus;
Hinsdale—Ellena Fairfield, Ellena Fairfield, Elisabeth Noll;
Holcomb—Carol Britton, Nancy Garlock, Ann & Alan Lerkins Family, Lowell & Evelyn Lovejoy, Nancy Norman Family, David L. Preston Family, Mrs. Russell H. Sage, Sandy Schlenker, Martha Stanton, Todd Stanton, Nancy Stewart, The Sykes Family, Denis Wheaton, Bruce G. Whitmore;
Holland—Frank & Lorraine Hahn, Brenda Hise, Charlotte Woodruff;
Holley—Karen A. Swanson;
Homer—Les Brock, Gary Harrington, Charles & Barb Jermy, Helen C. Perry, Laura Spencer;
Honeoye—Doris Miller;
Honeoye Falls—Martha D. Arnold Family;
Hornell—Shirley Burdett;
Horseheads—Ruth Hill;
Houghton—Robert Hagerdon;
Howes Cave—Shirley Bellinger;
Hudson—Karen Hewett McDonald;
Hume—Carol Arnold, Mae R. Stevens, Linda Worthington;
Hunt—Shirley Holly, Nancy Pattridge;
Ilion—Dorothy Dawson;
Interlaken—Howard Bassett, Heather Wilkins;
Ionia—Donald Parrish;
Irving—Jan Larson;
Ithaca—Rev. & Mrs. Erie J. Miller, Florence Peuther, Geraldine Prouty;
Jamestown—Carl & Peg Anderson, M. Bloomstoan, Floye H. Bloomstra, Megan Crandall, Mrs. Edward S. James, Jay Johnson, Ellis & Miriam Macey, Robert Roach, Ralph Stanford, Sandra A. Thunberg, Richard Tisth, Carol Trostle, Ann Weber;

Jordan—Esther Anthonson, Ellen D. Buckler, Kathy Cook;
Katonah—Howard & Roberta Fogle Jr.;
Kendall—Nancy Grah Family, Howard Patt, Ralph & Lorena Patt;
Kennedy—Mrs. Don Maloney;
Kirkville—Mr. & Mrs. Nathan S. Dunlap;
Knoxboro—Ernest & Bea Eaton;
La Fargeville—Bernadette Seme;
La Fayette—Mary Debottis, Harris Sloper;
Lakeville—Larry Dangelo;
Lakewood—Linda McCraw, Heleena Milan, June Wahlberg;
Lancaster—Betty Frey, Anne E. Gregory;
Latham—Katie Ring;
Lawtons—Frederick Haier, Cindy Kohn, Sue Niefergold, Florence Schmitz;
Le Roy—Grace Conklin, Donna Falkner, Liz Knitter;
Leicester—Lisa Cuozzo, Linda M. Hamilton Family, Bev Hart, Pamela & Holly Jacobs, Frank A. Milley, Mari Morgan, Don Popp, Kathleen Rawleigh, Shelby G. Sliker, Joshua Zambito;
Leon—James A. Baker;
Leonardsville—Dorothy A. Jones, William Lewis;
Lima—Livinia Curletta, Bev Gillette, Mrs. Carmen Gillette, Lois Lloyd, Jennifer Lusk, Sandra & Jessica Lusk, Jonathan Schwing, Sheila Seme;
Lindley—Doris Ferrier;
Little Valley—Dianne Beeman, Dorothy Dunn;
Livonia—Bonnie & Brian Stekl, Mr. & Mrs. Jason Stekl;
Lockport—Cheryl Krentz, Mrs. Charles H. Rigerman;
Lowman—Charles Pevnis, Calvin & Rachelle Purvis, Cat Purvis, Charity & Gene Purvis, Russell & Nancy Purvis, Ryan & Brittany Purvis;
Lowville—Ruth Berrus, Pat Call, Shirley Chambers, P. Miller;
Lyons—Alexandria R. Barner, Ruth Langdon, Paul L. Norton, Christopher M. Petty, Maurice & Sharon Schleede, Max Sontheim;
Macedon—Jennifer & Shane Dehn, Marion Ferris, Debra Howie;
Machias—Connie R. Chapman;
Madison—Patty Bikowsky, Janine Fuess, Carol J. Service, M. Umstead;
Malden Bridge—Louise Behn;
Malone—Evelyn Farley;
Mandana—Mrs. Burdette Gallton;
Manlius—Alice G. Mapes, F. Lillian Mose, Dorathy Moss, Jack Niles, M. Stables, Debbie & Ross Vilardi, Trevor & John Vilardi;
Mannsville—Richard Hughs;
Marcellus—Veronica Hughes, Helen Ramsden, Thelma Ramsden, Jason Wall;
Mariaville—Billie Black;
Marietta—Shirley Clark, Alma Dence, D.E. Fish, Theresa K. Fish, Sue Masters, Beverly Ann Porter;
Marilla—Margy Roloff;
Marion—Leona Frazer, Roger Larwwod, Letitia Turner;
Massena—Debra Howie;
Mayville—Jacquine Baker, Bill Paddock, Marian Scinen, Marian Scives, Hobart Weise;
Mc Graw—Lora Hall;
Medina—Paul Baker, Carolyn Squires;
Mellenville—Kathy McNamee Family;
Memphis—Maynard Bratt, Olive Bratt;
Mendon—Marguerite Alexander, Joseph Burnett, The Guilfoil Family;
Mexico—Wayne Cornell;
Middleburgh—Heinz Berkner, Pauline Mercer, Minnie Reinhart, Ed Waldron;
Millport—George Sydelko;
Mohawk—Betty Jane Brewer;
Moravia—Grace Conklin Family, Nancy Goodnough, Phillip Goodnough, Carol Hartnett;
Morrisville—Marilyn F. Griffiths, Joshua Schokker, Marianne Webb;
Mount Morris—Sharon & Thomas Coates, Joey Downey, Helen Peterson, Barbara Rudgers, Becky Wheeler;
Mount Vision—Laurie Kane;
Munnsville—Robbie Kiehn;
Nanuet—Laura Swanson;
Naples—Shirley Braun, Denise Wheaton, Lisa Woodard;
Nassau—David Dietrich, Charles Papa, W. C. Ransford;
Nedrow—Giselle Neu;
New Berlin—Harold Clarke;
New Hartford—Anne Koslosky;
New Lebanon—Edmond R. Lacasse;
New Woodstock—Mary Ellen Holmes;
Newark—Helen Blandino, Diana S. Jansen, Fred Miller, Edna H. Whyte;
Newark Valley—Gerald E. Strope;
Newfane—Susan Gardner;
Niagara Falls—Gerald Kraatz, Jerry & Bernie Kratz;
North Chatham—Merry Mitchison;
North Chili—Matthew & Hannah Brady, Jim Burkhart, Clayton Ess;
North Collins—Becky Awald, Edward & Millie Awald, Karen Niefergold, Gladys Taft, Virginia Winter;
North Java—Cecelia Conrad, Rosemary Schwab, Betty Suleski, Donna Ward;
North Syracuse—Harry & Pat Kilpatrick, Clifford Kingsley;
North Tonawanda—Jeanne S. Morris, William & Nellie Tubbs;
Nunda—Eleanor L. Gibson, Brandon Hadsell;

Gerald Hellickson

Oakfield—Milton Unger;
Olean—Jessica Fairfield, Cindy Wilson, Lucinda F. Wilson;
Oneida—Marlene Urtz;
Oneonta—Marie Gridley, R. Hart;
Ontario—Evelyn Bailey, Judith Boessmann, Elmer M. Schimerhorn;
Orchard Park—Nancy L. Conley, Heidi & Tim Gardner, Marjorie Lawson, Victoria Twarog;
Oriskany Falls—Bess Babcock, June Johnson, Allison P. Service;
Owego—Jake Rypkema, Francis Taylor;
Oxford—Grace Bartle, Mary Bliven;
Painted Post—George Halm, Marian L. Halm;
Palmyra—Linda B. Quadrozzi, Carl Root, Mr. & Mrs. Arnold B. Smith, Shirley Vanzandvoord, Stuart & Edna Warner, Russell Wendt;
Panama—Sandra Hoyt;
Pattersonville—William Black, Kyle & Abby Nelson, Nicole & Katie Nelson;
Pavilion—Marian Berkemeier, Alvin R. Bunce, Mrs. Gerald Copeland, Claxton Ewell, Willard Logsdon, Jim McIllroy, Bob Page, Peter D. Sherman;
Penfield—Lois Chase, Gladys Deveryst;
Penn Yann—B. Decker, Betty Frost, D. Hallenbeck, Glenn Lapp Family, Donna Mayo, Patti Phillips, Leanna Weaver, Roger Wright Family;
Perry—Cindy Clark, Randy Decker, Betsy Degroff, Tara Demers, Gerald & Pauline Foote, Anne Z. Koson, V. Link, Barbara Murray, Laura Myers, Debbie Page, Bradley & Chris True, Brian True, Diane True, Ruth True, Stephanie Wolcott Family;
Perrysburg—Merris & Dorothy Case, Carol Everetts, Theresa Frost, Mrs. R.D. Martindale, Pauline Pfeffer, Cindy Watkins, Tricia Watkins;
Peterboro—Janice Graham;
Phelps—Dawn Covert, Chris Dutcher, Mary Heffron, Frank Quiney;
Piffard—Everett Hunn, Gregory Martin;
Pike—Annabel Ayers, Ethel Camp, Doris Flint, Mrs. Frank Gillette, Ashley Hootman, Norma Stroud;
Pitcher—Warren Brown;
Plain City—Mrs. Alvin C. Gingerich;
Poestenkill—Shirley Lindeman;
Port Byron—Neal Becker, Barbara Black, Sally Smith, June Thomas, Agnes Turner, Mr. & Mrs. Edward M. Turner;
Portageville—Alicia Beardsley, Barbara V. Crosby, Waneta Krauss, Donna Rissinger;
Portland—Becky Boyland, Marie Emke, R. Patterson, Sherry Robbins, Sherry Robson, Jessica Salter, Sara Salter;
Portville—Bill & Helen Miller, Kathy & Jonathan Miller;
Poughkeepsie—Donald L. Schoenwald;
Preble—Jean M. Amidon;
Randolph—Betty Archer, Carol Hoxie, Tom Hoxie, Marlene Nieman, Cheryl Rockwood, Eileen Sickles;
Redford—D. Ward;
Red Hook—Anne Bauer;
Rensselaer—Bonnie Lee Hahn;
Richburg—Francis Bartoo;
Richfield—James Willsey;
Richfield Springs—Barb Kasprowurz, Cliff Oaks, Kelly L. Stone, Valerie Tanner, James Weeks;
Richmondville—Theresa McDermott, Lesley Sanders;
Ripley—Barbara J. Bovee, Lou Ann Henry, Barbara J. Lanphere, Bernard Lanphere, Sharon & Wanita Rogers, Carl Testrake, Prudence Waters, Dana L. Winkleman, Mrs. John Yusten, Jeffrey & David Zarpentine;
Riverhead—Shirley Braun;
Rochester—Melody Aldridge, James C. Clark, D. Clark Family, Bob & Beverly Evans, Wilson Fitch, Jean & Hans Gross, Rose Harshbarger, Diane Kacprzak, Dorothy Ketchum, Tammy McGarvey, Dorris Nash, Mrs. David Parmele, Frances Pautz, Brenden Ramsdell Family, Shirley Tschorke, Arnold & Florena Wage, L. Walsh, Lois Wendl;
Rome—Jean & Robert Ossont;
Romulus—Helen Kidd, Leaann Kidd, Mrs. Duane Lent;
Roscoe—Beatrice & Walter Stevens;
Rush—Peggy Nesbitt, Patti Page;
Rushville—Amy Daines, Mr. & Mrs. Leon Daines, Almira Jean Shaw;
Sanborn—Ken Wendt;
Sandadea—Grace Fowler;
Sardinia—Adeline Humphrey, Florende Rupert, Gladys M. Sears, Eddie Vacinek, Ruth Vacinek;
Sauquoit—Ruth Goldstein, Jim Mortis, Ryan Wilson;
Savannah—Robert & Pauline Judson, Robert & Dorothy Welch;
Schenectady—Don Bixby, Donna & Bob Pikcilingis, Heidi Pikcilingis, Julie & Brad Pikcilingis, Jan Simpson, Jean M. Sterling, Wayne Tompkins, Gail P. Vanpatten;
Schenevus—Milt & Olive Brandow, Margaret Green, Janette Peeters, Marian Peeters;

Barbie Howland

Schoharie—Edwin Grass, Eleanor Grass;
Schuyler Lake—Ida Davis, Kelly Stone;
Scio—Carol Abbery;
Scotia—Charlyne Bugg;
Scottsburg—Merle Frary;
Scottsville—Dorothy Leaton, Chris Oonk, Judith Seager;
Seneca Falls—Allen S. Burkholder, Barbara J. Clark, Mary Henry, Winfred Hilkert, Harriet H. Hoster, Jennifer Ann Millerd, Hazel Moses, Phil Rogers, Eleanor C. Shaffer, Alberta Shaw, Mrs. Alberta Stuck, Linda Stuck, Ellen & Joseph Ticconi, Ray Zettlemoyer;
Sharon Springs—Mrs. Edgar Handy, Walter Kahabka, Malcolm Lynk, Donald B. McCoy, Larry McFee, Nola Osterhoudt, Catherine Vandyke, Ginny Wilday;
Sherburne—Mrs. John Guter, William E. Hodges, Kathleen Moore;
Sherman—Janie Albrew, Clare Gulick, Elaine Kobielski, Louie & Laurajean Kobielski, Barbara Neckers, Helen M. Reynolds, Jason Yohom;
Sherrill—Johanna C. Wallace, Edna Walter;
Shortsville—Jenni Obryan, Philip Reed;
Siloam—Matthias Cordts;
Silver Creek—Lindsey Bonasera, Rose Crabb, Betty Delcamp, Arlene Mohart, Briana Palmer, Adam & Mellisa Sager, Darrell & Brian Sager, Marion E. Taylor;
Silver Lake—J. Maddison, Katherine Smith, Ruth Smith Family;
Silver Springs—Tom Bush, Floyd & Beatrice Chamberlain, Gloria Lanni;
Sinclairville—Andrew & Jean Abbey, Mary Dyson, Howard Gilbert, Clarice M. Larson, Garnet Millward, Glenn Millward, George & Audrey Prosser;
Skaneateles—Jean Bailes, Diane & Jessie Carr, Kelly & Carey Carr, Cathy Crary, Elaine M. Fey, Amy & Scott Flynn, Judy Frost, Rudy Gavurnik, Georgia & Allie Kennedy, Gina & Alli Kennedy, Becky & Amy Leubner, Irma Lukins, Muriel MacLachlan, Helen Newell, Mary Louise Osborne, Donna Porter, Lindsey Robertson, Jason Sheets, Tammy Slater, Eugene Springstead, Leland E. Springstead, The Sullivan Family, Nancy Thompson, James & Kimberly Tracy, James W. Tracy Family, John Tucker, Howard & Bessie Turner, Tim Vancamp, Nancie & Rich Way, Owen Wing;
Sloan—Kenneth & Linda Gribble;
South Dayton—Nancy Brisley, Sophie Fye, Nancy Howard, Tracy Leikam, Judy McGuire, Ruth Moore, Marc Nobles, Claudia Youmans;
South Lima—Mary A. & Matthias Cordts;
South Wales—Sharon Hawley;

Spencerport—Lilo Cordts, Ann Lerkins, Doris Ott;
Sprakers—Walter Cummings;
Springfield Center—Jeanette Dorn;
Springville—Margaret Brenner, Isabelle Charles, Jane Ciszak, Anita Domes, Marilyn Dye, Donald L. Fuller, George Keahm, Dorothy King, Ellie Kirkendall, Brenda Krzemien, Florence Land, Dorothy Lazell, Joyce Lis, Lucy Lux, Ralph & Dorothy Parsons, Marion Pearson, Fran Potter, Pat Riley, Mary Ruby, Ellen Schiester, Annabel Schmartz, Herman Schmitt, Ellen L. Schuster, Albert Underberg, G. Wilke, John Young;
Stafford—Tom Burns;
Stanley—Bonnie & Eric Bergstresser, Ina Gotts Campbell, Donald D. Gage, Lynn J. Miller, Joy & Jonathan Teet;
Steamburg—Betty Archer;
Stephentown—Patricia Spaniol;
Stockton—Karlene Taylor;
Strykersville—Bob, Donna & Logan Drummer;
Summit—Elaine Speed;
Syracuse—Betty Dejohn, Shirley Orzell, Donald D. Potter, Paul Rebuck, Mary L. Winters;
Troy—Margaret Fisher;
Trumansburg—Donald & Marcia Dimick;
Tully—Melanie Collis, Carolyn B. Gambell, Carl Henderson, Meghan Murphy, Kenneth & Lucy Winslow, Susan Wrisley;
Unadilla—Marilyn Tiffany;
Union Springs—Lucille & John Cardinell, Michael Cardwell, Phyllis & Arthur Gamlen Jr., Betty Jirinec, Doris Strayer;
Utica—Clarence Gates;
Valatie—Kathi Jonas, Phyllis Preuratil;
Valley Falls—Jack & Jenny Spink;
Van Hornesville—Sharon Galusha, Mariel Richardson;
Varysburg—Florence Almeter, Ethelbert Almita, Gloria Hoy, Andy Luce, Frederick Luce, Ray Luce;
Vernon—Bonnie Croft, Walter Fuller;
Vernon Center—Jean Langford;
Versailles—Donald Nephew;
Victor—Mr. & Mrs. Thomas Ewing;
Wadsworth—Trish & Melissa Boyd;
Wales Center—Beverly A. Dicardo;
Wallkill—Diana Jansen;
Walworth—Becky & Buzz Appleman, Beverly S. Trautman;
Wampsville—Barbara Hopsicker, Lainie Williams;
Warners—Earl Adams;
Warsaw—Christie Gerasimchik, Ruth Langdon, Marie Nevinger, Gene Prickett, Lucille A. Smith, W. Jerome Smith, Mrs. L. Stephen Snider, Ralph J. Vantyne, Ellen Whitmore;
Waterloo—Wesley Palmer, Gladys Sherwood;
Watertown—Barbara Kellogg;
Waterville—Shirley Kellogg, Virginia M. Leigh, Samuel J. Merriman, Sandra Oherien, Jimmie D. Riverburgh, Leona Root, Kelly Smith;
Watervliet—Stephen Gifford;
Webster—Harold Ball Family;
Weedsport—Marion Berry, Kathy Cook, Fred W. Kinney, Nellie G. Kinney, Rosamond N. Mason, Pat Smith, Barbara E. Stanton, Harold & Eleanor Sturgis, Linda Willis, Sheila Yoensky, Betty Zimmer;
Wellsburg—Leslie Kintz;
West Bloomfield—Katherine E. Nowack;
West Falls—Barbara Kruszka;
West Henrietta—Helen Howitt, Jeannette Symonds;
West Seneca—Lois Gislio, Marshall & Pearl Westphal Family;
West Valley—Carsyl Frank, Delores Hauri, Maella Hauri, Ray Williams, Peg & Michael Williamson;
West Winfield—Dorothy Andela, Marguerite Buss, Elsie Deboer, Rosemary Donahoe, Ann Pugh, Alfred Smith;
Westerlo—Bob & Jan Dietz, Susan Telfer;
Westfield—Barbara Bartlow, Sandra Cunningham, Alfred J. Deakin, Marie & Eric Edwards, David R. Eggert, Luanne Elder, Jean Foster, Pearl Kuhn, Marie Noble, Patrick Noble, Mary & Amber Perry, Claire Post, Esther Reardon, Ann Sherman, Art & Marion Sider;
Westmoreland—Carl Smith;
Whitesboro—Ruth L. Bliss, Marguerite Day, Wendy Washblion;
Williamson—Heidi Hoffman, Pam Sonneville, Marilyn Strickland, Jean Woodard;
Williamsville—Linda Rosser;
Wyoming—Deanna Berkemeier, Alvin & Marian Langdon;
Yorkshire—Shawn & Stephanie Johnston, Mr. & Mrs. Clare McVay, Maxine Morgan, Jennifer Newton, Mertie Peckham, Mrs. Clifford Zimmer;
Youngstown—Ray & Erva Graf.

North Carolina
Advance—Lindsay Smith;
Cary—Elizabeth Quigley;
Connellys Springs—Geraldine Segmon;
Fletcher—Earl Melton;
Germanton—Elmore & Cleo Redding;
Granite Falls—Betty J. Kistle;
Greensboro—Jean Anne Finley;
Jamestown—Nancy Ratcliff, Steve A. Ratcliff Sr.;
Misenheimer—Phyllis Houghton;
Morganton—Carl Bugg;
Raleigh—Emily Anderson;

Walnut Cove—J. Boles;
West End—Paul Hawkins;
Winston-Salem—The Adams, Shirley Cox.

North Dakota
Beulah—Herb & Catherine Scherbinski;
Devils Lake—Ragnheld Anderson, Arlene Kirk;
Glen Ullin—Paula Kobilansky;
Goodrich—Gerhard Freadrick;
Hope—Frieda Baldwin;
Jamestown—Barb & Pat Hogan;
Mott—Wilma Beckman;
New Rockford—Karen Hovey.

Ohio
Ada—Tami Anderson, Pauline Cribley, Andre Crouse, Janel Elwood, Russell & Mable Hathaway, Dorothy Jones, Hilda Mumma, Dorothy Rayl, Vera Schafer, Mrs. Robert S. Shanks, Gerald Trout, Wilma Willeke;
Adena—Alta Lorenz, Willard & Loretta Lorenz, Walter McAllister;
Akron—K. Coss, Sally J. Stronp;
Alger—Joan Faulder, Rick Jones, Phyllis Scott, Pauline Williams;
Alliance—Ralph B. Allen, Pat Boro, Pat Boyd, Mary Brogan, Arnold Burley, Sylvia Cline, Nancy J. Eft, Fran Faverty, Evelyn Flenniken, Casey Grant, Marleen Grant, Pam Hoff, Amanda Hoff, Cathy Hoff, Juanita Hoff, Judith Howenstine, Mrs. Ralph Kinser, Debbie Krug Family, Alva Markle, Pauline A. Miller, Barb Moser, Russell L. Newburn, Bill Oyster, Steven Oyster, Steve Oyston, Mr. & Mrs. William Redd, Samantha Riordan, Joshua Sabski, Marcia Schmid, Cameron Stolt, John Weaver;
Alvordton—Edwin St. John;
Amherst—Debra Pelton;
Andover—Ruth Band, Ruth E. Bang, Ashley & Jaclyn Beckwith, Charles & Bonita Brain, Howard Broughton, Ruth H. Brown, Clare Chapman, Kay Cork, Amy Eyring, Diane Furear, Doug Furman, William Griswold, Amanda J. Hilliard, Amiee Hofka, Jill & Derek Lewis, Denise Link, Donald & Ruth McMichael, Edna K. Moore, Lincoln Morris, Robert R. Payne Jr., John & Lola Racey, Timothy & Malissa Racey, Jeanne A. Schertzer, Rachel M. Wolfe, Toby J. Yoder;
Apple Creek—Ann Breneman, Ruth Hofstetter, William S. Nussbaum, Arthur Rurstutz;
Arcanum—Mrs. Chalmer E. Baker, Pearl Beckner, Esther Bowman, Merrie Brown, Margaret Cullers, Jesse Denlinger, Ralph Shively;
Archbold—Doris Nafziger, Irene Nafziger, Lawrence & Alma Smucker;
Arlington—John & Agnes Crosser, Cecil E. Fields;
Ashland—D Keith Ballantyne, Mildred Boehler, Virginia Brooks, Ben & Jacob Carpenter, Karen & Matt Carpenter, Janet Crist Family, Chad Draper, Cathy Emminger, Cathy Emoninger, Louise & Willis Esbenshade, Mervin & Donna Esbenshade, Brady Hardiman, Kara Hardiman, Doris Johnston, Jacob Lawrence, Miranda & Joslyn Lawrence, Janet Frew-Martin, Marge McBurney, Ruth M. Oberholtzer, Trent & Janice Oswalt, Helen Pifer, Velma Pifer, Betty Pifero, Dorothy Plice, Dona L. Roberts, Estelle Schenk, Donna Shaw, Paul Stephens, K. Roger Swineford, David Welca, Carol Wertz, Earl Witmer, Merle & Elaine Witmer, Jania Yeater;
Ashtabula—Teri Breedlove, Heathe Brock, Kerri Caudill, Joyce Enos, Patricia Guarracino, Roberta Kobernik, Terry Miller, James E. Prickett, Joanne Prickett, John Sandberg, Cheryl Lynn Wakeman;
Attica—Mildred Scott;
Atwater—Janie Goston, James Stricker, Martha Strickler, Beverly & Tom Whittlesey, Deloris Whittlesey;
Auburn—Sue Dunton;
Austintown—Betty Carson, Dana Fellows, Pat Marino, Betty Parson, Clarabell Sinn;
Avon—Herb Stockard, Mr. & Mrs. Joseph R. Wysocki;
Baltic—Rita Miller, Jean Shafer, Andrew Yoder;
Barberton—Carol Efaw;
Barnesville—Mary Shepherd;
Bay Village—Michelle Baukmett, Michelle & Kris Bauknecht, Irene Tiefenthaelfr;
Beach City—Kathryn Bixler;
Beaverdam—Earl Gossard;
Bedford—Ladimer Vitu;
Belle Center—Lois Stout;
Bellefontaine—Carolyn Deardurff, Charles Godwin, Harold Mills, Linda Sprague;
Bellevue—Danyell Falter, Clayton Miller, Steve Rogers, George Shane;
Bellville—Pat Dion, Maxine Hart, Carole L. Miller, Vickie E. Moran, Jean L. Reed, Paul & Ruth Williams;
Belmont—Charles Duvall, Sue Lofton;
Beloit—Brad & Virginia Bandy, M. Close, Melissa & Randy Crowe, Melissa Crowell, Paul & Mary Lou Hahlen, Rose Hahlen, Toni Henry, R.H. Hinton, Marjorie Hoffman, Ben & Abby Humphrey, Don Lane, Jancie Marling, Nancy Martig, The Martigs, Mr. & Mrs. John McCay, Joann Mehegay, Connie Phillips Family, Judy Schaeffer, Patty Sonor, Michelle Spencer, Betty Stewart, Rolland Stryfeler,

John Townsend, Mary Weatrick, Pat Weingart, Rebecca Wise, Mindy Wutrick, Freda Wyss;
Benton—Barb & Heather Biery;
Bergholz—Maxine Donaldson;
Berlin—Lois Basinger, Emma Clark, Brenda Patterson, Joanne Weaver;
Berlin Center—Harry Camp, Kelly Marie Conrad, Tracie Cummings, Jarrett Feller, Wendy Gfeller, Carolyn Hazzdli, Rosalie & Heather Hoffman, Edith Kale, Terrill Kale, David Kemp, George & Nellie Martinovich, Marlene Meek, M. Meier, Darlene Mix, Betty Noble, Mary Ellen Ripley, Joan Schuller, The Srocks, Jan Stiffler, Colleen Truitt, Doris M. Yeager, Marie A. Yong;
Berlin Heights—Robert Missig;
Big Prairie—Mrs. Regan Miller, Larry Alexander, Sophia Doyle, Chris Hayward, Kathryn Kemper, Luella Sage, Lee Smetza, Ruthie Tipton, George Trity, Larry White;
Blanchester—William Gilbert, Freda Jackson, Shirley Jackson;
Bloomdale—Lova Brandeberry;
Bloomingdale—Sheila Groves;
Bloomville—Zona Munro, Bradly & Ryan Schiefer;
Bluffton—Berdella & Byron Anderson, Marylin Basinger, The Houston Family, Lee M. Hursey, Casey Jones, Joan Carr Jones, Merlin Marshall, Herbert Reichenbach, Janell Reichenbach;
Boardman—Heather Leilt;
Bolivar—Kimberly Alspaugh, Bonnie L. Gooding, Maurice & Marylou Lundenberger, Mary Ann Schaar Family, Mr. & Mrs. Greg Young;
Bowling Green—Wayne & Alice Brueggemeier, Linda Cotrell, Rosemary Palmer, Shirley Woessner;
Bradford—Mr. & Mrs. Omer C. Holsapple, Eileen Whitmer;
Bridgewater—George Hardy Clan;
Bristolville—Donna Lindsay;
Brookfield—Rose Coryea, Herbert & Marcia Harrington;
Brookville—Mrs. Everet Brubaker, John & Darlene Denlinger, Mrs. Norman Denlinger, George Flora, Ann Marie Macy, Bill Mast, Labon & Camela Milyard, Nathan & Jason Milyard, Richard & Carol Milyard;
Bryan—Margaret Alvaney, Mrs. Evan Ballmer, Mrs. Arnold P. Ledyard, Mary Ann Schroeder;
Buckeye Lake—Harold Johnson;
Bucyrus—Erma Crabaugh, James Crabaugh, William K. Downing, Rosella M. Fither, Annabelle Gerhart, Bill & Eleanor Long, Craig Lutz, Warren E. Lutz, Pete Maynard, Ruth Metzger, Ryan Neidermeier, R.W. Oppenlander, Sarah Parker, Mrs. Victor Shultz, Paul R. Wagner;
Burbank—James B. Cool, Linda Lance, Linda Lauce, Ashley Nichols, Howard & Shirley Ream, Jessica Ream;
Burton—Eli S. Yoder;
Caledonia—Rodney & Mamie Baldinger, Dick & Sandy

Suzanne Brown

Holycross, Ken Huffman, Barbara Ann Reece, Donna Wade;
Camden—Ruby Bruner, Velma Major;
Canfield—Nelda Anderson, David Blevins, The Bricelands, John Lynn, Ada S. Miller, Margie Murphy, Wilma Rheil, Mary & Amanda Schaefer, Samantha Schaefer, Marie Seals, Helen Wack;
Canton—The Bagent Family, Joann Bagert, Edna McLean, Janet McLean, Robert Schwarz, Ray Stallman, Alvin B. Stauffer, Abby Steinmotz, Virginia Swart, Georgia Wilson, Richard Wilson, Mike Zelei;
Cardington—Bob & Eileen Chappell, Diane Clapsaddle, Jan Johnson;
Carey—Joanie Neiderkohr, Catherine Niederkohr, Steven Orians, Pat Seifert, Mary Jean Snyder;
Carlisle—Charles & Mae Thresher;
Carrollton—Donna Borland, Rick & Susan Borland, Katy Borland, Calvin Cain, Alice Cavitt, Barbara Coffy, Dorothy Giveen, Anna Grover, Mrs. Robert Gween, Berta Harsh, Mabel Hull, Robert & Shirley Lee, Frank & Shirley Mapes, Glenn & Shirley McCreary, Elizabeth Ann McLoney, Christina Mutigli, Robyn Shriver, Janet Thomas, Beth Zimmerman;
Celina—Glenna Bair, Mary A. Bollenbacher, Mrs. Henry Botkin, Carl B. Chiles, Nancy Desch, Laverne Dock, Mr. & Mrs. John Dresher, Jean Green, Wilma Heffner, John & Dorothy Hoenie, Nicole Kaiser, Harold Kinnison, Pat Leugers, Johanna Marbaugh, B. Nedderman, Sue Ransbottom, Sara Rayborn, Guy H. Schmidt, Marie Schroyer, Laurie Shaner;
Centerburg—Jessica & Justin Jones, Keith Jones, Marilyn & Juliana Jones, Darlene McGee;
Chagrin Falls—Harland Tracy;
Chardon—Glenna Alland, Glenn Peck;
Chesapeake—Homer Mays;
Chesterland—Mina Rock;
Chickasaw—Jean Liesner, Virginia Rosenbeck;
Chillicothe—Kenneth L. Coe, Amy Grim;
Cincinatti—Jeff Clark, Cathy Dahonick, Elizabeth Eggerding;
Clayton—Walter Bayer;
Cleveland Heights—Henry Warren;
Clyde—Sarah Durst, Kevin & Jennifer Eidt;
Columbia—Velma Lee Coaple;
Columbiana—Cleo Dietrich, Cecil F. Esenwein, Esther Fisher, Howard Herbkersman, Bruce & Dick Hetrick, Brittany Oliver, Courtney Oliver, Don & Grace Rupert, Mary Rupert, Eleanor Savage, Ashley Unkefer, Kristy Unkefer, The Weaver Family, Roxann Wellman;
Columbus—Christi Alspach, Kay Atkinson, Thelma Cooper, Velma Lee Cooper, Carmen & Carmelo Cubilla, Jayne McBurney Cubilla, Katherine Eley, Zoelouma C. Erwin, Marilyn Laucher, Leland E. Minton, Kathryn Petty, Carl Piper, Carol Piper, Margaret R. Planck, Carl & Carol Pyer, Alice M. Stoll, Barbara Wheeler, Jack Young;
Columbus Grove—Betty Basinger, Jacque L. Donavan;
Conneaut—Tim Baldwin, Lisa Branmer, Linda Cameron, June Chess, Arlene Cole, Janet Cole, Richard Cosner, Betty Dell, Rose M. Ensell, Evelyn Estes, Laura Fails, Ralph & Linda Fralic, Shannon Fralic, Jenniffer Grant, Flora Greenwalt, Kim Gregory, Julie & Gary Gritzer, Shirley & Chris Harco, Chris Harcy, Rev. Dwight & Maxine Hayes, Helen Hedderick, Nancy Herb, Mary Hicks, Ron & Colletta Hogle, Pam Hopkins, Sharon Hopkins, Eleanor Huston, Michael Jackson, Leon Jones, Ruth Knox, Sara & Riley & Kara Kreisher, Marie Lawson, C. Luce, Helen Mackey, George McCroskey, Robert L. McMillin, Willard Mullin, Marge Phillips, Corry Pifer, Karen Pulaski, B. Remaley, Connie Rodgers, Tom Rodgers, Emilie Sedmak, Bob & Lois Shumake, Grace Taylor, Hugh Vickery, Jason & Jessica Walker, Rick & Dianna Walker, Susan & Melissa Walker;
Continental—Marie Jane & Paul Schmidt, Ruth & Kenneth Spencer;
Convoy—Imogene Abbott, Jean Abbott, Mrs. Roscoe Abbott, Bonnie Beard, Connie Habegger, Deb Smith, Brent & Travis Swander, Brenda Valentine;
Cortland—Shirley M. Bacon, Anne Bates, Bill Bradbury, Cheryl Creed, John Forrest, Charles Goncz, Joan Haak, Betty Hyland, June Karovic, Mary Rider, Arlene & Geoffrey Roscoe, Mary Lou Safran, Courtney Sherretts, Linda L. Shipman, I. Smith, Beth Sprague, Michele & Travis Springer;
Cover—Shirley Tharp;
Covington—Elmer Fisher, John Fisher, Cedric Palsgrove, Robert Shellabarger, Clinton & Woneda Sink, Gladys B. Sink, Roy D. Sink;
Crestline—Isabelle Bray, Margaret Fetter, JoAnn Fisher, Mrs. Russell Fisher;
Cridersville—Isabelle Fockler, Deb Riepenhoff;
Croton—Paul & Marie Rhodebeck, June Smith;
Curtice—Mr. & Mrs. Albert Adam, Walter & Jeanette Humberger, Kelly & Matt Phillips, Bill & Delores Wilson;
Custar—Francis W. Flowers, Marvin & Betty Wilhelm;
Cuyahoga Falls—Alice Becher, Evan & Phyllis Case;
Dalton—Melody Amstuta, James & Marilyn Falb, Sharon & Roger Falb, Elmer Good, Kristy & Matthew Hofstetter, Misty Neuenschwander, Beth Odell, Tiffany Stein, Wilbur & Mary Wenger;

Damascus—Bergen Bauman, Hazel Bowersock, Christa Boyle, Erin & Natalie Cope, Amy & Jenni Griffith, Beth Grimm, Chris Loudon, Joyce Steergirls, Jan Zielke;

Danville—Howard & Helen Martin;

Dayton—Kody Apple, Merrill Hanger, Dorothy Hawes, Marvin Kidd, Mr. & Mrs. W. James Steen, John Wenger;

De Graff—Dorothy Sprague;

Deerfield—Tom J. Mix Family;

Defiance—Cindy Bentancur, John Dubar, Tammy Johnston, Dennis Tuohy, Wanda Jean & Paul Vogelsong;

Delaware—Kenyon Greeman;

Delphos—Vivian L. Adams, Steve Bockey, Dorothy Buettner, Ellen Gordon, Verna M. Kill, Mr. & Mrs. Joe Ratt, Ethel Schwinnen, Ray Shaw, Rod Tiernan, Alice Utrup, Evelyn Wurst;

Delta—Erin Binkley, Allyssa Lane, Becky & Andrew Tanner;

Deshler—Opel Casteel, James Finney;

Diamond—Sherry Maynard, Tabi Maynard, Wilma & Clyde Metzler;

Dola—Frank Hinkle, Dorothy Jones, Herbert & Dorothy Lenhart, Robert D. Ludwig, Terry Minter, Jane Ruppright;

Dorset—James Borsi, Linda A. Demanett, R.L. Robert, E. Spellman;

Dover—David & Rosemarye Archinal, June E. Becker, Neal Cole, Elizabeth M. Dougall, Andrew Dreher, Carl & Gwen Eichel, Gail Endres, Marianne Gordon, Jean Hall, Keith Joki, Mary Kandel, Tara Kittel, Florence & Linda Marburger, Norma Marlinko, Linda Maughan, Edison McDougall, Lindsay Miller, The Perkowski Family, Cindy Rainsberger, Patti J. Scharr, Lucille Steel, Nathan Steel, Kenny Swihart, Gail Walters;

Doyer—Armella Rieger;

Dublin—Mark Bradshaw, Carol Hoch, Margaret Moore, Mary K. Planck, Shirley & Duane Schirtzinger;

Dundee—Kim & Darren Frey, Pat Hamilton, Joseph Hershberger, Linda Mason, Martha Troyer, Erma Troyer Family, Ellen Yoder;

East Canton—Sandy Bellamy, Pearl Gailey, Francis Penergrass, Jim Shaw, Lillian Shaw, Bob & Shirley Starbey, Robert Starkey;

Eastlake—Betty Levkanich;

East Liberty—Carolyn Deardurff, Fred & Kathy Deardurff;

East Liverpool—Richard Chadwick;

East Rochester—The Baker Family, Howard W. Batzli, Lisa & Laura Bufford, John D. Burford, Judy Cooper, Matt Cooper, Nancy Cooper, Chris Douglas, Terri Elton Family, Twylla Hawk, Tiffany & Ryan Hayman, Laurena Kimble, Lyn Lutz, Vickie McDole, Mrs. M. Miller, Mary E. Miller, Rebekah Miller, Twila Miller, Sheri Saling, Dave & Sue Scharf, J. David Scharf, Edna Mae Speirs, Helen Stoudt, Wanda Zaugg;

East Sparta—Stephen Reidl;

Eaton—Jean & Marion Alexander, The Allens, Lisa Bower, Bonnie Sue Brubaker, Daniel Brunlin, Mr. & Mrs. James Potterf;

Edison—Jill & Bethany Gist, Rachel & Levi Gist;

Edon—Joe Allomong;

Elgin—Shirley Bolton, Jean Wentz;

Elida—Carol & Justin Angle, Hannah Angle, Michelle & Jacob Angle, David Bear, Dwight Bear, Virginia & Nelson Bear, Helen Beeler, Connie Bowers, Mary Bowers, Hannah & Rose Bowman, Sylvia Brock, Lou Cosyn, Gene Crisenbery, Anthon Denlinger, Runelle Dundridge, Joyce Exton, Mr. & Mrs. Jim Griffo, Ruth M. Grone, Jessica Hoover, Nina M. Jones, Terry L. Jones, William Lamon, Treva Lapham, Lynette Lewis, William B. Louth, Ashley & Galen Miller, Clayton Miller, Ruth & Lance Miller, Abe Peters, Heather Peters, Greg Rhoad, Louie Siefker, Edna Stemen, Janell Stockton, Karl Stockton, Carolyn Wilcox, Heather Wilcox;

Elyria—Margie Zalka, Margaret Zalks;

Englewood—Cherie North, Allen J. Yoder;

Etna—Ashleigh Bowers;

Farmdale—The Balentines, Marge Barry, Katherine Jackson, Mrs. Joe Kalas, Vickie Kuzmick, Carol Peska, Tracy Peska, Judy Piontkowski, Ivan Rose, Gerald Wildman, Sandra Young;

Findlay—Orva & Martha Armacost, Marilyn Beach, Theresa Bourret, Glenn Coats Family, Dawn Feller, Jill M. Gerding, Virginia E. Hiett, Lavaun Keller, Steven McCartney, Mary & Bob Pahl, Robert Pahl, Rhonda Simons, Betty Skinner, Susan Wiess, Homer & Lucille Willford, Olive Wiseley, Leon & Sally Wood;

Forest—Tara Dodds, Marlene Gillfillan, Ruby E. Heckathorn, Dave & Jeannette Kiper, Rachel Kiper, Tim & Ruth Kiper, Rachel Musgrave, Dale & Thelma Musselman, Sue Rickenbacher, Vincent Sherman, Marilyn Staley, Hazel Wilson, Florence Zingg;

Fort Jennings—Rita Beining, Ruby M. McKanna;

Fort Recovery—Paul Fullenkamp;

H. Woody Bailey

Fostoria—Josephine Bauman, Bridget Droll, Angela Fox, Mary Fry, Florence Norris, Pat Teinarend;

Fowler—Eleanor Clower, Mr. & Mrs. Robert E. McDonald, Nancy Wilhelm;

Franklin—Robert & Judy Hawkins;

Frazeysburg—Marie Dugan;

Fredericksburg—Abe & Edna Miller, Michael Miller, John Schlabach Family;

Fredericktown—Heather Craft, Raymond Hines, Cena M. Pridemore, Donald E. Walters;

Fremont—J.M. Knepper, Sally Miller;

Fresno—Esther Warren, Darlene Wills;

Galion—Jean Bane, Brenda Barile, Dylan & Kelsi Barile, Jim Grogg, Ryan Hoffman, Mrs. Lewis Kemp, Wanda & Clifford Landis, Arlene Layman, Hazel Patterson, Marion Patterson, Raymond & Eleanor Predmore, Marjorie Roesck;

Galloway—Eugene Kaderly, Jessica Meade, Misty & Megan Meade;

Lorene Henry

Geneva—Harold Berry, Michelle Berry, David Bowins, Mary Godwin, Earl Heaton, Bob & Pat Ostrow, Dorothy Rockow, Burnita Sample, Jeremiah Sample, Merritt & Alta Schaller, Louise A. Wineland;

Georgetown—Anna Lou Schmidt;

Gibsonburg—Kris Gerwin, Robert L. Gerwin, Eleanor Kniereim, Edith Linkey;

Girard—Michael & Laura Barrett, O. Jean Jones, Steven Terpin;

Gomer—Neva M. Stemen;

Grafton—Velva Mihalis;

Grand Rapids—Donna Vollmar;

Granville—Mr. & Mrs. Henry E. Whitehead;

Graytown—Helen L. Nowak;

Greenville—Herald & Perdita Baird, Melvin Benedict Family, Clint Bower, Pete Bussey, Keith Bussey Jr., Thomas Gibbons, Mrs. Alan W. Greiner, Philip King, Mildred Lanich, Nellie Leas;

Grove City—Marjorie Lightle, Don & Marie Schaffner;

Grover Hill—Joshua Lehman, Wilma Lehman;

Hamler—Mrs. Hugo Sonnenberg;

Hammondsville—Scotty & Laura Randolph;

Hanoverton—Pam Carnahan, Abigail & Sarah Carrahan, Karen & Joshua Kosko;

Harrison—Leo H. Rolfes;

Harrod—Delbert Binkley, Andrew Bohn, Marion & Bernice Criblez, Donna Faulder, Pat Geiser, Mrs. Roger Harpster, Mike Kessinger, Phyllis Marchal, Margaret McClain, Karla & Nocole Thomas;

Hartville—Albert Berchy, Joy & Gary Brothers Family, Lori & Christina Hoff, Andy J. Miller, Amanda Schlabach, C. Schlabach Family, Emanuel & Pauline Yoder;

Haviland—Lillian Eisenmann, Emily S. Toller;

Hayesville—Pamela S. Bright, William Glass, Jane Vangilder;

Hayster—Marie Sloat;

Heath—Mr. & Mrs. Donald Mohler, Dianna Thomas;

Helena—Rosie Reno;

Hicksville—Mrs. Robert Evans, Robert E. Evans, Howard Yoder;

Hilliard—Allen R. Hunt;

Hillsboro—Mrs. Carol Igo, Mrs. Raymond McCall, Galen Neal;

Hinckley—Leroy Jenkins;

Holland—Mrs. M. Biglow, Nancy Fletcher, Donna Kitchen, Frank Kitcher;

Holmesville—Lisa Yoder;

Homeworth—Randi Adams, The Austins, Denise Bryan, Julie Buttermore, Cindy Campbell, Jane Campbell, The Crist Family, Mandy Howenstine, Lee Johnson, Pearle C. Pieren, Joel Smith, Miranda Smith, Mrs. Nelson Stoll, Robert Sutton, Angela & Whitney Wiggers;

Hubbard—Mrs. Richard Stiver;

Hudson—Ben Danato;

Jackson—David Bowman, Patricia Kohr;

Jackson Center—Wayne & Ruth Ann Gerber, Linda Jenkins, Mr. & Mrs. William Knief;

Jamestown—Laurence & Ellen Liming, Carolyn Murry;

Jefferson—Shari Bailey, Freda Ebersol, Louise E. Ferguson, Lennette Hall, Phyllis R. Hall, Betty Helfer, Sara Helfer, Kathryn Hoffman, Judy Holik, Lisa Hurst, Melvin & Evelyn Marrison, Joseph Misinec Sr., Mary E. Paulson, Noble L. Smith, Hieda M. Springer, Barbara Tisch, Clarence Tyler;

Jenera—Mr. & Mrs. Harlow A. Rauch, Merritt Schaller, Nicolette & Brent Vonstein;

Jeromesville—Cindy Funk, Ruth & Courtney Haney, Lowell & Marjorie McFarlin Family, Michelle Mong, Mrs. Lorin Weaver;

Johnstown—Ada Cornwell;

Kalida—Diana Recker, Pam Strausbaugh;

Kensington—Dale Y. Brenner, Trudy Detchon, Dan Dryan, Janet Hays, Forrest Speirs;

Kent—Shirley Mains, Shirley McIntosh;

Kenton—Jamie Anderson, Ralph & Gladys Baughman, The Bolanz Res, Mildred Bridenstine, Mrs. Walter Bridenstine, Cheryl Brielmaier, Kathryn J. Buck, Geri Delong, Patrice Dugan, Janet Eibling, Judy Eldridge, Connie Gillfillan, Rita Goaasrd, Amanda Harp, Julie M. Hatcher, Zachary & Abigail Heilman, Carol A. Hensel, James Hommel, Nelle Keel, Tim Kiper, Joel Kuck, Carolyn Lawrence, Cindy Lease, Lowell B. Ludwig, Mary & Jessica Murphy, C. Musselman, Betty Pfeiffer, Courtney Rader, Shirley Riegle, Regina Roby, Peggy Rogers, Mrs. J.D. Schulmeyer, Ruth Schulmeyia, Tony Sherman, Linda Valentine, Maudie Williams;

Killbuck—Lisa & Jessica Shepler;

Kingsville—Brian Baird, Michelle & Jackie Baird, Courtney & Kris Gilkinson, Audra Hatch, Frank J. Mikolay, Judy Witt;

Kinsman—Diane & Jennifer Addicott, Joshua & Jessica Addicott, N. Darl Britton, Eleanor Brown, Janet A. Campbell, Amanda Carney, Rose Clute, Gilbert & Alberta Gates, Harmon P. Gates, Anne Gerzetich, Mildred Gregg, Heather Hall, Carlene Jones, Margaret C. Jones, Shirley B. Keeler, Junior Knepp, Lela

Betty Rolfs

Knepp, Linda Sue Knepp, Maerlin & Norman Mast, Mahlon Mast, Sueann Mast, Evelyn B. Mathews, Alma Mullet, Lynn Noxon, Diana L. Pelton, Mose Schlabach, The Sirrines, Deborah Smegal, Scott & Matt Smegal, Mrs. Lanny Tricker, Tammie Tricker, Richard White, Pearl Wick;

La Grange—Joe Cawley, Kathy Zalka;

La Rue—Vince Ciola, Sherry Denman, Lowell Murphy, Ima & Harold Robinson;

Lake Milton—Margaret E. Cline, Phyllis Gale, Jack & Phyllis Hales;

Lakeview—Doris Gratz, Geo E. Morris;

Lakeville—George & Marjorie Garver, Frank & Pat Gnizak, Louella Pyers, Lyle Reusser, Tim Sage, Carl Schlauch, Mary Spring, Maxine Young;

Lancaster—Joe & Pat & Nick Beiter, Emma Jean Curtice, Bob & John & Greg Huber, Steve & Barbara Huber;

Lebanon—Clayton Ivins;

Leetonia—Carla & Lila Shaum, Jeanette & Scott Watkins, Matt Weaver, Linda Woldgang;

Leipsic—Barb Steffen, Kayla Steffen;

Lewisburg—Mary Hypes;

Lewistown—Cindie & C. Lee Gibson, Diane Gibson;

Lexington—Helga Belt, Vivian B. Eckert, Judy Ehrensberger, Linda Huvler, Phyllis Newmann, Florence Popp, Kathy Schwartzmiller, John T. Simmons, Jackie Stout, Jewell Weiss;

Lima—Imogene Bassett, Dorothy Black, Beth Bracy, Sharon L. Collar, Shirley Dye, Peg Edman, Marguerite Edwards, Nancy Forbes, Kent Fry, Sharon Griffith, Vera Hadsell, Paul E. Hermon, Cecil Hicks, Mary Hoelscher, Bill Howard, George L. Klausing, Mr. & Mrs. Wilbur D. Lawrence, Benjy Lee, Amy & Cindy Miller, Kathryn Moritz, Eve E. Peters, June Polter, Cynthia Prye, Lucy Ross, Jean Schmidt, John D. Seitz, D.W. Staas, Mrs. Jason Stites, Jack Taylor, Andrea & Rich Traunero, Orlin Wertenberger, Lee Williams;

Lindsey—Arlyn & Carolyn Lipstraw;

Lisbon—Ernie Gouldsberry, Chris Liptak, Hugh Stewart, Kathy Strong;

Lodi—Duane & Mary L. Houston, Mrs. Donn Kindy, Ramona Mabry, Bill Nichols;

Logan—G. Russell;

London—Mr. & Mrs. Robert Wilson;

Lorain—Joe & Lynn Neuhoff, Pat & Paula Neuhoff;

Lordstown—Mr. & Mrs. William Bobst, L. Butler, Helen Byers, Judy & Josh Davis, Nancy Gentry, Tiffany Holton, J. Strodson, Brian Wells;

Lore City—Fran Hedleston;

Loudonville—Eulala Ballou, Betty Bookman, Esther Byler, John Delvillan, Jennifer Fisher, Wes & Patty Fliger, Norma Friestad, Rob Harris, Alice McDonald, Lenna E. Nowels, Judy Pollard, Judy Rafeld, Carol Rogers, Christian Savage, Dale A. Savage, Jodi & Ian Savage, Ruth Solon, Jan Strong, Bonnie M. Walker;

Louisville—Winnifred M. Belz, Jerry & Alice Bolanz, Mary Ann Bolanz, Joyce Doane, Susanne & Gary Gieseman, Richard & Diann Hartell, Diann Hartzell Family, Vincent A. Hostetler, Tracy Kerliy;

Lucas—Adam Backensto, Brigette Banks, Beverly Cole, Jeanne Elias, Laura & Sarah Flockenzier, Aaron Heuss, Richard Lehnhart, Robert R. Miller, Earl Oaklief, Angie Swank, Marilyn M. Zody, Reta & Todd Zody;

Lucasville—Janet Lewis;

Luckey—Lester & Ruth Meyer;

Lyons—Harold & Sue Holland, J. Holland;

Macedonia—Gabriel Adams, Ginnie & Joshua Adams;

Madison—Richard & Leah Hart, Stephen Hart, Dustin & Matthew Sample;

Magnolia—Don & Patti Howenstine, Mr. & Mrs. Robert L. Kemp, John F. Larson, Ruby Reidl;

Malvern—Dixie Hawkins, Rose & Bob Pierce, Florence Richards, Cathy Smith, Crystal Snyder, Leota Wetzel, Andrew Robert Woods;

Mansfield—Jo Altman, Helen Armstrong, Janice Baker, Janice & Merlin Baker, Delee Beal, Jean Becker, Thomas Bishop, Connie Blackstone, The Boehm Res, Kenneth Boyce, Ermibel Brickley, Cheryl Callis, Jan Distl, Lori Floro, C.A. Griebling, Beth Gross, Mildred M. Hamilton, Chuck & Karen Hardy, Melanie Hardy, Melanie & Lori Hardy, Helen Hevish, Billie Hoffer, Loetta Hoffer, Helen M. Hoskey, Dick Hosler, Jack A. Johnson, Lindsey & Doris Keiser, Clara Kissel, Crescentia Kline, Kimberly Kline, Leland Koppert, Jim & Ladonna Lotz, Abby Lowe, Anne Mandorsir, Anna J. Mandusic, Janell E. Marth, Mrs. Charles Martin, Alicia Milks, Kevin Rinehart, Mrs. James Secrist, Allison & Becky Sneeringer, Jeanett Strong, Cleo Thomen, Wesley Weiss, Tavo & Bonnie Zenil, Steve Zimmerman;

Marblehead—Bill Loudenslager;

Marengo—Delbert & Marlene Foos, Marbese Fors, Doris Mosher;

Maria Stein—Othmar J. Fullenkamp, Herbert Rolfes;

Marion—S. Beascher, Ellen Cawley, Joan Craig, Harold Davis, Harold Davis, Mary Dean, Brandy Eclard, Kathy Elkens, Erica Fairchild, Phyllis M. Fate, Marge Guider, Louise Haley, Norman Horne, Sue James, George Keener, Clara Ellen Laucher, Tony Lewis, Robert & Janet Lucas, Dean A. Minard, Lowell Munn, Gail Phillips, Carlisle & Betty Rife, Nancy Schiefer, Paul & Nancy Schiefer, Helen Schrote, Mary Severns, Mrs. Sheridan Severns, Harold Smith, Mr. & Mrs. Carrol R. Starner, B.J. Stover, Esther Tubbs, Jack Young;

Marshallville—Chad & Brandon Sidle;

Marysville—Donna Simpson;

Massillon—Lee M. Brenner, Beverly Easterday, Leona M. Hostetler, Harry Kutscher, Janet Starrett, Ed Steinbach, Larry & Kathy Volger, Richard Wolfe, Ruth Zimmerman;

Mayfield Heights—Lolly Mehling;

Mc Arthur—Carla & Kevin Teeters, Kayle & Rita Teeters;

Mc Comb—Don Courtright, Mable Courtright, Molly Farmer, Molly Farney, Mary Haley, Marilyn Oakes, Tammy & Derek Quiroga;

Mc Donald—Barb Thomas;

Mc Guffey—Evelyn Umphress;

Mechanicsburg—Philip R. Bumgardner;

Mechanicstown—Georgia Brothers Family, Alfred Schaal;

Medina—Mrs. Glenn Blair Jr., Lewis Jenkins, Georgia Ziegler;

Medway—Sue Lindeman;

Mendon—Mary Burnett, Joann Dudgeon, Marilyn J. Emans, Pat John, Martha Krick, Lester Miller, Jonathan Rickard, Larry Sapp, Lori Tobin;

Mentor—Lyle Jones;

Miamisburg—Vera Countryman, Dorothy M. Linville, Ed Linville;

Middlefield—Marilyn Anderson, Dan R. Byler, Kristi & Andrea Byler, William & Susan Byler, Janice Jonath, Anson Rhodes, Ralph Schwendeman, Doris & Ralph Schwindwam;

Middletown—John & Melanie Flower, Jeanne Snyder, Martha Jane Zecher;

Milford Center—Helen Wingfield;

Millersburg—Phillip & Sueann Beachy, Sue Ann Beachy Family, Esther Byler, Janice Finney, Bob Hanna, Alice Immel, Justine Kaufman, Mrs. Lovina Kaufman, Gail Mancuso, Rolland Mast, Ross & Rollie Mast, Lester McCune, Valerie McFadden, Alan Miller, Amanda Miller, Ella Miller, Joni Miller, Mervin Miller, Miles Miller, Nancy Miller, Paul Miller, Regina Miller, Sarah Miller, Betty Mullert, Robt & Cherolene Reidenbach, Kent Rodhe, Ann Stotler, Devon Stutzman, Heather Trubee, Gary Uhl, Mrs. Jerry Uhl, Tammy & Tel Vaughn, Mary Ellen Weaver, Ryan Weaver, Merlyn & Nancy Weitbrecht, Edna Yoder, Gloria Yoder, Irene Yoder, Junior A. Yoder;

Mineral City—David Proudfoot, Darlinda Schuartz, Pat Smith, Patricia Smith, Frances M. Willard, Francis Willard;

Minerva—Martha L. Blackburn, Roy Blevins, Mrs. Lawrence Brown, Beth Burchett, F. William Bush, Mrs. Ronald Cogan, Minerva Connestant, Melia Danner Family, Stella & Mike Dourm, Herbert Eglie, Jefferson Ellis, The Essick Family, Teri Essith, Mary Beth Gingerich, Robert Gingerich, Andrea & Shelly Grimm, The Hahn Family, Robert D. Harrell, Connie Hayman, Connie Haynam, Marie Johnson, Bill Leatherberry, Marjorie Manfull, Erin & Jenny Merrick, Ida Jane Miller, Christopher Ross, Jack Schaffer, Dorcas Sommer, Debbie Stoltzfus, Philip Stoltzfus, Dora & Maryanne Sutton, Keith Thompson, Norma Weaver, Merv White, Andrea & Emmy Yoder, Mrs. Alfred Zwahlen;

Mogadore—Leona Brown, Bud Persons;

Monclova—Don Stafford;

Moning—Erika Steiskal;

Monroe—Dale & Bertha Ridenour;

Monroeville—Eileen Simon;

Montpelier—Don & Isabel Imm;

Morral—Katherine Hunsicker;

Mount Blanchard—Avonelle Bateson, Carlton & Mary Gould, Sharon Umphress;

Mount Cory—Mrs. M.E. Boutwell;

Mount Gilead—Dave Cass, Judy Fetters, Amy Roach, Dorothy Scott, Alice Vannorn, Susan Windbigler;

Mount Orab—Barbara Cahall;

Mount Victory—Samuel A. Bontrager, Phyllis Wamack, Maude B. Williams;

Napoleon—Regina Germasen, Donna Dunbar, Abbie Fruth, Regina Germann, Marilyn Hershverger, Kristi & Ben & Brad Weddelman, Teresa Weddelman;

Nashville—Daniel Kirtlan;

Navarre—Joan Boron, Betty Z. Grewell, Gladys Smith;

Nelsonville—Anna Brewer;

Nevada—Beth Briggs, Harold Cover, Roma Cover, Tim & Nadene Cressman, Ed & Nina Leitzy, E. Lewis, Clifford W. Lutz, Lewis & Margaret Reber, Nathan Reber;

New Albany—Rolland & Marjorie Pestel;

New Bloomington—Jack Chambers;

New Bremen—Mary Lou Campbell, Wilton E. Dicke;

New Knoxville—Lindsey Meyer, Mark Varno;

New Lebanon—Howard J. Brunk;

New Madison—Keith Bussey, Virginia Fourman, Jesse Fourman Jr., William & Betty Riegle, Mrs. Norman P. Weimer, Paul E. Weimer;

New Middletown—June Barger, Pat Barger, Sophia K. Schmidt;

New Paris—Linda M. Pentecost;

New Philadelphia—Helen Ballard Family, Mr. & Mrs. Mark Beitzel, Dorothy Brandt, E. Cooper, Phyllis Eckert, Mary Horton, Ruth A. Irvin, Shirley A. Massarelli, David Oettinger, W.H. Oettinger, Anne & Leonard Snyder;

New Riegel—Dorothy Clouse, Wayne Gnepper, Dolly Smith;

New Waterford—Mike & Jackie Mayer, Pauleen Wolfgang;

Newark—Doris McGehee, Edith Murphy, Eloise Warfield;

Newcomerstown—Rheadon Roe, Roberta & Brandi Shingler;

Newton Falls—Donna & Tom Abel, Christine Adam, Pam Damico, Pamela Dunn, Dale Martin, Sue McCarthy, Mr. & Mrs. Don Rickert, Jill Ritchie;

Niles—Craig & Ryan Barrett, Arnold & Maryjane Veits, Janet & William Wiencek;

North Baltimore—June I. Crouse;

North Canton—Galen Alpeter, Susan Mudge, DeeDee Surtzback, Joann Theis, David Tidd;

North Fairfield—Joann Bond;

North Georgetown—Julie Hardy, Rachael Morrow, John Risbeck, Wilda M. Vogelhuber;

North Jackson—Ester Graham, Brad Herman, Robert & Dorothy Herman, Carolyn McCorkle, Sarah Miller, Barbara Nichol,

Sheila Roberts

Yori & Gary Riggles, Gary Ruggles Sr., Erika & Rachelle Stamm, Paula Vanauker, William & Diane Wilson;
North Lima—Bryan & Lindsey Hum, Dean & Joann Schultz;
North Madison—Bea K. Coss;
Norwalk—Agnes Linder, Betty Ross, Clair V. Ross, Sharon Ward;
Oak Harbor—Katherine Grimm, Norma Knipp;
Oakwood—Neocia Dimock, John & Donna Leatherman, Paul Reynolds;
Oberlin—Martha Zalka;
Ohio City—Linda Baker, Mrs. Ralph Evans, Paul Fauble, Jim Henrey, Martha Jones, Deanna Speelman, Sally J. Tickle, Ericka Williams;
Ontario—Eula Hisey;
Orangeville—Mary Ann Rufener;
Oregon—Irene Fahsholtz;
Orrville—J. David Risser;
Orwell—Audrey Bebout, Marion Day, Jason Knowles;
Ottawa—Kathy Dehnart, Mrs. Leah Dubry, Peg Niese;
Oxford—Audrey Brooks;
Painesville—Jean H. Gimbut, F. Glenn Haskins, A.R. Miller, Sandra Stalraher;
Palestine—Glenna & Clint Bowen;
Pandora—Mary Basinger, Tootie Schlumbohm;
Paris—Sarah Biss, Dale & Carolyn Caske, Stanley Gassman, Willis E. Gassman;
Paulding—Edythe Baxter, Marie Devers, Mrs. Doyle Johnson, Betty Klopfenstein, Viola Manz, Harlan & Dolores Riggenbach, Karen Schlatter, Willis Strabele;
Payne—Evelyn Copsey;
Peebles—Beverly Mathias, Melissa & Matthew Mathias;
Pemberville—Bernita R. Zellin, Robert W. Zellin;
Perrysburg—Janet Swartz;
Perrysville—Jenny Ayers, Paul Davis, Chis Dawson, Melinda Henwood, Clara Kiner, Tammy Kline, Nathan & Jessica Morris, Rilla Morris, Wyatt Morris, Marie Sellers, Kay Simon, Daniel Snyder, Roger Snyder, W.R. Snyder, Patti Spray, Jill Spreng, Bette Zody;
Pickerington—Paul & Peggy Kose;
Pierpont—Donna Bradman, Kathie Bradnan, Charlotte Carr, Norma M. Carr, Carolyn Chapman, Rachel & Cody Eager, Dana Greenlee, Susan & Dale Harvey, Chris & Marcy Koivisto, Carol Kowisto, Kim Marcy, Betty Obaker, Sophie Stajiak, Kathleen Zanzig;
Piqua—Ruby Bowman, Herman Brumbaugh;
Plain City—Mrs. Alton Beachy, Reba Durban, Al Helmuth, Eli A. Helmuth, Lee & Mary Alice Schacherbauer, Tommy Turill, Kaylene Yoder, Marlene Yoder Family, Gary Zerkle;
Pleasant Hill—Luther E. Angle, Luther Anhangle;
Poland—Mrs. William Hinson, Mrs. William Hum;
Port Clinton—Sue Aebie;
Prospect—Emilee Gustkey, Hubert Hoch, Nancy Shaffer;
Radnor—George R. Thomas;
Rawson—Dennis Vonstein, Stephanie Vonstein;
Raymond—George E. Eirich;
Republic—Danyell & Dustin Falter, Charita George, Joyce E. George, Mary Lou Neikirk, Mr. & Mrs. Grover Nickird;
Richmond—Marilyn Donohue;
Richwood—Nina Bumgarner, Ken & Charlotte Davis, Robert Howald, Joe Temple;
Risingsun—Delbert Wise;
Rittman—Barbara Camany, Kate Hartzler;
Robertsville—Vera Gerner;
Rock Creek—Pete Janson;
Rockford—Bill Bader, Abby Bollenbacher, Sally Dudgeon, Helen Heukle, Gertrude Hoblet, Helen J. McDonough, Mrs. James McDonough, D. Mihm, Doris Piper, Glenn Pruden, Raymond Pruden, Sondra Samples, Rufus & Martha Stober;
Rocky Ridge—Jerry & Shirley McNutt;
Rogers—W. Crawford;
Rome—David Beals, Sandra & Jennifer Beals, Shirley Potter;
Rossburg—Barbara Miller, Jacob Post;
Rushsylvania—Alice Bayliss, Betty Kennedy;
Russellville—John & Brenda Otis;
Saint Clairsville—John Graham;
Saint Marys—Marjorie Alspaugh, Charles & Mildred Botkin, Angela & Nick Kiel, Stacy Knatz, Kimberlee Koesten, Alice Noble, Dorothea Rupert;
Salem—Norma Althouse, Geri Anderson, Myrtle Bailey, Paula Bardo, Julie & Josh Bell, Roberta Bell, Christy Biery, Benjamin Blowens, Richard Bryan, Dan Cope, Stan Cope, Esther Coy, Amy & Erin Craig, Becky Craig, Lucille Duke, Ronald Edgerton, Vange Firestone, Wendy Frantz, Gayla Greenmyer, Paula Gregory, Becky Heffinger, David Herron, Becky Hiffington, Arla Hull, Susan Kaufman, Mrs. Carol Keir, Kimberly & Kelly Keir, Patti Knauf, Josh & Pam Leham, Katey Lora, Rose Lynn, Mickey McCoy, Elaine Medved, Steph & Elaine Nutter, Mildred Powell, Joan Rauch, Grant Reichart, Debbie Rhodes, Jean K. Rhodes, Mrs. John Rhodes, Shirley & Matthew Rill, Shirley & Sarah Rill, Evelyn Sidwell, Harold Sidwell, Ivan Snyder, Jodi Snyder, Ken & Deb Thomas, Melanie & Bryan Thomas, Marcia Todd, Shelley Wack, Ruth Wilhelm, Les & Neva Wilson, Robyn Winn, Clark Wiser, Clark Wisler Sr.;
Salineville—Charles Madison, Betty Twaddle, Duane & Lisa Ulman;
Sandyville—Shelley & Melinda Monroe;

Esther Gerber

Scio—Shirley M. Fisher, Clifton Kidd;
Scott—Henry Clark;
Sebring—Tim Burley, Mary Louise Ford, Eldon R. Groves, Tom Leach, Helen Paines, Megan Postiy, Patty Wallace;
Shelby—Jan Holden, Sherry Huff, Leonard & Julitta Kretemeyer, Debbie Ramey, William Ulmer, George Wagner, Larry Wagner, Doris Williams;
Sherrodsville—Twila Poole;
Shiloh—Sue Bauer;
Shreve—Seth Baker, Zack & Alex Baker, Leonard Bilek, Marilyn Chupp, Cindy Coy, Ethel Dravenstott, Lorrie & Corrie Menner, Loretta Miller, Katie & Maggie Snoddy, Sue Snoddy, Mary Wharton;
Sidney—Jerry & Doris Tangeman, Laverne Varno;
Smithville—Donald E. Howman, Kim Stoller, Linda Stoller, Mary Stoller, Phyliss Troyer;
Solon—Mary Ellen Sanislo;
Somerdale—Cade & Kari Adams, Ruth Draher, V. Shuman;
Somerville—Jewett;
South Charleston—Kenneth N. Paynter;
Southington—Ruth Noud;
Spencerville—Patrick J. Bonifas, Billie Core, Don Deger Family, Jim Eagy, Lois Ewing, Steve Howell, Pete & Dorothy Imber, Margie Kemp, Jodi E. Kill, Kristie Klausing, Dolly Martin, Charles Mowry, Paula Schumm, Sondra Strayer, Paul Swartz, Betty Whitling, David Wisher;
Springboro—Pearl Anspach;
Springfield—Cecil & Betty Baker, Mr. & Mrs. Raymond Currio, Clarence & Lola Jones, Forest R. Lightle, Bernie & Bill Wright;
Sterling—Jay Maibach, Robert Widmer;
Stone Creek—Vearl Specht, Sally Yoder;
Strasburg—Steph & Jessica Durbin, Lena Hilbert, Hazel Kreis, Scott Reifenschneider, Nancy M. Shaw, Allison Wardell;
Struthers—Mary H. Livak;
Stryker—Marcella St. John;
Sugarcreek—Andrea Adams, Mary E. Bear, David A. Brack, Deanna Burger, Pat Hamilton, Jason Hamsher, Reuben Hamsher, Chuck & Becky Jarvis, Ralph King, Mabel Milke, Leroy Miller, Mabel Miller, Nancy Miller, Stefanie Miller, Allen Mullet, Betty Mullet, Charlene Mullet, Mrs. Mattie Mullet, Ruth Mullet, Carolyn Simler, David & Erma Stutzman, Ada Troyer, Marilyn Troyer, Nancy Troyer, Cleone Widder, Janas R. Yoder, Mr. & Mrs. Leroy J. Yoder, Regina Yoder, Ruby Yoder, Diana Youngan, Diana Younger;
Sulphur Springs—Ralph Brause;
Swanton—Lytton & Grace Everett;
Sycamore—Esther L. Fry, Bernard F. Miller, Tristin Osborn, Melvin & Joan Ross, Lola B. Shellhouse, Bob & Marge Sowers;
Tallmadge—Herb & Jean Freyman, Mary George, Carroll & Gerri Jones, Joanne Turner;
Thompson—Lois & Perry Wilson;
Thornville—Kris Townsend;
Tiffin—Mrs. John Anway, Lorna Clem, Dow & Evelyn Creeger, Mr. & Mrs. L.D. Cruger, Dale E. Hoepf, Marilyn Kisabeth, Alam Lucius, Herbert & Juanita Miller, Rose Norris, Ardell Overbye, Lucille Smith, Dolores Weinandy, Mary Wetzel;
Tiro—Teresa Kaylor;
Toledo—Audrey Ball, Dorothy Fisher, Jennifer Gabe;
Toronto—Harold R. Clark;
Trotwood—John Heit;
Troy—Lowell Fisher, Allan & Virginia Miller, Darlene Mott,

Ruth Ann Scaggs;
Union City—Calvin & Beverly Bowman, Phil Bowman, Faith Smith;
Uniontown—N. Gingerich, Barbara Higgins, Martha Mertz, Mary Sommers;
Upper Sandusky—Dale Courtad, Jerry Hasting, Becky Krock, Ruby & Paul Krock, Franklin E. Leightey, Jim Petsche, Mr. & Mrs. Richard Pool, Shirley Pryor, Nathan Rober, Evabel Roszman, Lloyd Russell, Martha Russell, Emily Schoenberger, Jean A. Shumaker, Doris Smith, Rose Mary Weiland, Mildred Wentz, Rosemary Weyand;
Urbana—Richard E. Baker, Philip & Ruby Kauffman, Doris McGehee, John Sommers;
Utica—Mrs. Larry Houck, Ashley Jones, Maxine Kidwell, Kathleen Smith;
Van Wert—Dolores Keysor, Pauline R. Kundert, Mr. & Mrs. Donald Watson, Ericka Williams, Mark Wiseman;
Venedocia—Alice Gamble, Mike & Jay Hiett, Judi Richardson, Doug Ruen, Joe & Sharon Wright;
Vermilion—Ruth Huckeby, Gladys Moyer;
Vienna—Jason & Katy Anderson, Edna Ash, Carolyn Crew, Evelyn Crew, Patricia Kiser, Edgar & Norma Mealy;
Wadsworth—Danny & Marsha Houston, Mrs. George W. Leidal, Marion Rodgers, Paul Rodgers;
Wakeman—Gwendolyn Butler, Cheryl Price;
Waldo—Emma Jane Bumgarner, Lenny Cline;
Walhonding—Ruie J. Smith;
Walnut Creek—Rebecca Christopher, Jean Hostetler, Elicia Kandel, Levi & Orpha Steiner;
Wapakoneta—Roger Elsass, Barbara Engel, Harold J. Fisher, Hanna Hager, M.E. Koch, Mary Koch, Eileen Koepp, Phyllis Lunz, Kelly Mayson, Al & Dolores Meyer, Albert Meyer, Dean & Betty Place, Gene Pohlable, Bernard Schaub, Herman L. Schultz, Marjorie Settlemire, Lelah Steinmentz, Sayward Sunderlan, Mrs. Ralph Zimmerman;
Warren—Mrs. Carol Ady, Barb Allen, Sarah & Amy Allen, Mrs. Lois Barrett, Jason & Ashley Berecek, Traci Berecek, Bill Bixler, Nicole Brown, Mary & Herb Falkinburg Sr., Robby Fowler, Anne Gordon, Raymond & Kellie Kovac, Kris Kupal, Lillian M. Loudon, Mr. & Mrs. Leonard MacFarland, Thelma McLean, The Muir Family, George Myers, Janice Palm, Pauline Pesko, H. Peterson, Carol & Cordell Plant, Charleigh Raukovich, The Robinsons, Donna Romain, Scott & Marie Romain, Robert R. Rutan, Rachel Sabo, Joan Sawayda, Mr. & Mrs. Christopher Stern, Howard Stockton, Velma Walters, Virginia Whitacre;
Warsaw—Anna M. Donaker, Adam J. Smith, Ryan Smith;
Waterville—Janice Battin;
Wauseon—John Binkley, Harlen & Barbara Clark, Lowell Geringer, Velma Jones, Cecil & Pat Murry, Margaret Smith, Joan Tedrow, Becky Zumfelde;
Wayne—Cecil Sawyer;
Waynesfield—Becky Steinke, Lemaril & Kristin Walton, Mildred L. Walton, Pamela Walton, Gladys Werling;
Wellington—John Mihalis Family, Ted Pruitt;
West Alexandria—Ray Ashinger, Lester Bower, Denver & Ellie Crosier, Rita Deaton;
West Farmington—Lizzie W. Miller, Stanley B. Smith, Carol Troyer;
West Manchester—Donna Williamson;
West Mansfield—Linda Mathys;
West Salem—Josh D. Gilbert, Lyle Howman, Mrs. Robert Schmidt Jr.;
Westville—Connie Bigham, Mary Bigham, J.D. Counsil, Ted Pestel;

Westlake—Mr. & Mrs. Don Schmitt;
Weston—Pat Duron;
Wharton—Brady Darrah, Millie
    Dickinson, Donald & Janice Stark;
Wickliffe—Adrienne Armbruster, Lynn
    Armbruster, Lynn Karpoff;
Willard—Gayle Huffman, Roger Smith;
Williamsfield—Joe Barrett, Larry &
    Adam Bates, Brandy Cottman, Anna
    Hasson, David Kohta, Jeanette
    Nelliend, Mrs. Thomas Phipps, Jane
    T. Rossiter, Donna Singrey, David &
    Emma Troyer, Lori Troyer;
Williston—Roger & Phyllis Dehring;
Willoughby Hills—Lester & Char Foltz;
Willshire—Brenda Case, Nita & Ty &
    Taya Habegger, Clarence Hamrick,
    Linda Michaud, Mrs. Clarence
    Resor, Joan Riley;
Winchester—Pansy Juree Burns, Bob &
    Margie McRoberts, Donna & John
    Neu, The Semples;
Windsor—Ed & Marlene Lambert;
Winona—Dona Hardgrove;
Wintersville—Shirley E. Hibbits;
Woodsfield—Tony & Darlene Quails;
Wooster—Treva Joan Arnold, Glenn
    Chapman, Barbara Fickes, Bob Fisher, Susan Fullenkamp,
    Martha Jentes, Clyde Leatherman, Annabel Mays, Sadie
    Mays, Odella Reichert, David J. Skelly, Lucile Swinehart,
    Doris Lorraine Weaver;
Worthington—Frank Vanvoorhis;
Wren—Joyce Moser;
Xenia—Bob & Joan Greenwald, R. Greenwald, Donald C.
    Jones, Ken & Marjorie McCoy, Nick Rupert, Signa
    Zimmerman;
Yellow Springs—Ruth Colvin;
Yorkshire—Verona G. Kuether;
Youngstown—Mrs. J. Baginy, M. Borts, Virginia Freed, Ed
    Garback, Marilyn Ritchie;
Zanesville—Barbara Harris, David Harris;

Oklahoma
Alva—Pauline Holt, Bil & Marylou Witchey;
Antlers—Glen D. Fergason;
Bartlesville—Kacee Allison, Willie Johnstone, Betty Landes,
    Gus & Sandy Lefebvre, A.E. Skeen, Bobbi & Travis
    Turner;
Beaver—Arlyn Harris, Mary & Kenneth Sallee;
Boise City—Cindy & Heather Axtell, Remington Axtell, Luke
    & Catherine Biaggi, Mr. & Mrs. Dwight Bohn, Jay &
    Marlene Clark, Justin Clark, R.P. Crabtree, Lloyd French,
    Isabel Gonzales, Caroline Goodnow, Terrell Gray, Joshua
    & John Henley, Tina M. Jaques, Caleb & Amanda Manske,
    Holly Moore, Lyda Moore, Rebecca Poteet, Bonnie
    Powers, Fred & Jody Risley, Nicholas & Daisy Risley,
    Brenda Rodriguez, Lucy Schrayer, Laurena Snead, Linda
    Stewart, Sandra Thompson, Wallace Thornton, Pat & Hope
    Weldon, Ruby Yarborough;
Buffalo—Eva Lamunyon;
Cement—Greg & Janet Jantz;
Choctaw—Belle Stratton;
Dacoma—Shelby Davis;
Enid—Henry Buller;
Fairview—Herb & Inez Kliewer, Lavada Koehn, Harry & Viola
    Martens, Pauline Nichols, Don Nightengale;
Gate—Charlene Husted;
Guthrie—Leurs Bode, Derek & Brenda Owen, Ginger E.
    Patterson;
Hooker—Susan Wiens;
Isabella—Court & Layne Smith;
Jenks—Mrs. Roselle Watson;
Keyes—Phyllis Humphrey;
Laverne—Clinton & Carol Worth;
Medford—Doris Fair, John & Viola Friesen;
Mooreland—Earl Neal;
Morre—Helen Boarts;
Norman—Carlene Swain;
Nowata—Sandi Anders;
Oklahoma City—Eletha N. McCollum;
Owasso—Marie Marshall, Diana Wagler;
Ponca City—Jack James;
Sand Springs—Yvonne Marshall;
Seiling—Gene & Luella Childs;
Stillwater—John & Deborah Solie;
Texhoma—Betty L. Keylon, Kori Kincannon, Jay Marttax;
Tonkawa—Virla Smithheisler, The Smithheislers, Marilea
    Smithheisler;
Tulsa—Ciaro McKean;
Tyrone—Anita Faye Whiteby, Glenn Whiteley Family;
Verden—Chris Koehn;
Washington—Jeannie Martin.

Oregon
Coburg—Nina Dobbins;
Dexter—Joy Costello;
Eugene—Patricia Agee;
Florence—Margaret Hilliker;
Gresham—Chester L. Moran;
Klamath Falls—Nancy J. Bruceri, Sheridan L. Scott;

Mrs. Edward Waxham

Lebanon—Mr. & Mrs. Dean Gerig, Roy & Arlene Hostetler,
    Rosalie Weischedel;
Mc Minnville—Keith Snow;
Monmouth—Dave & Glenna Anderson;
Mount Vernon—Howard Gable;
Myrtle Creek—Judy A. Davis;
Portland—Gordon & Doris Hodson, Marge Moriarity;
Sweet Home—Hanley & Eileen Williamson;
Tillamook—Sharon & Don Reeves;
Waldport—Jim & Daisy Stoutsenberger;
White City—Pete Soots.

Pennsylvania
Adamsville—Angela Green;
Albion—Alice Bricker, Marie Bricker, Ramona Drury, Lou
    Dunn, Helen Harrington, Carrie Havington, Hilda Huston,
    Jean Merritt, Wayne Randall, Debbie Tercho;
Apollo—Mr. & Mrs. Eugene Hulty;
Atlantic—John & Winnie Morian, Lisa Morian;
Austin—John & Jean Herr;
Avella—Katie Brandenburg, Charles & Marjorie Zatta, Sue
    Zatta;
Beaver—Mary Lou Sherry;
Beaver Falls—Robert McConaughy;
Beaver Springs—Evelyn Wagner;
Bedminster—Tammy Stever;
Bernville—Wade Alsphugh, George & Darlene Longenecker;
Bethel—George Throne;
Bethlehem—Georgina M. Freed;
Bloomsburg—Barb & Doyle Dodson;
Blue Ball—Ruth G. Sensenig;
Bridgeville—Mary Stimson, Patty Simecak;
Brook Park—Lois & Ben Huffman;
Butler—Melvin & Mary Dodds, J. Gardner, Tom & Marge
    Nebel;
Cambridge Springs—Sally & Neil Morris;
Carlton—Jim & Joanna Schlabach, Mrs. Robert Stillsmoith;
Centerville—Donald D. Henton;
Chambersburg—Jenni Byer, Mary Beth Long, Omar R. Mart,
    Anna Blanche Martin;
Christiana—Ben & Mary Lapp;
Clarks Mills—Seth Arbackle, Jane Clark, Hazel McCartney;
Cochranton—Joey Gingerich, Samuel Gingervich, Lillian
    Grundy, Crist Kurtz, Janet Oakes, Verna Slozat, Ethan
    Wagler, Sylvia Wagler, Pete Wagner, Jacob A. Weaver,
    Clara Beth Yoder, Demas Yoder;
Columbus—Clair & Gloria Jaqueth, Clovis & Gloria Jaquith;
Conneautville—Dorothy Dart, Mrs. William Hritzay, Harriet
    McGee, Bonnie Russell, Barbara Varee, Mrs. Gerald
    Fuller;
Cooperstown—Laurence Shirley, Sonja Shirley, Charles & Iris
    Whitman;
Corry—Judy Allender, Shirley R. Stewart, Don Swart;
Cowansville—Ken Pfaff, Mary Jane Pfaff;
Cranesville—Denise Anselment, Evelyn Rogers, Jean Soltis,
    Charlotte & Gayle Suroviec, Heide & Melanie Suroviec,
    Jessica & Wesley Suroviec, Nathan & Darren Suroviec,
    Rachel Suroviec;
Dallastown—Carol Keeney;
Darlington—Charles McGaffick, Ann Mae McKenzie, Olive
    Weigel;
Dover—Joan Grace, Cindy Roach;
East Berlin—Dale E. King;
East Petersburg—David Gallton;
East Springfield—Nicole & Emily Drummond, Mary Ann
    Graham, Edith L. Ligheldon, Marga Rhoades, Carolyn
    Shaffer, Joyce Youngs;
Ebensburg—Gracie Furabaugh;
Edinboro—Bill & Evelyn Adams, Alyssa Dunn, Jill Walker;
Ephrata—Erla Mae Burkholder, Vernon & Vera Martin;
Erie—Rita Albrecht, Florence Allgerier, Mr. & Mrs. Clarence
    Bradshaw, Melody R. Brown, P. Bush, Barbara & Laura
    Chandley, Sharon Crowther, Bette Crynock, Robert

Domowicz, Judith Dundon, Esther Eller,
Marge Ferrier, Charles & Norma Fetzner,
Verna Fickenscher, Kevin Grace, Katie
Hatch, Bryan Kalgren, Louella Kightlinger,
Alicia Kreusch, Louise Loesel, Bill & Janet
Long, Joey Lopez, Frank Mentch, Jennifer
Morill, David Myers, Karen Narusewicz,
Ingelie Nordin, Kyle Peterson, Marian Pitetti,
Roberta Rager, Russell Raybuck, Mrs. M.L.
Rhodes, W. Schlabach, Rob & Pat Schodt,
Gilbert Smith, Jean Strong, David & Karen
Sundberg, Jill Sundberg, Karen A. Sweeney,
Joseph Tomasino, Angela Tucker, Angela
Turner, Carol Wood, Charles Zohns;
Etters—Janet M. Johnson;
Evans City—Janice Marburger, J. Martig, Nancy
    Nalepa;
Fairview—Colleen & Andy Bajarlh, Nichole
    Bayer, Betty Dusicsko, Ethel Dzmur, Mr. &
    Mrs. John Goluska, Brian Reitz;
Farmington—Simeon Winter;
Fredonia—Marcia & Les Maritella, Mary &
    Kristin Marstellar, The Welton Family;
Gap—Amos R. King, Christ Lapp;
Gibsonia—Rev. Byron & Mary McElroy;
Girard—Beth Ewig, Marilyn Herhold, Roberta &
    Marilyn Herhold, Ruth Olesnanik, James
Pazun, Nancy Sisson, Bertha Thayer, David O. Thayer,
Debra Warner, David Wayer;
Glen Rock—Ralph & Margaret Thomas;
Green Hill—Doris & Bud Kongher;
Greenville—Jackie Bennett, Frank & Patricia Cole, Myron C.
    Fasnacht, Mrs. Carol K. Forbes, Jennifer Forbes, Maxine
    Hasenplug, Mary H. Iffert, Anne M. Kiszka, Doris & David
    Kougher, Martha Linn, Mitchell Maybee, Robert &
    Carolyn Mitchell, Michelle Partridge, Joe Piper, William &
    Evelyn Powell, Julie Ryhal, Sandy Saxion, Mary Scott,
    Paulette L. Young;
Greenwood—Joseph Piper;
Grove City—Edward W. Carlson, Kelly R. Cloves, Clara &
    Chester Coulter, Tom Coulter, Burton Rea, John E. Wilson;
Guys Mills—Allen Mast, Ray Miller;
Hadley—Dah Brychik, Andy Mullett, Mary & Garth Shay;
Hafuy—Jason Coblentz;
Hanover—Sarah M. Bair;
Harborcreek—Robert W. Bird, Christ & Amy Burns, Glenn
    Goodenow, Barbara Gross, Deborah Huck, Nancy Thomas,
    Nancy Wood;
Harleysville—Catherine Derstine, Mark H. Free;
Harmony—Ashley Getsay, Gertrude Getsay;
Harrisburg—Betty Jeffery;
Hartstown—Shirley Hackworth;
Hermitage—Joe & Annete Selenchiks;
Homer City—John Goral;
Hookstown—Bob Irons;
Jackson Center—Grace & Sarah Magargee, Richard & Carolyn
    Magargee, Jim & Ruth McKinley;
Jamestown—S. Davenport, Loretta Enterline, Janet Gibbons,
    Janet Gilburn, Harriet Liszka, Terri Livingston, Sara Miller,
    Shirley Patton;
Kane—Lorraine Oakes;
Kempton—Mrs. Willis Henry, Willis R. Henry;
Kutztown—Cindy Rothermel;
Lake City—Jessica Dusicsko, Kelly Koble, Janet Richardson;
Lebanon—David M. Eggert, Lizzie Stoltzfus;
Lenhartsville—Audrey Meikel;
Leola—A.M. Martin;
Lewisburg—Sally Miller;
Linden—Shirley Smith;
Linesville—Helen Flickinger, Alice Heald, Margaret Lisk,
    Norma J. Thompson, Joanne Valentine, Edna Woodard;
Lititz—David D. Hess;

Gary Gieseman

Ludlow—Kay Nonnenberg;
Luthersburg—Maxine Cramer, Steve Cramer;
Manheim—Elwyn Estabrook, Lloyd Keller;
Marble—Carolyn Beichner;
Markleysburg—Fred J. Kamp;
Mars—Marion Clever;
Meadville—Kelly Crouch, Glenn Custard, Violet Hilliard, Bertha Mesarch, Daniel Miller, Helene Morneneck, Judy Morneweck, Ralph & Zona Spring, Carol Wells;
Mercer—Ida Darraugh, James & Josephine Lutes, Betty Lou Stoops, Courtney Urey, Nancy Wilson;
Mertztown—Esther Mae Zimmerman;
Meshoppen—Alice Sherwood, Karl Sherwood, Roy Sherwood;
Meyersdale—Perry R. Millard;
Midland—Marian Justice;
Mifflinburg—Samuel Horning;
Milan—Theodore S. Roy;
Millmont—Eli M. Martin;
Milton—Almaretta S. Hupp;
Mohnton—Catherine Unger;
Monaca—Charles & Jean Thornburg;
Monroeville—Ruth E. Pitts;
Mount Bethel—Paul Schmidt;
Mount Joy—Mr. & Mrs. Dale Martin;
Myerstown—Bertha Brown, Harvey Brown, Shirley M. Kreider, Elam & Miriam Stoltzfus, Samuel Stoltzfus, Kathy Weik;
Naryon—Omar Fischer;
New Brighton—Betty Cogliate;
New Galilee—Lois McAnlis, Wayne McAnlis, Delores McCullough;
New Holland—John Beiler;
New Ringgold—Jamie Shoemaker;
Newburg—Sandy Moose;
Newburg—Samuel J. Fischer;
North East—Ruth Ann Bartlett, Nancy Beeman, Jalisa Boll, Janet & Jacinda Boll, Jeffrey & Janae Boll, Pat Bowman, Mary Ruth Burnham, Kim & Breann Chesley, Irma Colligan, Jessica & Georgie Dohler, Mary & Andrea Dohler, Michael Drabic, Ashlee Eisaman, Kay Eisaman, Gerri Ellsworth, Gerrie Hutchinson, Carolyn Mikytuck, Haley Mix, Jeremy & Zachary Mix, Shelby & Jesse Mix, Sandy & Maggie Neil, Tony Neil, Chuck & Darla Parmarker, Yvonne Peck, Roy & Jane Peters, Ctystal Pratt, Fern Reslink, Carolyn Schermerhorn, Paul M. Schroter, Karen Sharling, Debra Warren, Robert Zeigler;
North Springfield—Katie Donahue;
Oley—Lillian Hetrick Family;
Oxford—Becky Myers;
Palmyra—Hank & Elaine Sell;
Pennsburg—Larry & Christena Boardman, Wylie & Mary Overly;
Philadelphia—Joseph R. Marbach;
Pittsburgh—Elizabeth Barngrover, Sue Graham, J.A. Hollister, Sis McKenna, Sandy Stiffler;
Pittsfield—Shirley Rutsky;
Pleasantville—Carol Clark;
Pottstown—Jeremy & James Zimmerman;
Prospect—Emilee L. Gustkey;
Punxsutawney—Jeromy & Sarah Anderson, Kelly Anderson, Lester & Maryelle Anderson;
Quarryville—Mannie Stoltzfus;
Richfield—Heidi & Heather Gingerich, Nina Kay Graybill, Lois Lauver;
Roaring Spring—Mr. & Mrs. Ron Dilling;
Russell—Adam & Benjamin Vanord;
Saegertown—Rita Bernoski, Gerald Schlosser, J. Schlosser, Melvin Schlosser;
Saint Marys—The Garners;
Salisbury—Krist Yoder;
Sandy Lake—V. Beougher, Bob Kimmel, William F. Kines, Rollie & Bonnie Smith, Kim Smith Family, Beverly Thompson, Marie Vandervort;
Seneca—Joe & Lillian Drozdo;
Sharon—The Beers, Florence McCartney;
Sharpsville—Vicki Colapietro, Michelle Joseph;
Shippensburg—Marie Stimson;
Shrewsbury—John & Charlene Miller;
Springboro—Franny Kenyon, Nick Kenyon, Tami Mritzay;
Springville—Robert Wheeler;
Stoneboro—Ray & Margie Gaus, Marsha & Billy Graham, Jacki & Ashley Opitz;
Telford—Beulah Clemmer;
Templeton—Felina Gundlach;
Tidioute—Lorraine Genard;
Tionesta—Roxanna Johnson, Judy Whitton;
Titusville—Gayle Christy, Dorothy Hasbrouch, Jerry Knickerbacher, Marion L. Sloan, Harrison Zacherl;
Towanda—Tom Cook;
Transfer—Maxine Hasenplug, Katy & Michael McGrat, Nancy McGrath;
Tunkhannock—Bob Smales;
Union City—Harvey H. Ganoe, Lynda Luba, Harvey & Joyce Nye, Marsha Tomcha, Roger Wetmore;
Uniontown—Eleanor Jenkins;
Utica—Bethany Covert, Brian Covert, Christopher Graham;
Valencia—Mary Ann Wiliams;
Venus—Dick & Donna Morrison;
Waterford—R. Blass, Fritz & Gladys Bliley, Kendra Christansen, Linda & Chelsea Christiansen, Carl D. Eliason, Ronald E. Eliason, Barb Fitting, Eleanor Heidecker, Cynthia Kreider,

Esther Gerber

Marjorie L. Kreider, Dana Twaroski;
Wattsburg—Mary Austin, Helen Orton;
Waynesboro—Harvey E. Rice, Jean & Robert Rice, Robert L. Rice;
West Springfield—Jen Barrante, Elaine Brockett, Becca Camp, Betty Chiro, Peggy Haykins, Robert Hopkins, Kristi Keeler, Christa Klein, Faith & Phillip McDonald, Matthew & Carolyn McDonald, Diann Menosky, Dorothy Porter, H.G. Whitney, Harley Whitney;
West Sunbury—Ella & Harold Barkley;
Wildwood—Virginia Greenwald;
Williamsport—R. Shoemaker;
Worthington—Mrs. Oren J. Claypoole;
York—Ruth Keenet, Mrs. Walter Keeney;
York Springs—Everett Weiser.

Rhode Island
East Greenwich—Shirley Ridley.

South Carolina
Easley—Jan Jackson;
Liberty—Norma Mapes.

South Dakota
Box Elder—Lila Miller;
Nemo—Dick & Rosie Seaman;
Stratford—Lloyd Jark;
Sturgis—Heidi Hatzenbuhler.

Tennessee
Chattanooga—Virginia Macnaughton;
Clarkrange—John & Betty Miller;
Knoxville—Garvin & Sandee Greene, Katherine Greene, Marjorie Robbins;
Kodak—Glen & Louise Burchby;
Linden—Charlyn Martin;
Mount Juliet—Becky Stofira;
Murfreesboro—Gen Womack;
Newbern—Florence & T.J. Merryman;
Oak Ridge—Don & Debra Carpenter;
Trimble—Marvin & Louise Bradford, Helen & Reed Walton Sr., Dorothy West;
Whitesburg—Mr. & Mrs. Earl Young.

Texas
Alamo—Mary Curtis;
Amarillo—Pete Bitela Jr., June Bohrer, Lindy & Jamie Busby, Inez Dent, Josh & Jason George, Audra Hampton, Emily Jaramillo, Betty A. Jones, Donna Miller, Mary Montoya, Linda Pack, Shantel & Mark Wilson;
Austin—Lynette Brannon, Nancy Kwalleck;
Blossom—Vera Withers;
Brookston—Vernon & Lillian Koehn;
Canyon—Janet Freeman, Jimmy Northeutt;
Carrollton—Mattie Hildebrand;
Colleyville—Pearl Dearing, Sheila Waltke;
Dalhart—Carol R. Artz, Erinn Lynn Campbell, Dexi & Elliott Chase, Mike & Sally Chase, Tiffany Crawford, Lisa Demots, Jean & Ashley Duschl, Marie Foshee, Carol Herreman, Karla Hoehn, Rainee Ingram, Sandra Kasten, Shawn Kimber, Ora Mcmains, Vera C. Pollan, Carren Ranay, Wanda Robertson, Tana Roves, Corinna Smith, Les & Tim Smith, Roy Stout, Robin Vela;
Denton—Susan Sponsler;

DeSoto—Mrs. Gene Foster;
Detroit—Rachel Koehn;
Driftwood—Vaughn M. French;
Dumas—Hannah Guest, Frances Holden, Owayne & Joe King, Carrie Usher;
Edinburg—Ken & Gina Moore;
Fort Worth—Von Dunn;
Galveston—Mr. & Mrs. J.G. Picone;
Gardendale—Cathy Adams;
Garland—Janiece Loveland;
Grapevine—Nathan Conner, Tom & Sarah & Kris Louderbach;
Harlingen—Russell Shafer;
Hartley—Sue Cunningham, Stewart Mininger, Peggy Pippin;
Hereford—Lindsey & Whitney Goforth, Larry & Betty Harris;
Killeen—Barbara R. Crawford;
League City—Cara Langton Family;
Lefors—Ralph Alexander;
Levelland—Tina Majors;
Liberty Hill—Becky Bradley;
Littlefield—Mr. & Mrs. K.O. Lynn;
Livingston—C.W. Neal;
Louise—Evelyn Miller;
Lubbock—George Davis, Molly L. Davis;
Medina—Marie Rivas;
Midland—Ray Holder;
Milano—Eldon Ball;
Muleshoe—Pete & Ettie Jesko;
Odessa—Ann Becker;
Pampa—Charles J. Albus, Leslie Whitten;
Perryton—Gordon Todd;
Plainview—Clareen Borron, Lena Chiddix;
Richardson—Annette Reynolds;
Royse City—Myrna Reynolds;
Sadler—Coleman & Robert Barnes;
San Antonio—Ilene M. Dyer;
Stratford—Alton & Francis Brewster, Mildred Carroll;
Sunray—Jim Ferguson;
Sweeny—Karen & Patrick Whorrall;
Texline—Sherri Eads;
White Deer—Paulett & Sammi Cotton.

Utah
Kaysville—Alan Manning;
Ogden—Elaine K. Burkey;
Orem—Kevin Satterfield;
Salt Lake City—Lorraine M. Cutler, Georgia B. Miller;
Scipio—Robert & Mary Cook, Anna May Keesey;
West Valley City—Lucille Jones.

Vermont
Arlington—Olga Hagelberg;
Colchester—Barbara R. Howard;
Johnson—E. Garfield;
North Pomfret—Leon & Betty Stetwon;
Vergennes—Floyd Sipley;
Williamstown—Gloria Winters.

Virginia
Dayton—Roy Rhodes;
Farmville—Barb Nelson, Kris Palmer;
Free Union—Roger L. Byers;
Glen Allen—Brad & Ryan Booth;
Harrisonburg—Chester G. Leaman;
Independence—Marvin Carrico;

Oneida—Elmer Keithley;
Richmond—David & Marcus Hensel;
Sterling—Justin & Drew Eggleton, Victoria
Eggleton.

Washington
Auburn—James Wood;
Battle Ground—B. Wilson;
Bothell—Iva Metz;
Bremerton—John Lawrence;
Delhart—Wanda Weller;
Everett—Marian Harlander;
Four Lakes—Rev. & Mrs. Terry R. Major;
Greenacres—Ann M. Nap;
Kalama—Shirley Northness;
Longview—Ruby & Roy Stiebritz;
Marlin—Clint & Evelyn Claassen;
Moses Lake—Verline Murray;
Poulsbo—Penny Reynolds;
Puyallup—Eric Boettcher, Heidi & Linda
Boettcher, Florence Garrick;
Seattle—E. Boger, N. Wayne Pierson;
Spokane—Jack Derawe;
Stanwood—H.W. Lilgreen;
Tacoma—John Garrick;
Vantage—Catherine Stockdale;
Wilbur—Terri Edwards;
Yakima—Harold Alderson, Chuck Butler.

West Virginia
Charleston—Byron & Grace Rinehart;
Chester—Curtis Ralston, Ford & Merle
Ralston;
Elkview—Fred & Willadean Radabaugh;
Parkersburg—A.L. McCoy, Ruth McNara,
Ruth McNemar.

Wisconsin
Alger—Pauline Willimas;
Appleton—Audrey J. Patterson;
Baraboo—Melvin Brandt, C.P. Fox;
Beloit—Marilyn Cade;
Black Earth—Philip Skalet;
Blair—Robert Jennesan;
Blanchardville—Mary & Gene
Hendrickson;
Boyd—George & Dorothy Burke;
Brandon—Cheri Sharp;
Brillion—Roy & June Bastain;
Bristol—Glenn Gillmore, Allen & Shirley Kirchner;
Brodhead—Henry & Susan Prien;
Cedar Grove—Clarence Meeusen, D.V.M.;
Chippewa Falls—Arlene Melville;
Clear Lake—Walter & Ardella Monson;
Clinton—Walter Schwengels;
Columbus—Justin & Heather Gronholz, Sue Gronholz;
Cross Plains—Russell & Ruth Williamson;
Dallas—Stan & Karaleen Sternitzky;
Dousman—Maldwyn Inez Morris;
Downsville—Don Bertelson;
Eau Claire—Elvern Kranig;
Evansville—Frank Leeder;
Fall Creek—Carol Strasburg;
Fence—Mrs. M. Dziewiontkoski;
Fond du Lac—Jerome A. Fox;
Granton—Lila & Jerry Schmitz;

Shirley Lorance

Green Bay—Carl F. Boser;
Greendale—Roy & Bobbi Reiman;
Hewitt—Richard Spindler;
Horicon—Mr. & Mrs. Norbert Koysill;
Hortonville—Mildred Hedtke;
Janesville—Jim Johnson, Loren R. Johnson, Leslea Kincaid;
Jim Falls—Clark & Shirle Davis;
Madison—Lynn M. Pomplun, Ralph Yearous;
Markesan—Dorothey Brown, Tom Miles;
Medford—Walter & Margaret Balcier, Emil & Gladys Paur;
Mequon—Bill Luebke;
Milwaukee—Marjorie Turk;
Minocqua—Jean Allen;
Neenah—Alvin Elliott, Evelyn & Earl Luebke;
Oak Creek—Carol Pettis;
Onalaska—Angela Brandt;
Oostburg—Gen Hubregtse, Ronald Huibreger;
Osseo—Karen Wagner;
Owen—Claire Milliren;

Poynette—William Priske;
Racine—Dorothy J. Nelson;
Readstown—Vivian Guist, Gayle Smith;
Reedsville—Theodore Smucker;
Salem—Harold Sheen;
South Wayne—Dorothy & Francis Fox;
Spooner—Bev Schluter;
Spring Valley—Anita M. Sebron, Earl Sibis
Stratford—Richard Spindler;
Strum—Sylvin Olson;
Watertown—Wes Kron, Larry Simons, Nell
Simons;
Wauwatosa—Tom Dallmann;
Webster—James & Thelma Cutler, Jim
Cutler;
Willard—Ron Klinke;
Wind Lake—Jim & Bonnie Fredrick, Dan &
Elaine Lecus;
Wittenberg—Laverne Rosewow.

Wyoming
Cheyenne—June & Marvin Bristow;
Evanston—Christene Salamon;
Laramie—Carolyn Abernethy.

Alberta, Canada
Bawlf—Irene & Bill Murphy;
Botha—Dan & Marie Barnec;
Edmonton—Bill Wythe;
Fort Saskatchewan—S.J. & Edna Melville;
Lacombe—Ethel Thompson;
Leslieville—Helen & Paul Zander;
Linden—Allen & Justina Ensz.

British Columbia, Canada
Crofton—Mrs. D. Bayko;
Nanaimo—R. Bianchin;
North Vancouver—Sharon Ellington.

Manitoba, Canada
Winnipeg—Alice Doerksen.

Ontario, Canada
Markdale—Craig Dennis;
Newton—Ray & Lillian Kuepfer;
St. Thomas—Marie Scott;
York—Joyce & Ab Collins.

Saskatchewan, Canada
Alsask—Lewis Pierce;
McCord—Vernon Eklund.

England
Mary Bray.

Russia
Roman Borukhov, John Caemmerer, Alexander Vladimirovich
Dmitriev, Serguei Petrovich Druganov, Michail Sergeevich
Kozlov, Alexander Valerianovich Petrovsky, Sergei
Alekseevich Ponomarev, Vladimir Alexandrovich Rizhkov,
Aleksey Anatol-Evich Sapojnikov, Alexander Ruslanovich
Saraev, Stepan Stepanovich Sulakshin, Michail Evgen'evich
Surin, Iouri Nikolaevich Tortoukov.

Switzerland
Mr. & Mrs. Jorg Muller.

Mrs. Arthur Whi